Mexican Karismata

Engendering Latin America

EDITORS:

Donna J. Guy
*Ohio State University*

Mary Karasch
*Oakland University*

Asunción Lavrin
*Arizona State University*

# Mexican Karismata

*The*
*Baroque Vocation*
*of*
*Francisca de los Ángeles,*
*1674–1744*

ELLEN
GUNNARSDÓTTIR

UNIVERSITY OF NEBRASKA PRESS

LINCOLN • LONDON

∞

Library of Congress Cataloging-in-Publication Data
Gunnarsdóttir, Ellen, 1967–
Mexican karismata : the baroque vocation of Francisca
de los Angeles, 1674–1744 / Ellen Gunnarsdóttir.
p. cm.—(Engendering Latin America)
Includes bibliographical references and index.
ISBN 0-8032-2199-1 (cloth : alk. paper)—
ISBN 0-8032-7113-1 (pbk. : alk. paper)
1. Angeles, Francisca de los, 1674–1744.    2. Catholics—
Mexico—Querâtaro—Biography.    3. Catholic
women—Mexico—Querâtaro—Biography.
I. Title.    II. Series.
BX4705.A5925G86 2004
282'.092—dc22
[B]
2004052616

# Contents

# Illustrations

# Preface

Spain's empire in the Americas was not built solely on the shoulders of bureau-crats, bishops, military commanders, and successful miners and merchants. The cultural edifice of Hispanic society rested upon a broad base of people who lacked exalted rank or position. A great many of these, particularly in New Spain, were residents of those quintessentially Hispanic communities: the towns and cities. These urban dwellers were a diverse lot—Creoles, penin-sulars, mestizos and mulattoes, laymen, and members of various religious orders. In their spiritual strivings toward God, these men and women became the foot soldiers of the Counter-Reformation in the New World, laying the foundations for the baroque Catholic culture that persists in Mexico with great vitality to this day.

This is a study of the life of one such foot soldier. Francisca de los Ángeles (1674–1744) was a *beata* who was born and lived her entire life in the humble provincial city of Querétaro, then a stronghold of Hispanic culture on the northern frontier of New Spain, now central Mexico. But Francisca's charis-matic gifts propelled her toward an unusual life for a woman in colonial Mexico, and the extensive body of writings she left behind affords an un-commonly intimate and detailed first-person perspective on the culture and religiosity of a dynamic and expanding Hispanic society.

In its outlines hers is a relatively straightforward story. In the northern city of Querétaro, a notably pious and observant community, missionaries newly arrived from Spain discovered in the person of an adolescent girl from a poor Creole-mestizo family a soul especially favored by God. Under their protection, Francisca undertook spiritual labors, mixing—like Saint Teresa of Ávila—her visionary and mystical experiences.[1] Already as an adolescent she had gained a reputation as a holy woman. Relics blessed by God during their unions were said to work miracles, and stories of her bilocations to Texas, where she claimed to have converted thousands of Indians, circulated widely. As she grew older, Francisca worked with her mentors to establish a religious institution, which, after decades of hardship, finally found official sanction as a Royal College in 1729. She served as its headmistress until her death in 1744. She was renowned for her virtue and piety, adherence to the sacraments and liturgy, as well as for her obedience to her superiors and the doctrines of the faith.

We know about Francisca's life because she, like many holy women, wrote regular accounts of her soul for her confessors. Her letters, written over the course of nearly half a century, describe her visions, mystical unions, religious practices and spiritual feats, and also recount many details of the more mundane aspects of her life and administrative duties. After her death, Francisca's name and her writings, like those of many other religious women, were overshadowed by the biographies of virtuous nuns from aristocratic convents written by their confessors for public edification, not to mention by larger-than-life figures like the nun, poet, and scholar Sor Juana Inéz de la Cruz.

This is one of the principal reasons that Francisca's record of her own life is so noteworthy and valuable to us now. In strictly practical terms, it is crucially important and quite remarkable that so many of her writings, encompassing virtually the whole of a very long life, survive. But one of the great merits of her letters is that they have not been expurgated of the more mundane, problematic, and often heretical elements of her life. The tidying up that a conscientious spiritual director of the Counter-Reformation inevitably undertook when transforming a protégée's correspondence into hagiography erased such complexities from the public version of a holy woman's life. Francisca began compiling material for such a hagiographic work, and her biography was indeed written after her death. However, it was never published, and the only manuscript one can find record of seems to have been lost on a journey from Mexico to Rome.

Although it was not what Francisca wanted, it is perhaps fortunate for us, from a historical perspective, that her version of her life is the only one that we possess. Her rather untidy and uneducated correspondence throws light onto the popular but unruly landscapes of early modern Catholicism. Her writings are testimonials of a baroque religious culture that, in common with many of Francisca's contemporaries, permeated every aspect of her internal life and daily activities. One moment we can find her languishing in bed, transported to the divine regions, while in the next she is sitting at her desk efficiently drawing up lists of how many pounds of wheat, sugar, and beans she would need for the weekly maintenance of her community, or carefully crafting a letter to one of her many benefactors. And while she strove to present the acceptable, standardized version of her interior life, she was also unable to refrain from documenting with interest her own fallible and contradictory human nature. In addition, her accounts are liberally sprinkled with contemporaries' views of her as they appear in Inquisition records and letters, documentation that is usually deliberately excluded from hagiographic literature.

The copiousness and comprehensiveness of Francisca's writings and the broad nature of their content practically demand as little interference as possible from the historian. They certainly will be of interest to literary scholars and historians of gender. In this study, however, I have opted for the methods of biography because they offer the surest means of doing justice to the haphazard but also very personal and detailed version of events that the *beata* herself presents. We have the good fortune to have a woman who lived three hundred years ago recount a great deal about her life; I believe we should let her speak in her own words as much as possible. This approach enables us to capture the ambiguities and inconsistencies of a life in ways that a more theoretically constricted approach might not. I have tried to stay faithful to the rhythms of Francisca's own narrative and have arranged the study into chapters that encompass distinct periods in her life, which she viewed as a journey toward spiritual perfection.

What I have tried to provide the reader with is a coherent, chronological narrative of Francisca's life within the context of an expanding colonial society that was an integral part of the broader Hispanic world. In so doing, I hope to allow the modern reader a glimpse of how ordinary people in peripheral places like provincial New Spain were affected by and helped to direct the larger forces at work in the fitful world of a Catholicism faced with such adversaries as the Reformation and the emergence of science. Though Francisca's life played out in the backwaters of the Spanish empire it took its inspiration not merely from its immediate surroundings but from a much grander theater originating in distant Europe. Indeed, I believe it is necessary to begin her story almost half a century before her birth by taking the pulse of the Counter-Reformation in Rome.

# Acknowledgments

I can safely and without pretension say that this book would never have been written without the help of several generous people. This applies most literally to Fray José Luis Soto Peréz, O.F.M., archivist of the Franciscan convent in Celaya. I first knocked on his door as a PhD student searching for information on the Santa Clara convent in Querétaro. Padre Soto not only allowed me access to the archive but showed me Francisca de los Ángeles's correspondence, neatly cataloged and maintained in brown carton boxes. I did finish my thesis on religious institutions for women in colonial Querétaro, but retained a fascination with these letters. When I finally returned to Celaya to work on them my situation had changed radically, for I was the mother of a four-month-old boy who was not much impressed with his mother's preoccupation with archives. It was then that Padre Soto demonstrated what a generous man of God he is. He not only transferred the correspondence, box by box, to the Concepcionista convent in San Miguel de Allende, which is situated only a few blocks away from my doorstep. He also later allowed me to photocopy what remained of the correspondence to be transcribed and bring the copies with me to my new job in Iceland. I literally owe Padre Soto everything when it comes to this book, and I extend to him my most heartfelt gratitude.

A second crucial person is my Cambridge supervisor, D. A. Brading, who in an elegant and understated manner put me through the grind of learning the historian's craft and taught me that the story speaks for itself. Asunción Lavrin has provided me with humor, professional advice, and constant encouragement during our correspondence over these past few years and has played a pivotal role in bringing the manuscript to the attention of the University of Nebraska Press. I could always count upon my mother, Unnur Úlfarsdóttir, without exception, to entertain her grandson through long winter afternoons when his mother was working. And finally, my husband, Edward M. Farmer, throughout the years, and in particular through the writing of this book, has been my editor and provided me with shelter and direction in every sense.

There remains a multitude of people to thank, among them, my father, Gunnar Gunnarsson, for his all-encompassing interest in his daughter's prospects as a writer; my sister, Halla; friends Berglind Bragadóttir and Ragnhildur Zoëga.

On the academic front, I thank the examiners of my PhD thesis, Brian Hamnett and John Lynch, for their good advice and encouragement, and Nora Jaffary, Antonio Rubial García, and my dear friend Susie Minchin for providing me with manuscripts, articles, and books of great value for this study. Historians Clara García Ayulardo and Marta Eugenia García in Mexico I thank as good friends and companions, and Enrique Florescano I thank for his generous hospitality. The directors and staff of every archive and library I have been to during this research have been more than forthcoming with help. I wish to thank in particular Fr. Mauricio Portillo, O.F.M., of the library of the Pontificio Ateneo Antonianum in Rome; Manuel Ramos Medina at CONDUMEX in Mexico City; and the staff of Archivo General de la Nación in Mexico City and Archivo de Notarías in Querétaro. As for research facilities, I wish to thank the nuns of the Concepcionista convent in San Miguel de Allende for their gracious hospitality; working in their tranquil and sunny visiting quarters with a view of their lovely orchard was more enjoyable than words can describe. In Iceland, I wish to thank Rannís (the Icelandic Research Council), for a research and travel grant, and my colleagues at the University of Iceland's Spanish Department and Center for Humanities, in particular Sigríður Matthíasdóttir.

At the University of Nebraska Press I owe particular thanks to Elizabeth Demers for her interest in and encouragement of the project, as well as to the anonymous readers for their valuable comments for revision.

Finally, I dedicate this book to the memory of my grandparents, Unnur, Úlfar, Salmanía Jóhanna, and Gunnar, all avid readers of biography.

# Mexican Karismata

# Introduction

In 1632, the pious Pisan academic Galileo Galilei, friend to popes and cardinals, faced a Roman tribunal of infuriated Inquisitors for maintaining that the sun was at the center of the universe. These scholastic defenders of the faith had in their hands none other than Holy Scripture to contradict him. Among the many groups that threw themselves into the fray was the recently established Congregation for the Propagation of Faith (Propaganda Fide), the papacy's new missionary sword. The Congregation consulted the Jesuit scholar Cardinal Robert Bellarmine who assured them that Galileo's fanciful flights of imagination did not challenge such natural truths as the location of heaven and hell. Hell, for example, remained where it always had been, at the center of the earth as far as possible from the angels and blessed souls who inhabited heaven.[1] Armed with such reassurance, Propaganda Fide would battle its way through a seventeenth century gripped not only by religious wars but by the emergence of science, personified in such figures as Descartes and Newton, who stripped God of omnipotence and tried to situate Him within mathematical logic and the human intellect.

Thankfully for the Congregation, God's creation was large. Across the Atlantic loomed the New World and its Spanish possessions, steeped in orthodoxy and governed by Iberians, the most enthusiastic defenders of the Catholic faith. As the Counter-Reformation had gathered full steam in the late sixteenth century, its Spanish clergy undertook a full-fledged "spiritual conquest" of the pagan lands of the New World, which prompted the famed Italian reformer Carlo Borromeo to remark that "the clergy of Spain are the nerve of all Christendom."[2] Around the time of Galileo's trial the inhabitants of New Spain had begun to venerate the image of Our Lady of Guadalupe, whose miraculous appearance in 1531 to a poor Indian on a hillside outside Mexico City heralded, according to seventeenth-century Mexican theologians, nothing less than the transfer of divine favor from heretical Europe to the New World.[3] Other regions of America were similarly favored. In Lima, four saintly personages from the early seventeenth century would eventually be canonized, among them, in 1671, the region's first woman saint, the Dominican tertiary Rosa of Lima (1584–1617). Across these diverse lands the success of the Tridentine emphasis on the inculcation of orthodoxy through imagery was evident in the widespread use of household altars with their images and crucifixes as well as in the elaborate religious festivals common to cities and villages. Here, the Lutheran heresy seemed a strange dream to a church so firmly in control of its parishioners' piety; the devotion to the sacraments was a distinguishing feature of the colonies' ritual life, and saints and martyrs were a comforting presence in its households. At the same time, this New World offered exciting possibilities for ardent missionaries. Its original inhabitants, referred to as Indians by the Spaniards, had been found, in spite of their apparent proclivity for religious devotion and acceptance of the Christian God and his court, to slyly venerate their gods in secret. And if the shadow cast by pagan darkness over this land of evangelical opportunity was not enough to attract the attentions of Propaganda Fide, the Inquisition's archives contained mountains of paper demonstrating that the devil was hard at work among the Creole (Spaniards born in America) and mixed populations of the cities, encouraging witchcraft, superstitious practices, and false piety.[4] Across the Atlantic then, European missionaries could find exciting contrasts between the "New Jerusalem" in Mexico City and the "Blind Babylon of Idolatry" in the Peruvian Andes.[5]

It was not until the late seventeenth century, however, that the opportunity presented itself to Propaganda Fide to conquer the New World. It came in the person of an enthusiastic Spanish Franciscan, Fray Antonio Llinás, who had spent several years in New Spain and returned to Europe convinced that the colony's wild northern frontier, boundary of the Christian world, needed a forceful missionary hand. Llinás was given permission to recruit in Spain, and eventually two missions were sent, one to Peru and the other to New Spain. The latter group settled its center of operations in the northern city of Querétaro, which opened onto the expanse of the empty northern frontier. In New Spain, the missionaries encountered an urban population which, in spite of its penchant for vice, would have been genuinely aghast at the rational and intellectual God proposed by Europe's "new men of science." Its God was a thunderous and almighty monarch who hurled warnings of His wrath at humans in the form of natural disasters and epidemics, or expressed His pleasure with abundant rain and through the mouths of visionaries. To be sure, some marginal and dispossessed figures flirted with the devil in the hope that he might take on the divine tyrant, while a few members of the elite also timidly savored the fresh gusts of intellectual winds coming from Europe.[6]

Mexican baroque society was obsessed with creating order in the midst of the chaos of an Indian, European, and African New World. Anxious Spaniards created a myriad of categories with which to classify the baffling variety of resulting ethnic mixtures, and they strove to uphold a caste system to shore up the logic of their supremacy. As a result, the tension between order and chaos permeated every aspect of Mexican colonial culture, prompting Thomas Gage, the seventeenth-century traveler, to note that "Sin and wickedness abound in Mexico, yet there are no more devout people in the world toward the Church and clergy. In their lifetime they strive to exceed one another in their gifts to the cloisters of nuns and friars. Some erect altars to their best devoted saints, worth many thousand ducats; others present crowns of gold to the pictures of Mary, others lamps; others repair them; others at their death leave to them two or three thousand ducats for an annual stipend."[7]

High and low, this complex society lived within the medieval intellectual perimeters of scholasticism, which held that absolute truth was to be found only in divine revelation as transmitted through the writings of the fathers of the church. Answers to any and all intellectual questions were thus to be found there; it was useless to look for them elsewhere. New World scholastics achieved dialectical excellence, and the celebrated minds of the epoch were those who could memorize gargantuan texts and regurgitate them to a dazzled audience in the richly adorned halls of the university. In a society "oriented towards opposing modernity, not achieving it"—to borrow Octavio Paz's words—the talent of New Spain found expression in the truncated wildness of the baroque.[8] Verses, novels, treatises, chronicles, and pamphlets were published in prodigious amounts in florid and dense language, a verbal thicket too full of thorns for most modern readers to even contemplate entering. The baroque's style, in the words of David Brading, was "classical epithet . . . piled on classical epithet, with metaphors multiplied beyond control, meaning was sacrificed to literary effect, and critical acumen destroyed by the imperatives of eulogy."[9] Verbal raptures were reproduced in the interiors of churches, where the array of richly adorned images of saints and sprawling canvasses of biblical paintings relieved only by gold-leaved columns, cherubs, and flora provided a religious theater as satisfying to the senses as the frequent bullfights, fireworks, comedies, and *mascaradas* (parades) on offer in the streets. According to Thomas Gage's account, Mexican nuns at times staged the children under their care in popular theatrical acts: "They teach these young children to act like players; and to entice the people to their churches, they make these children act short dialogues in their choirs, richly attiring them with men's and women's apparel."[10]

Asceticism was an integral element of this drama, which was as extravagant in its flair as the best of baroque theater. It was practiced by people of all stations, from the impressive peninsular Juan Palafox y Mendoza, bishop of Puebla and viceroy of New Spain (1600–1659), who fasted, wore silices, slept on boards, and flagellated himself, to the most humble urban hermits, who lived modestly in family homes or in groups without financial resources, education, or official church sanction.[11] Austerity mixed with emotional extravagance and affective piety pervaded this baroque society, and its churches were filled with the murmur of exclamations of love and suffering and devotion to the Virgin and the saints. Men such as Palafox were fired in their pity by the example of church history's greatest protagonists, as Brading articulates it: "a formidable army of martyrs, confessors and other holy men and women, whose lives and works constituted the proof that the Catholic church still enjoyed God's blessing and was still animated by the Holy Spirit."[12]

Into this fertile ground the Spanish missionaries of Propaganda Fide brought their powerful and mysterious medieval God, embattled at home but enthusiastically accepted by a people already well versed in Tridentine traditions such as *imitatio cristi* (imitation of Christ), the Stations of the Cross, and the Eucharist. The region must have seemed promising indeed to natives of a seventeenth-century Spain that was well past the "heroic age" of Tridentine reforms and was struggling with general poverty and the decline of religious institutions.[13] In his study of popular devotion in southwestern Germany in the seventeenth century, Marc Forster identifies a "drive to provide more diverse and intense religious experiences" within the communities. The new missionaries in New Spain belonged to that movement in an Iberian context.[14] They promoted faith in, and fear of, their almighty patriarch through such tried Counter-Reformation tools as communion, captivating masses, and increased and more intensive confessions. Apart from the few disgruntled secular clergy who were annoyed by the triumphalist evangelism that had characterized the "spiritual conquest" of the preceding century, the new missionaries made quite a splash in these foreign lands. Upon their entry into Mexico City they made such an impression that a mission—consisting of sermons, confessions, and penitential processions—they had planned to preach in the cathedral eventually had to be expanded to include every church in the city as well as all convents of female religious.[15] The missionaries became legends in Central America and Texas and were even more successful in their missions to the faithful. Many became the stuff of edifying biographies, and through the years they succeeded in recruiting Creole friars who would acquire fame throughout the colony.[16]

Francisca de los Ángeles was one of the missionaries' more successful recruits. She was not merely obedient and contemplative as befitted a good nun but the recipient as well of visionary experiences that fired her active nature to champion the sort of reformist evangelism within Querétaro's female community that her mentors were undertaking in the colony at large. Her commitment and activism are mirrored in her long career as a writer; her correspondence spans approximately forty-eight years. Although it contains rather typical accounts of visionary experiences and mystical practices, it is also colored by her particular situation. Most of the Spanish-American religious women who have left accounts of their lives were nuns living in cloistered, elite convents. In an age when models of exemplary lives were held up for the general public's adulation and emulation, these women were aware of the objectives of their narratives. In most cases, they constructed autobiographies that began in childhood and followed hagiographic parameters through adversity, diabolical torment, and divine illumination, closing at moments of maturity with a sense of having overcome hurdles on the *camino de la perfección* (the road toward perfection). The perspective is thus that of the already holy protagonist looking backward at the tumultuous process that eventually led to the elevated state of her soul.

Francisca had none of these trump cards up her sleeve as she started to write. At the age of eighteen, she was already recounting visions and favors from the divine for her confessors, and she continued to do so almost daily for several years. Although at times she attempted to begin the construction of a *vida* narrative, these efforts quickly floundered. She changed confessors frequently and thus found herself needing to adapt to their different styles and temperaments. Since her relations with her mentors did not center solely on the direction of her soul, but on friendship and their support for her bourgeoning community, the letters contain references to most aspects of her experience of life. Hence, her correspondence lacks cohesion and a unified objective. After her death, it was not edited but archived in its entirety— amounting to thousands of letters—by her Franciscan mentors. This provides the modern reader with enormous advantages, for Francisca's monumental legacy is a porous construction through which the spectator can glean intimate glimpses of a baroque life.

This life is a microscopic hodgepodge of contradiction. After two close brushes with the Inquisition for heresy she remained nevertheless a favorite *hija espiritual* (spiritual daughter) of the most famous Propaganda Fide missionary in the New World, Fray Antonio Margil de Jesús. He himself became a subject of scrutiny by the Inquisition, which was his order's closest ally in the battle for Christian souls. In this New World inversion, a woman who by all accounts would have sounded the bells of suspicion among the brethren in Spain for her frequent visionary inconsistencies, long disputes with her confessors, and overly affective piety held sway over an elite gathering of men sent across the ocean to combat not only pagan darkness but precisely such individualistic and unorthodox tendencies in the faithful. She was a mystic who described herself as possessing a "heart of stone" and little given to tears in a period when the mystic "gift of tears" was highly prized. She confessed to a "spiritual mania" but condemned the sort of excess and "exteriority" that led to demonic possession. Finally, she professed to have a merry heart but a melancholy nature. Humility and obedience did not prevent verbal battles with her superiors, and mystic retreat did not preclude administrative excellence. Such attributes might have dampened the devotion of any ordinary ecclesiastic attuned to more accepted American models of female holiness such as Santa Rosa de Lima whose tortuous, ascetic sanctity led her to an early death.

The Carmelite tradition, after the death of Saint Teresa, imitated her mystical ecstasies but placed less emphasis on her apostolic experience. As Marina Caffiero argues in the context of Italy, this became the dominant model for female religiosity in the High Baroque era.[17] But to the Spanish friars, Francisca's character must have presented a dim but hopeful echo of female apostolic exemplars such as that hero of the Counter-Reformation, the splendidly Castilian Teresa. She combined a reformist energy and sociability with mystic rapture and disdain for the world to create a reputation as unorthodox to some as inspiring to others. The writings of the famed Spanish mystic Madre María de Agreda, who had experienced bilocations to New Mexico where she preached and converted thousands of infidels, were read daily at Propaganda Fide's convent in Querétaro. Madre Agreda insisted upon an expanded role for the Virgin as "co-redemptress" and promoter of the primitive church. As devotees of her texts, the Franciscan missionaries might have agreed with the seventeenth-century abbess of Fontevraud, Jeanne-Baptiste de Bourbon, who argued that "if in the order of nature, God has given some preeminence to men rather than women, that was within limit and measure. But in the order of Grace he has communicated his favors to women without restriction or limit such as in his elevation of the Virgin above all those who are not God."[18]

The peninsular missionaries who became Francisca's protectors most likely nursed an appreciation of reformist women regardless of their class. Nevertheless, they would probably have agreed with the opinion of a Jesuit friar who stated in a 1627 sermon in honor of Saint Teresa that "sanctity in women usually consists in being quiet, obeying, staying in a corner and forgetting about oneself."[19] The paradox dissolves in the light of the Franciscan triumphal and decisively medieval apostolate: if God, who obeyed no human rules or opinions, chose to propagate their mission through a mere woman, thus converting her weak, susceptible self into a spiritual *varón* (male) then they would participate in the enterprise.

Further, in their writings, the Franciscan superiors of Francisca de los Ángeles frequently expressed a desire to revert to the pure and ecstatic apostolate of Christianity's first centuries.[20] In Mexico's northern desert, far from the heresy and bloodshed of Europe, they saw a millenarian opportunity to resurrect that world in which the divine spirit at times had erased barriers of institutions, class, and even gender. It is likely, based on their behavior toward Francisca, that their spiritual formation owed much to such late antiquity attitudes that had loomed large in the centuries before the Reformation. Through ascetic practices and prayer males or females could achieve a holy state that transcended the ego and obliterated gender. Spiritual virility could thus save a woman, as stated by Jerome: "As long as a woman is for birth and children, she is as different from man as body is from soul. But when she wishes to serve Christ more than the world, then she will cease to be a woman and will be called man."[21] A *mujer varonil* (manly woman), in spite of the weak female trappings of her flesh, could therefore become a kindred spirit with that of a male in the quest for God. This opinion was echoed by Teresa of Ávila's biographer, Francisco de Ribera, who claimed that "women who with fortitude overcome their passions and submit to God must be called men."[22]

There was nothing overly unorthodox about this in New Spain, where the reputations of pious nuns were eagerly assimilated into local pantheons and served to buttress a sense of orthodoxy in the insecurity of distant lands. Friars and seculars formed intense spiritual relationships with nuns and *beatas* whose holy example was thrust at the populace through sermons, *vidas*, spiritual guides, and common gossip. But such women gained preeminence in a cultural climate that was far more complex and ambiguous than that which gave birth to Jerome's simple maxim. Between them lay over ten centuries of the history of women's participation in the Christian cult, during which layer upon layer of attitudes and opinions on female piety had been laid to create a cornucopia of conflicting and contradictory perceptions. Female spirituality expressed itself in the austere and the rich nun, *beata* and Beguine, saintly laywoman and the witch. It was exalted and repressed, admired and despised, welcomed and repudiated. But through the complicated tapestry of women and Catholic religious culture ran the solid thread of acknowledgment— at times tacit and reluctant or vocal and enthusiastic—that while women's fallible natures were easy prey to the devil these very vulnerable attributes could also lead them straight to God. The much admired state of virginity combined with these mysterious female elements to propel some women to fame and authority. Celebrated holy women such as Hildegard of Bingen and Teresa of Ávila framed their writings in this tradition, referring to themselves, paradoxically to a modern but logically to contemporaries, as weak and "wretched" while at the same time speaking and preaching with divine authority.[23] This strain of thought ran through colonial Mexican assumptions regarding holy women. A populace attuned to the climactic convulsions of baroque religious and secular drama followed with relish the dark and heroic battles of women suffering from inherent weakness in flesh and spirit with Lucifer, erotic tortures and humiliations, and the final, blazing glory of victorious entry into the divine world. The women who succeeded in winning critical acclaim were those who followed the prescribed methods outlined by their confessors and spiritual guides to proceed on this tortuous path. Others, too arrogant, too eager to give orders, not careful enough to stay within the prescribed perimeters, and not safeguarded by the institutional cushion, fell victim to the Inquisition.

Francisca de los Ángeles knew this terrain well and followed its guidelines dutifully throughout the narrative of her life. But her terror of the devil is not convincing enough, nor are her illnesses and self-depreciation, and her efforts at prescribed modes of spiritual exercise quickly floundered. What is convincing in her letters is her sense of apostolate to the living and the dead, her energetic and anxious quest for God, and, in spite of her protestations to the contrary, her pragmatic delight in earthly existence. Her sociability combined with visionary fervor certainly attracted many a cleric to her door, but upon close inspection the flaws in her orthodox narrative might have repelled an ordinary confessor nourished by local texts on holy women. But the Spanish missionaries of Propaganda Fide were not ordinary men. Instead, they were the representatives of a "Baroque papacy" that in the words of R.

Po-Chia Hsia "presided over a heroic Catholicism, peopled with missionaries, martyrs, converts and living saints."[24] They recognized in Francisca at an early age a spiritual virility desirable to friars who fervently believed that they were being given an opportunity to resurrect the primitive church in the American desert. As the inheritors of a Franciscan tradition that scorned intellectual endeavors, they had faith only in knowledge that came straight from God. This tradition found its mystical flowering among pre-Reformation Franciscans on the peninsula such as the early-sixteenth-century friar of Escalona who moved his pulpit to the center of his church in order for the congregation to better observe his ecstasies and raptures; and the celebrated Cardinal Xímenez de Cisneros who found such enjoyment in watching the celestial dances of the visionary María de Santo Domingo and protected her from the assaults of the Dominicans who accused her of false piety.[25] María de Santo Domingo's *Libro de la oración* was published in Spain in the early century with the enthusiastic introduction of a cleric who proudly maintained that the "unlettered are those with acquired learning and in terms of infused learning, the Holy Spirit bestowed as much on His handmaid as on any other."[26] In this context, it seems almost logical that the doors to individual expression that Propaganda Fide helped close on Galileo Galilei in the first half of the seventeenth century were opened wide at its end to a humble and uneducated Mexican *beata*. Like the Jesuits, the Franciscan missionaries, in spite of their papal affiliation, concerned themselves more with the salvation of individual souls than the execution of institutional reforms.[27] Indeed, Francisca de los Ángeles was allowed entry into this most elite of armies by surprisingly unruly soldiers.

Gender, religious culture, and the church in Mexico is a theme that has received plentiful scholarly attention. Josefina Muriel (1946) and Asunción Lavrin (1967) pioneered the field with their studies of female religious institutions and culture. They have produced convincing narratives of these institutions' flowering in New Spain and their participation in diverse aspects of colonial life: religious cult, economy, education, and cultural formation.[28] A proliferation of subsequent studies has demonstrated the importance of convents and other religious institutions for women in perpetuating colonial hierarchies of class and caste, not only in Mexico but in colonial Spanish and Portuguese America.[29] Further innovations include studies that use Inquisition records to analyze the baroque religiosity of urbanites accused of false mysticism, and detecting in such sources evidence of widespread popular cultural practices.[30] Of particular interest for this study is the growing body of work on the autobiographical and biographical narratives of nuns, *beatas*, and their confessors.[31] Here, attention has focused on distinguishing the particular features of female mystical writings. Particularly among literary scholars, the dominant perception has been that early modern Catholicism's strange mix of repression of and admiration for religious women spurred a new genre of female mystical writing that fitted itself tightly within the parameters of orthodox hagiography while combining the theme of the "wretched woman" with visionary authority.

A nun or a *beata* did not sit down to write the story of her life simply because she felt she had something to say but because the man in her life, that is, her confessor, deemed that she had something *exemplary* to say. However dependent and admiring they were of their *hijas espirituales*, confessors provided— sometimes literally—paper and writing plume, and had the power to withhold them. The confessor therefore had to be persuaded of his protégée's virtue and special standing with the divine and at the same time soothed regarding the potential heresy of her experiences. While men's biographies extolled their achievements as missionaries, reformers, and founders of institutions, women's narratives turned inward, eschewing details of earthly life in favor of the mystical realm, a more open field of opportunity. Their *vidas* thus focused on extreme ascetic practices and self-deprecation, which were considered acceptable channels to heroic achievements of virtue.[32] Many admiring men supported their *hijas* down a road that led directly to Inquisitorial dungeons; others were tortured by suspicions of the devil's hand in the intense bond that united them. A more fortunate group managed to keep the enterprise within an acceptable norm, meticulously copying visionary experiences that earned their protégées a local reputation and contributed to the greater glory of the church.[33] Should the collaboration succeed and produce an orthodox *vida*, as Ibsen argues, it served not only as religious exemplum but constituted political capital as well. Like the Virgin of Guadalupe, visionary women were native treasures of the New World and symbols of God's favor.[34]

Much current scholarship, mostly in the form of literary critique, thus holds that religious women's *vidas*, however narrow and male dominated the confines of the genre, provided their cloistered and humbled writers with power and authority over the establishment that sought to control them. Like Saint Teresa who provided female writers of the Counter-Reformation with the most successful model of a *vida*, religious women of the era used the maxim of their natural inferiority and "wretchedness" to cloak the divine treasures given them with orthodoxy. A wretched, useless woman merely wrote down what was dictated to her by the divine so it could be examined and verified by more erudite, learned men. As long as she dutifully labored as God's scribe, transmitted messages without deciphering them, obeyed her male ecclesiastic superiors and did not let fanciful ideas of authority get a hold of her, she would earn the opportunity to narrate a dramatic story in which she acted as chief protagonist. Discussing the paradox of the wretched woman and authoritative visionary, feminist literary criticism has identified such modern concepts as "agency" and "resistance" in the writings of colonial Spanish American nuns. McKnight, for example, in her excellent work on the famous Colombian nun Madre Castillo has identified in Madre Castillo's writings parallel themes: the first is the language of "self-censure," while the second reveals the writer as "an instrument of God." In Madre Castillo's case, by comparing the *vida* narrative with the known facts of the nun's life and rise to political power within the convent, McKnight has fleshed out what she sees as a strategy of "subtle resistance" to the male power structure that dominated the writer's life. A similar view is expressed by Ibsen who sees in the writings of the women she examines the "notion of agency as the writing subject attempts to transcend the limitations imposed on her discourse by strategically situating herself in a position that permits access to power while satisfying the demands of both her real and implied readers."[35]

I do not doubt the usefulness of using gender as an analytical tool in telling the story of female religious writers. In Francisca de los Ángeles's case, for example, the term *gender* is of clear significance to her spirituality and relationship with the institutional church. Nevertheless, it is my opinion that a more fruitful perspective on her life and character is that provided by her particular historical moment: High Baroque Mexico, an open and vibrant society in spite of its neomedieval character. In other words, if it is important to see these texts in the context of the hundreds of female writers laboring in colonial Spanish America, to see them not as unique but to restore them, in Kathryn Joy McKnight's words, to their "feminine milieu" it is equally important to see lives such as that of Francisca de los Ángeles as the expression of a baroque society, a New World hybrid of the European and the indigenous. As Octavio Paz notes in his study on Sor Juana de la Cruz, while Catholicism was on the decline in Spain in the late seventeenth century and much of the eighteenth, it was "a creative force in New Spain", a "new religion" being crafted through popular participation. Indeed, Paz contends that the baroque period was not only "long-lived and rich" but "strikingly original."[36]

Francisca's texts are evidence of the originality of this society. Her life is not only marked by strategies of resistance to a closed-off male establishment but by a remarkable and baroque openness. In spite of her faithful adherence to a story line that casts herself as a wretched and humble woman inexplicably singled out for divine favors, Francisca devoted her true writing energy to an altogether different rhetoric. Indeed, what defines her writing career is the arrival of European missionaries to a small but prosperous city on the doorstep of a pagan desert, men who were intent upon salvaging the kingdom of God in this divinely promised but strange territory. It is in this encounter between the New and Old World that a local woman, combining prudence and charisma, finds surprising opportunities for a vocation not at all in accordance with the maxims of her epoch. This story then, should be seen in the context of the renewal of lay religious experience in the world of the Catholic Counter-Reformation. More importantly, it provides a "view from below" on early modern Catholicism in Mexico. Francisca occupied a lowly place within the church as a tertiary who for most of her life did not live in officially sanctioned enclosure. But she is one of many such figures who defined popular lay piety in her age.[37] The Counter-Reformation's effect on her life is much more evident as dynamic spirituality than institutional reform. In this sense, Francisca's story is emblematic of H. Outram Evennett's view of the Counter-Reformation as first and foremost a "spiritual renewal."[38]

From this "view from below" Francisca's holiness is not entirely in line with Tridentine policy. Indeed, the shadowy narrative that emerges parallel to the one that would stake her claim to holy status reveals a woman with one foot in the supernatural and the other in the natural world, but both equally firmly on the ground. To contemporaries, Francisca's achievements were not visible in her emaciated body, public trances, and prophesies but in the continual growth of her community and its reputation, the comforting vision of its humble poverty during public processions, and the security it provided poor Creole *doncellas* with no other recourse. Her talents were obvious in her confections and in her orchard, inherited from her father, from which she produced a wide variety of fruits and vegetables, presented as gifts to her visitors. These attributes were considered important enough evidence of Franciscan holiness. After her death, her fellow *beatas* took care to underline her miraculous skills as a gardener, and one of her benefactors brought her figurines of the Child Christ, made of sugar, to boast of during a visit to the court in Madrid.

The intent of this study then is to delineate a colonial life that is singular for its expression: not a carefully formulated narrative but a day-to-day enterprise describing the process of survival—spiritual and material—of a soul alert and sensitive to the opportunities and dilemmas of divine and earthly existence. It is a baroque life in all its contradictions, but its overarching focus is the journey to God. The florid Hispanic tradition of female mystical writers initiated by Saint Teresa focused single-mindedly on that aim. Modern scholars discerning strategies for self-expression and authority in such writings should not forget that the *self* expressed by these women was most often a mystical creature, lost and struggling to get back to its creator. Francisca's mystic journey was an improvised and often haphazard pilgrimage, at times dwarfed by her natural sociability and busy schedule as foundress of a religious community. In her youth she was boastful and arrogant, convinced of God's favor. As a result, her visions focused on her own elevated status in the court of heaven. Under the direction of the famed missionary Fray Antonio Margil de Jesús her natural evangelical tendencies were intensified. In his company and that of his disciple Fray Antonio de los Ángeles, she began to cast herself as a penitent focused on the eradication of the ego, who by living continually in the passion of Christ brought humanity closer to God. Earthly life then became exile, a "Calle de Amargura" (Street of Bitterness), through which the Lord led those willing to live in Christ's passion: "let the Lord lead us up that street, where we are beaten and stoned and continually falling down," she preached to one of her confessors. The motherland was the supernatural world, entry to which could occasionally be gained for a glimpse of what awaited the *bienaventurados* or blessed souls.

Unlike the young Francisca, who slipped effortlessly back and forth between the two worlds, the mature woman of the 1700s and 1710s found that these apertures were only available to her through suffering, melancholy, and illness. That said, the moments of entry did present themselves at the strangest of times, such as when filling her pitcher of water at the fountain her gaze brushed an image of Christ engraved on its wall. Nor was she alone in her travails. In addition to her guardian angels, the nine choirs of the angels in heaven, the one thousand guards of the Virgin, she could list sixty-six saints as her guardians, including such global celebrities as Saint Francis and Saint Clare, but also local personages such as Bishop Palafox and the Querétaro nun Antonia de San Jacinto. These celestial representatives could be reached through prayer but in a more spectacular way through octaves and novenes, which she used not only to lift her spirits but to secure assistance in mundane tasks such as looking for her keys.[39] This is the mystical journey Francisca de los Ángeles embarked upon in her mature years, one in which, despite her confessor's continued interruptions, she placed all her energy and faith.

Above all, she trusted in God, a trait that she believed rendered all creatures, even of the weak female sex, equal before Him: "Many times I have heard that it is easy to deceive us women; in my opinion that is entirely possible, but I cannot escape the thought that he who does not want to be deceived enjoys the protection of God, our Lord. I know myself, and I know that my will is strong; it is to serve God in all things and thank him for all that he has done for me. I know that I do not want and have never wanted to be deceived."[40]

Indeed, as she neared the end of her life, Francisca had the sense of having mastered her unruly self in the quest for God. Sometime in the 1720s she wrote to Fray Juan de Ortega of Propaganda Fide: "Only by keeping to a strict regime spiritually have I been protected from the spiritual melancholy born of my bad nature."[41] In the baroque narrative that dominates her letters then is the story of a yearning for the sublime and an earnest search for God, a devotion that does not result in the destruction of the body and mind but in the dedication of a life. It is an ordinary story, similar to hundreds in the history of the church, and yet compelling for the charisma with which its protagonist confronts her New World baroque time and place.

# 1 Baroque Querétaro

# 1   The Emerging City

*Querétaro is the largest, most beautiful and opulent city in the arch-*
*bishopric of Mexico, owing to the great many sumptuous churches*
*that adorn it, the order of its streets and squares, its perfect residences,*
*the large number of Spanish families . . . as well as its good climate,*
*abundance and pleasantness.*

José Antonio de Villaseñor y Sánchez,
*Teatro Americano*

### Childhood: The Setting

Francisca de los Ángeles was born in 1674 in the city of Querétaro in the region of the Bajío, an intermediary zone between central Mexico and the great arid plains of the north.[1] It is dryer than the more temperate valleys of the center, but its soil is a fertile mixture of the alluvial mud and volcanic ash that settled and intermingled when the zone was a great lake lined by volcanoes. This fertility and potential for mixed agriculture differentiates the Bajío from the northern plains, which are suitable mainly for raising cattle. Before the conquest it was inhabited by nomadic and seminomadic tribes whose habits differed radically from the sedentary, highly organized population of the center. The Spaniards came to call these tribes collectively Chichimecas.[2]

The conquest and colonization of the Bajío became an important objective of the Spanish Crown from the mid-sixteenth century onward, and by the end of the century indigenous resistance had been largely quelled. The Bajío quickly developed into the most dynamic area of colonial Mexico, becoming, in the eighteenth century, the "pace-maker of the Mexican economy."[3] Its success derived from a mixed economy based on cattle and sheep raising, intensive cultivation of cereals, commerce, and a highly advanced urban textile industry.[4]

Even by the mid-seventeenth century the Bajío's social and cultural composition was notably heterogeneous and fluid. This was in large part due to its origins as a nomad zone and to the fact that the traditional patterns of Spanish colonization were not applicable to local conditions. Only two *encomiendas* were granted in the area, and neither was passed to the *encomenderos'* heirs. Rather, settlement was centered on the creation of new towns endowed with land by the Spanish Crown. As a result, the Bajío became an area of immigrants, in which Tarascans, Otomís, and the conquered Chichimecas blended with Spaniards. Separated from their original societies, the Indians of the Bajío did not retain the ethnic and social cohesion that, in spite of the chaos of the first century after conquest, characterized the settled societies of the center and south. While serious economic opportunities remained as closed to mestizos and most Indians as in the rest of the country, the mestizo population of the Bajío by the early eighteenth century seems to have been far more mobile than in other areas. It could easily move, for example, from one locality to another in search of better economic opportunities.[5] Importantly, the development of gigantic latifundia, which characterized the northern plains in the sixteenth and seventeenth century, and the subsequent creation of a peon class tied to the estates did not take place in the Bajío.[6]

Querétaro, the symbol and epicenter of the fluidity and dynamism of the Bajío, is situated on the eastern frontier of the region in a valley formed by mountains to the south and north. To the west lie the rich plains that form the basis of the area's agriculture, extending to Celaya, Irapuato, Salamanca, and León. The first settlement in the area after the Conquest was founded by an Otomí cacique, Hernán de Tapia, who fled his home in Jilotepec in the vicinity of Mexico City with thirty Otomí families when the Spaniards arrived in the area. He traded peacefully with the Chichimecas and lived in independence until he bowed to the power of, and joined forces with, a Spanish *encomendero*, Hernán Pérez de Bocanegra, and set about colonizing the area.

By the time of Francisca's birth, Querétaro seemed a very promising place indeed. Almost two decades earlier a group of hardy Creole and peninsular settlers had pooled their resources to buy, at the cost of five thousand pesos, the title "*Ciudad muy noble y leal*" (very noble and loyal city) as well as a handful of titles such as *regidor, depositario,* and *alferéz mayor*.[7] In doing so, they achieved the recognition they believed they deserved for their hard work and effort. The town was probably founded between 1540 and 1541, and its population remained for a few years largely Indian in composition.[8] After 1546, with the discovery of silver mines in Zacatecas, however, the town underwent a rapid transformation. One of the main routes linking the new mining settlement to the urban centers of the south passed by Querétaro. This created a new economic raison d'être for the town, which soon became an important trading center, both as an extension of the network created by Mexico City merchants and by virtue of its own food production. By 1580, Querétaro had over eighty Spanish inhabitants, whose main occupations were stock raising and trade.[9] By 1590, John Super estimates that the total population of the town had reached one thousand people of diverse ethnic origins. By 1642, the population had grown to five thousand, two thousand of whom were Spaniards.[10] From the middle of the sixteenth century onward, the Spanish Crown began to grant individual *mercedes* in the form of *sitios de estancia*. The land was initially used for raising cattle, horse, and sheep, and by 1639 *vecinos* of Querétaro possessed over one million head of sheep.[11] Descriptions of the period portray a fringe of wheat haciendas bordering the town to the west, while the land closer to the town and in the canyon was devoted to small gardens and *milpas*.[12] The richness and complexity of the area's agriculture was described by the Franciscan chronicler Alonso de la Rea in 1639: "surrounding the city there is not a foot of land that is not cultivated with seeds of all kinds, beautiful gardens, large vineyards that yield a good grape harvest, together with all sorts of Castilian fruit trees."[13]

The urban economy of Querétaro experienced an equally dynamic growth that was in large part derived from commerce, which in the course of the colonial period became ever more complex and profitable. Socially, merchants became members of and enjoyed close ties with the local elite and often served in important political posts in the town.[14] Textile shops appeared in Querétaro by the end of the sixteenth century, raising many a newcomer to the social status of merchant and landowner.[15]

The Spanish population was positioned at the top of the social ladder, mostly in such occupations as miner, merchant, hacendado, lawyer, bureaucrat, and clergyman. Owing to the town's origin as an Indian pueblo, however, its inhabitants did not live in entirely segregated areas. While the elite houses were concentrated in the center around the Plaza Mayor, it was not uncommon to find Creoles, Indians, and mestizos living on the same city block.[16] This was the environment in which Francisca de los Ángeles was born. Her family belonged to a middling stratum of artisans, carriage makers, mule drivers, and servants. It was a hybrid world of poor Creoles, mestizos, and mulattoes, quintessential products of the urban fluidity of the Bajío.[17] According to her chronicler, her mother, Antonia de Herrera, was a Creole of a "noble" but poor family. Her father, Juan Alonso, was described in Inquisition records as a mestizo.[18] The family was quite large—with nine children—and struggled to sustain itself. Juan Alonso made ceramic pots and sold fruit from his orchard.

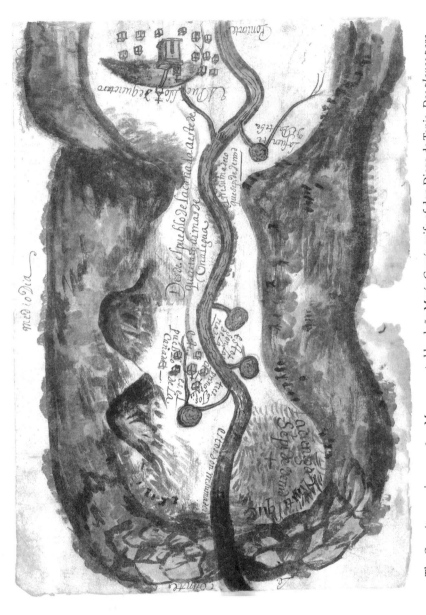

The Querétaro region, ca. 1620. Map presented by doña María García, wife of don Diego de Tapia. *Dos planos para Querétaro*. Querétaro, El Gobierno del Estado de Querétaro, Archivo Histórico de la Provincia Franciscana de Michoacán, 1999.

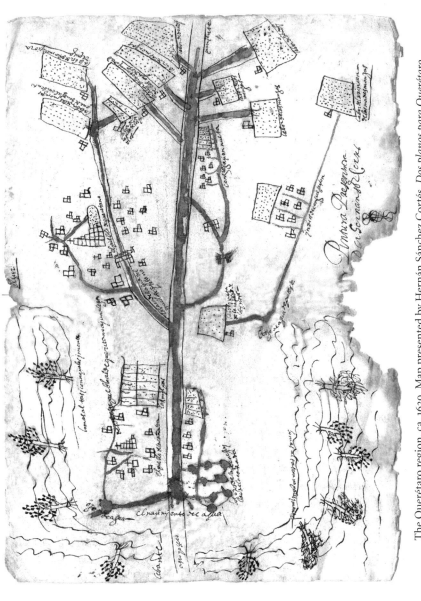

The Querétaro region, ca. 1620. Map presented by Hernán Sánchez Cortés. *Dos planos para Querétaro.* Querétaro, El Gobierno del Estado de Querétaro, Archivo Histórico de la Provincia Franciscana de Michoacán, 1999.

They lived on the western outskirts of town in a neighborhood that was both mestizo and Indian. While undoubtedly poor, Francisca's family probably did not live in squalor. Indeed, in the late seventeenth century, before the city's population boom began to strain the supply of housing and water, conditions seem to have been relatively good for most of its inhabitants. In 1689, Carlos Sigüenza y Góngora said of Querétaro: "There is no house, however small it may be, that does not have access to water that comes from wells or is conducted by masonry troughs that pass through the streets of the city. . . . As a consequence of these facilities and the fertility of the soil, one finds everywhere delicious gardens and pleasing and productive horticultural plots that have no equal in Mexico."[19] The gardens in turn produced such exotic fruits as "*el criollo, chirimollas*, avocados, white *zapotes*, bananas, *guayaba*," as well as the Spanish varieties of peaches, *membrillos, chabacanos*, and apples.[20]

Francisca's own account of her childhood is so hagiographic as to render obscure the facts. Nevertheless, it is highly probable that she grew up in considerable freedom given that both her parents were constantly at work and she probably had to shoulder the responsibilities of looking after younger siblings. Her childhood memories do indeed include wanderings into the countryside with a younger sister as well as visits to neighbors and family.[21] As she grew older, however, it rapidly became clear to her mother that it would be impossible to rely on Francisca to contribute to the family's survival. She did not fare well with household duties and showed no talent or interest in womanly occupations. Instead, she spent a large portion of her time gazing up at the stars, leading her father to brag to his friends that his daughter would become an astronomer. Friends made gentle fun of such an ambition. Certainly, in Francisca's childhood games the element of the heroic is obvious. She pranced around the orchard like a tomboy, sun-browned "like a soldier in Flanders or a Moor," which prompted family friends to maintain that she had been endowed with the wrong sex.[22]

In what seems to have been, for a time at least, a tempestuous household, Francisca may have gleaned from her parents glimpses of contrasting but equally dramatic religiosity: the rapidity with which the devil snatched a weak soul, the slow penitential ascent back to God's graces, as well as the rewards of constant and ascetic piety. Francisca's father, Juan Alonso, seems to have been of a "harsh and severe" disposition, a source of great distress to his wife according to her own account to the *beata* María de Jesús, future chronicler of the Beaterio of Santa Rosa de Viterbo. In Antonia's *vida*, it appears that neighbors also accused him of thievery, thus causing the pious lady one more mortification. It is difficult to know whether to take this account as fact. The entire *vida* is composed around the theme of Antonia's holiness—thus her reluctance to marry, her constant mortifications during the marriage, and her central role in the redemption of her husband's soul through her constant prayers. Furthermore, as Juan Alonso was a mestizo the Creole María de Jesús may have invested him with the characteristics commonly attributed by Spaniards to this ambiguous caste—dark, violent, criminal, as this would only serve to enhance Antonia's martyrdom. But if we give some credence to this account, it is clear that Francisca lived with a rather tormented father figure who in the end found peace and was "reborn" as a Franciscan tertiary, praying and practicing penance in a hermitage he constructed at the bottom of the family orchard.[23] Francisca was his favorite, according to her own account. He later told her that when he received her from her godparents' arms after baptism the sight of her had filled him with joy and he had known that she was something other than what she appeared. When he turned to the religious life, she became his main confidante. On Saturdays the two fasted and distributed bread and plates from Juan Alonso's ceramics shop to the poor. They also fasted together on particularly important novenas. And Francisca became her father's steady companion in his long final illness.[24]

In contrast with her close relationship with her father, Francisca did not have much in common with her mother. Antonia was the exemplary living martyr. With nine children, a difficult husband, and faced with constant poverty, she was the kind of woman constantly occupied in menial tasks, only sitting or kneeling to nurse, bake, sew, confess, pray, or attend mass. When Francisca was a young child, her mother's spiritual counselors and only consolation were the Carmelite friars whose monastery was nearby. She took her daughters there at an early age to receive religious instruction. Yet the defining religious influence of Francisca's childhood seems to have been her father's more tormented, dramatic religiosity.

When Francisca was five years old, the Child Jesus stepped out of the sunrays and presented himself to her as she played in the family orchard. From that time onward, Francisca's precocious nature embraced the Holy Trinity, the saints, and the angels, a divine world with which she communicated daily with vigor and enthusiasm. Later in life, in letters to her confessor she refashioned her childhood memories into exempla fit for a saint's life. One day, when her mother and sisters were busy with other tasks, Francisca was charged with making bread buns for the family. Worried that she might ruin the baking, she asked God for help. As if in answer to her request she saw a hand bless the bread as it went into the oven. When her parents came to look at the results of her baking they realized that she had baked twenty extra buns without touching more of the flour than she had been given. They decided to sell the buns, but at Francisca's insistence gave her two to distribute to the poor. The miracle of multiplication was repeated, and Francisca managed to feed up to sixty beggars for two days on her two bread buns. When an incredulous neighbor asked Francisca's mother how they could afford such extravagant charity, she answered philosophically, "the dough rose."[25] According to her narrative, on two separate occasions, when she was three and six years old, Francisca raised other children from the dead, and in another instance she returned sight to a group of blind men. In the fashion of other holy women, Francisca scorned the company of other children but spent her time in the company of the Child Jesus, who became a substitute for her family. She later recalled that on one occasion as a very small girl she had disturbed her father in his hermit's cell at prayer. She had asked him to teach her to "pray well," but he told her to leave him in peace.[26] But if her mortal family did not recognize Francisca's sense of mission, her celestial family articulated it for her. One day the Child Christ confided in her that his Divine Father had charged Francisca with a garden of souls. Thus, she became a gatekeeper of salvation just like any priest, her priesthood handed to her from God.[27]

### Institutional Culture: Splendor and Ritual

Baroque Querétaro provided fertile grounds and ample opportunities for an emerging woman mystic. A small provincial society bound together by family and business ties, its members were anxious to uphold its Spanish traditions despite its location at the edge of a wild frontier territory. The bellicose stance of the Indian groups inhabiting the impenetrable Sierra Gorda region—almost on the city's doorstep—only served to accentuate the need to erect an oasis of orthodoxy in the middle of the desert. Signs of divine pleasure or displeasure were thus anxiously watched for, while the citizens devoted their energies to building monuments to Catholic civilization.[28] Querétaro's churches contained not merely traditional iconography such as the passion and crucifixion of Christ, his baptism, the Holy Family, and legends of the Virgin but also such Tridentine themes as visionary saints like Teresa of Avila, Ignatius of Loyola, and Filippo Neri in ecstasy; the Eucharist; purgatory; and miracles.

Happily, there were signs that God looked favorably upon the devotion and hard work that had enabled the Spaniards to settle the area. The surest evidence of this grace was the existence of a miraculous image of the Virgin, named la Virgen del Pueblito, housed in the Indian village of San Francisco Galileo on a hillside two leagues from the town. According to popular legend the Virgin had sympathized with the labors of Franciscan friars working to convert the local Indians. In 1532, a Franciscan friar placed an image of the Virgin at the site the Indians used to worship their old gods. The local people began to venerate the image, which resulted in the "banishment of the devil" from the area. Word of the miraculous power of the image spread, attracting the Spanish population to its sanctuary. The image was known to sweat and shed tears, to heal the sick, to aid women during labor, to bring the city rain during the dry season, and to halt epidemics. On feast days the image was carried in a solemn procession to Querétaro where it "converted the sinful to virtue" and performed various other miracles. In 1686, a *cofradía* was founded around the image and became, in the course of the eighteenth century, one of the largest in the city.[29] The pious did not have to search far for further proof of divine benevolence. In 1613, for example, as farmers in the Querétaro valley faced worsening water shortages, a natural dam burst, providing the dried riverbed with abundant water for irrigation.

Throughout the colonial period, Querétaro became known as the "holy city of the interior."[30] The proliferation of saints' feasts in the early modern church was eminently visible in the city's cultural life. Public occasions such as the reading of the *edictos de fe* of the Inquisition provided opportunities for the town's foremost citizen to parade through the main streets in their finest livery. On the morning of these announcements, a band of trumpet and drum players led members of the town council, officers of the militia, and the Indian governor. All on horseback, they were accompanied by servants carrying their insignias and "damask robes," notaries, and priors of the religious communities to the house of the Inquisitor. From there they marched, watched by the general public, through the colorfully decorated main streets of the town on their way to the parish church of San Francisco, where the edict was read. The spectacle was a demonstration of the city's prosperity. The militia officers, inevitably among the richest and most prestigious citizens of the town, rode horses bedecked with "cloth embroidered in gold and silver, richly dressed, followed by their footmen."[31]

During the first century of Spanish settlement in Querétaro the situation of the religious orders was a precarious one. The Augustinians, who established their mission there in 1570, were repeatedly attacked, and several friars and Christian families were killed by the Chichimecas.[32] By 1600, however, as Spanish society began to take root, *queretanos* ceased sending money for pious works in Mexico City and refocused their energies on adorning their own locality with religious buildings.[33] By the late seventeenth century the religious orders as well as the secular clergy had acquired a permanent and meaningful presence in Querétaro. The most powerful group were the Franciscans, who had served as advisors to Hernán de Tapia when he founded the town. The impressive chessboardlike grid of the city streets, laid out from east to west and north to south, was the work of a Franciscan friar. The Franciscan monastery was the city's first religious institution, and its friars learned the Otomí language to minister to the indigenous population.[34] Situated in the heart of the city, the monastery's parish dominated the social and cultural life of the town for most of the colonial period. The wealth generated from the Franciscans' monopoly on baptisms, marriages, and funerals was evident in the adornments of their church and convent.[35] Between 1607 and 1630, five churches were built in the city, including the Franciscan convent of Santa Clara, the Carmelite convent, and the Jesuit college. Between 1669 and 1756, another ten churches and convents were built, the most famous of which was that of the secular congregation of Santa María de Guadalupe.[36] In 1739, a chronicler of the city commented proudly on his motives for writing his narrative: "by revealing to the world a city so populated by benefactors and monuments of religion and Christian piety the world would see that the city of Querétaro in spite of being young and founded on the edge of civilization, is so Christian and devout and pious that by maintaining at its expense so many churches and religious communities it deserved from the all powerful the many benefits that it receives from God in the form of so many miraculous religious images, which the liberal hand of the Almighty had favored it for its refuge, aid, and defense."[37]

Churches and convents were not the only symbols of Querétaro's piety. The city also boasted numerous lay religious associations and confraternities. By the end of the sixteenth century, four Spanish confraternities had been established. These were followed by Indian, mestizo, and mulatto associations. Some were mixed; others were segregated by ethnic groups and professions. A chapter of the Franciscan Third Order was founded in 1634 and remained one of the city's most powerful organizations. It attracted the city's most elite citizens well into the eighteenth century.[38] The orders and the confraternities devoted their activities to sponsoring masses and religious festivals, maintaining their churches, attending to the sick, and assisting the poorest among their members.[39] During religious festivals they paraded their images around the town's main streets, and during epidemics members of the Franciscan Third Order took out its image of Jesus Nazarene and walked with it barefoot, whipping themselves in public penance.

By the time of Francisca de los Ángeles's birth, then, Querétaro was a landscape in which the pious would not have to walk far to find haven in the cool interior of a church or a chapel. Nor would they have had to wait many days to see a baroque procession of miraculous images to exhort them onward along the road to perfection. Church bells calling the faithful to service marked the passing of the day and religious festivals the passing of the year. Clergymen and friars were a daily presence in the city's streets, and the townspeople used the imposing churches and convents as points of reference when describing locations in the city. There existed no distinct boundaries between the secular and the religious. Guardians of convents, the ecclesiastical judge, and the Inquisitor were all important figures in the town's political life, and friars and clerics influenced and took part in the decisions and everyday existence of the populace. Elite members of Creole society, for their part, provided inspirational examples of lay piety. The extravagantly wealthy militia captain, Juan Caballero y Ocio, founder and benefactor of over ten convents and churches, became a priest. The rich Marquis de la Villa del Villar del Águila constructed a house next to the Capuchin convent so he could enjoy the company and spiritual comforts of the nuns he revered so greatly. And the illustrious Col. José de Urtiaga Salazar y Parra became friend, benefactor, and advisor to the Franciscan friars of Santa Cruz.[40]

The life cycle of a large number of illustrious Querétaro families was woven into the existence of its religious institutions. Many members of the elite wore the habits of the Third Orders and perpetuated the religious culture of the town by joining multiple confraternities, often in the churches that belonged to the orders of which their family were members. They sponsored religious festivals and masses and founded chantries. Upon their death, they were buried in tertiary habits (a common tradition even if the person had not belonged to the order in his or her lifetime). The wills of *queretanos* frequently reflect these complex cultural connections with religious institutions. In 1678, for example, when the Creole *doncella* and Franciscan tertiary Ana de Lezea made her will, she left an allowance for two hundred *misas resadas*, donated her jewels to the cult of a saint's image in Santa Clara, and founded a chaplaincy for the Jesuits.[41] In this manner, Querétaro's aristocratic families were thoroughly integrated into the Tridentine church and its sacramental order. They demonstrated an orthodox faith in the redemptory intercession of the church before the divine patriarch, accepting its power in all walks of life.

Popular Culture

Interwoven with piety and righteousness in the fabric of Querétaro's baroque culture was a delight in bullfighting, gambling, public bathing at the reservoir, and dancing. *Queretanos* also shared with their fellow colonials a taste for theater. During the 1680 consecration of the sumptuous Church of Guadalupe, for example, the ceremonies were not limited to pious rituals. At the entry to the church, on an ornate stage, costumed actors performed a piece by the high priest of baroque theatre, Calderón de la Barca. The following days were taken up by such secular delights as bullfights, poetry competitions, and evening fireworks. The festivities were crowned by an elaborate *mascarada* (parade) that began with a thrilling display of the contrasting elements of their fragile, frontier world: a group of almost nude, aggressively painted Chichimeca horse riders and a band of Indians dressed as other famous Chichimeca and Aztec kings and emperors accompanied by an orderly procession of Spaniards in their finest livery. These were followed by a lone horse rider in the guise of Charles V. Completing the *mascarada* was a carriage covered with a model of silvery, white, and blue waves that supported an ornate boat strewn with flowers. On the boat was raised the image of the Virgin of Guadalupe, sheltered by a large seashell against a background of colorful silk. At the foot of the image knelt a small girl dressed in sumptuous Indian attire, symbolizing the New World's complete subjection to the Virgin. To underscore the notion of popular adoration, the girl held the image of a heart in her hands.[42]

Such colorful devotion did not necessarily translate into full adherence to church-imposed restrictions on sexuality. *Hijos naturales* was a common term in the baptistery registry of Spanish parishes in the late seventeenth century, and it did not usually convey any stigma on the honor of the child or its parents.[43] Rather, such amorous liaisons between unmarried couples in effect fueled enthusiastic gossip. In 1669, doña Maria Sanchez de Azevedo y Mendoza of neighboring San Juan del Río sued don Francisco Xavier Hurtado de Mendoza for having seduced her under the promise of marriage, and then reneging when she became pregnant.[44] In 1682, José de Casaos, a Creole, was thrown into prison to force him to marry a woman he had been living with for several years.[45]

Gambling presented another of the devil's more effective temptations and led many pious *queretanos* astray. Chronicles and town records are full of such cases. In 1678, for example, *alferéz* don Phelipe de Arroyo Sandoval, commissioner of the Inquisition in Querétaro, made a pledge—even registering it with a notary—to quit gambling altogether for three years. His pledge stipulated that if he broke his promise his self-inflicted punishment would be a one thousand–peso donation to the convent of San Antonio.[46]

Another much-traveled road to perdition amongst *queretanos* was superstition and a widespread belief in witchcraft. Indeed, this pious city, so notable for its charitable support of the clergy, was permeated by popular traditions reminiscent of Spain before the full thrust of the Counter-Reformation.[47] The few unlucky perpetrators who went too far or who for some other reason were denounced to the Inquisition were mostly city-dwelling mestizo women of humble means. The most sought-after skills in such *hechiceras* were mixing and preparing the powders that pacified difficult husbands and brought back unfaithful lovers. They also used peyote and other indigenous ingredients to cure all sorts of ills, whether mental or physical. In 1689, da Juana de Tovar, a Creole widow who lived on the edge of town, was prosecuted as a *supersticiosa* and *sacrilega*. Doña Juana freely doled out powders for various amorous problems, used magic wands blessed by friars to find buried treasures, stuck needles in wax dolls to hurt her enemies. She also used peyote and unearthed secrets and foretold the future with the help of broken porcelain pieces thrown into a pitcher of water. Once the edict containing the accusation against Doña Juana was read in the pulpit at the city's main churches, throngs of people, from Creole *arrieros* to African slaves, came to give their testimony.[48]

But the humbler elements of Spanish society were not the only ones to get into trouble for their faith in superstitious practices. In 1709, for instance, Magdalena de Zárate, member of an established Creole family, denounced Juana Molina, also a Spaniard, for persuading her that there was a treasure hidden under her house that could be found with the help of a magic wand said to have belonged to Saint Peter Martyr. Involved in the case with Juana were several upstanding personages. One was a Franciscan tertiary, another was the nephew of a rich merchant, and yet another was described as a distinguished citizen of town who also wore the Franciscan tertiary habit.[49]

Baroque Querétaro thus fostered a delight in worldly pleasures, a taste for theater and splendid ritual culture, orthodox piety, superstition, witchcraft, and heresy. But in the last two decades of the seventeenth century the most prominent feature of the city's cultural life became the religiosity of its female population, from the rich nuns of Santa Clara to humble *beatas* and extravagant heretics. This Querétaro formed the adult Francisca de los Ángeles.

## 2   Women in Baroque Querétaro

### Santa Clara

By the latter half of the seventeenth century, cultural life in Querétaro presented a broad spectrum of female spirituality, from the rich nuns of the convent of Santa Clara de Jesús to a curious mixture of pious *beatas, curanderas,* witches, and heretics. It included women of all stations and ethnic mixtures, many of whom acquired a local reputation. At the apogee of this little world was the splendid example of female monastic life in Querétaro, the rich, elite convent of Santa Clara de Jesús.

Like the myriad of female convents that had been established in the colony by the end of the seventeenth century, Santa Clara was a source of pride, a symbol of orthodoxy, and a central player in the reproduction of culture and society for Querétaro's elite.[1] In effect, it served as no less than a justification to the divine eye of the town's existence. Most of New Spain's inhabitants in the seventeenth century would probably have agreed that there was a need to maintain an army of religious, male and female, who would pray around the clock to soothe celestial fury and ensure the welfare of the colony. The female convents in particular served the important role of praying for the success of their brethren and the welfare of the community.[2] They contained personages famous locally for their holy example, sheltered and raised children in a most desirable cloistered fashion, and served as ritual centers for the cities. But in the most baroque of twists they were also romantic places where young men courted blushing young nuns across the convent rails, where scandalous behavior and the relaxation of rules provided excellent fodder for town gossip. While nuns could be austere, forbidding people they could also be compelling figures. In 1650, the "lieutenant-nun," Catalina de Erauso, a runaway Basque novice who was reported to have spent eighteen years in Spain and its colonies disguised as a man, died in Mexico. Her story would be immortalized by playwright Juan Pérez de Montalban and was probably known by the late seventeenth century to a great many people in the region.[3] Almost two centuries later, in 1840, the Englishwoman Francis Calderón de la Barca described the sight of the young novices of the Santa Teresa convent in Mexico City—grouped together on a *matte Turque* while she sat in a luxurious chair before a table loaded with "cakes, chocolate, ices, creams, custards, tarts, jellies"—as the most picturesque scene she had ever laid eyes on.[4]

Among the great variety of conventual foundations in the colony, Santa Clara occupied a rather middling position. A provincial convent filled with daughters of rich families, its religious culture, aside from a few ascetic examples, was genteel and permissive. The convent was founded by the cacique Diego de Tapia, son of the city's Otomí founder. He had only one child, a daughter named Luisa, who was raised in the convent of San Juan de la Penitencia in Mexico City. When the time came for her to *tomar estado*, that is, to marry or take the veil, a close adviser of his, the Franciscan friar Miguel López, persuaded Diego to found a convent in his native town where Luisa could become a nun. The Tapia family possessed great estates around Querétaro; all of Diego's sisters were childless and contributed some of their property to the foundation. Don Diego himself donated ten of his haciendas on the condition that he and his daughter would be registered as the founding patrons.[5]

In the early seventeenth century the Spanish population of Querétaro had grown considerably. Apparently, there were at least two hundred Spanish *vecinos* who proclaimed their willingness to support the foundation financially on the grounds that their daughters would one day enter the institution.[6] As the town was growing, and did not as of yet have any religious institutions for women, royal approval was promptly granted.

The new foundation took the rule of the urbanist Clares. They were allowed to possess property, a necessity for a convent founded in order to shelter elite women. Santa Clara slowly expanded to accommodate its ever growing population.[7] During the colonial period it occupied over four modern city blocks so its walls contained a bustling town of streets, gardens, public fountains, over sixty individual "cells" large enough to house the nuns and their company, and ten chapels.[8] While the founding nun had been Indian, no other Indian noblewomen professed in the convent. Its administration was taken over by Spanish nuns who came from the leading families of the town. During the seventeenth century the convent came to house a large religious and secular population. In 1639 there were already 60 nuns and 130 laywomen, mostly servants but also girls and women, residing in the convent.[9] By the end of the seventeenth century that number had grown to a little under 100 nuns and 600 servants.[10]

Santa Clara rapidly produced icons of female religiosity to serve as role models for the pious and yet worldly population.[11] When Antonia de San

Jacinto, a poor nun in Santa Clara, died in 1682, a cult instantly formed around her saintly memory. On November 20, 1683, the one-year anniversary of her death, the Santa Clara convent in Querétaro called its faithful flock to mass with mourning bells. The city's elite, clad in black, emerged from its residences in the streets surrounding the convent and made its way to the church where a multitude had gathered rapidly. The crowd eventually filled the church and its entrances, forcing many devotees to turn away.

Famed throughout Querétaro in her lifetime for her virtue, Antonia had been a poor nun whose saintly ways and hermetic nature had so distinguished her from the other nuns that many had tried to persuade her not to profess. She died when Francisca de los Ángeles was nine years old. Whether she knew or had caught a glimpse of the icon, we do not know, but it is likely that she had heard of her reputation, especially since Antonia's biographer, Fray José Gómez, enthusiastically spread the word of her holiness. According to his biography of the nun, Antonia "was always in the presence of her husband, working to please him as much as possible in her mortifications of discipline, cilices, fasts and vigils, with the practice of silence, withdrawal, humility, and prayer."[12] Conscientious and obedient, she attended all masses conducted in the church, prayed in the lower choir from nine to three every night, and humbly adored and obeyed her confessor.[13] Intensely mystical, her energies focused on constant fasting and self-mortification. The Eucharist effected mystical union with God, and according to a witness her face glowed like "polished silver" whenever she received it. At times her hunger for the host could only be satiated by taking communion on two consecutive days.[14] In the nun's struggle for saintliness she fought the classic battle with the devil, who had persecuted her since childhood, staged accidents in which she hurt herself, and haunted her so persistently in her daily conventual activities that it became common knowledge among its inhabitants.[15] The nun's life, in Gómez's version of it, thus contained all the hagiographic elements necessary for the creation of a proper Tridentine icon of holiness to be held up to women like Francisca de los Ángeles.

Nevertheless, a more careful reading of Antonia's biography reveals assertive aspects of her piety that would also characterize Francisca's future relationship with the institutional church and its male members. In Antonia, should Francisca have observed her from afar, she would have caught a firsthand glimpse of the other side of the feminine coin. Antonia evaded the authority of the church, refusing—although diplomatically—to partake in the communal office of oral prayer, saw prophetic visions, cast herself as

God's messenger to men, and reversed her role as a nun and disciple to become the spiritual teacher of her confessor and other clerics. This saintly nun then flirted with *alumbradismo* as it had been defined by the Holy Office.[16] According to Gómez, Antonia was so enraptured in "continued contemplation that she could not recite the Holy Office vocally."[17] In an age when a direct communication with God lifted a person to a level above his or her peers, such experience offered a perfect excuse to evade a communal ritual. During her raptures Antonia saw visions of souls ascending from purgatory, and on one occasion she saw a vision of Christ falling to his knees under the burden of the cross, which told her that he could no longer support the sins of priests, nuns, and monks.[18] By virtue of her undisputed and privileged communication with the divine, Antonia was thus able to formulate criticisms of the church. Her critical eye could also be turned toward the townspeople. On repeated occasions, for example, she saw a vision of a recently deceased prominent Querétaro citizen wearing rich attire and sitting in a carriage consumed by flames.[19]

In the security of her orthodox reputation Antonia could take further, independent steps by counseling male ecclesiastics. It is clear from Gómez's account that he was enraptured by the spirit of his protégée; he found that "her lips were instruments through which God announced [his sentences]."[20] On many occasions, he confessed, "by reason of impulses that I could not resist, I found myself going to the Church of Santa Clara, to find there Mother Antonia by the rails of the lower choir and she would say to me, here I am, waiting for you because I asked God to bring you to me."[21]

Gómez was not the only one to enjoy the fruits of Antonia's special relations with God. She commonly gave advice to the younger nuns in the convent and, on one occasion, taught the mistress of novices the techniques of mental prayer by accompanying her in prayer until two in the morning every night for many days.[22] We know from Gómez's account that Antonia was revered by Querétaro's priests and friars. One comment of his is particularly revealing: "a priest, attempting to perfect himself, communicated with Mother Antonia for some days and then ceased seeing her, and entering carelessly into the Church of Santa Clara, and not realizing that he would see her, the first thing offered to his eyes was Mother Antonia by the grilles of the choir and she asked him how he was? Words did not come to him immediately to tell her of his state of affairs and then Mother Antonia said laughingly: 'If you don't do what I tell you, how are you going to take advantage of it? [her teachings].'"[23]

Antonia finally died "a heavenly death" in her closed cell into which she allowed only her confessor and the town's most illustrious friars and priests. The Franciscan commissary general, visiting Querétaro at the time, had questioned the nun on her religious spirit, declared her *en-diosada* (possessed by God), and asked to be with her at the hour of her death.

After her death and well-attended burial, Antonia's cult grew rapidly within conventual and town society. Bits of her old habits were used to cure the ill during an epidemic that hit Santa Clara, and were solicited by the laity for that purpose. The anniversary sermon extolled her virtues, poverty, and constant battle against the devil and moved churchgoers to tears, many of whom besieged the nuns for some of Antonia's relics. The sermon was so successful that the town's wealthy cleric, don Juan Caballero y Ocio, had it printed at his own expense for public edification. With such encouragement Antonia's cult grew over the years, and in 1686 her remains were excavated and moved to a more prominent and distinguished place in the church. In saintly tradition, her body was found to be uncorrupted, and once the abbess and friars were out of sight the nuns and Indian workmen began to tear pieces of her clothing and wrap them in paper as if she were already a recognized saint.[24]

Antonia was not the only Santa Clara nun to enjoy a saintly reputation. A Santa Clara abbess of the period, María de la Presentación, was reputed to possess the power to wake people from the dead, to call animals magically, and to receive visions and favors from the divine. The nun owed her fame to Col. José Urtiaga, who possessed her mystical writings. Urtiaga was so successful in his efforts on her behalf that the viceroy, persuaded of her powers, demanded through royal patronage that she be elected abbess of Santa Clara.[25]

The mystique of such women and their connection to the divine was further imparted to the populace through sermons at profession ceremonies and funerals of nuns. When Teresa, daughter of the illustrious Querétaro citizen Juan Martínez Lucio, professed in Santa Clara in 1719, her brother, who preached the sermon, impressed his audience with a poetic image of his sister ascending to heaven and being received by her divine groom: "Do you not see her? Do you not see how she takes her eyes off yours? Do you not see how she lifts them to the Empyreum? How, using a cloud as a beautiful white veil she hides in it so that already we begin to lose sight of her? Look carefully at this cloud: look how she leaves the crudities of this earth to ascend to the Supreme Region."[26]

Such sermons clothed the life of the nun in biblical images, relating it to the passion of Christ and the sorrow of Mary. Martínez Lucio proudly declared that just as Christ had earned divine glory in his sacrifice so would Teresa through the "holocaust" of her religious vows. When the orphan Ana María de los Dolores professed in 1712 she was reminded that her most important religious duty was to weep, like Mary, for the crucified Christ.[27] These words were pronounced not merely for the edification of the novice but also for the benefit of the public. They articulated to the congregation that the city's convents were sacred territories in which the divine and the mortal were interlaced, apertures into the supernatural world. As members of a network of extended familial and entrepreneurial relationships, the Creole citizens of Querétaro most likely felt that they had a share in a family's sacrifice whether they were blood relations or not.

Santa Clara and its nuns thus exemplified to the humbler elements of Querétaro's citizenry, such as Francisca de los Ángeles and her family, this society's collective piety and its Iberian cultural ancestry. The sacrifice of their daughters to a life behind walls affirmed the cultural leadership of elite patriarchs. It demonstrated not merely their pious unselfishness but also their family's closeness to God, achieved through their nun daughters' elevated status.

### Worldliness in "Paradise"

Nevertheless, as with Antonia de San Jacinto's religiosity, institutional religious life in Santa Clara presented its less hagiographic elements. In this "heavenly garden" of Christ, worldliness was an inescapable baroque element of the equation. As daughters of prosperous families, the majority of the nuns received capital endowments on their families' estates that generated a yearly living allowance of 150 to 300 pesos.[28] Many members of this group received estates instead of endowments for these purposes, and others inherited estates while they were nuns.[29] They lived in cells whose value averaged between 800 and 3,000 pesos, or several times the price of a good house on the Querétaro property market of the period.[30]

In their daily activities, the inhabitants of Santa Clara were not separated from the bustle of life on the other side of the convent's walls. In fact, several of the cells were built into the outer walls surrounding it, directly facing the street. The convent endured constant street traffic as nuns, servants, laywomen, and girls as well as visitors such as doctors, priests, and artisans went about their occupations.[31] In a religious community whose rules required extended silent periods of prayer and meditation, the constant circulation of people resulted in slack observance of these regulations and became an incessant source of admonishment from the provincials. They complained of servants chatting in the plazas during silent hours and of the presence of pets such as cats, dogs, and monkeys, which made the convent resemble a "farmhouse" rather than a religious institution.[32]

With the movements of laypeople, worldliness flowed into the convent. Every day, a small market was set up in the cemetery outside the convent's *locutorios*. Here, the servants purchased household necessities and chatted with the vendors, from whom they brought the nuns news of the world. The servants' movements were not restricted to the market; they entered and left the convent freely and often lived there with their children.[33] The nuns traditionally enjoyed warm friendships with their doctors and confessors, who frequently made long visits to the cells. At times, they stayed longer than needed to drink chocolate and chat, and their social manners were sometimes those customary in the outside world, including greetings with kisses and hugs.[34] At the close of their day, workers laboring on construction within the convent grounds brought water to the nuns. Musicians came to teach laywomen and nuns to play instruments and broke convent rules by giving private lessons in their individual cells rather than in the *rejas* under the scrutiny of other nuns.[35]

The dress of laywomen, girls, and servants brought yet another reminder of the world. Because it emphasized individual style and reflected the fashions of the period, their appearance became a constant source of criticism by the provincials. In this aspect at least, class lines were blurred, and the friars, desperately trying to maintain a semblance of class order, instructed the abbess that only women and girls of high social rank should be permitted to wear elaborate clothing. The servant girls were found to wear indecent attire such as pearls, broaches, necklaces, earrings, and skirts with slits in them.[36] The residents, who consisted of women of every age, wore low-cut blouses and open shoes.[37]

Such individuality in attire was not merely characteristic of the lay population. Many nuns, whose dress was uniform according to their regulations, added a personal touch to their attire. They were found to embellish their habits with wide skirts, ornate blouses, lace, and even silk stockings. In 1709 the provincial ordered that the nuns' habits be simplified: "ceasing to use any adornments, the skirts and habits should be smaller in diameter . . . and that the abuse of worldly shirts cease but if they have to be used instead of the tunics that should be used according to the rule, they should be used

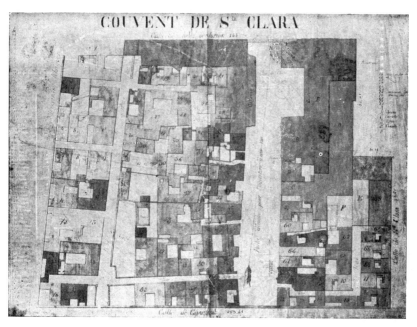

Map drawn by the French army in 1864, showing the maze of buildings and streets that was the convent of Santa Clara. *Cartografía de Querétaro, colección de 35 planos de la ciudad capital y del estado.* Facsimile, 2nd ed., Querétaro, El Gobierno del Estado de Querétaro, 1978.

as remedies, honestly, not symbolizing the victory of vanity."[38] Complaints over appearance were a constant theme of the dispatches from the provincials throughout the century. One friar's indignation reached such a pitch that he exclaimed, "You were called to religion to serve as brides of Christ, therefore please try to pay more attention to religion and not to what you wear!"[39]

Finally, worldly festivities were an integral component of conventual culture. In 1742, the provincial banned the practice of celebrating nuns' twelfth year in the convent with fandangos and other "profane" music in the *locutorios.* On abbesses' birthdays the creativity of the nuns took a more extravagant turn. According to Fray José Santos, all classes of the convent's population—nuns, servants, and residents—dressed as men and sang and played music.

### Witches, Heretics, and the Franciscan Friars of Propaganda Fide

While Francisca undoubtedly had the opportunity to observe the strange mixture of splendor and earthiness, austerity and extravagance, that characterized life at Santa Clara, she herself belonged to a world from which sprang a more radical, and hence heretical, female religious culture. It was from Francisca's social milieu of poor Creoles and people of mixed ethnicity that Querétaro's *curanderas* and witches emerged.

This group, predominantly composed of women—although men were sometimes noted *hechizeros*—was largely left to its own devices by the Inquisition. The exception were cases when it was proven that they had made a pact with the devil. Indeed, the devil seemed to lie in wait on all street corners of this pious town. He seduced men and women of all stations and ethnic groups. The aforementioned doña Juana de Tovar, like Francisca's family, lived, for example, on the outskirts of town and associated with poor mestizos and Indians. Her punishment was measured by the fact that she had clearly made a pact with the devil. She was thus paraded through Mexico City in an *auto-da-fé*, taken around the streets with the mark of *supersticiosa* sown into her clothes, and sentenced to one year of forced labor at the Hospital de Dios in the capital as well as a six-year exile from Querétaro.[40] In 1675, a Creole dance and music teacher named Domingo de Silva was accused of putting a spell on people after making a pact with the devil.[41] The devil's power was well known, and in moments of desperation people were willing to trade in their piety for quick and successful action from the other side. In 1663, for example, Pablo de Casas, a Creole merchant in Querétaro, was losing heavily in a game of cards one Saturday morning when he was heard to grumble: "The mass of Our Lady, do you hear me, take it." A scandalized player immediately denounced him to the Inquisition.[42]

Beginning in 1686, however, the devil began to orchestrate vehement attacks on the God-fearing populace. In that year, a scandal brewed as a twenty-year-old mestiza, Josepha Ramos, servant of the local apothecary and wife of an Indian shoemaker, presented herself to the Querétaro Inquisitor. It seemed that town gossip had blamed her for the illness of her ex-lover, the Creole barber Juan Patino, as well as his sister-in-law. According to Josepha's testimony, a Creole woman had furnished her with powders to mix in her lover's chocolate so he would be unable to consummate the marriage he was about to enter into with another Creole woman. Having spent three consecutive nights with his bride without being able to consummate the marriage he begged Josepha to release him from her spell, a plea to which she acquiesced. The newlyweds were then able to have marital relations, but a few days afterward Patino fell gravely ill with a high fever. On that day, witnesses saw Josepha come to the house and embrace the bride's younger sister, who promptly fell ill with similar symptoms. The bride's family petitioned the ecclesiastical judge to order Josepha back to the house to release the sick from their pains. A notary brought her back, but at that point the plot thickened, for this was no case of ordinary witchcraft. Josepha declared that she really had no authority in the matter because the devil had come to her one night in the form of a man, promising to hurt her lover's new family should she pledge to become his slave. Josepha neither accepted nor denied his offer, and the next day she found that witnesses had seen her embrace the sister-in-law. Her argument was thus that the devil had worked his evil deeds in her likeness. While obviously terror stricken, Josepha clearly enjoyed the awe and fear with which her lover's in-laws regarded her. She set about anointing the sick with herbs; feeding them liquids, which only seemed to aggravate their condition; and, with rosary in hand, cried out to those present in the house that she had just seen the devil present. In a few days, the townspeople "spoke of nothing else," and the Inquisitor busily set about taking testimonies. The curious asked Josepha if she really "communicated" with the devil, and what he looked like. Happily feeding their imagination she informed them that he had come to her as a large man with the mask of a bull. The Inquisitors were also curious as to what exactly took place during her conversations with the devil, and in 1688 decided to interrogate her further, but by that time Josepha had quietly left the city.[43]

It was not until 1691 that the Inquisition, with renewed vigor, hunted Josepha down. By that time her case had become far more interesting. A large group of virtuous Creole women had emerged in Querétaro claiming to be possessed by the devil. They all blamed the *maleficio* on Josepha. By that time Josepha Ramos must have thought that she had mercifully evaded the attentions of the Inquisition. She had gone away to live in neighboring Celaya with her husband. The couple had had a son and then peacefully returned to Querétaro to work for the local apothecary's family. Although Josepha was known in the town as an *hechizera*, people seem to have avoided her rather than taunt her. But unbeknownst to Josepha, Querétaro's cultural life had undergone profound changes that were to drastically reverse her good fortune.[44]

In 1683, a year after Antonia de San Jacinto's death, and three years before Josepha first came to the attention of the Inquisition, a group of peninsular friars arrived in the city. They came from special recollect monasteries of the observant provinces of Spain where friars had been leading particularly meditative and ascetic lives since the monasteries' founding in the early seventeenth century. The arrival of the Franciscans in New Spain was due to the efforts of friar Antonio Llinás from Mallorca, who came to the colony in 1664 and spent over a decade in Valladolid, Celaya, and Querétaro. The neighboring Sierra Gorda region, with its unsubjugated and loosely organized Indian tribes, captured his apostolic imagination. When he returned to Spain in 1680 to attend the general chapter of the Franciscan Order, he succeeded in persuading the minister general, Fray José Ximenes Samaniego, that it was imperative to rescue the Sierra Gorda mountains from the dark grasp of the devil. It was a compelling argument at the time since in that same year twenty-one Franciscan friars had been killed by Indians in New Mexico. Llinás's romantic idea was to pluck eleven apostolic friars from convents in Spain and take them straight into Sierra Gorda. His evangelical dreams undoubtedly focused on the restoration of the Franciscan "Golden Age" of the first century after the Spanish Conquest, a phenomenon since dwarfed by the achievements of the Jesuit Order. The more sophisticated Samaniego immediately understood that the plan was suicidal and advised the conventional method of obtaining royal permission to found apostolic colleges. The most convenient location due to its proximity to the mountains would be Querétaro.[45] Llinás could not have applied at a more opportune time. Both Crown and papacy were anxious to see some progress in the evangelization of the New World following a long lull in which parishes had been filled with overly comfortable clergy. And Samaniego had known the famed Madre Agreda, who during her spiritual bilocations to New Mexico had encountered multitudes of Indians living in pagan darkness.[46] Llinás campaigned successfully to persuade friars from recollect convents in the peninsula to dedicate either half of each year or a decade of their lives to the preaching of the Christian doctrine.[47] He then obtained papal and royal approval for a college in Querétaro, which was placed under the papacy's missionary department: The Congregation for the Propagation of Faith.[48]

The twenty Spanish friars accompanying Llinás arrived in New Spain in 1683. They quickly dispersed throughout the country, traveling on foot, preaching, and founding new colleges. The first college was inaugurated in Querétaro in 1683, the second was founded in Zacatecas in 1707, and a third was opened in Mexico City in 1731. The friars emulated the style of the original Franciscan mendicants. Carrying only a cross and a breviary they entered the towns singing the litany of the Virgin, preached in the churches, and confessed the townspeople. In this dramatic manner their missions and colleges had a profound impact on the religious and cultural life of the colony in the eighteenth century.[49]

As soon as the Franciscan missionaries arrived it was evident that they differed greatly from the other religious communities already established in Querétaro. The rules pertaining to the size and behavior of the community were already a clear indication of this. No more than thirty friars were to reside in the college at one time: twenty-six missionaries and four lay brothers whose duty was to beg for alms for the community. They were to observe the rules of the Friars Minor with its focus on poverty and communal life. Prospective missionaries were to undergo thorough training in preparation for their mission and learn the indigenous languages of the region in question.[50] The Propaganda Fide chronicler, Fray Isidro Félix de Espinosa, noted that "as the missionaries came from foreign regions, the inhabitants of Querétaro listened to them as if they were men of another world."[51] For their part, the friars found that in Querétaro—so close to the devil's territory and so far from the purifying influence of the Mother Church—Indians and Spaniards alike had fallen en masse into the grave of worldliness and sin. On the important Holy Cross feast day, the townspeople, rather than congregate quietly and reverently in the churches, built an extravagant cross and monument on the town square, where they reenacted the battle for Querétaro that purportedly had occurred on the site. Afterward, they stood vigil around the cross throughout the night with torches, music, and dance, creating a splendid social affair in which young upper-class women used the rare opportunity to flirt in freedom with their *galanes*. As for the Indians, the scandalized friars maintained that the men pawned the dresses off their women and went out drinking and carousing with prostitutes while their women, naked at home, could not even attend mass. Alcohol-induced homicides were rampant among the indigenous population according to the friars, who later boasted of having curbed Indian criminality through their rigorous indoctrination.[52]

Querétaro thus provided an excellent training ground for the zealous Franciscans on their path to greater glory among the *infieles*. Formed in the climate of post-Tridentine Catholicism in the mother country, they placed special emphasis on securing the ties between Christians and the church. They did this through severe religious indoctrination in which they followed popular devotions such as the Stations of the Cross and the penitential mission that focused on effecting mass demonstrations of penance through the preachers' dramatic sermons. Michael P. Carroll has noted how effective the preaching orders of Counter-Reformation Italy were in joining the post-Tridentine Church's "dynamic christocentrism" to popular traditions based upon the visual such as processions and passion plays. This union of "official" and "popular" Catholicism lay at the core of Propaganda Fide's mission in New Spain.[53] Like the Jesuits, the most successful proponents of Catholic renewal, their priorities lay in preaching and working among the laity rather than dedicating their energies to communal liturgy. The friars were all young, on average in their mid- to late twenties, and turned energetically to the task of winning *queretanos* over to their side.[54] On the first Sunday after their arrival they gave the townspeople an indication of the rhetorical *blitzkrieg* they would employ to win them back to God. They mounted every pulpit in the city and raised their voices in thunderous and theatrical sermons never heard before in this relatively comfortable town. For the benefit of those who could not be dragged to church, several friars walked the streets and preached.[55]

The mission lasted an entire month, after which, in the chronicler Espinosa's opinion, inhabitants at the very least took care to sin in secret.[56] Querétaro's surrounding haciendas did not escape the friars' attention either.[57] Scandalized that the town's churches were not open all day on important occasions such as Holy Thursday, they threw open the doors to their church day and night. In response, *queretanos* as well as the inhabitants of neighboring ranches and haciendas thronged their church throughout Lent, day and night. The friars offered further spectacles to the bemused populace by regularly performing the *via crucis* in their cemetery before large audiences. They continued to preach on street corners and plazas and set an example in their own mode of life by taking religious practices such as fasting and mortification to an extreme form. For example, they regularly deprived themselves of sleep, whipped and beat themselves, and carried heavy crosses and crowns of thorns.[58] Catching the town's sleeping inhabitants unaware, two or three friars would walk the streets at night singing psalms and preaching in loud voices on the street corners.[59] Their influence on Querétaro's traditionally festive town life was such that when an inhabitant who returned to the city after a long absence asked a passerby for news, he replied: "Sir, Querétaro is no longer Querétaro, for some Fathers of the Cross have arrived and they are so impertinent that now everything is very sad, one cannot hear one harp, nor one guitar, all is prayer and sermons."[60]

The friars specifically targeted women in their teachings, encouraging townswomen to abandon their household tasks to attend their sermons. Women flocked to their confessionals and remained for hours in intimate and emotional discussions. A large group of poor *queretanas* also frequented the steps of the Santa Cruz chapel, where the friars would always give them food.[61] Among the most devoted and favored female devotees of the Franciscans was

Francisca de los Ángeles. Nine years old at the time of their arrival, she was so taken with their dramatic and elaborate preaching on the city's streets that she managed to persuade an aunt who frequented Santa Cruz to take her to mass there. The Carmelite friars who confessed her family told her not to bother, for the friars would be away constantly on mission.[62] Contrary to her family, which had always remained loyal to the Carmelite convent, Francisca began confessing with the friars of Propaganda Fide. Her independence, however, was short lived. On one occasion the mass at Santa Cruz lasted long into the night, and her scandalized father prohibited her from attending further services. Francisca nevertheless persevered in insisting that she confess with the Franciscans and waited patiently for them while they were away on mission. She thus invited the wrath of her former Carmelite confessor, who refused her communion. In the end, however, she succeeded in persuading her whole family to turn to Santa Cruz for religious services.[63]

The missionaries immediately recognized in Francisca signs that she had been chosen by God. From the moment of her first confession in Santa Cruz in 1683 the Franciscans treated her with special affection and attention. Taking advantage of their independent status—for they had been placed directly under the authority of the Franciscan Commissary in Mexico City—they acquired written permission from the capital to confess her.[64] Her first mentor was one of the most prominent friars of the college, Fray Pedro de Sitjar. They also persuaded her reluctant father to allow Francisca to take the habit of a Franciscan tertiary while still a young girl. By becoming a tertiary Francisca thus joined a long tradition of female religious who were not institutionally bound by lifelong vows to a cloister and were thus as a rule more charismatic and independent in their religiosity. Such women followed prayer practices and routines that were not necessarily prescribed by the institutional church, nor were their lifestyles uniform. Some lived and practiced their religion in the shelter of a family house; others grouped together and made their own living. In the thirteenth and fourteenth centuries, such groups put their stamp on urban life in northern Europe and were called Beguines. In 1230, for example, Beguines constituted 15 percent of the adult female population of Cologne. In Italy and Spain, such women were called intermittently *beatas* or tertiaries.[65] Francisca embraced her vocation with ambition and rid herself of whatever material items she possessed, save images of Christ, the Virgin, and Santa Rosa de Viterbo, her favorite female saint; a terrine; a pillow; a wool blanket; a habit and two tunics; two petticoats and kerchiefs; as well as headdresses and sandals. Although she lived with her family, she nevertheless survived off ecclesiastical charity. The former provincial of the Franciscan Order in Querétaro daily sent her some mutton and two buns of bread and provided her with a new habit every year. The same friar seems to have made some vague promises about taking her to Mexico City and obtaining entry there for her into a convent, but the plan was never carried out.[66]

Why did the Santa Cruz friars not enter Francisca into the convent of Santa Clara as a lay protégée of a nun so as to find her a rich benefactor she might later profess under? After all, the friars enjoyed intimate friendships with the nuns. Perhaps her mestizo background presented a hindrance, although that is unlikely since many of the Santa Clara nuns in all probability had similar backgrounds. It is more likely that in Francisca they recognized charismatic gifts that made her unsuitable for conventual life, and perhaps they wanted to keep this potential treasure chest of mystical knowledge within easy reach. Throughout the ages, women like Francisca had attracted groups of male devotees, "spiritual directors" like Antonia de San Jacinto's Fray José Gómez, who were more interested in approaching the divine mysteries through their disciples than steering their souls.

In any case, the friars most likely taught Francisca how to read and write (though she later noted that she had taught herself) as well as some rudimentary Latin.[67] Sometime in the 1680s Fray Pedro de Sitjar began to command Francisca to write down the miracles she performed and visions she experienced, and for that purpose he sent her *cuadernitos* of paper. While the order demonstrates the Franciscans' interest in their new protégée's experiences, letters were a time-tried method used by spiritual directors to regulate the problematic spirituality of women.[68] The letters were then copied and probably edited and kept under lock at Santa Cruz. But while Francisca de los Ángeles was engaged in apprenticeship as a holy woman under the tutelage of the friars, other female followers of theirs went much further and in a more blatantly heretical direction. Concerned as they were with putting the fear of God in the populace and strengthening their position in town society, the friars paid particular attention to the devil, elaborating on the subject in their thundering preaching. Their success in capturing the imagination of townswomen became evident when, in the fall of 1691, a crisis of diabolical possession erupted in Querétaro. The possessed women were devotees of the Franciscans of the Colegio de Santa Cruz, and their numbers had so increased during the autumn that by December the city's Inquisitor reported that a new case emerged every day.

The affair began in late summer 1691 when Juana de los Reyes, a young Spanish *donzella* of an impoverished family with elite connections, suddenly fell into a stupor. Her frightened parents called the guardian of Santa Cruz, Fray Sarmiento, to administer the last rites. Sarmiento, a veteran in matters of diabolical possessions by virtue of his experiences in Spain, immediately thought he recognized signs that demons had entered the girl's body. For several days the girl lay immobile and unable to speak, and when she finally regained consciousness she would only speak to Sarmiento. In the fall of 1691, Sarmiento and a small group of Franciscan friars began to spend "day and night" in Juana's house exorcising her. The girl emitted strange objects from her body, such as toads, balls of wool, and nails. The devil often tore her clothes to shreds in the presence of the friars and spoke through Juana, curiously enough only in Spanish and not Latin as was his habit. He could however understand rudimentary Latin, which reinforced the friars' conviction that the possession was real. Shortly thereafter, another Spanish maiden, Francisca Mexia, fell ill with the same symptoms and was also exorcised by the friars.[69]

Juana and Francisca were followed by other women, mostly Spaniards from middling and poor families, many of them Franciscan tertiaries. The women all showed hysterical contempt for the sacred objects used during religious services and many spat on the priests. After their sermons, which lasted until eight or nine o'clock in the evenings, the Franciscan friars staged public exorcisms that imbued the populace with terror: "as people considered that these women were possessed, when they heard them raise their voices, which they usually did at the end of the sermon, and with the darkness of the night, [the spectacle] caused them great fear and such horror that the mob tried to flee."[70] At gatherings of the Third Order, many women would stand up when the preacher was elaborating on doctrine and scream, "Shut up, shut up, do not listen to this," thus scandalizing onlookers.

By the end of the year the city was in a state of terror. Novenas were organized in the city's churches; its friars and clerics staged a solemn penitential procession in which some went barefoot, others lashed themselves and wore cilices, and women accompanied the crowd with "great silence and example." For more than three months nobody spoke of anything but the possessions, and many curious made their way to the public exorcisms and even to the women's houses to watch the friars perform. The one source of comfort provided to the townspeople was the devil's disclosure that the saintly nun, Antonia de San Jacinto, had indeed interceded and obtained divine approval for the temporary exit of the demons from Juana's body. But such comfort was short lived. In the midst of all this chaos, terrifying rumors circulated in the city. One maintained that the devils were so powerful that not even the Virgin could fight them. The Santa Cruz friars exacerbated all this by declaring in the pulpit that one of the devils had announced that the world was coming to an end, and that the day of judgment was near. They also complained that the reason their exorcisms did not work was that the populace did not believe wholeheartedly in the possessions. When one of the friars present at the exorcism asked the devil why God had chosen Querétaro for this scourge, the answer was chilling: because there were so many witches and sinful people living there. Finally, to crown the entire affair, it soon emerged that seven nuns in the convent of Santa Clara were also possessed.[71]

Throwing himself into the fray, the town's sheriff acted on the testimony of Juana and Francisca that the entire affair had been started by the unfortunate mestiza Josepha Ramos by arresting her as well as a group of mestizo and Indian women. She was taken in his carriage under public scrutiny to his house where she was interrogated and beaten into admitting that she and a group of other witches had orchestrated the entire affair, having made a pact with the devil. Every day, a crowd of people gathered in front of the alcalde's house, and on one occasion Fray Bonilla of Santa Cruz even paraded the demented Francisca Mexia in front of the house where she screamed that the "*chuparatones*" (Josepha) was the one behind it all and that she should not be set free.[72]

Losing their patience with the Franciscans' antics, the other religious orders, already irritated by the new arrivals' closed-off attitudes and elevated status, complained to the Inquisition in Mexico City.[73] According to their testimony the friars were adding to peoples' confusion by claiming that anyone who did not believe in the possessions would be punished by God.[74] Hence, confessors of other orders had to contend with public fears, and the tension in the city escalated to the degree that an exasperated Carmelite friar commented that "the city of Querétaro is undergoing a most painful tribulation. . . . Men are disconsolate, women are afflicted and souls everywhere riddled with doubt. The holy religious orders are nearing a very grave confrontation which is emerging from the disunity and the differences of opinion over the recent happenings. Already there are signs of disturbances and controversies from which very harmful scandals can ensue."[75]

In December 1691, the Querétaro inquisitor, don Juan Caballero y Ocio, asked his superiors in Mexico City to investigate the matter. The Inquisitors promptly ordered edicts to be read in all pulpits and hung on all church doors banning the use of peyote and other indigenous herbs. However, the case reached its climax when on January 2 Juana de los Reyes gave birth to a child. The next morning a chastened Fray Bonilla intruded upon a mass given at the convent of Santa Clara to beg God's forgiveness on this grieved city, and quietly asked the Inquisitor to accompany him to the house of the Reyes family. As Caballero y Ocio left the ceremony, "the entire congregation and the nuns were left in confusion upon the departure of the most important personages who had been summoned to the mass."[76] At Juana's sickbed the Inquisitor found a group of defiant Franciscans—surrounded by the triumphant heads of the other religious orders—who insisted that the devil had inserted semen from a man into the woman's body without her knowledge. To support their case they had carefully laid out all the objects (toads, nails, etc.) emitted from her body.[77] The unfortunate circumstances of the labor nevertheless contained tragicomic elements. The midwife who delivered the baby testified that having been summoned with haste to the Reyes house, she found Juana's father and Fray Bonilla desperately trying to choke a writhing shape under Juana's habit, thinking that she had ejected yet another demon, this time in the shape of a pig. The midwife's long experience saved the child, which survived for three months in the care of a family friend.[78]

With the childbirth, town gossip reached a new pitch. In spite of the Franciscans' insistence on the infant's diabolical origins, the religious orders complained to the Inquisition with renewed vigor. The tribunal in turn acted swiftly, and on January 18 Juana and two other women were formally accused of feigning diabolical possession. A year later Juana was brought to the capital where she confessed to mimicking her symptoms to hide the fact that she was carrying her brother's child.[79] The scandal affected the Santa Cruz friars deeply. The guardian of the college himself, Fray Sarmiento, was severely reprimanded along with a group of other friars, and one Franciscan was arrested.[80] Juana herself was sentenced to appear at an auto-da-fé in a Mexico City church, after which she was cloistered in the convent of Santa Clara for one year. Josepha Ramos did not fare as well. She was sentenced to appear at a public auto-da-fé with the sign of witch sown into her clothes. She was then paraded through the streets nude above the waist and received two hundred lashes. To crown her punishment she was condemned to five years of forced work in the Hospital de Dios in the capital and ten years in exile from Querétaro.[81]

But while the Mexico City Inquisitors were swiftly dealing with the troublesome female heretics of Querétaro, another case of a Franciscan devotee came to their attention. Although she had no ties to the group of demoniacs, Francisca de los Ángeles was nevertheless denounced in the autumn of 1691 as a *falsa beata* to the Inquisition. It is in the documentation of her case that we catch the first glimpses of the adult personality of the emerging "holy woman."

## 2  The Holy Woman

# 3  Heresy

## The Inquisition Case

Francisca's case was based on the testimony of a resident of the capital, Francisco Borda de Coronado. Judging from his declaration, her fame as a holy woman had begun to spread beyond the boundaries of the city by 1690. Corresponding with a friend in Querétaro, a Franciscan friar of the Colegio de Santa Cruz, he had learned that Francisca, who confessed with another friar of the college, had received indulgences for the friars' rosaries from Christ himself. When Coronado later traveled to Querétaro to visit his dying friend, he found a group of Franciscans making signs of the cross over the sick man with a bronze crucifix. The friars assured Coronado that the object would help his friend to *bien morir*, for it had been taken to heaven by an angel known to have aided the young *beata*.

The dying friar graciously bequeathed the object to his friend who had come all the way from Mexico City to see him. Following the friar's death, Coronado returned to Santa Cruz to fetch the crucifix. At the college, however, no one seemed to be willing to give the object to him, and every friar he spoke to claimed that it had been passed to someone else. Coronado gradually learned that the object was being circulated among people in the town and that he would be unable to locate it. But the woman's fame, Coronado discovered, had spread to Mexico City. Three weeks before entering the office of the Inquisition he had been in the accounts office of the Real Hacienda where he noticed an official holding a bronze crucifix in his hands. Asked where it came from, the official responded that he had received it from his superior but that it originally came from a "holy woman" in Querétaro who had dispatched it to heaven to be graced with indulgences.[1]

Having listened to his accusations, the Inquisitors in Mexico City decided to gather information on Francisca de los Ángeles and begin preliminary interrogations of townspeople in Querétaro. But when the Inquisitor in Querétaro sent his agents to Santa Cruz, the result was disappointing. The friars unanimously praised Francisca's virtues and humility and avoided comment on her visions and experiences.[2] Nevertheless, the visit seems to have induced one of the friars, Fray Diego de Salazar, to express his reservations about Francisca's actions and her public reputation. On November 25, 1694, he gave testimony before the Inquisitor in Querétaro.[3] Salazar had begun to wonder if Francisca was not spreading the rumors of her own holiness, for her confessor, Fray Pedro de Sitjar, had denied having spoken to anyone on the subject.

Another of Salazar's main concerns was that from his own experience Francisca's saintly reputation could not be substantiated. It was, for example, commonly believed that Francisca had traveled with her guardian angel to the hostile territory of Texas, where she engaged in missionary activities among the Indians. Santa Rosa de Viterbo had taken her place in Querétaro in order that her absences should not be missed. The missionaries so steadfastly believed in her account that they even asked her to write a guidebook of the territory for the friars who were about to make the long voyage. Salazar, however, had spoken to the friars upon their return from Texas, and they informed him that Francisca's account had proved to be worthless, even if the Indians confirmed that they had seen two missionaries before. Another event that heightened the friar's suspicions was a tale told by another *beata*, Felipa, of the divine favors that Francisca had received on Palm Sunday. Francisca agreed to write for the friar her own account of what had happened, but when he compared it with Felipa's tale he found no similarities.

Other fragments of the friar's testimony, coupled with examples of Francisca's own letters to him, which he brought before the Inquisition, and her confessor's papers, all reveal a vital aspect of her character: she used her status as a holy woman to voice and lend authority to opinions and to exercise power that otherwise would have been forbidden to her. In 1689, Sitjar commented that Francisca had scolded a fellow *beata* at a mass at Santa Cruz for being vain about her clothes and appearance. Known for her prophetic gifts, Francisca had looked at the beata and had seen flames emanating from her.[4] On one occasion Francisca informed the Santa Cruz friars that one of her confessors was still suffering enormous torments in purgatory owing to his having left the college in Querétaro and his mission in León before he died. Such open criticism of an illustrious friar by a mere *beata* would have been an unthinkable transgression had she not possessed a direct channel of communication with God. In her own letters to Salazar, Francisca went even further. She claimed that one of the crosses blessed by God would ensure a safe childbirth to any woman who had it laid across her chest and would gain five thousand years of absolution from sin to anyone who held it. More spectacularly, she attested that any priest who wore the cross while saying mass would gain a greater indulgence than if he had made a pilgrimage to

Jerusalem. Thus, Francisca, who by virtue of being a woman would never be able to say mass herself, attempted to insert her own presence into the priestly office. Not content with merely associating herself with the power of male ecclesiastics, she also assumed the authority of the Pope by claiming that one of her blessed rosaries, if held during the saying of a *padre nuestro* and an Ave Maria, would gain "all the favors and indulgences and remission of sins and crimes which the Popes have conceded to all the religious orders."[5] Here, she was on dangerous ground. In 1598, for example, when the Mexico City *beata* Marina de San Miguel was tried and condemned for illuminism, part of her offense was the granting of indulgences from God obtained through her intercession. Had her story been known to Francisca, warning bells undoubtedly would have begun to ring for the young *beata*, for her predecessor had been enthusiastically received as a holy woman in her neighborhood, but once the Holy Office became involved approval quickly gave way to a torrent of denunciations.[6]

On the day of Salazar's testimony, Fray Francisco Estévez, the guardian of Santa Cruz, sent a letter to the Querétaro Inquisitor asking that Francisca and the fellow *beata*, Felipa, be examined. He was worried that they were both *ilusas*, a common seventeenth-century term to describe female "pseudosanctity."[7] Estévez confirmed that the rumors about Francisca's holiness had been circulating in the town for five or six years. It was known that she had prophetic visions, could wake people from the dead, and received special favors from God, such as the stigmata that were proved by her bloodied habits, safeguarded by her mentors. He attested that one of her confessors, Fray Escaray, had exclaimed "that this Francisca was so favored by God that aside from the Holy Virgin no holier woman could be found."[8]

Having seen the testimonies, the Inquisitors in Mexico City decided to open a case against Francisca and Felipa as well as against a Santa Clara nun who had also been mentioned in the documents. They instructed the Inquisitor in Querétaro to interrogate Francisca's present confessor, Fray Pedro de Sitjar. But surprisingly, dispatches from Querétaro ceased for the next three years. In 1697, following renewed orders from Mexico City, the testimony of another member of the Santa Cruz community, Fray Antonio de los Ángeles, was taken. The friar praised Francisca's virtues and modesty in all matters and denied any knowledge of her supposed communication with God. At this, the investigation ceased again. In 1703, the Mexico City Inquisitors dispatched a letter to Querétaro ordering that the proceedings continue. Their efforts did not bear fruit, however, for in 1708 the new Querétaro Inquisitor sent a note asking for facts on the unconcluded case. The note was filed with the rest of the papers relating to Francisca's case, but her name did not appear in Inquisitorial records for several years.[9]

The Mexican Inquisition, overwhelmed with cases from its enormous jurisdiction, was not overly effective. Indeed, only one-sixth of cases brought to its attention between 1571 and 1700 were processed. Nevertheless, these proceedings seem rather sloppy.[10] Why this delay? Why did the Querétaro Inquisitor seem so reluctant to conclude the case against Francisca? The answer illustrates how important she had become to Querétaro's religious culture and society at large. The Inquisitor at the time was don Juan Caballero y Ocio, a wealthy priest and the most generous benefactor of convents and churches in Querétaro. He had known Francisca since her childhood, had supervised her earliest religious education at the Carmelite convent, and, according to one chronicler, the two enjoyed "an intimate friendship."[11]

Thus, the Inquisitor himself, whose duty was to prosecute Francisca, believed fervently in her worth as a religious figure and so succeeded in thwarting the case against her by ignoring orders from his superiors in Mexico City. Another witness in the case, Fray Antonio de los Ángeles, was at the time corresponding with authorities in Mexico City to secure a license for the foundation of a Franciscan convent in Querétaro for Francisca and other *beatas* living with her.[12] Thus, it is clear that the townspeople of Querétaro, including the Santa Cruz friars, took pride in Francisca's special nature. She had originally been accused by an outsider, and it was not until the Inquisition in Mexico City had set the wheels of the case in motion that the two Santa Cruz friars expressed their reservations. Fray Salazar's testimony was probably induced by the recent memory of the demoniac scandal and his consequent anxiety not to arouse the ire of the Inquisition yet again.

At no stage did Francisca's critics seem to have truly doubted her powers. Coronado attempted to gain ownership of the crucifix and did not denounce Francisca until after the Santa Cruz friars had denied him this powerful relic. It is highly likely that Coronado's testimony was induced by anger and a desire for revenge for having been deprived of it. Even Salazar, who expressed doubts about the truthfulness of Francisca's experiences, was revealed by another friar's testimony to have expressed his belief that her stigmata were genuine.[13]

Rather, concern seems to have been directed at the widespread reputation that Francisca's holiness had earned. Coronado had found her crucifix being passed between high officials in Mexico City, and Salazar was mainly perturbed that such grave religious issues had become material for common gossip: "by being so public it has offended his scruples seeing such lofty matters which should be concealed becoming an entertainment."[14] Furthermore, knowing the weak nature of women, he worried that their notoriety might cause Francisca and Felipa to "become imbued with diabolical vanity and that which could be good would become vice."[15]

Francisca's religiosity as it appears in the testimony of the aforementioned men had thus transgressed the limited space allotted to her in the Counter-Reformation Church. She devoutly attended mass and communion and humbly obeyed her confessor. However, she also took unauthorized power in her own hands by casting herself as capable through her direct communication with God of endowing objects with the powers of indulgence. Hence, she seized a prerogative that the institutional church zealously monopolized as one of the fundamental elements in its role as intermediary between God and mortals. But not only did Francisca transgress, her transgressions had become public rumor beyond Querétaro, and her relics were being passed between large numbers of people. As Salazar's concern shows, the public nature of the case constituted a threat to clerical authority. Before the outbreak of the Inquisition case, the Franciscan order had shown some concern over the Santa Cruz friars' famous *hija espiritual* in Querétaro. As bloody tunics began to arrive from Fray Escaray in Querétaro each year after Easter, the Franciscan commissary ordered that they be hidden and then interrogated Francisca himself in Querétaro. He found her spirit satisfactory, but the examination shows that the order realized the possible repercussions of her fame well before she was reported.[16]

That Francisca should be afforded protection by Querétaro's religious and secular hierarchy is indeed extraordinary in light of the humiliating crisis endured by the city during the demoniac scandal. Between Francisca and the possessed women there existed only vague boundaries. Both communicated with the supernatural world, and like Francisca the possessed women professed to know the will of God, albeit transmitted through the devil. Indeed, in the baroque religious culture shared by these women's contemporaries in Europe and the New World, demonic attacks represented necessary obstacles and challenges along a path that could also lead to sanctity and intimacy with the divine. Caroline Walker Bynum notes that by the fifteenth century in Europe, saint and witch had begun to resemble each other.[17] Women who communicated with God and women possessed by the devil equally inspired fear and awe in the common people and gained a stature above that of the rest of God's flock.[18] Women pursuing the path to holiness were thus constantly engaged in a balancing act between sanctity and diabolical possession.

During this period, women's religious expression faced an ambiguous and contradictory response from the Catholic hierarchy. On the one hand, many male ecclesiastics admired and respected these women's ability to enter the supernatural world; on the other, their freedom and individuality of expression aroused distrust and anger. Of course, misogynist attitudes within the church had a long tradition. Their foundations lay in Greek thought. Aristotle in his *Politics* asserted that "the slave is entirely without the faculty of deliberation; the female indeed possesses it, but in a form which remains inconclusive," and in his *History of Animals* he concluded that women's inferiority was the work of nature.[19] It was an attitude perhaps best expressed by Thomas Aquinas, who acknowledged that women could receive prophesies "since in the matter of the soul woman does not differ from man." Nevertheless, he continued, women could not be permitted to express these experiences "addressing themselves to the whole church."[20] When female mystics took one step too far in an independent direction the church moved swiftly to denounce and prosecute them.

During the Middle Ages, women's mystical raptures and revelations had been enthusiastically accepted by many as signs of God's benevolence toward his flock.[21] Nevertheless, public opinion of such women was fickle, and since the signs of divine ecstasy so resembled those of demonic possession it could easily turn against a figure it had formerly revered.[22] At the end of the thirteenth century social change in Western Europe resulted in greater institutionalization of the church and its separation from the populace. The result, in the words of Michel de Certeau, was that "mysticism came to designate what had become separate from the institution."[23] Unencumbered by institutional confines, popular culture, embraced by the high and low, enthusiastically continued to regard female mysticism as a navigable channel to God. The female piety of the Beguines was suppressed by the Council of Vienna in 1311–12, and around the same period some female mystics were burned at the stake.

In spite of the church's attacks, the culture the Beguines propagated continued to flourish on both sides of the Alps. By the fifteenth century, northern and southern Europe was bursting with enthusiastic, reform-minded groups of men and women whose aim was to revitalize the sagging church with Early Christian apostolic zeal. In Italy new types of conventual institutions were founded, and the old were reformed. Among the former the tertiary communities, based on simple vows and an open and active Christianity, were the most common.[24] But as this reformist zeal developed on the northern side of the Alps into a full-fledged criticism of—and consequent split—with the papacy, ecclesiastical attitudes changed further toward mysticism.[25] As a movement whose purpose was to defend Catholic society and culture from the Protestant north, the Counter-Reformation further propagated an intolerance against individualistic expressions of piety and communications with the divine that did not take place through church rituals.[26] Tertiaries, the uncloistered emblems of popular devotion, presented a particular threat. In 1575, Seville Inquisitors condemned a group of *beatas* for their open lifestyle and frequent communion, which to them reeked of false piety.[27] The Inquisitor of Seville described the problem: "These *beatas* who promise obedience to particular persons should not be allowed; it is the invention of the *alumbrados* of this epoch with which they distract daughters from the service and obedience to their parents and women from their husbands. . . . it is an invention of the devil and of vain men who under the guise of sanctity and religion want to be served and obeyed by simple women."[28]

In his analysis of female saints' *vitae* from the period, Rudolph Bell shows that their content and style changes after 1500. In place of emphasizing heroic deeds of virtue aimed at edifying the lay populace, the *vitae* show an increasingly "didactic" content aimed at showing clerics the pitfalls that women, by virtue of their sex, faced in their pursuit of the divine. Similarly, Bell demonstrates that after Pope Urban VIII instituted new canonization rules in the early seventeenth century requiring proof of doctrinal purity the number of Italian women who gained the Vatican's recognition for their holiness fell.[29] As Bynum has noted: "By the time of Catherine of Siena, Bridget of Sweden, and Joan of Arc the influence—even the survival—of pious women depended almost wholly on the success, in ecclesiastical and secular politics, of their male adherents."[30] Ironically, the seventeenth century, which saw the mysticism heralded by Saint Teresa and Saint John of the Cross flourish, also witnessed greater institutional restrictions placed on women as a result of the Council of Trent's policy of cloistering all female religious, lay or regular.[31] The church that saw in the cloister great potential for "moral regeneration" in a society under siege by heresy, refused mystics the freedom of total abandonment to the will of God for fear such individuality would weaken its defending ranks.[32]

In Spain, the cradle of Tridentine spirituality, renowned religious women fell under the suspicion of the Inquisition. Between 1544 and 1546, Magdalena de la Cruz, abbess of the Santa Clara convent in Córdoba, was tried in a highly publicized trial. For over thirty years her prophetic visions, which she disavowed after her arrest, had attracted a distinguished group of followers, including the empress and the Inquisitor general of Spain. Inquisitorial interrogation also revealed that she had indeed been possessed by the devil. The case caused disbelief and horror throughout the country. Saint Teresa herself said of the nun: "I never remember her without trembling."[33] Indeed, Teresa's body of work aimed at finding an acceptable channel for individual visions and mystic experiences in a church bent on curbing the dangers of such practices. Thus, her sainthood did not come about solely thanks to the great mystic heights she ascended, but due to a prudent life's work as a conventual reformer whose activities were marked by constant caution and reference. To win the freedom for her writing and foundational activities, Saint Teresa had to defer to the authority of her superiors, consult them on the orthodoxy of her religious practices, and refer to herself as a simple, "wretched" woman to alleviate their suspicions. This ambience persisted after her death. Only seventeen years before her canonization theologians suggested that her writings should be destroyed. They linked her to the *alumbrados*, contended that she had been deluded, and argued the dangers of setting the example of a woman teaching men.[34] When she was finally canonized in 1622 the image of her presented in the papal bull was radically different from that emerging from her own writings. She was applauded for her lack of self-will and obedience to superiors, for her commitment to physical mortification and prayer to atone for the sins of the unfaithful, and her adherence to the doctrines of the Roman Catholic Church, confirmed by her mystical life.[35] In a 1627 sermon in her honor, a Jesuit accentuated the unusual and active character of Saint Teresa's virtues by stating that "sanctity in women usually consists in being quiet, obeying, staying in a corner and forgetting about oneself." Alison Weber argues that "her rhetoric of femininity, which served her own needs of self-assertion successfully, also paradoxically sanctioned the paternalistic authority of the church over its daughters and reinforced the ideology of women's intellectual and spiritual subordination."[36]

A common definition of women's heresy of the period was *alumbrada*. The heretical sect of the *alumbrados* had emerged in the first decades of the sixteenth century, in Guadalajara, led by a Franciscan tertiary, Isabel de la Cruz. The *alumbrados* supported mental prayer and individual spirituality as opposed to vocal prayer and public religious ceremonies, and their leader developed her own particular doctrine of *dexamiento*, or the abandonment of human will to God. The movement quickly gathered followers but was repressed by the Inquisition in the late 1520s and its leaders flogged in an auto-da-fé.[37] Nevertheless, from 1570 onward, in Extremadura and later in Seville, the *alumbrados* continued to gather converts, and the Inquisition found itself more and more occupied with *beatas* who followed the movement.[38] This religiosity was carried over to the colonies and left to flourish there in the New World's relative isolation. Nevertheless, the colonial Inquisition sporadically roused itself from its stupor. In Lima, home of the famed mystic Santa Rosa, several cases of *alumbradas* were tried by the tribunal between 1580 and 1620. In a paradox appropriate to the epoch, a group of women reconciled in an auto-da-fé in Lima in 1625 were all devotees of Rosa's.[39]

The Mexico City Inquisitors of the seventeenth century shared this distrust of women and their piety. As Dr. Luis de la Pena was known to have commented, "women are not only weaker and more susceptible, but are humid, crass and viscose by nature and because of this temperament are not only subject to lunatic impressions but are easily overcome by passions of hatred, love, happiness and sadness." Given these shortcomings, he concluded, their visions and raptures should not be trusted.[40] Nevertheless, on another occasion he demonstrated his personal confusion in the matter by arguing that the perfect female visionary was a woman who experienced numerous visions but "based on a life of virtue." Their visions' contents should be orthodox and not attempt to create new doctrine or contradict sanctioned models of sanctity.[41] The same confusion as to the nature of women's relationship with God appeared in a guidebook on mysticism by the Jesuit Miguel Godínez, first published in Puebla in 1681. In answer to the question why "women, in spite of being less saintly than men, received more favors and gifts [from heaven]" he noted that as water assumed the form of a glass, so did the divine spirit fit perfectly with women's malleable and loving natures. Furthermore, since God honored his friends, he endowed women who could not receive favors such as entering the priesthood or preaching the doctrine, with the privilege of visions, raptures, and revelations.[42]

The paradox is evident in the fate of a three-volume, one-thousand-page hagiobiography of Catarina de San Juan, a popular holy woman of Puebla who died in 1688. While the first volume was approved by the highest-ranking authorities in New Spain—a bishop, the viceroy, and a *calificador* of the Inquisition—it was subsequently banned by the tribunal.[43] Around the same time, Francisca's renowned contemporary, Madre María de San José, a Puebla nun, was forced to have all her religious writings circulated among the city's clergy in order to verify their orthodoxy.[44]

The Mexican Inquisition in the seventeenth century not only banned writings by and about *beatas* but frequently prosecuted women for being *falsas beatas*, tertiaries who feigned divine visions.[45] In the seventeenth and eighteenth centuries, forty-five women convicted of false mysticism ended their journeys toward the divine in Inquisitorial dungeons.[46] Indeed, it would have taken an inordinate amount of luck for the Querétaro *beata* to escape the attentions of the Inquisition altogether. The tribunal by this time had become increasingly preoccupied with "false mysticism" on grounds that had little to do with the reasoning its Iberian counterpart used in its sixteenth-century drive against *alumbrados*. As Jaffary has demonstrated, in the second half of the seventeenth century a subtle shift occurred in the arguments the court used against the men and women accused of false mysticism. They were increasingly designated as *ilusos*, or people who "feigned mystical experiences" rather than *alumbrados* who propagated heretical forms of piety.[47] Jaffary sees the shift as evidence of the court's preoccupation with the growing number of urban Creoles who lived in humble economic circumstances in close proximity with the castes. Many such urbanites somehow slipped through the safety nets constructed by the colony's social hierarchy and acquired a reputation and a following among the devout for their privileged relations with the divine.[48] As representative of the colony's peninsular elite, the tribunal was concerned with stifling disorder within a community threatened by its close proximity with African and indigenous elements as well as by the growth of a Creole society beginning to take on a vitality all of its own.

By the time of Francisca's trial then, Inquisitors in Mexico City were not altogether as concerned with theological questions as they were with a troublesome element of the population who simulated gifts that were not theirs to possess by birthright. "False mysticism" was considered among the gravest crimes brought to the attention of the tribunal. While only 2 percent of cases brought to trial resulted in convictions, in the case of "false mysticism" nearly 65 percent of court cases terminated in convictions.[49] The irony in this context, explains Jaffary, is that the majority of those tried exhibited their adherence to and acceptance of orthodox Church doctrine. Their misfortune stemmed from the creativity with which they blended elements of their own daily lives and social circumstances into their interpretation of the mysteries of the faith or became overly ambitious when it came to self-promotion. Claiming to be able to interpret visions became more dangerous than actually experiencing them. Indeed, it is likely, argues Jaffary, that this group of people represented religious practices common to New Spanish urban populations at the time.[50] Francisca's social circumstances combined with her confidence in and self-assured interpretations of her visionary experiences certainly place her in this category of colonial Mexican society. At the same time, comparing her spirituality and religious practices as they appear in her letters with those of the defendants Jaffary analyzed shows that while she hovered constantly on the edge of danger there were certain limits she did not overstep.

Almost half a century before Francisca came to the attention of the Inquisitors, the tribunal had condemned and imprisoned two sisters from the capital and their male *devoto* for false and deceitful piety. Their story throws into relief the security and singularity of Francisca's position. Josefa and her younger sister, Teresa, derived from the same impoverished Creole background as Francisca, and like her they attracted at a young age the attentions of ecclesiastics for their visions and raptures. Like the young Francisca, Josepha attributed extraordinary powers to herself as messenger of God, freed thousands from purgatory, brought news of the dead to their families, and rapidly acquired with her sister the reputation of a "*santita.*" Both women used their status to criticize the ecclesiastical hierarchy, but at the same time their rhetoric professed complete adherence to orthodox doctrine, and both were admired for their virtuous pronouncements. But at that the comparison stops. While Francisca toiled obediently as a tertiary under the wing of her powerful Franciscan protectors and embraced the holy poverty they preached, the Romero sisters accepted jewels, expensive clothes, and money and refused to become tertiaries, preferring the autonomy and liberty of the secular state. Josefa, the leading figure of the duo, demonstrated publicly her raptures and histrionics as she was possessed by the divine spirit, which spoke through her mouth and engaged the spectators in conversation. Her theatrical flair also produced sessions in which she donned a stole and washed and kissed the feet of twelve clerics and laymen. Such behavior is absent in any documentation about Francisca. Josepha fell in love with a young, peninsular seminarian whom she made her secretary and who industriously copied every word that escaped her mouth during her trances. Her conflictive and passionate nature finally became her nemesis. She began to sow seeds of doubt in her devotees when she suddenly began to show intense symptoms of demonic possession, and her sister Teresa accused her of falsity in retaliation for receiving a jealousy-motivated beating. The end came when her amorous advances toward her secretary during one of her raptures drove him into the arms of her twin sister, María. Josepha's uncontrollable jealousy propelled her to denounce both of them to the Inquisition. After the group's sentencing, Josepha languished in an Inquisitorial dungeon for six years until her merciful death.[51]

That Francisca possessed qualifications that separated her from the more unfortunate members of her sex is reflected in her escape from the Inquisition and the lengths to which Inquisitor Caballero y Ocio, a prominent member of the colony's Creole elite, went to protect her. Had members of the Querétaro elite been given the opportunity to insert their opinion into the documentation they might have replied as had the fifteenth-century Italian prince of Ferrara, Borso d'Este, that it would be "a great setback to the city to lose a saintly woman."[52] As the inhabitants of an emerging and prosperous city, they were likely gratified at the existence of a "holy woman," which affirmed the benevolence with which God viewed their activities. Querétaro might be a young city, distant from the heart of the colony, but its ambitious citizens undoubtedly longed to put themselves on a par with cities such as Puebla, which had produced so many saintly personages.[53]

Unlike her sophisticated *capitalino* predecessor, the potential transgression of Francisca's extravagant rhetoric was neutralized by her complete obedience to superiors, her institutional stature as a tertiary, and her renowned poverty and virtue. Like her Spanish role model, Sor María Agreda, whose more unfortunate youthful spirituality had swung from ecstasies to demonic possessions, Francisca emerged in the end unscathed from the dangers of spiritual adolescence. And unlike Saint Teresa, who had struggled to control her raptures in public, Francisca did not seem to suffer such inconveniences.[54] But most importantly, her mentors and protectors were mystics and devotees of popular traditions. The Spanish missionaries were also, as emissaries of Propaganda Fide, members of an "elite corps" of what Patricia Wittberg defines as the "Apostolic Era" (1500–1800).[55] In the New World, the post-Tridentine Franciscan warriors declared war upon the devil. They set themselves apart from the complacent clergy and espoused rustic life and folk wisdom, and they enchanted congregations with their own raptures and trances in the pulpit as well as their public penitences. Their message conformed entirely with the objectives of their mission, that is, to revive the fear of God and respect for the church. In this spirit they supported and protected an uncloistered beata's apostolic mission because they were convinced of her dedication to their battle for fickle souls. In this frontier city that opened onto the expanse of the great deserts of the north, unencumbered by the splendor and institutional authority of the capital, Francisca could thus continue on her ambitious path, relatively free of the restrictions imposed upon similar women in the Old and New World.

## A Writer's Beginnings

In 1689—two years before the outbreak of the demoniac scandal and the Inquisition proceedings—when Francisca was fifteen, her life as a religious woman suddenly took a new direction. In that year, her father, Juan Alonso, having led a recluse's life in his last years, died, aided on his deathbed by a group of Santa Cruz friars. He was buried in the convent's cemetery.[56] His death left Antonia, Francisca's mother, and her three daughters in dire financial straits. It was then that Francisca's intimate ties with the Santa Cruz friars and her reputation as a religious woman offered the four women an honorable exit from the vulnerable situation they found themselves in. The women all became Franciscan tertiaries. Adjoining their small house, the missionaries helped them construct four cells, each with a small bed, a desk on which they placed their religious books, and a tiny altar for prayer. Under the direction of the Franciscans the women then settled down to a life of rigorous religious exercises, including long hours of prayer, meditation, mortification, and fasting. They took communion daily at Santa Cruz and on special occasions such as Easter they remained in the church from Thursday to Saturday: "the days and nights, they used to accompany His Majesty in the early hours of his sorrowful passion."[57]

The women sustained themselves at first through charity. Clara, the oldest daughter, for example, begged for alms on her way to church in the mornings. The women also made small Christ images out of wood and flower decorations and sold them for their sustenance. In spite of her youth, Francisca quickly emerged as the small group's leader. The fortunes of the women depended to a large degree on her, for it was her relationship with the Santa Cruz friars that provided the underpinnings of the group's survival. And this relationship she cultivated assiduously. Everyday she walked from her home on the western outskirts of Querétaro, through the center, and up the long hill to Santa Cruz where she met with her spiritual director, Fray Sitjar. They entered the confessional, but since Francisca always had an infinite amount of information for her director, he commanded her to write down her experiences and visions. Consequently, the letters poured forth, written in torrents without punctuation or other relief for their poor reader and the friar who was assigned to copy them in a neat, precise script that almost contradicted the extravagance of their author.

The letters were what mattered, for with them Francisca laid the foundation for her claim to entry into that privileged group of female protagonists within Western Christianity known as "holy women." In every nook and corner of the Christian world such women had existed throughout the ages as living examples to their contemporaries of divine grace. These "almost-saints" might perhaps make it to sainthood posthumously; most of them did not. In the world of the Counter-Reformation, Saint Teresa of Avila stood as a shining example to any would-be saintly woman, a reminder of the infinite possibilities for recognition that existed should the right path be chosen. In her writings, Teresa had managed to champion a fervently individual and mystical path to God, defending visions and mental prayer while skirting the Inquisition and remaining a "Daughter of the Church."

In Spanish America, the Iberian nun's example was avidly followed. What united most colonial "holy women" was their talent for writing and a vision-ary imagination that set them apart from the pious masses. Armed with such tools, they succeeded in engaging the attention of their male ecclesiastical readers who had the power to destroy or elevate these women's reputations by burning, circulating, even publishing (though usually their own accounts based on the material) their supernatural experiences and pious practices.[58] To the New World clergy the production of edifying life stories of virtuous women served the noble purpose of convincing a distrustful European read-ership nourished on myths of the region's morally corruptive climate that it was capable of nourishing holiness.[59]

Should a "holy woman" aspire to such heights the path was a tricky one. In good contradictory baroque fashion, she had to convince the expectant friar or priest of her absolute humility, obedience, and self-deprecation, while simul-taneously defying such categorization by asserting an extraordinary closeness with the divine that effectively granted the authority to interpret his will—thus violating that sacred prerogative of the male clergy and flirting with heresy. Writing had to constitute yet another sacrificial enterprise, undertaken solely as a result of a woman's vow of obedience to her spiritual director.[60] It was in this context that charismatic women in the colonies undertook their individ-ual *caminos de perfección*. For example, Francisca de los Ángeles's Colombian contemporary, Madre Castillo, the mystic nun of Tunja, scaled the heights of political power within the elite convent of Santa Clara as its abbess, held other positions of power, and wrote a *vida* as well as several accounts or *afectos* of her spiritual life that eventually were published—albeit posthumously. By framing these achievements in constant suffering and anxiety she thus stamped on her life's work the virtues of humility and obedience, creating an "autohagiography" that secured her a reputation that lives to this day. The same could be said for the Puebla nun María de San José, another of

Francisca's baroque contemporaries. The martyrdom of an early religious vocation ignored by her family, followed by a tortuous battle to enter a convent, and crowned by mortifications within the convent generated a figure of such rich and authoritative spirituality that one of her confessors reportedly kept her at the writing table twenty-three hours a day, and her writings circulated amongst influential local clergy.

Francisca de los Ángeles may never have heard of these contemporaries, but she would have known from the outset what her objectives should be and the tools to be used for such ends. Indeed, the entire process was clearly delineated step by step in hagiographies of Counter-Reformation saints. In these textbooks of virtue, the personal element had been blotted out in order to make space for standardized qualifications for sainthood that would meet with the approval of a Church single-mindedly rising from the ashes of its encounter with the great Lutheran heresy. Francisca rarely discussed what she was reading at the time. However, it is highly likely that she had ample opportunity to read given the copious output of religious texts from New Spanish printing presses and the flow of such readings from the peninsula, which produced more than half of all New Spain's publications between 1500 and 1670.[61] The models for exemplary behavior for Counter-Reformation saints were clear. They belonged to the clergy, and in particular to the new orders such as the Jesuits, the discalced Carmelites and the Oratorians, amongst others.[62] They were founders and reformers, many of whom combined their reformist spirit with an ecstatic mysticism, such as Saint Teresa and her friend Peter of Alcantara, Tridentine bishops, and missionaries.[63] As for women, the papacy's approval of cloistered spirituality was clear. Four of the five women canonized in the period were nuns, while the remaining one, Santa Rosa de Lima, nevertheless provided an inspiring example of lay spirituality.[64]

The tools available to would-be female religious writers were rather restrictive, however. As mentioned, the genre of the *vida* or autohagiography called for a personal narrative to be squeezed into an unvarying organizational structure whose fundamental markers were an early religious vocation, adversity in pursuing it—due in large part to the persistent temptations of the devil, self-deprecation, and the inexplicable spiritual gifts from God. The less biographical *afectos*, however, opened up wider possibilities. These shorter segments of writing recounted visionary experiences without a necessarily fixed structure. This was a genre that could thus be molded to individual passions and ambitions.[65] Moreover, the rhetoric used, in spite of its emphasis on humility, obedience, and docility, nevertheless provided space to flex creative muscles. Francisca almost certainly did not read tracts on the composition of devotional literature, but from her religious upbringing attending masses and reading the lives of the saints she would have understood the power of the written word to play upon human emotions. In 1567, in his *Ecclesiasticae rhetoricae*, Fray Luis de Granada set down guidelines for such literature. They included using verbal acrobatics to produce dramatic, visual images in readers that would shock them into an altered state of consciousness, preparing the ground for the emotional rather than intellectual absorption of doctrine.[66] The baroque literature of New Spain, sacred and secular, echoed this stance. It employed, in the words of Octavio Paz, "wit" and "conceit" to reach an expression that Paz considers more authentic to Mexican society than later literary trends. Its delight in "recording picturesque details and in highlighting specificities," in Paz's opinion, mirrored the condition of the Creole in a strange New World not yet his own.[67] Never sanctioned as a preacher, Francisca took to this baroque style with gusto, using it to construct the hero theme of her life story, though framing her narrative with the appropriate usage of self-deprecatory rhetoric.

Guidebooks and spiritual directors throughout New Spain informed aspiring souls as to the necessary stages of the journey: the purgative, illuminative, and unitive states. The purgative state was to rid the soul of the excesses of the self and the ties that bound it to the *siglo* (lay society). It was thus a process that involved penitence, mortification, and self-abasement. Should the soul successfully traverse it, the illuminative state provided the rewards of vision and ecstasy, of seeing the divine world in colors and light that were not earthly. Finally, the unitive stage brought a union with God that was a rapturous obliteration of the self, an experience thought to be beyond words, a flight of the soul from the body, a release from earthly chains. Once the union was over, the soul was left with total contempt for the world, which in the words of Saint Teresa was of no "avail to it in its torment."[68] As Asunción Lavrin has shown, the writings of Mexican nuns followed this scheme closely. They expressed, in her words, "the best tradition of sixteenth-century recogimiento even though sometimes dressed up in baroque garb."[69] Their narratives express an unrelenting tossing from the purgative to the illuminative state and back, with dramatic rhetoric that tries the patience of even the most devoted reader.

When Fray Sitjar began to order his protégée to put her experiences on paper, we do not know whether she harbored an idea of herself as a *vida* writer.

What is clear from the outset is her ambition. At the age of only seventeen she had already converted herself from a poor *donzella* of ambiguous mestizo-criollo background with no hope of a good marriage or conventual dowry into a "holy woman" convincing enough for male members of the city's elite to go out on a limb in protecting her from the all-powerful Inquisition. By the time of that landmark event in her life, she was already providing her Santa Cruz confessor, Fray Sitjar, with *cuadernitos* describing her divine experiences. There is evidence, however, that Francisca began her writing career within the *vida* genre. The first papers of her correspondence are written by Sitjar and contain the narrative of her childhood, a story that, in effect, has the stamp of the beginnings of an autohagiography. Whether Francisca continued on this path we do not know. Her recollections of her childhood cease there, and by 1689 she is writing letters in the *afectos* style rather than a *vida*.

### El camino de la perfección *and the Certainty of God's Love*

In her *afectos*, Francisca provided evidence to her confessors of her progress toward *perfección*, defined in the religious thinking of the period as consisting of a "high degree of saintliness and habitual grace," which then lead to "supernatural life."[70] Saint John of the Cross, a powerful Counter-Reformation saint, accentuated the anti-intellectual nature of mystical rapture at this level. According to him, true mystical visions could not be put into words. His practice derived from a long-standing contemplative monastic tradition that had been practiced throughout medieval Europe and England. Its focus, formulated by a late-fourteenth-century English priest, lay in searching for God in the darkness, in the "cloud of unknowing" that separated God from humans, and relinquishing all earthly ties. It thus advised abnegation and austerity as the most efficient method of contemplation.[71]

In her *Interior Castle* Saint Teresa described the progress for religious women in the following manner: The castle represented the soul, its outer walls the body, and its innermost chamber the space "in which things of great secrecy between God and the soul occur." Entry into the castle was obtained by prayer. The soul then made its way slowly through its mansions until, having overcome the necessary obstacles, it was pulled toward the divine. Teresa thus expressed to her "sisters" the logic of religious enclosure. By forgetting about the body, the outer walls of the castle, the nuns would, for the first time, learn to enter into their souls, which were made in the image of God, what Michel de Certeau named "the other of yourself." By confining their bodies, nuns thus achieved freedom of the soul and were assured by Teresa that "without permission of the superiors, you will be able to enter and go for a walk at whatever hour."[72]

In the popular piety advocated by the Counter-Reformation, the "flight of the soul" took place not merely through meditation but through the dramatic imagery of baroque religious art. In 1563, during its twenty-fifth session, the Council of Trent decreed that "the images of Christ, of the Virgin Mother of God, and of other saints are to be placed and retained especially in the churches and that due honor and veneration is to be given them."[73] Ecclesiastics were instructed in particular to use religious images to demonstrate the miracles performed by God through the saints.[74] On the veneration of relics the council stated: "The holy bodies of the holy martyrs and of others living with Christ, which were the living members of Christ and the temple of the Holy Ghost, to be awakened by Him to eternal life and to be glorified, are to be venerated by the faithful."[75]

But by encouraging the imaginative use of religious art, the Counter-Reformation sanctioned mental prayer as the foundation of popular piety. The sainthood of Ignatius of Loyola was further confirmation of the process. During mental prayer the rational mind became vacant while the imagination was heightened and began to experience the divine. In 1605, a Spanish Jesuit, Luis de la Puente, described the classic baroque method of mental prayer, founded on the exercises of Saint Ignatius: "imagination . . . is of great help if one can easily form within oneself some figures, or images, of the things one is to meditate on: because it is like . . . spiritually placing in front of the soul the thing which is to be meditated on, as if it were present . . . with as much liveliness and propriety as possible. If I have to think of Hell, I will imagine a place like a dungeon, dark . . . and horrible."[76] Thus, the baroque centered on escaping the earthly boundaries of the rational mind and imagining the supernatural; miracles, magic, and the force of the devil were its essential elements. The pious sought to imitate the passion of Christ through self-mortification and fasting. Within seventeenth-century Spanish convents such mysticism was rampant. The church recognized the phenomenon and tried to co-opt its potentially dangerous, heretical tendencies through institutionalization. When the Pope decreed new rules for the Order of St. Clare, they included obligatory mental prayer, fasting, and discipline.[77]

In the colony, this baroque culture shaped the childhood and adult life of the religious women of Querétaro.[78] A late-seventeenth-century account from the convent of Santa Clara mentions that hagiographies were normally read to the convent's inhabitants in the evenings. Providing visual inspiration were the robed, bejeweled saints' images whose maintenance was the nuns' responsibility. The same chronicler noted that mental prayer was a popular religious practice, with the more accomplished nuns teaching the methods to others less naturally enraptured.[79] Spiritual guidebooks for women employed mystical but quotidian imagery such as that used in the guidebook written for inhabitants of Santa Clara by Fray Diego Mendívil, entitled "The Laws of the Wife." The book was constructed as an intimate conversation between Christ and his bride. Christ, the husband, admonished the nun, his wife, that she could not serve two masters but was to dedicate herself to supporting him in the battle against the devil, "because I raised you so that you could work against and gain victory over the enemies."[80]

The little we know of Francisca de los Ángeles's early religious education follows this pattern to the letter. Free to roam the streets, Francisca would have had the opportunity to become a connoisseur of the baroque art and ornamentation displayed by Querétaro's various churches. The church of Santa Cruz with its religious imagery provided a principal source for her visionary imagination. Adoring its images and monuments, and reveling in its rituals, revelations came upon her, such as the vision of the Child Christ in the host and the Holy Trinity in his Sacred Heart. On the day of Saint Michael, she gazed with wonder all day as the statues and images in the church were joined by a large crowd of saints and angels. And like the saints in the *retablos* she drank the blood that dripped from Christ's wounded side.[81] Perhaps the most appealing testimony of her affection for the old church is her description of how the sight of it would stave off the demons that usually approached at dusk. On one or two occasions as she kneeled by her window gazing at the distant temple on the hill she suddenly saw it open and reveal in a brilliant light His Divine Majesty, surrounded by saints and angels that played music. That this was not a flight of Francisca's fancy was certified by her sister Gertrudis who, seeing her thus enraptured, had asked what she was looking at. Then looking toward the church Gertrudis too had seen it open with a great light emanating from it. At other times the power of the church was such that having just exited her door to begin her long journey to Santa Cruz, Francisca would feel as if she were already at its altar.[82]

While the Querétaro baroque had not yet reached the greatness in art and architecture that it would achieve in the eighteenth century, there was still plenty of imagery to admire and draw inspiration from. For example, the interior of the church of Santa Clara, a fifteen-minute walk from Francisca's home, presented all the necessary exempla of saint's lives, biblical scenes, and the divine world. In an undated letter found among her papers from the end of the century Francisca listed her most cherished objects, thus revealing the fundaments of her devotion: an ivory crucifix, images of Saint Joseph and Nuestra Señora de la Concepción, two stained-glass images, and two statues, one of bronze and one of ivory showing Nuestra Señora de los Dolores. She also possessed a few small devotional prints and books, some of her possession and others on loan. Among these were the writings of the famous Spanish nun Madre María de Agreda; those of the Madre Antigua, called the *Mill of Prayer*; as well as a book of hours; a spiritual guidebook called *The Intimate Life of the Spirit*; and *Battle of the Spirit*.[83]

In her writing, Francisca tread the path between affective piety and heresy, humility and authority, with care in order to create an orthodox narrative of her mystical journey. In its early years, however, the *beata* demonstrated altogether too much self-confidence and gusto in her use of extravagant, worldly language to describe heavenly scenes to succeed in portraying herself as a "wretched" woman and orthodox mystic undergoing the purgative preparation for illumination. Instead, she cast herself as an author in the long-standing mystic tradition that was a chiaroscuro of divine ecstasy and devil-induced depression. On one occasion she lamented that she had ever taught herself to read and write because unlike other children who are taught these things by their parents, her determination to acquire such skills on her own amounted to the sin of self-love. She also used the occasion to beg her confessor, Sitjar, to allow her more time in the confessional since writing was her greatest torment.[84] At the same time, it was an heroic activity, one that only the strongest of spirits could endure. In an undated letter, Francisca claimed to have noted the occasions on which she sat down to write, unfortunately without specifying the length of time. In all, she counted 305 writing sessions, during all of which she suffered "exquisite contradictions" only believable to someone who had experienced them. As soon as she sat down to write, she felt herself wedged between two tribunals. In one, a severe judge informed her that God commanded her to write, while on the other side a multitude of ministers disrupted her activity and inflicted confusing torments on her that cannot be described as anything but ecstasy. At this point, she became invisible to her own eyes, which in turn saw only the paper and the inkpot.[85] At other times, the devil craftily spirited her writings away, to the great displeasure of Sitjar, who at one point commanded her to demand the return of the letters.[86] During dry periods the Lord took pity upon her and sent her splendid visions that immediately renewed her writing fervor.[87]

She was a spontaneous writer, and at times would find that she had used up the paper allotted before getting to her point.[88] And when inspiration burst forth, she praised the Lord for firing her pen with his grace: "I take up the notebook and the pen without remembering anything, feeling like a dried stick; . . . it seems that the Lord finds it useful to bring it back to my memory so that I comply with the virtue of holy obedience." Similarly, writing led to an enhanced understanding of the things of this world: "As I am writing, this is what has occurred to me; . . . it seems to me that an entire world can live in one wretched soul, and it lives only in that soul and not in the world at large," she wrote in 1706.[89] And should the friar be left in any doubt about God's insistence that she write and His pleasure with her writing, there was always the monumental proof conferred upon her one day when she repeatedly tried to throw her papers into the river only to have them always come back intact without the ink running. Although she demanded that the friars burn her papers she was probably aware of how carefully they were stored and locked up. Many years later a hint surfaces in her letters that she might have liked to keep them herself to reread. On March 2, 1714, she asked her confessor to send all her letters back to her so that she could burn them. She cited as her reason for not asking him to burn them himself the terrible smell they emitted when burning.[90] And to emphasize that the command to write came not only from her confessor, she also related a vision in which the three Maries educated her on the virtues of writing as a way to exercise humility and contribute to the building of the mystical church.[91]

The devil's great strength, however, lay in his persistence. While other people found the sound of children playing outside their window disturbing when they tried to concentrate on writing, Francisca had to contend with the infernal noise of hundreds of devils raising havoc outside her cell. She longed for ignorance, for it brought the obliteration of *entendimiento*, a source of constant torment.[92] During such periods she often found that her only solace lay in writing verse.[93] Self-deprecatory remarks were strewn throughout her texts in the appropriate places. In the midst of a particularly torrential letter vividly describing her experiences during Easter, she complained: "I feel terrible about writing such extraordinary things [the visions] for the most ordinary thing in me is not knowing how to express what I receive." But not only did the floodgates of language open to Francisca; she also possessed a knack for telling a good story and building the pious reader's anticipation, particularly when it came to describing the devil's never ending tricks. Never eloquent according to the fashion of the period, her style is colloquial and her sentences, often characterized by repetitive confusion, run into each other. Nevertheless, her writing flows—particularly when read out loud—and the task of transcription may not have been an overly cumbersome burden for the Santa Cruz scribe.

At least it seems to have captured Sitjar's attention, for he kept Francisca at her task in spite of her repeated objections and complaints. He was particularly interested in her experiences over Easter, when she received stigmata and accompanied Christ in his passion, as well as in physical descriptions of her guardian angel, heaven, hell, and purgatory. In 1693, Sitjar was clearly in the habit of sending her blank pieces of paper daily, with the order to fill them. It was an order she did not always succeed in carrying out. And when she tried to excuse her lack of obedience in the confessional by blaming it on the devil's taunts, he told her harshly that it would be better for her to leave him forever than to start lying to him. When she did comply with his command to write, he was often annoyed to find that her descriptions were incomplete.[94]

Picking up the "hero" theme of Counter-Reformation devotional literature, Francisca's letters are logs of the daily strife that was *el camino de la perfección*. Her weapons in this battle were, of course, her confessor and her writing, but also an array of devotional objects given to her by benefactors. Armed with these weapons, Francisca launched into a pious wrestling with God in order to bring humanity closer to Him. Wrestling with God meant fending off the constant attacks of the devil who acted as His servant to test her faith, as well as begging His mercy when He was angered and using His more gracious moments to obtain the release of souls from purgatory. This relationship had its constant highs and lows, for Francisca's God was alternatively a thundering, bearded patriarch lashing out with fire from His throne at the cowering, sinful humanity before Him, a warrior-king surrounded by a *caballería* of martyrs, or the *fin amant* of Beguine literature, whispering sweet words in her ear during unions illuminated by an indescribable light, His mystical face in her hands. At other times, He was a father endowing His daughter with treasure.[95]

In spite of her dutiful adherence to the required narrative of mystical torment, the underpinnings of Francisca's youthful spirituality was an unquestioning faith in her elevated status in the eyes of God. Indeed, the great patriarch in heaven kept a book on the favors bestowed upon her, which contents she had timidly scanned over His shoulder. The favors were a burden to bear since she was naturally the most sinful and vile creature that ever lived on earth. But incomprehensibly the flow from heaven remained constant, providing her with an understanding of the mysteries of the faith that could not be obtained from her mortal confessors. At such a young age she had already ascended to an understanding comparable to that of that celestial upper class into which the friars had little hope of achieving entry: the saints. Like Saint Rita and Saint Catharine, Francisca had been granted the grace of understanding the mystery of the holy faith and of receiving indulgences directly from God. The Lord allowed her to drink from the cup of eternity and thus to understand the mystery of the Holy Trinity, her soul suspended "in the state of God almighty." As a result of this divine education she could understand the friars' incantations in Latin on the passion even though she had never studied the ancient language and could understand the apostles singing the Lord's praises through the song of birds.

She also received assistance for more practical, day-to-day matters, for the Lord taught her how to do particular religious exercises according to His way and not in the manner taught by the guidebooks. He also propelled her forward when she proceeded through the Stations of the Cross.[96] The culmination of the progress finally came when she understood "what God is, and what is sin against God." Her confessor, however, most probably felt relief when Francisca found herself unable to put this knowledge into words since this protected her potential heresy with the orthodox cloak of the "cloud of unknowing." Or Sitjar may also have felt annoyance for Francisca's seeming knack for whetting his appetite and then refusing to disclose what she understood. In her letter from October 18, 1697, for example, she states that she had been granted an understanding of several mysteries over Easter, but she did not feel the *animo* to disclose them.[97] On other occasions, however, her descriptions leave unsaid no details about the graces bestowed upon her in heaven, as in her description of October 24, 1697, of the renewal of marital vows with her divine groom, which took place on the day of All Saints in an elaborate ceremony attended by the saints and the angels. The splendor and romance of the ceremony only underlined how far away the friar was from the possibility of such intimacy.[98] While Francisca could not harbor any hopes of ever becoming the center of such a glorious public spectacle as a nun's profession, in heaven such prospects were easily realized. One of the advantages of her heavenly marriage was that when her earthly travails got the better of her, her divine husband consoled her. Thus, she could triumphantly inform Sitjar on several occasions when he had been harsh with her that Christ had comforted his *beata*, sometimes appearing as a beautiful young man. On another occasion, when Sitjar had not allotted her enough time in the confessional, she retorted that the Lord had brought her comfort.[99]

Carefully establishing her authority throughout her correspondence Francisca felt free to divulge, in extravagant, chatty language, the drama and splendor of the otherworld. Inhabited by angels, devils, saints, cherubims, and the godhead, the baroque imagery of this world echoed the visual flights of fantasy offered by religious art to her contemporaries. In 1693, at Sitjar's request she labored for several days on a description of her guardian angel, her most reliable ally in heaven. With the stature of a boy of fourteen years and dressed in a tunic the color of sunrays reflecting off a mirror, her angel was a baroque figure with shoulder-length golden locks, pale but flushed skin, a cross plastered over his forehead, and his arms crossed over his chest in the manner of Saint Francis. Nevertheless, Francisca went to great lengths to emphasize that her angel was a truly mystical figure and not the product of the religious art visible in churches. Thus, his wings "did not resemble in any manner those which the painters paint on their angels." Instead, they did not have feathers and did not move during flight. The angel came to Francisca in a small white cloud, bringing gifts and news from up above, and facilitated her experience of the passion of Christ by giving her a bitter drink. He also helped the *beata* in more earthly endeavors such as finishing her daily load of laundry, "stretching" and "folding" the linen, and accompanying her to the church. More importantly, he exhorted her to persevere in her faith and escorted her to the divine presence. [100]

To her mentors then, Francisca projected divinity in highly material terms using a popular rhetoric that to many a learned ecclesiastic would reek of heresy. But thankfully, Francisca's protectors were the men who had inspired the demoniac scandal of Querétaro, men whose own piety straddled the dangerous boundaries between orthodoxy and heresy.

## 4   The Evangelist

### The Critic

The arrival of the Propaganda Fide friars in Querétaro probably opened a path for Francisca that otherwise would have remained closed to her. We know of the other religious orders' disdain for the friars' dramatic excesses in the pulpit, and in particular for their role in the demoniac scandal. Deprived of her mentors, Francisca might not have found a sympathetic ear, one disposed to spreading her fame among the town's other religious orders. Confident of the protection of the Santa Cruz friars and other ecclesiastics, Francisca could not refrain from portraying in her letters opinions and sentiments that belonged to this world. Behind the required facade of humility and passivity, she frequently found cause to find fault with her benefactors and meddle in their affairs. Her confessor, Sitjar, for example, was not the most ideal mentor when it came to the drama of popular piety. In the chronicle of the college he is described as a learned man, a scholar of literature who the community chose to engage in its dialogue with the local Jesuits on intellectual matters. He devoutly followed the liturgical hours and was untiring at the confessional. [1]

Sitjar's more passionate *hija espiritual* was often quick to retort to a criticism. In 1693, Francisca wrote to him that Christ had informed her of the virtues necessary to become his bride, which were humility, resignation, and patience. Then Christ had brushed away the latest conflict between Francisca and her confessor, assuring her that it only served to "adjust in me." While Sitjar may have been scolding her for her lack of humility, Francisca here played her trump card, for the ultimate judge had not seemed worried about her shortcomings. [2]

In spite of her little *delitos* Francisca seems to have felt confident enough of Sitjar's admiration and trust to allow herself a little meddling in his job as her spiritual supervisor. Sometime in 1693, Sitjar confided in her that he was anxious about the coming chapter at the Santa Cruz convent because the friars were in discord on the subject of the missions. The second group of missionaries Sitjar brought from Spain in 1692 was profoundly disgruntled after hearing of their brethren's legendary adventures in Guatemala, Costa Rica and Nicaragua. All had arrived with dreams of quick glory in the south, but to their disappointment only two more friars were needed to support the southern missions. They felt cheated and hemmed in, confined to missions among the Spanish population and Christianized Indians.[3] Francisca consoled Sitjar with a vision in which God's grace infused the friars with light in spite of the devious devils who had infiltrated the group. Finally, God sent a dove that settled on one of the friars' heads (to Sitjar's chagrin Francisca said she did not know which friar), signaling His satisfaction with their choice of guardian. She also assured Sitjar that she prayed constantly that the conflict be resolved without damaging him. To emphasize how hard at work she was for his sake she noted that she had planned to pray the *camandula* for thirty-three days with thirty-three Lord's Prayers as well as five Ave Marias. Through such efforts she would try to secure three things: first, that Sitjar allow her to confess as often as she wanted; second, that the Lord put her troubled confessor's mind to rest; and third, that the Lord give him the strength to govern her soul. The puzzled Sitjar may not have understood how her prayers for God's help in the troubles facing the Santa Cruz friars might have led to soliciting an improvement in their relationship. However, the anecdote shows that Francisca was always on the alert to opportunities that might provide her with greater freedom and power with her confessor.[4]

Indeed, she was not averse to prodding Sitjar lightly when she felt that he was not inspired enough in his direction. In one instance, she informed him that Fray Ortega, who had confessed her during Sitjar's travels to Spain, had understood a vision of hers before she had even uttered more than a few words. To contrast this with her frequent exasperation at Sitjar's lack of imagination, she informed him in another letter that the devil had whispered in her ear that confessing with him was like beating against a stone wall.[5] She later wrote to him that it had become more and more difficult for her to relate her experiences in the confessional, for it was as if she were "obliged to speak to a person that I had never seen or known." While the devil's interference was implicit in the problem, the point was nevertheless made clear.[6] But such outbursts were tempered by a normally admirable show of humility in relation with her confessor. On one occasion, during the feast of the Cross, Francisca stayed in the church for forty hours fasting. This impressed Sitjar to such a degree that he gave her a bread roll he had saved from his supper.[7]

Repentance was also a powerful tool in calming her confessor's irate nerves. In 1696, one of the Santa Cruz friars, the lively and inspiring Fray Francisco Frutos, had managed to persuade Francisca to come into his confessional on a few occasions. He and other friars had reputedly given her bad advice (regarding what she does not reveal). In her letter of June 1, she begged Sitjar to forgive her, even implying that she had not known that it was Frutos on the other side of the screen.[8]

But Sitjar could not prevent Francisca from communicating with other religious men. Such a step would have been physically impossible since she was not a recluse and spent large portions of her days in the Santa Cruz church. Aside from Fray Juan de Ortega, Fray Francisco Frutos, and a group of unnamed Santa Cruz friars, Francisca does not describe her relationships with religious men, but we know from other sources that pious young men wrote to her for spiritual advice and that the devotional objects blessed by God during their unions circulated among the town's ecclesiastical and secular community. It is likely that benefactors visited, as well as pious people simply needing a good spiritual talk.[9] In addition to her circle of friends, Francisca probably knew a great many people because she frequently complained of her constant engagement in conversations in the streets and plazas, during which, she maintained, she stayed solitary in the presence of the Lord. Likewise, given her intimate friendships with priests and friars of all orders and the turbulent politics between those groups, Francisca was probably embroiled in a hotbed of gossip and criticism. In July 1699, for example, she informed her confessor that a Carmelite friar had confided in her his displeasure with the Santa Cruz friars. Characteristically, she was not averse to stirring up already existent hostilities between the orders.[10]

And while Francisca took care to dot her writings here and there with statements asserting her orthodox passivity in the face of the divine or her incapacity to understand His messages or transmit them in words, she simply could not refrain from interpreting them or using them as fuel for criticism. Her critical eye most frequently turned toward male religious who would bear the brunt of her assaults. In a vision she saw a Santa Cruz friar with the stains of sins on his robe, discerned the devils trying to destroy the frail community, and communicated with a deceased friar who suffered the most terrible torments in purgatory for his sins. To crown her body of evidence against the pious friars she asserted that the Lord had told her how revolting He found it to watch a sinful priest handing out the host. Considering that the Santa Cruz friars were her principal benefactors, Francisca demonstrated great audacity indeed.[11] But her freewheeling visionary criticism did not stop at the Santa Cruz friars. In October 1697, she informed Sitjar that in a vision she had seen Juan Caballero y Ocio, Querétaro's most distinguished cleric and her friend and benefactor, standing next to the archbishop of New Spain among the saints who assisted God on his throne. His presence at the celestial court signified God's pleasure with his charitable activities, particularly the construction of the church for the newly established secular Congregation of Guadalupe. Nevertheless, the Virgin had communicated to Francisca that Caballero y Ocio was not at all secure in God's graces in that it was known up above that many of his pious works were spurred by vanity. Reassuringly, however, the Virgin promised to watch over him and give him a nudge in the right direction should he stray too far. In this letter, Francisca demonstrated considerable political skills, for while Caballero was a man above criticism and a financial backer of missions, he was the leader of the town's secular clergy, which was irritating the all-powerful Franciscan Order that monopolized the parish church by demanding to take over more and more of their duties. The vision may have been highly gratifying to Sitjar because while it did not condemn Caballero y Ocio it hinted that earthly success might not translate into salvation.[12]

Nor was Francisca able to refrain from interpreting her visions in a manner befitting a preacher. During Lent of 1693, she saw a great cross extending to the sky that was covered with people, some climbing up, others falling down, still others sitting on the ground deriding the climbers. For the edification of Sitjar, she asserted that those climbing were the virtuous who followed the path of God, those falling were the sinners who had failed in this struggle, while those sitting on the ground were the lowest of all sinners, those who laughed at the preaching of the friars. But the charity of God was boundless as was attested by another vision of a hundred fountains reaching up to the sky, which symbolized the "ardent charity and love" of the "son of the eternal father."[13]

### Apostles in a Supernatural World

Francisca de los Ángeles and her mentors belonged to a culture that focused intensively on tangible symbols of devotion such as Christ as a human being, his passion, the saints, and the relics and holy sites. Their spiritual life centered on a literal interpretation of scripture that maintained that the Bible presented only true facts rather than symbols of religious truths. Karen Armstrong has observed that during the Counter-Reformation, while Muslim spiritual leaders placed emphasis on symbol and imagination and the importance of finding the divine within the soul, Christians, as demonstrated in the trial of Galileo, held that—following scripture—places such as heaven and hell were to be found in actual geographical locations.[14] In Francisca's mental world supernatural life was not an abstract phenomenon of the soul but was contained within material, everyday reality in a parallel orbit that intersected only with earthly life through the grace of God. Just as the images of saints could come alive before her very own eyes so could biblical scenes take place on the streets of Querétaro, visible and audible only to the favored visionary few. On Good Friday, for example, Francisca was in the habit of following in the footsteps of Christ's passion through a grand tour of Querétaro's religious landscape, in which she carried out each station of the *via crucis* in a different church.[15] On the streets and plazas Francisca saw and heard the noise of the crowd as they sneered at her, as they had jeered at Christ. Her jailers beat her and prodded her on as they had with her beloved. Her martyrdom was not over until three o'clock in the morning when she regained consciousness in the Santa Cruz church and hobbled home across town, exhausted by her efforts.[16]

Fray Ortega was an interim confessor with whom Francisca had formed an immediate spiritual bond and with whom she had regularly prayed. He had been at the church of San Antonio on one particular Easter when Francisca had passed by to perform a station of her *via crucis*. Early the next morning, as they met in his confessional, he had asked, "Ay, Francisca, what was that last night, do not deny it, for it has me preoccupied." It emerged that the friar had heard the noise of the manic crowd following her, but to their mutual relief it seemed that only two men in the Calle del Carmen had been frightened by a noise of unknown origin that day.[17] Thus, this supernatural "theater" was always present, disguised in the folds of physical reality.

This sentiment was shared by her mentors at Santa Cruz. Indeed, in Querétaro, no group of religious personages was more devoted to the theatrical aspect of baroque religiosity than the friars of Propaganda Fide. Their daily devotional practices in the cloister were probably an endless source of fascination to townspeople, and it was from these men that Francisca found the protection and example for her own ambitions in the spiritual realm. Most of the original Santa Cruz missionaries were learned men who had received substantial theological training during their years as students and novices in the peninsula. But as ardent evangelists, their natures veered toward the affective piety propagated for the masses by the Counter-Reformation, with its emphasis on images, mental prayer, and active engagement in *imitatio cristi*. Such piety, of course, was not merely the reserve of the poor. At the heart of the Counter-Reformation, in the Vatican, the seventeenth-century pope Alexander VII kept a coffin in his bedroom and a skull on his writing table, while his greatest baroque architect, Bernini, was an ardent devotee of *imitatio cristi.*[18] The missionaries of Propaganda Fide, elite soldiers of the Vatican, would have to be men whose natures conformed to such practices.

Undoubtedly, the first missionaries who arrived with Fray Antonio Llinás in 1683 regarded the New World as a divine opportunity offered to sinful and heresy-ridden Europe to renew its Christian zeal and purity and create the earthly paradise that had so utterly escaped the Old World. The constitutions of the college listed its raison d'être as being their sorrow that "such a multitude of Indians, redeemed with the precious blood of Jesus Christ would live submerged in the darkness of their heresy, deprived of the light of the gospel due to a shortage of missionaries, and thus so many suffer so miserably."[19] Such an impression was echoed more than half a century later in the letters of their successive brethren in New Spain to friends in the mother country. While Fray Francisco López Salguero described the New World as "full of iniquity, vice, idolatry and sin," his compatriot, Fray Pedro de Barco, found that it had given him the chance of a rebirth as a Christian. In the civilization and tedium of Spain, he realized that he would inevitably be competing for honors, but in the land of "barbarians," where he was but one of the multitude, he had found his true calling. For each soul that he had left in the mother country he had found a hundred in the New World, "in which beautiful variety there is to be found copious material for praising the work and providence of the Lord . . . pure Indian, mulatto, mestizo, coyote, morisco, and Spanish souls."[20] The language echoes that which Jacques Le Goff terms the "ideology of the desert" of medieval Europe. It reveals a fascination that runs through Christian culture from Christ's temptation in the desert, the "epic of the desert" created by fourth-century Eastern hermits, to the holy men of European forests and isles. The desert-wilderness was the antithesis of the city-culture, a place of wild beasts and demonic temptation but also a source of holiness and regeneration for Christians. This idea had its revival in the fourteenth and fifteenth centuries, especially among the Franciscan order, and it is likely that the Spanish missionaries of Propaganda Fide spread out in New Spain's northern wilderness were profoundly influenced by it.[21]

For the original Propaganda Fide missionaries, then, the opportunities were greater and the stakes higher in the Indies. The intensity of the battle between good and evil grew in proportion. Already during the Atlantic crossing they had begun to practice their rhetorical fluency by preaching a mission to the crew and passengers.[22] Upon their arrival in Veracruz on May 30, 1683, their worst fears were confirmed. There they witnessed the power of the devil in the New World. They entered a city in terror after one of the worst pirate attacks of colonial times by the feared buccaneers Lorencillo, Nicolas Van Horn, and Michael Gramont. The city was held hostage from May 17 to May 31, when a ransom finally arrived from the capital. Hundreds of citizens were dead, others were held hostage, women were raped, and churches were despoiled.[23] The stench was intolerable as the friars tried to make their way barefoot along the city's corpse-strewn streets. Moved to tears by the sins that had clearly caused the "divine indignation" that had permitted such atrocities, Llinás determined to undertake a mission among the remaining citizens to induce general penance. He was dissuaded by a more sensitive local priest who begged him to not arouse further lament among the traumatized citizenry. Nevertheless, Llinás used the situation to edify his companions about the trials that awaited them in the Indies: "Life in the Indies is to suffer travails: What I offer you are thorns not comforts." Thus, the enemy would be vanquished with the primitive weapons of the first apostles. In the privacy of a convent cell, the twelve men stripped themselves of the last vestiges of their institutional life in the peninsula. By changing their habits for the simple tunics of traveling evangelists, they were thus "making primitive war with the naked enemy, fighting with equal arms in the nudity of their vestements."[24]

In Querétaro, despite evidence of the success of the devil's efforts in the wilderness of the northern regions, the friars discovered that the site of the convent that was to house their *colegio* was also vested with miraculous powers. The convent church was situated on the stage of a battle between Spanish and Indian settlers and the region's original inhabitants, which through "divine intercession" had been won by the settlers. It housed an old wooden crucifix constructed by an early missionary to commemorate the event. The cross quickly became the object of Spanish and Indian worship and worked miracles that attracted frequent pilgrimages. Appropriately then, the friars found themselves inhabiting one of the places that symbolized in local myth the righteousness of Christian claims to the territory.[25]

*Imitatio cristi* was taken to spectacular lengths within the convent, and on occasions outside it. The Santa Cruz friars followed the liturgical hours prescribed to their order as well as they could, considering the long hours they spent in the confessionals—it was their policy never to turn penitents away due to time restrictions—and awarded two hours minimum a day to mental prayer. In practice, however, mental prayer and the adoration of images consumed whatever free time they found when not on mission. The most important addition to the observation of regular hours was their practice of the *via sacra* at two-thirty every afternoon. At that time they gathered in the cloister and reenacted Christ's suffering by ordering the lay brothers to "slap them, pull on them with ropes and tread on them."[26]

How much of this was observed by Francisca is impossible to know. Obviously, she could not enter their cloister, but she did watch their public demonstrations of penance and was probably informed by her confessors of the practices prevalent in the ritual life of the convent. These practices she copied studiously, wearing hair shirts, sleeping naked on a cold stone floor in the posture of a cross with her mouth to the floor, fasting, and engaging in other penitential exercises. Although she showed considerable enthusiasm—at the very least in her letters—for these practices, physical mortification did not blend well with her active nature. Doing without hot chocolate in the mornings simply would not do, she complained in one letter, since the lack of it caused terrible headaches throughout the day. Instead, she was more interested in an active apostolate as a preacher and evangelist.

Perhaps Sitjar understood Francisca's evangelical leanings, for he provided her with letters written to him by the legendary founder. The letters have been lost, but judging by the chronicler Espinosa's description of the saintly friar, they probably contained the sort of rhetoric that would inspire Francisca's. She also corresponded with the lay brother who accompanied Llinás in his religious exercises and could thus receive firsthand knowledge of the master's methods. Like other members of the Santa Cruz community, its founder used physical mortifications to experience the suffering of Christ. He took such practices a step further, entering into partnerships with lay brothers who pulled his hair, beat him, and even, on one occasion, dragged him naked in the middle of the night, with a rope around his neck, to a public plaza. But Llinás distinguished himself further as a mystic by experiencing recurrent raptures and trances that rendered communication with him impossible for hours on end.[27] An equally inspired preacher, his congregations were often treated to spectacular experiences. Espinosa's *Crónica*, for example, includes a hagiographic account of a sermon in Mexico City where the entire congregation was left in suspense while the friar seemed to levitate in the pulpit with his arms outstretched.[28] Undoubtedly, audiences in Querétaro, Francisca among them, were not unaffected by the friar's rapturous rhetoric. And in Llinás's writing, Francisca would have found a spiritual soul mate, for he recognized that the greater the favors from heaven, the heavier the burden for the soul. Like him, Francisca the mystic was the victim of alternating ecstasy and depression.

In the spirit of her mentors, then, Francisca took on the multiple roles of intercessor before God's wrath for the souls of sinners, a humble bride of Christ, and thundering evangelist suffering for the crimes of humanity. Throwing herself into a role exercised by religious women throughout the ages, the *beata* established an "apostolate to the dead." As apostle to the dead, the mystic used her privileges and special communication with God to aid souls in their release from purgatory. In this sense, she followed a particular female piety that flourished in medieval Europe and found widespread acceptance among women in the New World. It was based on a tradition, with roots in the thirteenth century, that recognized that between death and judgment there existed an intermediary sphere that some scholars like Jacques Le Goff consider to obey the limitations of time and space, where sins are purged through suffering, usually in fire. Quantitative measures were used to match the severity of the sins with time in purgatory, which, although perceived differently by the suffering souls, could be measured by those on earth in terrestrial days.[29] Evidence of a feminine preoccupation with alleviating the sufferings of the dead through self-sacrifice is noted by Barbara Newman in the second-century Eastern text of the *Acts of Thecla,* as well as in an early-third-century narrative, the *Passion of Saints Perpetua and Felicitas.* In the twelfth century, Hildegard of Bingen composed a tract on purgatory, and the feminine "apostolate to the dead" became an integral element of saintly women's hagiographies. Women who pursued an active devotion such as the Beguines considered prayer for the souls in purgatory as a central part of their vocation.[30] The medieval church, which monopolized the most effective means of liberating souls from purgatory, namely, the requiem mass, did not object to this quiet apostolic vocation in women. As Newman argues, it "constituted a safe, invisible, contemplative mission that could put women's devotion and compassion to work without violating any gender taboos."[31]

On the other hand, Tridentine sacramental piety had substantially eroded religious women's power for redeeming suffering souls with their prayers.[32] In distant Querétaro, however, under the guidance of her charismatic mentors, Francisca practiced a full-blown medieval apostolic vocation to the souls in purgatory.[33] To her mind, the place recalled various meanings and usages. It could be an underground cavern full of suffering; a desert of ragged, weary souls; or a state of mind. In 1698, for example, Francisca spoke of having entered purgatory of her own volition in order to "make penitence for my sins, to cry for them as well as for those of my loved ones."[34] As a frequent visitor to purgatory she was familiar with the desperation of the souls suffering there. On one occasion they came to her "like birds through the air, I felt their solid weight as they hit me on the chest and shoulders, one placed himself on my head."[35] Taking on some of the sufferings of those stuck in purgatory, she succeeded in hurrying their stay. Indeed, salvation—of living souls and those in purgatory—presented a complicated open market system in which exchange rates were all important. Masses, prayers, communion, prostrations, penitential practices, and spiritual exercises presented the currencies in use. Every inch gained on the spiritual battlefield would be applied for the benefit of the souls of living friends or departed ones.[36] The prayer of San Francisco, Ave Marias, as well as visits to altars were also among her most favored remedies.[37] A day of contemplation and spiritual exercises was not purely beneficial to the practicant. In the larger scheme of things its hard work earned respite for many a surrounding creature in the supernatural and natural realm. Thus, the Santa Cruz friars often sent Francisca messages informing her that they had applied a particular mass for her salvation.[38] She in turn applied many exercises, prostrations, or prayers for their souls or of those in their charge. When it occurred to her that pronouncing the name of the Lord out loud on earth would be heard by and so alleviate the souls in purgatory she decided one day to "bless the name of Holy Mary" three hundred times. To her great surprise she was informed from up above that one hundred souls would exit purgatory, thus bringing the exchange rate down to an advantageous three Ave Marias for each soul.[39] On one occasion, for example, it seemed enough to suffer for one night for one soul, for after three nights of burning she saw three souls ascend to heaven.[40]

She was always aware of the exchange rates her endeavors might earn, and did not neglect to credit her own attendance at masses at the town's various churches for the benefit of her needy, departed protégées. Thus, Francisca paid homage to the longstanding tradition that Newman terms "co-redemption," or a partaking of Christ's passion of the cross to redeem the souls of sinners.[41] She often reported enduring excruciating and protracted pain for the souls of departed loved ones, usually the terrifying sensation of burning up in fire. Even the stifling heat of midsummer could present a venue for salvation, for by suffering it in patience Francisca was convinced that credit would be applied to the souls in purgatory.[42] Should her efforts come to fruition all the suffering was worthwhile. She would regularly see souls dramatically transformed from wailing, tortured entities into white doves ascending to heaven.

Francisca had orthodox confidence in the sacramental power of the mass to salvage souls from purgatory. In one case it was clearly the holiness of the friar saying the mass that caused, according to Francisca, eight souls to be released from their suffering.[43] On another occasion she recalled having been called by her mothers and sisters from the tranquility of her hermitage on the orders of the Santa Cruz friars. They had promised five masses to Saint Augustine "*para una necesidad*" and required her to go to one of them.[44] Her presence there was a supporting feature of a joint enterprise of salvation. Public processions could reap great rewards for their sheer scale. On the day of Corpus Christi, on the advice of a confessor, Francisca always asked the Lord to apply the indulgences gained for the benefit of the entire populace of the city.[45]

Purgatory, as the anteroom of paradise, functioned according to its own logic, however. The long line of waiting souls moved slowly forward as a result of the efforts of the living. Thus, Francisca had her own understanding with the divine judge: if she applied a mass for a certain soul but there was another almost on the brink of release, God then applied the credit Francisca had gained to this first-in-line fortunate soul.[46] The magnitude of sins to be redeemed, however, might become almost too great a challenge even for Francisca. On one occasion she recorded having prayed energetically for a whole year before she finally saw the soul leaving purgatory and, in company of five others, ascend to heaven. Prayer alone, of course, did not work in most cases. Francisca once begged Sitjar for permission to embark on a series of elaborate exercises to save a soul suffering "the greatest and most cruel tortures." She had seen the soul in the form of a woman, richly dressed, trapped in a dark cave surrounded by devils. Her plan included performing the *via sacra* every morning and every night, performing discipline several times a day, wearing a silice, and visiting the altars of the churches every day to pray for the woman.[47] After such pain and suffering, the rewards were undoubtedly great, and Francisca often luxuriated in the lovely perfume a soul's exit left in her cell for days after the event.[48]

Deathbeds presented a particular challenge for her powers. She had been informed by the Lord that the person who repents and grasps the light just before dying considerably shortens his or her stay in purgatory.[49] In the course of her day, Francisca would thus always stay on the alert for the bells of the parish church signaling the death throes of a parishioner ("*tocando agonías*"). At the sound, she would drop whatever she was doing to prostrate herself in the shape of a cross, and say three Our Fathers and Ave Marias.[50] In 1697, she wrote to Sitjar of an extended battle she had fought with several demons during a vision of the bedside of a dying Santa Cruz friar. The friar had appeared to her confessing that he had never loved God and had never repented of his lack of love. Francisca begged the Lord, reminding him of "the life, passion and death" of his holy son, to shine his light on the wayward friar. But if the friar was intransigent, the Lord showed himself even more severely, and it was not until the Virgin decided to take the case that some progress was made.[51] Characteristically, and in spite of her bravado, Francisca found it difficult to go to the extremes of suffering experienced by many famous holy women, such as the celebrated Golden Age Spaniard Juana de la Cruz. Juana filled her bed with stones, either burning hot or icily cold, and lay on them like a mother hen in the belief that each and every one contained imprisoned souls whose release she could effect, as her fellow nuns read her passages on Christ's passion. All things considered, Francisca argued that since God had a preference for the simple, he would be happier with "one Ave Maria, one act of love" than with dramatic penitential practices.[52] Unlike many holy women who found pleasure and union with Christ through the painful gifts of their longstanding illnesses and sufferings, Francisca was decidedly more comfortable with action.

Saving souls at death beds was not a purely supernatural experience. Francisca's letters from this period contain suggestions that her presence was frequently required at death beds and that she had seen many deaths. On one occasion, she recalled a particularly difficult battle with the devil over the soul of a woman in her last agony:

> one or two creeds before giving her last breath, she called me, I went to her, and found her very smiling and happy. Admiring her joy, I asked her of its cause. She told me, well do you not see what beautiful silk cushions and lovely rugs I have here . . . . two others heard her words, I told them: look this is the devil at work distracting her, bringing her these apparitions . . . and without her noticing I threw blessed water on her and we recited the creed at which her face changed expression and I asked her where were these things she was telling me about. She told me: no I see nothing. I exhorted her not to remember anything of past vanities, that she give her heart to God, that it was now time to go and give him an account of her soul. Pressing her to make acts of contrition she died in a short while.[53]

Francisca's presence at the side of death beds advertised her capacities to the wider populace. She was also a messenger to the living of the fate of their loved ones. At times, that role could be a delicate operation. In June 1696, the repentant *beata* told Sitjar that she had caused great pain to the family of a young Spaniard in Querétaro, recently deceased. He had appeared to her suffering the particularly creative torment of being locked in a dark, humid cave one moment and suffering in flames the next. The next time she saw his sister, Isabel, Francisca informed her that her brother suffered in purgatory and that it was up to them to free him. The sister then told her mother of this, who shed bitter tears for an entire night and begged Francisca for a solution. Francisca recommended commissioning a novena for his soul, but suffered guilt for having caused the mother such pain.[54] In these capacities, as intercessor before God of souls approaching death and as messenger between the realm of the living and dead, Francisca rendered great service to the people of Querétaro. She provided a type of "life insurance," similar in principle to that which daughters in religion rendered to their parents.[55]

### Tejas

From an early age, Francisca's piety was driven by a view of mankind as exiled from its natural state. In June 1699, she wrote to Fray Antonio Margil de Jesús, her new confessor: "I would like to go out speaking in voices that told everyone to wake up from the state of oblivion in which they find themselves not minding the end for which we were all raised in the world."[56] Such sentiments led her to a more radical form of internalized evangelism than that of saving souls in purgatory, namely, her spiritual travels to the region now named Texas. Her bilocations, which took place on Thursdays while Santa Rosa took her place in the house, are the supreme expression of Francisca's vision—after a Teresian fashion—of the cloister as a missionary battlefield. Among the most intriguing sections of the Inquisitorial stack of papers for 1692 is that dealing with her role as a guide to Franciscan missionaries attempting to win the territory of Tejas for God. Thankfully, Francisca's own letters, beginning in 1689, elaborate further on the subject and provide her own account of events.

As noted earlier, the convent of Santa Cruz seethed with men who were prepared to endure uncommon hardships—from traveling on foot over vast expanses of desert and braving death—to help souls whom they considered to be innocents who had been lured by the devil from seeing the light of the one true God. Francisca corresponded with and formed friendships with these men, and from them took her own rhetoric. The intensity with which the Propaganda Fide friars launched into the reclamation of orthodoxy in Querétaro was replicated in their evangelical efforts among the more challenging Indian nations. In Talamanca, the Lacandon area, and Costa Rica it was reputed that they had converted over forty thousand Indians. In their own writings they established a mission myth that mirrored the Franciscan Golden Age after the Conquest. Fray José Díez, for example, in his chronicle of the college noted how their single habit became so patched and battered by years of traveling through mountains, deserts, and jungles on foot that not a single thread of the original material remained. According to the friar, the missionaries in these wild regions lived mostly off roots, yucca, and an occasional toasted corn cob, while in better times they were allowed the luxury of beans for lunch and bread dipped in hot chocolate at night. His one-sided triumphal accounts of the missions include descriptions of mass processions, confessions, and night-long penitences by the men locked in the churches with the friars.[57] Their style was aggressive, and they were seemingly adept at using local guides and inter-preters to communicate with otherwise unapproachable populations.[58] Once established in their mission they demonstrated that they were rustic men who grew their own food and were not parasites on the native population. Their missionary principle, formulated by Fray Joseph Castro, was to leave behind them "[intellectual] speculation, for even if it is by the most learned men in the world, the practice of a rustic is enough to turn it to dust."[59] To such apostles the pulpit lay at the center of their mission. Their rustic oratory conformed to their wild surroundings: down to earth and descriptive. According to Díez the "pulpit was the arena in which as messengers of Christ, they exalted his Word and brandished the sword of the Divine Word, to declare war on the Devil and his allies, with such courage and constancy that they would rather forsake life than the preaching apostolate."[60]

Francisca probably found such doctrine thrilling, but her own confessor, the learned Sitjar, was less inspiring as a missionary in the New World. It was probably for this reason that she began to correspond with Fray Francisco Frutos, the Santa Cruz friar who had lured her into his confessional and was one of the *colegio*'s legendary missionaries. Frutos, one of the original Santa Cruz friars most beloved by the citizens of Querétaro, distinguished himself as a confessor and was famed for his ability to gently steer recalcitrant souls into reconciliation with their creator in their last moments. In company with another Santa Cruz friar, Frutos had traveled on foot across the region of New Galicia preaching to all ethnic groups in the cities, towns, and ranches. The simplicity with which he taught the crowds the elements of mental prayer, the exercise of the *via sacra*, and the act of contrition purportedly made the crowds hysterical. The scenes at times would resemble an image of Judgment Day: women and men kneeling on the floor, beating their chest, and wailing over their own sins. Frutos also faithfully propagated the Santa Cruz friars' penitential practices while on mission. Three times a week he ordered the population of the pueblos in question to separate into groups of men and women to perform penitential exercises. According to the *Crónica* of the convent of Santa Cruz, the missions were so successful that people traveled over sixty leagues to confess with him and his companions.[61]

Frutos was also known for his diligence in steering young, pious women to the tertiary life. Given his enthusiasm for the spiritual life of women, it is most likely that Frutos took an interest in Francisca from the start.[62]

Upon their return to Querétaro, the missionaries undoubtedly recounted their adventures to Francisca, leaving her to dream of performing similar feats for the faith. As Vera Tudela notes, the exoticism of the New World and the "desert" opportunities it offered to the mystic had already been incorporated into colonial hagiography, such as in the narratives of transatlantic travel of Spanish nuns described by admiring biographers as *"verdaderas apostólicas."*[63] Many religious women in New Spain nursed such ambitions. The Puebla nun Francisca de la Natividad, writing in the middle of the seventeenth century, saw visions of Indians begging for religious indoctrination and declared that she harbored a "holy jealousy" of missionaries. For that purpose alone, she said, she wished that she had been born a man. María de San José, a contemporary *poblana* nun, characterized herself as an "encloistered missionary."[64] And Catarina de San Juan, another holy *poblana*, reported bilocations to the northern borderlands where she aided Jesuit missionaries.[65]

In 1688, when Francisca was fifteen years old, prodigious news reached the *colegio* that would give her an opportunity to explore the daily reality of evangelical work. One of its missionaries, Fray Damian Mazanet, who had been occupied on mission in Coahuila, had been informed by some coastal Indians that about a 130 leagues north, by the Bahía del Espíritu Santo, they had encountered some Frenchmen, Spain's rivals in the region. Fray Damian immediately informed Capt. Alonso de Leon, the governor of Coahuila, who in turn informed the viceroy, the Conde de Galve. Concluding that the French in all probability were the much hunted expedition that had landed at Matagorda Bay in 1685, the viceroy ordered the governor to investigate the matter. Thus it was that Fray Damian found himself traveling north with Spanish troops to reconnoiter the area.[66] After finding some French corpses within a burned fort, the Spaniards encountered, some forty leagues north of the fort, a group of seemingly friendly Indians of the Affinais nation. In response to questions as to their nation and disposition toward the Spanish, they answered *"texía, texía,"* signifying, according to chroniclers, "friend" in Affinais. They freely offered information on their region through an interpreter and seemed interested enough when queried if they would adopt the Catholic faith.

The governor and the friar returned to Coahuila. There, the governor composed an *informe* that the friar took with him to Mexico City for the viceroy. Resting at the college on the way to the capital, Fray Damian gave his eyewitness account of the Affinais's great desire to adopt the true doctrine. The friars immediately discerned the hand of divine providence. Ever since its foundation the College of Santa Cruz had repeatedly begged to be allowed to enter the northern wilderness and establish missions but had been denied the opportunity since its services were much in demand among the faithful.[67] At the viceregal court, the order was immediately issued to prepare a fourth expedition into Texas. On March 27, 1689, the expedition set forth from Santiago de la Monclova in Coahuila, and was joined in Texas by regiments from Nueva-Vizcaya. It was a success, capturing French leaders who were interrogated in the capital that summer. A year later, in March 1690, a much larger expedition set forth from Coahuila, accompanied by veteran missionaries from Santa Cruz. By May, they had thrust deep enough into the territory to be greeted by an Indian chief whom the Spaniards decided must be the governor of the Texans. He led them to his pueblo in a valley covered with maize and bean fields. There, curious scenes took place of the kind that would be held up to inspire subsequent waves of missionaries. At his modest house, which the Spaniards noted with pleasure was spotlessly clean and proper, the newcomers were treated to tamales and *atole*. The next day the friars, accompanied by the governor and the Spanish troops and followed by some curious Indians well furnished with gifts, held a procession around the pueblo that ended in a Te Deum sung by the friars at the governor's house. The next day, the Spanish soldiers constructed a small chapel to celebrate the coming feast of Corpus Christi.

Corpus Christi, the twenty-fifth of May, became the high point of the expedition. Again the governor, friars, and the soldiers accompanied by caciques, and a multitude of Indians in formal dress, formed a procession that ended with the governor bowing to the authority of Carlos II. At this triumphal moment it was decided to found a mission among the Texans, and after the soldiers had constructed a small wooden convent at a central point between the pueblos of three valleys, the expedition returned to Mexico. They left behind the three friars and a few solders, and took with them four Indians, some of whom were relatives of the "governor's."[68]

Sometime in the summer of 1690, Fray Damian arrived with his new companions at Santa Cruz in Querétaro and caused quite a stir. It was commonly agreed that the Indians possessed a "lovely physique and disposition." They became the most sought after dinner guests in town, a privilege that was only afforded special benefactors of the *colegio*. But if the Indians were thus paraded publicly, Francisca, as a spiritual daughter of Sitjar and confidante of other friars, must have caught a glimpse of them. As the greatest missionary feat of the college, there was probably talk of little else among the community and its intimates for days and weeks.[69] The event at least had profound effects on Francisca, for it was some time after this date that she began to experience constant bilocations to Texas where she converted and pacified thousands of hostile pagans.

A second expedition, which set out in May 1691, was a failure, however. In October 1693, exhausted by their efforts and with no hope of reinforcements, the missionaries buried their sacred objects and church bells and began the slow trek back to Coahuila, accompanied by the few Spanish soldiers who remained.[70] The memory of that first glorious entry into the wilderness of Texas and the endless possibilities offered by the Divine Father for evangelization among its numerous population nevertheless stayed with the Santa Cruz community, which tried repeatedly to obtain support to revive the missions. Such efforts were fruitless, however, until 1716 when the story took a new turn.

The bitterness of disappointment did not fade quickly at Santa Cruz. On February 14, 1698, five years after the return of the last missionaries from Texas, Francisca wrote a fascinating letter to Sitjar that throws light on her rather ambiguous role in the affair. In the letter, Francisca saw reason to defend herself against grave rumors clearly circulating in the convent, and probably in the town, that she had been the instigator of the missionary effort. A group of friars had clearly questioned her on the subject, for Sitjar was curious as to her response. Unfortunately for the friars, Francisca could remember little of what she had said so many years ago. Equally fortuitous for her own cause was the miraculous coincidence that she could remember facts that exonerated whatever guilt she might bear. First, she was careful to note in her letter, she had not known Fray Damian before his first entry into Texas, and thus could not have counseled him to do so—as the allegations asserted. Second, when Fray Damian returned to prepare his second mission, she did not disclose to him any revelations as to the fate of the effort. Thus, it was unfair of her accusers to maintain that it was because of her revelations that the viceroy had funded the expensive second expedition.

From these curious denials the confusing facts of the story began to unfold in the letter. Apparently, upon his return from the first triumphant expedition to Texas, Fray Damian, hearing of the fifteen-year-old holy woman graced with direct access to the divine, sought out her advice with his group of missionaries. At first, Francisca had demonstrated the proper resistance. She responded to the friars that she simply did not understand anything, and was "*una ignorante*," who did not even know how to cross herself properly. The friars impatiently brushed away such modesty: yes, yes, but even if it was so, she should tell them what she thought without leaving any details out. Alas, her youth had led her astray and made her commit such "*tonterias*," which the mature twenty-four-year-old religious woman writing the letter would never have imagined performing "for the experience and knowledge I now have." But at the age of fifteen she simply could not resist the sight of such illustrious friars hanging on to her every word. They seemed each and every one like a San Francisco Xavier. Later, of course, she realized that the impression of their saintliness had been an illusion, for "faced with hardship they came back and left everything."[71]

But these mirror images of San Francisco Xavier had prodded her with straightforward questions. Would it be convenient to venture deeper into the territory than their present mission? Should they make a rush to explore the hinterland or take their time and traverse the territory first? Should they enter by sea or land? Would the pagans convert? The stunned adolescent tried to respond to this barrage of questions to the best of her capacity. The result, according to her, was bland. Yes, it would be a great service to the Lord if the missionaries entered into these territories and converted the pagans. And since she did not receive any message from the divine as to the methods to be employed—the quick thrust or slow exploration—she simply said that it would be a good thing to do. And concerning the question of entry by sea or land, there was silence up above (it probably did not help that Francisca had never seen the sea), forcing her to offer the dubious opinion that with "good current and some stability it would be possible because even if it was costly it would be highly advantageous, but lacking these elements it would not be convenient." And finally she flatly refused having said anything about whether or not the pagans would convert. Even if she had been informed in a vision that all the pagans she had seen on her bilocations would in the end convert, the Lord had of course not deigned to use earthly time measures for such things. As a result, she did not know if it would take two years or twenty-five.

In the end, Francisca conceded that it had been because of her avid desire to see these pagans brought into the fold of the true religion that she had given these answers. But as for blaming her for all the costs undertaken by the viceroy and other elite Spaniards for the expedition, such an accusation was ridiculous. Besides, in her opinion, it was "a great *rateria* grumbling over whether money was spent or not, when so much is spent on the vanities of this world . . . when God, our Lord did not hesitate to give his life and the last drops of his blood to save our souls."[72]

The blandness that Francisca tried to ascribe to herself at this age does not coincide with the image of the fiery prophetess seen in the 1691 Inquisition documents. And, indeed, her own letters to Sitjar confirm this discrepancy. In one of them she conceded that "when you asked me these questions on the *cuadernillo* which you showed me, I have to admit that I cannot remember well if what I said here was noted in it . . . Please show it to me, and I shall try to clarify to you Sir what I understood in prayer, and what I said according to my own opinion." It thus appears that what Fray Sarmiento had complained about to the Inquisition was true: Francisca did write down her experiences in Texas during her bilocations for Fray Damian and his fellow missionaries. Modesty could not stifle the torrent of her pen when thus provoked. And should she be left in any doubt as to the profound importance of her mission to Tejas there was always the savage Indian riot that caused many casualties on Querétaro streets in 1690 to serve as a cautionary tale.[73]

We do not possess Francisca's guidebooks, but we can surmise what they contained from her later descriptions of the region of the infidels. Bilocations, or divinely aided travel that allowed one to visit faraway places without undertaking the actual voyage in one's body, were not at all uncommon within Catholic religious culture. In such cases, absences would not be noted since a favorite saint would commonly assume the person's physical appearance, while the traveler—or voyeur—would fly to his or her destination. Living witnesses to such experiences could be found within the community. Fray Francisco Casañas de Jesús María, Protomartyr of Propaganda Fide in the Indies, had been among the second wave of Santa Cruz missionaries to enter Texas. While residing at Santa Cruz after his return, he experienced bilocations that took him further east and north of the reconnoitered territory, where he converted thousands of pagans.

At Santa Cruz it was known that the community's great role model, Madre María de Jesús de Agreda, the famed Spanish nun, had experienced such bilocations to New Mexico between 1620 and 1631. With the help of angels she had been taken to several faraway kingdoms located beyond hostile lands. In the process, she had converted thousands of pagans to the faith and induced them to seek missionaries to baptize them. Powerful men within the church, both in the colony and Spain, had found her tales intriguing. Memorials of them were printed in over four hundred copies and circulated in Spain and brought to Rome.[74] Agreda's bilocations, as noted by Clark Colahan, presented powerful political capital for the Franciscans as proof of divine pleasure with their efforts. Through her mentors, Francisca must have been aware of the nun's enthusiastic reception by King Felipe IV himself, who established with her an intimate epistolary friendship and congratulated her on her eventual escape from the Inquisition's clutches. Indeed, the Holy Office questioned the nun at length, worried that she might be suffering from diabolical delusions that could lead to false trances and consequently forged bilocations. When it did it found her to be charming, obedient, and humble. Astutely, Madre Agreda hinted that perhaps her bilocations were simply owed to God's awareness of her intense evangelical desires, which had led Him to allow her to believe that they were true.[75] Her examiners concluded that the blame should be placed upon her Franciscan mentors for encouraging exaggerated accounts of her missionary work, and they left her convent laden with crosses as souvenirs of this holy nun.[76]

Francisca had the good fortune to evade interrogations by the tribunal on her bilocations, but in the previously related letter to her confessors she took Madre Agreda's tack of diluting her experiences with doubt and caution. According to her descriptions to another more trusted and less critical confessor, however, she went a step further than her Spanish model: she baptized her own Indians and provided them with the sacraments. Francisca's bilocations must have begun early since she was able to write down guidebooks based on her experiences before the second Propaganda Fide mission. Indeed, in a letter to Fray Antonio Margil de Jesús from the turn of the century, she attested that these experiences had begun long before the first missions to Texas. As with Madre Agreda, it had pleased the Lord to show her all the lands of the world where infidels were portrayed as shadows aimlessly wandering about the earth in the dark night of their sad state. At first, these travels took place during dreams. She found reason to doubt them since she had been taught that the devil might easily use dreams for his deceptions. Then they began to take place in trances during waking hours. The power with which the Lord pulled her into the supernatural world caused her to vomit continuously, and her general health deteriorated to the point that a doctor told her to reconcile herself since the end was drawing nearer. For two months she was only able to partake of hot chocolate, which she unfailingly vomited.

In the end all these troubles paid off, however. Francisca finally felt herself being transported bodily across the region, walking on foot but with exceptional speed. In this respect, she showed herself far more confident than her distinguished Spanish model, who claimed to be unsure as to whether she had traveled in body or not.[77] To verify the orthodoxy of her experiences Francisca told first her confessor and then the Franciscan commissary general, to whom she wrote regularly of her spiritual experiences. Both exhorted her to resign herself to the will of God who would not permit her to err.[78] In the midst of her confusion, Francisca decided to visit a leper woman who lived in a nearby carriage house, avoided by people due to her pestilent odor. Having been overcome with such divine favors Francisca's instinct was that it would please the Lord if she cleared her active mind of such thoughts and gave herself totally to his will. But the visit was to have fateful consequences since it seemed to please the Lord to use the opportunity to inform her of her evangelical destiny. As she kneeled by the woman's sickbed she saw a tremendous vision of the land of converted pagans. God then made her understand that these were infidels who would in the future convert, and that it was her duty to carry out the conversion. Francisca saw His words like sun rays that covered the world. Their power was such that she fainted and came to in the arms of a female passerby. Having exhorted the sick woman to resign herself to the will of God and to keep the Lord Jesus Christ in her heart always, Francisca departed for home with a renewed sense of mission.[79]

It was in a spiritual manner that God first brought Francisca to a land of pagan Indians that turned out to be the region of New Mexico, which she probably had read about in the famous Madre Agreda's texts. There, the divine being showed her a baby girl being born to an Indian woman. The girl, God informed Francisca, would be left there to die by her mother. Taking her by surprise He asked her if she wanted to baptize the baby to ensure its entry to heaven. When His protégée replied yes, God sent her down with her angel with a jar of blessed water to baptize the girl, who appeared to be the great granddaughter of people who had taken part in the slaughter of missionaries in the region decades ago. With the baptism of the baby girl, Francisca took her first step as evangelist and took up the path in which less successful missionaries had failed.[80]

Eventually, however, Francisca was taken bodily to New Mexico. There, she and her angel were welcomed by a group of thirty people who were so inviting that the angel suggested that Francisca baptize them. Eagerly seizing the opportunity, Francisca preached to the Indians as to "who is God, and how there exists another life in heaven, and how hell is full of pain, and how the purpose of our life here on earth is to serve and love God as his law and his Church teaches us so that when we die we go straight to heaven where one can gaze at and revel in God with a feeling even greater than that which we experience when admiring and enjoying the sun; and those who do not want to follow that path, their soul will go to hell."[81]

In spite of such simple rhetoric, Francisca's first audience does not seem to have understood very well. Along with her angel, the missionary stayed for a few days with the newly baptized, but when she decided it was time to leave they would not let her go. She informed them that her Father demanded that she go back, a tactic that worked well since, according to her, children of the *naturales* obeyed their parents with great humility. Thus, the evangelist learned to establish communication by appealing to the traditions of her flock.[82] Francisca continued to return to New Mexico, where she met with old people who she claimed had been baptized by Madre Agreda. The nun herself had cautiously stated, however, that she had only taught the catechisms and prompted her congregation to seek baptism. In one instance, Francisca gave last sacraments to an old man who had been baptized by her famed predecessor but who had then returned to his pagan ways in his adult life. By administering the last rites Francisca thus crowned the evangelical work of the Spanish nun and established herself as her successor.[83]

Francisca the preacher was active, virile, and ingenious, as opposed to the self-image she liked to project: the contemplative, humble, and obedient *beata*. These new features of her character were male in nature according to her culture. Thus, it quickly came about that the Lord endowed her with the form of a friar, which allowed her to travel the roads north from New Spain to New Mexico and eventually to Texas undetected. In the land of the *infieles*, however, there existed some confusion as to Francisca's sex. The Indians named her intermittently, *señora*, *madre*, and *padre*. The fact remained, however, that Francisca left behind in Querétaro the femininity of the retired life.[84]

But her bilocations seem to have continued after the final return of the vanquished missionaries, and were perhaps intensified by their failure. In her letter of February 14, 1698, Francisca used the opportunity to remind Sitjar that on one of her travels she had seen a splendid light rising to the sky. It signified the burial site of Fray Miguel Font-Cuberta, president of the first mission in Texas, who had died there before the arrival of reinforcements, and was now a *bienaventurado*. Shouldn't the missionaries return to this place, she had asked the Lord. The immediate answer was that that would be very pleasing, but alas, "since the means to do so is in the hands of men, much of what God desires is lost."[85] But Francisca did not give up hope. At the end of her letter she suggested indirectly that her knowledge might be of great use for future missions since God had taken her to various regions where "there are to be missionaries, others where there were, and yet others where there never will be."[86]

With the hindsight of several years, Francisca could now model her experiences in Texas on the legendary stories told by the missionaries and probably known to most *queretanos*. In her account she paid attention to detail, such as the regional differences between the different nations of the territory. Patiently, she explained to her readers that just as New Spain was composed of many independent entities, that is, cities and villages, so the territory of Tejas was composed of different groups, who all used a similar word to describe their larger surroundings. Thus, some used "Tejes," others "Theche," and others "Tejas."[87] It was a large territory according to the *beata*. Its rough roads and wide and deep rivers presented innumerable difficulties to the evangelization effort.[88] Early on, then, Francisca seems to have decided to focus her energies on a limited population. Having been given the privilege of watching the first missionaries in action, she was able to build on their efforts.[89] Thus, her energies were mainly spent building a small chapel, saying the holy office, congregating the Indians, catechizing, and baptizing. Francisca even inserted a dramatic account of an epidemic that closely resembled the *tabardillo*, which had struck during the second mission. Like her role models, she welcomed the opportunity to baptize innocents before they were taken away, thus ensuring their direct ascent to heaven.[90]

It seems that throughout the 1690s, Francisca traveled frequently in spirit to Tejas to maintain the wrecked missionary effort there. In one instance, she mentions departing every Thursday; Santa Rosa of Viterbo took on her likeness to cover up the absence. In another, she mentions having traveled eight times to Texas over a period of three months. The frequency of her travels also depended on the needs of the Indians of her congregation. Should the need arise, her guardian angel would serve as a messenger. At times she would rouse herself even while sick in bed. The prospect of a mission never failed to charge Francisca's body with energy and lightness that allowed her to travel large distances.[91]

In Tejas, unencumbered by controlling friars, Francisca assumed their roles. Having drawn the inhabitants of the region to her thundering preaching, she set her protégés to work building a church. Never having left the region of Querétaro, Francisca naturally used the religious landscape of her native town as a reference for her constructions. Thus, having moved their modest church three times, just as the Santo Domingo in Querétaro had been moved, Francisca's converted Indians finally settled on a location that facilitated access to the local population. There, Francisca built a replica of the church of Santa Cruz, her favorite place of worship, although slightly more modest in size. The church, according to Francisca, was made of "adobe walls on the inside, supported by sticks like those used in bullfights . . . the roof is very well made, it looks like *otate* [grass used for weaving baskets], but looking at it it seems like a marble veined cloth." It contained five altars, the principal of which was adorned by a miraculous crucifix which Francisca had found in a cave by the sea. (She may have been thinking of sacred objects left by the friars after their retreat.) Another of her church's cherished images was that of Saint Francis, whom she had encountered while trying to traverse a great river. As she stood on the riverbank, frightened by its power, the image had appeared to her and led her across. Afterward it had settled in the characteristic posture of the saint, arms folded across the chest and hands bearing stigmata facing upward, and it allowed her to tow it to the church.[92]

It is clear from her rhetoric that Francisca took her mentors' view of the character of the Indians. The Franciscans of Propaganda Fide were anxious to revive the spirit of the first century after the Conquest with its massive conversion effort. Its thrilling impetus was that the Indians were innocent, noble children of God who had been led astray by the devil but who, once turned to the right path, would supersede the peoples of the Old World in their natural inclination for devotion. Another view emerged as the euphoria of the sixteenth century waned and the greater stability of the seventeenth century unearthed fundamental cultural antagonism between Indians and Spaniards. It held that Indians were active devil worshippers with very little hope of salvation.[93] In a letter of April 2, 1699, Francisca recorded her mentors' preference for the former view. In it she quotes her deceased friend Fray Juan Capistrano, who was in the habit of saying "that if our Father San Francisco were alive in these times and if he had worn the costume and led the life of the Indians, he would have taken it and taught it to his friars." Francisca's friend had "loved the Indians very much." He would fill his sleeves with sweets and go to their casitas to give them away.[94] His protégée espoused the same principle of evangelical simplicity. In April 1699, she gave her confessor Fray Antonio Margil de Jesús some advice before he left on mission: "the Lord wants his ministers to execute the ministry of preaching the truth of the *evangelio* with *desnudez* and poverty which is the most effective way to be of profit to souls."[95]

As for her Texan and New Mexican protégées, Francisca concurred with this view: "I have considered that our Lord has endowed the naturals with humility and self-deprecation." And in comparison with the Christians of her own society, they were much more receptive to God's word. In August 1699, she told Margil that she had seen this contrast in a vision. God's aid to humans she had seen in the form of soft rain so fine that it could not reach the ground since from the earth rose a terrible smelling vapor that stopped it. However, in the land of the *infieles*, the rain did reach the ground, "and our Lord made me understand that these poor things are more capable of receiving the light of the *evangelio* and that many will be converted to his holy law."[96] Nevertheless, at times Francisca found them to be like unruly children. The men had sexual relations outside of marriage, and incest was not uncommon.[97] "The poor things are so materialistic," she complained, that it had been necessary for the good Lord to demonstrate to them concretely some of his prodigies—naturally, in cooperation with his apostle. Thus, she had congregated the grumbling inhabitants and ordered them to try and carry the crucifix from the church. Should it not move, she warned them, it was a clear sign that God wanted to stay in their midst. According to Francisca, the immobile crucifix quickly quieted any voices of discontent among the new parishioners. They might also become dangerously enamored of her devotional objects. On one occasion they tried to tear her rosary from the rope she wore around her habit, but again she used the same trick. Finding that the rosary simply could not be ripped out, they settled for a promise of new ones the next time she returned.[98] Saint Francis also lent a hand in regaining the unstable affections of the Indians during times of famine and disease. On one such occasion Francisca carried the image out of the church and fell on her knees, at which the image opened its arms, turned its eyes toward heaven, cried and emitted blood from its wounds. The gesture assured the return of the dispersed congregation and the conversion of many more. With her devoted flock, Francisca experienced exhilarating miraculous episodes that brought her back to biblical eternity. Thus, like Christ, Francisca managed to multiply one *fanega* of maize to feed five hundred parishioners. In this visionary realm it was not difficult for Francisca and her protégés to surmise the presence of God. In one instance, for example, the Indian groups of the region clashed resulting in the massacres of innocents. Divine fury was unleashed as the heavens opened and the infidels were struck by fire.[99]

Overcoming language restrictions, Francisca the missionary managed to organize her congregation into a fixed schedule of ritual and prayer. Ingeniously devising signs by which she signaled fasts, holy days, and vigils, she taught her disciples to erase each sign after the day had passed to keep up with the Catholic ritual schedule. Thus, during her absences her flock would not be confused as to their duties. And for her strenuous efforts there were ample rewards. Newborns were brought to be baptized, and young girls educated by Francisca cleaned and decorated the church. The high point of it all was reached when new converts were taken into the congregation. At such moments, Francisca herself led her flock in saying the creeds, pronouncing doctrine, and praying.

Thus the Francisca that the Mexico City inquisitors gleaned from their stack of papers was a precocious young woman, bent on emulating the example of her famed mentors and not in the least retiring when it came to the undeniable heresy of assuming the powers of the sacrament. In the span of twenty years—from the arrival of the Santa Cruz friars to the eruption of the demoniac scandal and the bilocations to Texas—Francisca had been transformed from a "special" sort of a nine-year-old into a full-fledged prophetic saintly woman who had acquired education, skills, and a network of religious and secular admirers and friends who shielded her from the harsh gaze of the Inquisition. Judging by the details of the Texas life provided in her letters, it is likely that Francisca dazzled audiences, religious and secular, with her descriptions. Thus, she became not only a channel to the divine world, but into another even more mysterious and impenetrable reality: that of the dark regions of the *infieles*. Moreover, Francisca enjoyed more freedom of movement and speech by virtue of her special status as a Santa Cruz protégée than even the elite nuns of Santa Clara could ever hope for.

By the turn of the century, then, Francisca de los Ángeles stood relatively unchallenged and full of confidence in her own authority. But the year 1698 brought an encounter with one of the most famed missionaries of the New World, Fray Antonio Margil de Jesús. The event would effect dramatic transformations in her religious persona.

# 3   The Foundress

## 5  Francisca and Margil

*If all the musical instruments of the world and harmonious voices*
*would join while one is in rapture they would not be enough to detach*
*the soul from that intimate and close union which it is enjoying with*
*the Higher Good, absorbed in its sweetness and drowning in the*
*abyss of Divinity.*

Fray Antonio Llinás,
*Crónica apostólica*

One day around the turn of the eighteenth century, Fray Antonio Margil de
Jesús, guardian of the Santa Cruz convent of Querétaro, visited Francisca de
los Ángeles at the recently established *beaterio* of Santa Rosa de Viterbo.[1] He
came to help her install a sun watch in her garden, a skill for which he was
well known. Upon completing his labor, the two sat down in the community's
chapel and began to speak of spiritual matters. Suddenly, the friar stood
abruptly up from the bench, his arms and legs seized up in a spasm, and for
over an hour he was rendered immobile in divine ecstasy. Although Francisca
was aware of the supernatural cause of his state and had seen him in similar
circumstances before, she fainted from the intensity of the experience, and her
fellow *beatas* had to carry her to her cell.[2] Friar and disciple often shared such
moments of sudden entry into the supernatural world—indeed, Francisca's
mentor often levitated in her presence—and inevitably, once Margil came out
of them, the two would cry together.

   The friar had become Francisca's confessor on the death of Sitjar on May 8,
1698. Born in 1657, in Valencia, Margil was forty-one years old when he began
to confess the twenty-four-year-old Francisca. According to the hagiographic
account of his childhood provided by one of his biographers, Margil had
shown the sort of religious precociousness that characterized also Francisca's
youth. In 1673, a year before Francisca's birth, he became a novice in a convent
in Valencia, but his "ardent apostolic vocation" led him to join Fray Antonio
Llinás ten years later in his mission to found the Propaganda Fide colleges in
the New World. He thus became a member of the first group of friars to take
possession of the Santa Cruz convent in Querétaro.[3]

The missionary: Fray Antonio Margil de Jesús. *Crónica
del Real Colegio de Santa Rosa de Viterbo*. Edited by Josefina
Muriel. Querétaro, El Gobierno del Estado de Querétaro, 1996.

As noted by Antonio Rubial García, Margil was not only the perfect missionary of the Counter-Reformation church, but his activities evoked images
of that glorious "Golden Age" of the Franciscans in the New World—the
sixteenth century—and its missionary feats.[4] Pushed by fierce evangelical
impulses, he had not been content with the relatively tranquil life led in
Querétaro. In 1684 he had embarked on a series of missions to the Indians in
the deep jungles and mountainous terrain of Central America, covering the

territories of present-day Chiapas, Guatemala, El Salvador, Costa Rica, and Nicaragua. He pushed as far south as Panama, always on foot, and became over the years a living legend in the area. Margil was a missionary in the truest sense of the word, for he did not merely preach but taught by example, living in holy poverty and fixated on the devotions he propagated. A small, frail man, his energy was boundless. In their testimonies during the failed process to win Margil his sanctification, witnesses recalled the astounding speed of his walk, which they could only attribute to divine causes.[5] He would walk chanting into Indian villages, drawing curious crowds. They would then be treated to his furious and inspired preaching, peppered by self-whipping and raptures.[6] A "lion" in the pulpit, Margil possessed the desirable missionary characteristic of sweetness in the confessional. An energetic director of souls, he could confess hundreds in a day, an occupation that was the bread and butter of his vocation as a priest.[7] Contemporaries described him as a humble, loving, and gentle man, graced with a lightness of temperament: "He was cheerful and *bromista*, and peppered his talks with old refrains and sayings."[8] Margil's powerful political instincts nevertheless made him one of the most important and prominent figures in the colony, both for his reputed evangelical talent and for his ability to communicate with, and endear himself to, rich and poor alike. This accessibility was reinforced by his image as an outsider to the ecclesiastical hierarchy, for he was known for his complete negation of the material. He refused pecuniary remuneration for his missionizing efforts and, according to testimony offered during his process for sanctification, could not distinguish precious metals from ordinary ones.[9]

In 1697 Margil was forced to return to Querétaro upon his election as guardian of the Santa Cruz convent. On the *camino real* outside Querétaro he was greeted by the entire Santa Cruz community and hundreds of curious queretanos who had heard of the famous man. To many, he must have been an awesome and romantic sight. According to a witness he arrived "bronzed by the sun, with a patched habit, a hat slung over his shoulders, and from the rope around his waist hung a skull."[10] Once settled in his post, Margil turned his forceful attention to the townspeople. He devoted a large part of his day to the confessional and frequently preached the main mass of the day. When not bound by his duties as guardian, Margil took to his old missionary habits. He preached every Sunday on street corners and plazas, visited criminals in the jails, and accompanied the condemned to the gallows. He walked long distances at night to be with the dying and became a frequent guest in the town's rich and poor households.[11] Wherever there was worldly merriment

Margil seemed present with his denunciations. At the reservoir in the gully on the outskirts of Querétaro where townspeople liked to bathe and have picnics on holidays, he reputedly preached one day, which caused the damn to burst a few days later. The rumor spread like wildfire around town that this friar "was indeed holy."[12]

Margil's confessional style was warm and intimate. He would take his disciples' hands in his, look them straight in the eye, and cry with them for their sins. He preached and practiced a highly affective spirituality: a purging of the self through mortification and humiliation and a complete identity with Christ and his tortured body. A fervent practitioner of mental prayer, Margil's obsessive focus on becoming an empty vessel for the will of God at times approximates the quietist heresy. His rhetoric of penitence and sacrifice echoes feminine spirituality throughout the ages. As a result, women flocked to his confessional, and he rapidly acquired a following of female devotees.[13] Ironically, Margil, undoubtedly the perfect Counter-Reformation missionary, best exemplifies the medieval spiritual traditions that infused the group of friars of Propaganda Fide.

Francisca was probably introduced to Margil upon his arrival in Querétaro and must have listened to his sermons. She would have found him endlessly fascinating for his past evangelical feats, his appealing character, and his apparent vitality as guardian, in which capacity he quickly launched efforts to revive the northern missions.[14] There exist no accounts of him taking an interest in Francisca at all; after all, she was Sitjar's spiritual daughter. But Francisca had her ways, and used her talents to gain his attention. On May 29, 1697, she wrote to Sitjar of a very disturbing vision she had just experienced. Fray Francisco Escaray, an old friend, had appeared to her, suffering excruciating torments in purgatory. Why did the saintly friar suffer pains imaginable only for the worst sinner? Because the holy community of Santa Cruz had permitted discord to infest its otherwise pious operation. A group among the peninsular newcomers of 1692 had left the college in a climate of hostility and mistrust. Francisca and Sitjar had discussed the college's problem, which affected her greatly. Now her grief had received divine confirmation. She had been allowed to experience only a semblance of what Escaray was suffering, but that was enough for her to beg Sitjar to do something about the matter. The remedy, according to Francisca's most trusted counsel, her guardian angel, would be to charge Sitjar, the vicar, and the new guardian, Fray Antonio Jesús de Margil, to use whatever means were at hand to bring back the stray sheep. Should they not comply with such orders, a warning had been inserted in the divine message: "look, if I punish him who bears little guilt, what will await him—unless he mends his ways—who carries it all?"[15]

It was such a tremendous message that Francisca confessed that she simply could not bring herself to relay it directly to Margil, "a father whose style I do not know."[16] Two days later the message had clearly been relayed to the new guardian, who was highly perturbed by the news. "*Padre mio*," Francisca wrote to Sitjar apologetically, "I have been greatly preoccupied with the difficulty which the matter of my deceased Father has presented to the Father Guardian."[17] But instead of easing his worries, the *beata* turned up the heat. In the latest vision the poor repentant friar tried to put up a brave front, but his ever greater torments did not escape Francisca's discerning eye unnoticed. Ten days later, the matter had not been resolved to her satisfaction, while Escaray continued to suffer in limbo. Moreover, his devotee, who suffered with him, found herself burdened with more divinely designed and innovative torments such as that of "always going about like an impatient person, not because I am impatient, but because it is a way of suffering which I understand the Lord wants me to go through in order to be of any help to this soul."[18] Francisca exhorted Sitjar to "please tell the father guardian from our Lord not to be afraid of this act of charity for this soul," for it was imperative for him to write to the provincial on the matter. And if anyone were left in doubt as to the veracity of her messages, she added the new torment suffered by Escaray, namely, "a great flat iron weighing on his chest which melts in the fire and enters his entrails to be regurgitated through the mouth and once again returns to the chest. " This new torture was not even suffered for his own sins but for those of the friars who had left the college.[19]

Whether Francisca made any progress at all in lobbying for Escaray over the summer is unknown, but her efforts clearly caught Margil's attention. At some point over the summer, the two formed a *hermandad*, promising to pray constantly for each other's well-being. Having thus sealed their relationship, Margil approached her and asked "with great humility" that she tell him whatever she learned from God concerning his own person. On August 20, she sent her reply, though prudently through Sitjar. Having overcome the proper feelings of not being worthy enough to receive divine news concerning such a saintly man, Francisca launched into the long message from God. But if Fray Antonio hoped for some information regarding his own person he was disappointed for the Lord—through San Juan Capistrano—took this opportunity to divulge his wishes as to the administration of the saintly college. First, the duo Sitjar and Margil were to love each other, work in unison, and concentrate on preaching the love of God within the community, "in the pulpit, in the confessional, and in talks to seculars." Second, the friars were to fight to retain the unity of the college. The "Infernal Dragon" was trying to destroy it, a result that would leave souls in worse darkness then before the "light of God" was emitted to them. Then Margil was instructed on the means to achieve that end: he was to stand up in front of the entire community and reiterate the things that he had told personally to Francisca about the love of God. But such a measure would not suffice since the troubles at the college simply would not go away. Rumors circulated that some of the discontented friars were planning to travel to Spain to obtain a papal bull dissolving the community, since it no longer went on missions and quarreled. For this reason, Francisca argued, it was imperative to send a friar to the general chapter of the order in Spain. It pleased the Lord to choose Fray Juan Capistrano, her good friend, who had often spoken of the necessity of such a measure. In regard to the missions, although some friars were discontented with merely preaching among Christians while their real desire was to convert *infieles*, they should be made to understand that preaching among Christians was a necessary preparation for that other, higher stage of the evangelical life. Finally, as an afterthought, Francisca added that the Lord had indeed informed her of many truths concerning the persons of Margil and Sitjar, "but it is enough that I know them and give thanks to the Lord that mortals should exist who please him."[20]

It is difficult to assess whether the bond formed between Francisca and Margil over the summer of 1697 had any effect on the selection process of her new confessor in the spring of 1698. According to the friars who witnessed the event it seemed that divine providence had already made up its mind on the matter. Margil and Fray José Díez, as the most senior members of the college, with great ceremony put on their surplices and placed several slips of paper in a chalice on which were written their names. No matter how often they drew, Margil's name always came up, and thus he became Francisca's confessor.[21] But the loquaciousness the *beata* demonstrated in her early counsel to Margil quickly faded when she first came face to face with him in the confessional. Probably for the first time in her life, she was sincerely unsure of herself and felt a "great hole in the heart."[22] Immediately, she decided that this new relationship would be a disaster. It had seemed to her that in spite of speaking a lot she had not said one thing that came straight from the heart. Nevertheless, she felt great internal stirrings, and the second occasion in the confessional established an immediate and intimate bond between Fray

Antonio and Francisca. "The second time that I bowed before his feet my soul felt a stirring faith from which I received a remedy from my desperate grief and thus I became determined and told him with simplicity of my past travails. I told him with such naturalness as if I were truly at the feet of Jesus Christ and I can attest in truth that I did not feel another presence than that of his Divine Majesty. He listened to me with his accustomed charity, cried his innocent tears and thus exhorted me to resignation."[23]

Francisca loved Fray Antonio Margil de Jesús passionately and expressed these sentiments in a correspondence that lasted for almost thirty years, or until his death in 1726. In 1708, she described this feeling vividly in a letter to Fray Juan Alonso Ortega: "I love my confessors with fine and reverential love and since our Father is so attractive it did not take much for me to love him thus, but I felt particular light and peace in all his counsel; indeed, the Lord favored me so much in this respect that I began to feel the peace and serenity [with him] that I normally feel in the most secretive of prayers."[24] As she lay sick in her cell, exhausted and fearing herself to be near death, the arrival of the friar was announced.

> it seemed to me that they did not tell me that he was mortal . . . but our lord Jesus Christ. I wanted to hold him in the greatest love and I carelessly wanted too much to see him. I mortified myself with this thought and I wanted to repress this pleasure. I did so for a little bit. . . . I left repressing my delight in order to not allow myself too much rejoicing, in all things I was so afraid that it seemed to me that I was always committing offences. . . . He embraced me but I was so afraid that I could not say a word, we went to the cell and as the father said that he had something to tell me everybody left the cell and I was left with the father. He gave me an embrace and another and another and I still could not say a word to him.[25]

In 1701, she described the intense relationship that had developed between them to her interim confessor, Fray José Díez. According to Francisca, Margil was endowed with a supernatural understanding of the workings of her soul: "Many times, without saying a word to him, and only by arriving at his feet, did I feel bathed in security in the midst of my fears, in peace in the midst of my tribulations, comforted in the midst of my afflictions."[26] Another episode in the confessional resembles a passionate exchange between lovers. Having attended his mass in Santo Domingo three days in a row, on the day of Santa

Catarina she saw Margil at the altar bathed in "crystalline light." When the friar sat down in his confessional after the mass Francisca was quick on her feet and entered before anyone else. As she looked up at him Christ appeared to her in all his glory in Margil's person, and when she told him of her vision of him at the altar, the friar responded tearfully: "You have me here, the trials of my love are over, embrace me and let us join together to never be separated." His passionate speech had such effects on her that she felt as if "my heart would burst from my chest."[27]

Other visions followed of Margil as living embodiment of Christ her beloved. In December 1698, a few months after becoming his disciple, she saw him as Christ entangled in gigantic thorny bushes wailing with pain. She marveled at the great tortures the soul had to go through to achieve one instant of union with the divine.[28] A few months later, in April 1699, that impression was strengthened when she saw the Lord change into Margil in a vision. The presence of God in Margil was verified the next time she saw the friar, for he appeared to her a changed man, with greater strength and joy than before.[29] And alone in the Santa Cruz church one night, Francisca saw Margil suspended above the floor, intertwined in sweet union with Christ on the cross.[30] Margil's favored place in celestial circles was also confirmed in a vision that portrayed him being dressed in rich priestly robes by the Holy Trinity and the Virgin. In August 1698, Francisca told her new confessor that he had been revealed to her as a heart with a mouth and eyes in the breast of the Lord. That his preaching was the true interpretation of God's word was affirmed in the same vision when God showed her the Bible. In each and every page she had seen Margil.[31] This was further confirmed by a vision of the doctors of the church in the court of heaven espousing the Propaganda Fide friar's love of rustic wisdom. They informed her that Margil's faith was so strong that "it penetrated all that the saints had written, and in his knowledge of God he was perfect."[32] When she was physically separated from him while he was away on his various missions nothing could stop her from traveling in spirit with her angel to distant locations to see him.

The raptures they experienced together must have increased their intimacy. Indeed, Francisca's mentors placed great value on raptures. Their authority on such phenomena was a lay brother of their order, Fray Senso, who had been an expert in distinguishing between the three different states of rapture. The first was induced by feeling pain at humanity's sins; it was expressed as a state of bitterness and was not very common. The second was a rapture induced by the experience of "compassionate pain" at the thought of Christ's passion and was a sweet and common state. The third was born "of consideration of the Highest Being . . . in Whom the soul rests as if in its center." The three stages of rapture resemble the purgative, illuminative, and unitive stages of prayer common to most mystics. However, they are much more ecstatic, and indeed more extrovert in nature. The friars enthusiastically observed these states in each other. The chronicler Espinosa, for example, when relating a rapture experienced by Llinás at the convent of the Carmelites in Mexico City, proudly declared that it was "in all its circumstances admirable."[33] Francisca was introduced to these wonders for the first time in the confessional after a particularly passionate session between the duo and God, and it terrified her. In the midst of her doubtless extended recounting of sins and favors, Margil suddenly began to suffer spasms, his bones creaked, his hands became cold and deathly pale, and sweat and tears began to pour down his face. Understanding what a holy episode she had been privileged to witness, Francisca managed to keep her senses long enough to give the Lord thanks for this gift. But while in the presence of the master the protégée mostly limited herself to watching, she frequently experienced raptures in the privacy of her cell or before a limited public of her own *hijas*. The raptures continued into her old age, and after her death the *portera* of the *beaterio* of Santa Rosa de Viterbo attested to having found *su merced* standing in the middle of the reservoir, the water reaching to her waist, her hands extended to her sides, her eyes fixated on the sky. It took three more *beatas* to haul the enraptured foundress out of the water, one pushing from below and the others pulling from above.[34]

Like most love affairs, however, this one harbored fears, suspicion, and anxiety. While Margil evidently placed his trust in Francisca's privileged relation with God, he did not find her humble enough. During one of their first confessions he took both her hands in his and told her to prepare for the trials and tribulations that awaited her.[35] The friar did not exaggerate and promptly launched Francisca on a path of self-humiliation that was intended to test her faith and lead her to modesty. Among other trials, Francisca had to crawl on her knees from the doors of Santa Cruz to the confessional every day for three months. She endured her penitence admirably, even during periods of torment such as when the women who came to be confessed by Margil—many of whom knew Francisca personally—began to gossip and mock her.[36] Francisca's public penitence came to an end when, desperate and sure she had had enough, she got up from her knees and exited the confessional before Margil had given her permission. But in that moment he showed the attributes that had made him so beloved by many and called her back with the words, "Come back, you crazy woman, calm yourself, I will not mortify you anymore."[37] At this early stage in their relationship Francisca was overcome with frustration. She had the nagging feeling that Margil was not really that interested in what she had to tell him in the confessional.

Her trials, however, were over one day in the confessional when Margil divined a *cosita* on her mind that she had not been able to put into words for him. After that she trusted him fully and remained secure in the knowledge that he visited whenever he possibly could.[38] Francisca later described the initial troubles between them as arising from her inability to face the truth that he presented her with, "for the truth is always bitter in the beginning."[39] And in language echoed by modern popular psychology, Francisca claimed that Margil succeeded in opening her soul, thus aiding in "unearthing from my suffering heart the fears and anxieties I harbored."[40]

Margil was the ideal confessor for a visionary like Francisca for several reasons. His missionary feats were inspiring to the ordinary Catholic, but even more so to a woman endowed with a sense of her own apostolic mission. And if his ascetic practices concurred with those already described in relation to the first Propaganda Fide missionaries, Margil seems to have superseded his community in his desire to live in the passion of Christ. In Margil's orbit, Christ was in every human being and animal. Thus, he explained to his protégée, he did not worry about failing in his vow of obedience while traversing the jungles and deserts of the New World, for in each Indian, and each animal he found a superior. And when he found himself at a fork in the road, undecided which path to follow, he usually made it his habit to follow the next goat or sheep since "that is where the Lord wants us to go." His faith in the Lord invariably paid off because using this method the friars usually found the *camino real*.[41]

Like Francisca, Margil was not sufficiently careful with his words. In 1697 the friar was denounced for his public condemnation of several (although unnamed) civic leaders, ecclesiastics, and laymen during a sermon he gave in the church of the Congregation of Guadalupe.[42] As in his protégée's case, his reputation prompted Querétaro authorities to protect him from the Holy Tribunal.[43] In Francisca's view at least, this close brush of the saintly friar's with the Inquisition tied them closer together. She consoled Margil that the Lord was not in the least pleased with the head of the town council, clearly the main instigator of the reaction to the mass.[44]

*Padre* and *hija* were sociable and spent long hours of their days in the company of others. As a novice, Margil was notorious for spending the greater portion of his free time during the day in the church rather than in the seclusion of his cell. This practice was to characterize him throughout his life as a man of God, whether it be in the confessional, saying mass, performing the *via crucis*, or praying. Their baroque striving for holiness did not translate into withdrawal, but rather an embracing of the world. An anecdote told by a witness in the proceedings for Margil's sanctification is particularly revealing about his view of the purpose of his vocation. The witness was the wife of a Querétaro hacendado who invited the famed man for dinner. At the table, the woman watched Margil intently to see if he would eat. Noticing that he ate heartily from all platters offered to him, she thought to herself that rumors of the man's holiness had to be exaggerated. At that moment, Margil fixed her with his gaze and said: "I am only complying with my obligations; if we do not feed the mule he will slow us down on the way." And at that, he continued to eat merrily.[45] Judging by this account, Margil operated on the practical grounds that rather than allowing fasting and the mortification of the flesh to reduce the body to incapacity while the spirit soared in mystical passion, the best way to serve the Lord for a man like him was through the physical labor of evangelization. He was a reformer in the Teresian tradition. The strict parameters set by hagiographic literature could not encompass his particular baroque blend of mystic and activist, spiritual and earthy being. Another anecdote, told by Francisca herself, during the same interrogations further demonstrates the friar's earthiness. While his chronicler maintained that Margil habitually deprived himself of sleep, including the siesta, Francisca recounted an occasion when he had stopped by the *beaterio* to take a nap in the hot afternoon. Escorting him to her cell, she had been wondering whether to offer her bed or a bench. Turning, the friar had said, "that is none of your business, you crazy woman".[46]

### The "Wretched Woman"

The starting point of Margil's spiritual efforts, in the tradition of the great Iberian mystics Saint Teresa of Ávila and Saint John of the Cross, lay in the destruction of the ego and its appetites. This was also the focus of the observantist movement within the Franciscan Order in the sixteenth century. Francisco de Osuna's *Tercer abecedario espiritual* (1527) and Bernardino de Laredo's *Subida del monte Sion* (1535) both preached the soul's detachment from all things created, a state of nothingness, or "*no pensar nada.*" Only as an empty vessel could a man's soul feel moved by the passion of Christ. Perhaps Margil's spiritual objective is best expressed by Jo Ann Kay McNamara in her discussion on post-Tridentine mysticism: "The mystic's ego, dissolved into the divine intention, closed a circuit and conducted grace back to the troubled world."[47]

But ego was something Margil's new spiritual daughter possessed in abundance. In Francisca, Margil's Old World spirituality encountered a boisterous New World mysticism that in the words of Van Deusen focused "on contemplation, revelations, ecstatic states, visions, and physical ailments" instead of "meditating on nothing."[48] Repeatedly, the holy man reminded his confident disciple that her ultimate goal had to be a spiritual state of "*nada.*" And in spite of his clear faith in her visionary powers, Margil followed time-tried methods employed by confessors of holy women since the late Middle Ages. The tactic was explained by Jean Gerson in *De probatione spirituum* in 1415: "if you listen or give advice to such a person, be on your guard, so that you do not applaud her, praise her, or look upon her as a saint worthy of revelations and miracles. Better still, contradict her, scold her severely, ridicule her as one whose heart is proud and her eyes lofty and who deals with matters too great and wonderful for her."[49]

Margil stuck to this advice. Allowing himself to assure his *hija* of his continued affection, he nevertheless remained steady in his continued care to suppress her ego. Repeatedly, he reminded Francisca of the dangers for a mystic of self-love: "This road followed in the school of mysticism . . . even though many find it rugged for all the obstacles that the enemy places in that road such as thorns, they do not run a risk following it who never allow themselves to be deceived by self-love and who are always immersed in the profound knowledge of their misery." Thus, a truly spiritual soul had the obligation to remind itself of its wretchedness constantly. On one occasion in the confessional Margil gave Francisca a memorable demonstration of such a ritual. Lamenting how many Christians did not love God he reminded his *hija espiritual* that the two of them had "a greater obligation." Subsequently, he said, almost beside himself, "Wretched is Fray Antonio, say yes daughter." Shocked, Francisca protested "no," but the friar only repeated his claims until the *beata* understood the rewards reaped by such self-humiliation. In a vision she saw God blessing her soul and taking possession of the friar's heart.[50] Thus, she learned that only through the obliteration of the personality would she succeed in opening the soul to God. When Francisca asked Margil how it was that so many people maintained that he was able to read people's souls and their secrets he attributed it to his complete abandon to God: "As I have given God my heart, my soul, my body, with all its senses, when God wants to speak and say what it pleases Him to say, my nothingness allows Him to do what He wants with this creature, and I am like a boy who hears his father speak." Francisca believed that this characteristic of Margil's had resulted in his particular preaching style, for the friar was famous for crying and laughing whenever he spoke of God, a well-known indication of sainthood. On another occasion, Margil told Francisca: "Look, girl, I have made a pact with God that Fray Antonio does not speak or look or do anything unless his Majesty is preaching, speaking, listening; God is everything and Fray Antonio is nothing, nothing."[51] In this manner, Margil transmitted to Francisca the doctrine of Saint John of the Cross, who lamented those souls who "instead of abandoning themselves to God and thus helping themselves, hamper Him by indiscreet actions or lack of actions, resembling children who kick and cry when their mothers want to carry them in their arms."[52]

Such rhetoric, with its emphasis on man's wretchedness and "the dark night of the soul" before God, was a cue eagerly seized by Francisca. The first letter that survives to Margil, written in April 1698—immediately after Sitjar's death—demonstrates with its dramatic change of tone her astute insights into his character. It is a letter written by a "wretched" woman, a broken-hearted lover who has scaled the heights of divine passion only to be cast away into the dark dungeons of despair. "The more vivid my love is, the more tremendous is my affliction and sadness at seeing God so distant, so that it seems to me that heaven and earth are closer than my soul is to God," she wailed to her new confessor. The root of the problem was very clear to her, however: she had used God's favors, so generously bestowed, very poorly indeed and had not paid any heed to repent of her sins. Her past life had been a disgrace, and she now found herself an outcast with no friends to pray for her soul. Having found Margil, Francisca now renounced her past life and boastful mysticism, dying only to be reborn under his tutelage.[53] In this spirit she set about, under his instruction, composing a *vida*, commenting how astonishingly easy it was compared to when Sitjar had assigned the same task. By this time, she may also have been more aware of the need for restraint in the composition of a narrative that eventually would serve as the basis for her posthumous reputation, and indeed cult. In 1696, the biography of Catarina de San Juan, the saintly *poblana*, was banned and her cult repressed by the Inquisition. The reasons were complex but included official aversion to the overly baroque narrative of her miracles, visions, and raptures and its lack of historical "rigor." There is no evidence in Francisca's letters to suggest that she knew of the case, but she was on familiar terms with the Querétaro Jesuits whose brethren in Puebla had been the holy woman's mentors.[54] Furthermore, her own Inquisition case was still technically open at this time and probably served as a reminder to tune down her rhetoric. This time, then, she approached her task in a comprehensive way, carefully accentuating her "chosen" status through the early favors received while merely a child. Unfortunately, Francisca had not yet reached her youth in her account when Margil was suddenly called back to Guatemala.[55]

In the next letter, the holy man's new *hija* reaffirmed their union in the eyes of God and against the devil. Angered by one of Margil's particularly good deeds, the devil had stabbed her foot with a metal rod, and the tip had got stuck there. But God's pleasure with the friar in the end rescued her and healed the wound. Margil, obviously content with this story, must have decided that a little explanation was needed to convince readers of the letters. At the foot of the letter he thus added a little note clarifying the part about how the metal got into her foot and confirming the gravity of the wound.[56]

In the third letter (July 1698), Francisca took stock yet again of her past in preparation for the renewal of her vows of spiritual union with Margil. She begged him to grant her a leisurely confession in order to purify herself before the event, and reconsidered her concept of property. Offering to part with her favorite devotional objects such as the image of the Child Jesus in order to free herself from the chains of *propio*, Francisca nevertheless could not refrain from philosophizing on the question. If they could not own property, then whose were the few material things they used, clothes, devotional objects, and the like? She decided on a compromise: "I think on this point, that I have to use property as people use the water that flows in the river, or the ground which they tread on. Of the water they only drink what is necessary, and of the ground they only touch the ground that is needed in order to make their way. That is how I would like to get by, and that is how I will get by with devotional objects which in my opinion is the water, and in clothes and such things which are the ground to be treaded."[57]

Questions and ideas such as these were simply not to be found in the Francisca who was Sitjar's devotee. The rapidity with which the change occurred testifies to the impact of Margil's preaching and example on his new disciple. The overarching themes of her correspondence during the first two years of her relationship with her confessor are insecurity and wretchedness in the search for God, as well as a burning desire for evangelical action. Practically gone are the entertaining and appealing descriptions of the celestial court and its workings. Instead, there emerges a recounting of penitential practices, of extraordinary affliction at the hands of the devil, an emphasis on the nothingness (*nada*) of the self (*yo*), and frequent denunciations of the sinners of this world. Finally, Francisca now began to write longer, more comprehensive letters, which were aimed at producing a larger picture, so to speak, than her snippets to Sitjar. Further, her language changed, reverting more and more to symbols to explain her experiences. This change reveals Margil's influence. Judging by his letters, he followed the example of John of the Cross and Teresa of Avila in using symbolism in lieu of the complex and florid language of scholastic theology. In this expansive context Francisca is granted the exquisite grace of constantly accompanying the Lord Jesus Christ in his suffering and passion and is charged with the task of spreading his word to Christian and pagans alike. The precocious but spoiled daughter of God who spent her energies on visions of herself ascending to and mixing with the celestial elite in a manner forbidden to her in society as well as convincing her confessor of her separate and elevated status has now been converted into a penitent and an apostle who desires nothing more than to suffer for the sins of mankind. The Counter-Reformation's focus on Christocentric piety had thus been firmly implanted in Margil's Francisca.

### Partnership

Whether it was because of her love for Margil or this new role, Francisca in her letters to her new confessor placed greater emphasis on the partnership between them and between her and the Santa Cruz community. Indeed, at times her intense involvement in the affairs of the *colegio* seems to have tired her out. On one occasion she confided in Margil that the devil had whispered in her ear that now that the friars were going away on mission, she could finally rest.[58]

At times, Margil complained that her letters were too long and that she often forgot where she had left off in the last letter.[59] But the partnership was a reciprocal one, and Margil was full of questions for his spiritual daughter: How would God like him to interpret a certain piece of doctrine? What was the fate of dear friends in purgatory? How was Margil to quell discontent within the recently established *beaterio* of neighboring San Juan del Río? Her end of the bargain was to retain the attention of the divine ear and secure for Margil the privilege of suffering with the Lord Christ for the world's sins. And should she feel that Margil was neglecting his duties as her spiritual director she did not hesitate to remind him of them. In November 1698, she gently scolded him for not giving her enough time in the confessional. "I admit that I am rustic when I speak . . . but it is for this reason that you are my Father, and after God I have no other light and comfort than that which his Majesty endows me with through Your Paternity." Thus, she reasoned, since he had not been willing to listen to a matter of great seriousness in the confessional she would simply write it down for him.[60] A month later a much graver discord had clearly arisen between them. "I wish for some space to speak to Your Paternity, and when I say space I mean it not in your way but mine," she began her letter. "I admit that this is self-love, may it please the Lord to rid me of it." It appears that Margil had sent her instructions that she simply would not carry out, after which he sent her another message advising her not to come to his confessional the following morning since he would not be there. Worrying that this was a trick of the devil's she went nevertheless, but to no avail. Forgetting about the instructions, she did not remember until the following day, but was nevertheless reluctant to carry them out since she wavered in her reading of the message. At times it sounded like typically sound advice from her favorite mentor, but at others it sounded terribly uncharacteristic in its demands. All this confusion in the end, she asserted, arose from his not wanting to speak to her in the confessional: "He who does not enjoy a frank communication with his spiritual director is close to falling into temptation," she warned him darkly.[61]

The partnership, at least from her point of view, must have been strengthened by their shared apostolic fervor. After the Querétaro demoniac scandal of the early 1690s Francisca's mentors probably forbade any mention in her letters of her bilocations to the land of the *infieles*. Margil, however, had no such qualms. His missionary zeal whetted his curiosity as to her experiences, and he commanded her to write them down. Francisca embarked upon her task with enthusiasm even if he at times complained that her writing was too long-winded. While the details of the bilocations have been described in the preceding chapter, it is of interest to note here the care that went into her evangelical narrative. The information presented is carefully organized, and there is none of her characteristic straying into new territory until she has forgotten where she started. Instead, the experiences, the scruples with which they were put down, and the rhetoric used to portray them all combine to set Francisca on a footing equal to Margil. Like Margil, she received her evangelical mandate from God, but unlike him, her order came not through the church but directly from the divine. In a sense, then, Francisca's bilocations not only raised her to Margil's level but above it.[62] In the letters she also espoused the sort of rhetoric that Margil undoubtedly used to describe his missionary experiences. Francisca's Indian congregation, for example, was based on the Franciscan ideals of the noble innocent Indian of the Spiritual Conquest who, having been led astray in his innocence by the devil, was nevertheless more pious by nature once he had been brought back to God than was the vice-ridden European. There was no evidence as of yet of the inherent devil worshipper that characterized Spanish cultural perceptions of Indians in the eighteenth century. And it was from Margil that she took her rhetoric on preaching. A good preacher, according to her, "should preach the bare truth with the most honest and prudent terms required by the divine language." At that she repeated Margil's motto on preaching the word of God, "that it seem to the senses and touch the hearts like a clarinet."[63]

### Belittling the Devil

Margil's influence was evident in his disciple's treatment of the devil, who began to be given greater consideration as she grew older. As Francisca reached puberty the Christ of her childhood, her playmate and companion, began to leave her, and instead she found herself a victim of horrible visions of the devil.[64] In her "career" path as a holy woman, Francisca espoused the notion of the devil common in early modern conventual piety: a powerful instrument of God sent to amplify the suffering of the pious on their *camino de la perfección*. As had the possessed women of the Querétaro demoniac scandal, Francisca understood the degree of holiness conferred on those chosen to suffer his torments. The devil sent whole armies of demons to beat her and abuse in the darkness of her orchard, even going so far as to try to drown her in the river. At times she was so physically exhausted after these episodes that she could not get out of bed for days. But at this point, she parts ways with the possessed women of Querétaro. Unlike them, Francisca already enjoyed power. She was a friend and confidante of several priests and friars and regarded as a special friend of God. Possession was not a necessary means to fame and recognition as it was with the female demoniacs and at least partly with their Propaganda Fide mentors.

Throughout Francisca's early correspondence there is an unease with the devil. Meticulously strewn here and there are references to the torments suffered at his hands, but her youthful self-confidence could not quite accommodate him in her upwardly mobile scheme. In this sense, she was likely more influenced by the popular culture of the age than by the piety practiced by the austere elements within Santa Clara's nun population. Judging by the Inquisition records already studied here in relation to baroque Querétaro, its mixed population approached the devil much as did the hybrid culture of Europeans, Amerindians, and Africans who characterized the region of central Mexico (marked by Michoacán to the south and Zacatecas and Nueva Vizcaya in the north.)[65] From this medieval notion of the devil as a folkloric figure, often of ridicule, and mixed with the magical beliefs of non-European cultures, the devil emerged as a rather mild figure to be called upon should God and the saints fail. As Spaniards attributed other cultures to demonic power, the oppressed could however invert that notion as a means to combat Iberian dominance. On the doorstep of Querétaro, for example, Chichimeca territory was known to be full of caves and holes inhabited by the devil in whose power its local *curanderos* trusted to fight Spanish incursions and to which the local populace in times of need turned to make a bargain against God. In 1657, for example, a mulatto shoemaker desiring to become a great bullfighter sought the help of an old man in a cave near Celaya who introduced him to horned devils to whom he presented a writ of slavery.[66]

In Francisca's devil all of these elements mixed. Her fundamental assumption regarding the devil, however, was the concept at the core of Christianity's attitude towards him throughout the ages, namely, that he was subservient to God, to be used as his tool. As Cervantes notes, early Christian theologians concurred in the notion that the devil had limited power over people's souls since "he was a creature of God with an essentially good nature that he had merely deformed through his own free will."[67] Francisca was at ease with this notion, but at times, in all probability influenced by her mentors, she carried him toward the extremes that had gotten the Propaganda Fide friars in trouble during the demoniac scandal.[68] On April 2, 1699 she wrote to Margil of a vision that troubled her greatly. She had seen a young girl sitting on his divine majesty's knee, drunk with His love as He breathed on her face. But, strangely, as He continued to bathe her in His breath, the girl took on an ever more intense expression of suffering, ceasing to move until Francisca assumed she was dead. Then a great number of demons came to the Lord's side; He gave the lifeless girl to them and ordered "let fire consume." The demons then worked their tortures on the peaceful girl while God watched contentedly. Afterward, He ordered them to bring her to Him. Taking her in His arms again and tormenting her with His own hands he permitted her to experience the "suffering and wounds of His Passion."[69]

In this vision the relationship between God as Lord and the demons as His servants is crystal clear and the holy purpose of the torment beyond doubt. Yet there is something unnerving about God's pleasure as He watches the girl's pain. Indeed, there is an echo here of the unjust and arbitrary God so brilliantly fleshed out by Cervantes from the Franciscan rhetoric of the Querétaro demoniac scandal, "a tyrant" who employs the devil as "a cruel chief of police." This devil was derived from an early modern nominalist tendency that took the Augustinian separation of the natural and supernatural to its extremes. He was no longer a free agent whose power was derived from divine will, but a slave to God. Thus, God's justice was "arbitrary" and no longer based on what humans might see as just principles.[70] Many of Francisca's mentors accepted this philosophy and saw it as sound, for they were only interested in experiencing the passion of Christ. As Cervantes notes: "Their central concern was not whether God's will was just or unjust, but rather whether it would allow them to undergo sufficient suffering for their sanctification and the salvation of those around them."[71]

As evidenced in the vision just described, Francisca dutifully followed these guidelines regarding the devil and, like many of her fellow sisters in religion, welcomed the extreme tortures that the Lord visited upon her through him. Nevertheless, it was beyond doubt against her active and optimist nature to allow herself anywhere close to demonic possession. That was not God's plan for her since she was after all an evangelist put to good use among the thousands of Indians in Texas. Indeed, Francisca was simply incapable of embracing a theology that so detested human nature and the body and allowed the devil such free rein in his attack upon the senses.

In Cervantes's opinion the demonology evident in the Querétaro scandal was based on a theology "where grace no longer perfected nature but destroyed it and replaced it. The pious Christian should decry human nature as the basis for any kind of spiritual truth." But to Francisca it was precisely her own nature, perfected by God's grace, that allowed her victory over the devil. Her devil at times shows his power as supreme torturer of souls, but most of the time he is a sly adversary that her battle-hardened self is constantly on guard against. In effect, he resembles much more the folkloric devil of local Inquisition cases who appears in the form of a fellow human than the Satan of the demoniacs.[72]

From the beginning of her relations with Margil, Francisca took care to distance herself from the kind of spirituality that aroused the demoniac scandal. Her superiority over the devil is without doubt in a vision she recounted to Margil on November 4, 1698. Fearing that the devil with his torments had taken away some of the "gains" earned through her arduous efforts, Francisca was comforted by a vision in which God assured her that the devil had not succeeded in his plan. To prove it to her he gave her permission to tie the devil in her cell like a dog for as long as she wanted to. At his summons an army of demons brought her a man who approached her in an arrogant manner. With swift speed Francisca untied the rosary on her belt and threw it around his throat, bringing him to his knees. The devil thus subdued, she uttered the words "In the name of the Lord, by virtue of his Majesty and in reverence of the purity of our Lady do not move!" Feeling that keeping the man tied up with the rosary was indecent, she replaced it with a belt and kept her prisoner for days in her cell. He changed forms several times from man to dog and cat, making such terrible noises that she worried that her fellow *beatas* would notice his presence.[73] During one of Margil's visits he had been present in the form of a dog, tied up to the altar. She gave him blessed water to drink but refused all his requests for food. At times though, the nagging thought came to her that keeping the devil tied up in her cell for that long might present a temptation, a fear that was confirmed when he began to tell her such funny things that she began to smile while praying. While there is certainly something of the erotic in this experience, its main message is Francisca's superior ability to keep the devil at bay through her favored position with the celestial court.

Indeed, the frequency with which the devil appeared to her in the form of human or animal indicates his limited power. In March 1699, she had undertaken a forty-day retirement in preparation for Easter but dutifully attended mass at Santa Cruz during the prescribed days of communion. In a letter to Margil from the period, however, she complained of the constant presence of a neatly dressed woman in the church waiting for confession. The woman approached her every time and disturbed her praying. At first Francisca had listened to her in admiration only to realize later that the woman was filling her with lies. Nevertheless, she could not be certain that it was the devil in the shape of a woman since she did see her going into the confession booth. But as a result of all these perturbations Francisca asked permission to confess and take communion in the Dominican church, which was much closer to her house and more advantageous during her withdrawals in the hermitage. In another instance she had hired a day laborer who had presented himself at her door to do some work in the orchard only to realize later that he was the devil in the shape of a man. Both these cases present attempts by the devil to get under her skin through an innocent disguise, but the threat never really amounted to much more than annoyance.[74]

Francisca's view of the devil as a sometimes mediocre evil was reinforced by Margil's tutelage. In contrast with his brethren involved in the demoniac scandal Margil clearly veered toward the medieval notion of a devil "trickster" employed by God for various ends, but who could be held at bay through liturgy.[75] In January 1700, when Francisca was suffering unusually severely at the hands of the devil, Margil sent her a note advising her to just "humiliate the dogs." He also taught her to say simply "*fiel es el señor*" whenever she felt his presence. While it was a common thing to say, Francisca believed in its power as it had been taught to her since Margil always said it with a special *afecto*.[76] In this sense, both Francisca and Margil adhered to the culture of the mixed population of the towns and ranches, the world described by Cervantes as the "*demimonde*" with its almost pragmatic approach to the devil as a creature of limited power. While Margil certainly adhered to the asceticism of his Franciscan brethren he, like his female disciple, was first and foremost an active evangelist. It is impossible to distinguish in him a hatred of the body and the natural realm as the anecdote regarding his appetites clearly expresses. Just as mentor and disciple used the tools available at their disposal to win infidels to God, so did they use the methods made available to them in their fight against the devil. Francisca, for example, was convinced of the power of confession to fight the devil. On one occasion she asked Margil to write down for her the *Magnificat* as well as a magic spell he had told her about to help her fight against Satan. Indeed, the devil's attacks at times merely signaled the success of Francisca's participation in Margil's work to save souls. In June 1699, for example, she mentioned that the devil's attacks had been fierce lately because Margil was driving him crazy with his evangelical successes. Thus, taking the suffering upon herself, she gave her beloved mentor the space to continue his evangelical activities.[77] The battle against the devil was another element in Francisca's baroque hero narrative, which united the two.

Should she be in the mood for it, Francisca, like many religious women, was not above using the devil as a comfortable foil for criticizing her mentors. In a rare fit of insecurity the devil came to her and told her that she was being ridiculed by her trusted mentors. He, however, would take her to a faraway place where she could give herself completely to God and never be forced to write.[78] Thus, Francisca typically inserted various cultural tendencies into her own approach to the devil. Her exuberant nature could not quite embrace the terrifying and all-consuming tool for sanctity that early modern conventual piety held the devil to be. She used some of its elements for her own ends, but her instinctive response to the devil—like Margil's—was an echo of a much milder medieval notion blended with elements of New World lore. Always influenced by her mentors, her social background and particular nature nevertheless prevented her from feeling the temptation to follow many of her fellow *beatas* on the path to possession and damnation.

### Religious Practice

If Francisca was not willing to go the path of demonic possession, she was eager to follow whatever challenges her confessor had in store for her on her *camino de la perfección*. Margil set a high standard with his own penitential practice. He used a sleeveless *jubo* of bristles and a knee-length *silice* made of knotted wires. At times Francisca would get a firsthand glimpse of these treasures as he sent them to her to be washed. She later testified that they were very worn and had to be replaced frequently.[79] With great ambition he imposed such disciplines on his protégée. In the morning she would put on her *silices* for the climb to Santa Cruz, and for three hours a day she would have to arrange herself in a cross, her hands looped through two hoops fastened with thick nails to the wall, from Margil's own collection. She found the exercise too arduous and obtained permission to divide it into two hour-and-a-half periods. Margil himself, however, was reputed to take these instruments with him on his voyages. He would drive his nails and hoops through tree trunks and hang himself there during breaks on the road.

Francisca never took to physical penitences in Margil's manner, and they do not seem to have been effective in aiding her entry into the divine sphere. Although her letters frequently refer to future penitential plans they contain few accounts of actual performance. Without spiritual aptitude such practices in her opinion were not of much use. Her views were echoed by holy personages such as Saint John of the Cross who in his "Ascent of Mount Carmel" attributed such extreme practices to dangerous appetites and exclaimed it "sad to see the ignorance of those who burden themselves with extraordinary penances and many voluntary exercises; they think this ought to be sufficient to bring them to union with divine Wisdom."[80] In 1713, she remarked to Fray Ángel, a new confessor, that in spite of repeated attempts she had never really succeeded at penitences but instead had "always been more inclined to ponder divine love in prayer."[81] "As for fasts and other penitences," she noted in October 1698, "I find them ruinous in the extreme, for if I do not drink hot chocolate in the morning it is certain that I will suffer from a headache and at times it provokes me to vomit." Thankfully, in this matter, as in others, divine guidance was provided: "the Lord spoke to me and amongst other things I understood that he did not want me to fast or do anything else of what I had planned for this novena."[82] God thus kept her from going to extremes in her physical mortification and safeguarded her health, keeping her fit for her various activities. Indeed, Francisca does not seem to have been ashamed of her earthly pleasure in chocolate. When it pleased the Lord to take away her sense of taste, she found it to be a punishment not a grace. On another occasion, Francisca manifested concern with her health. In December of that year, she felt a fire in her interior. At first she thought that it might be a mystical revelation, but quickly realized that it was a flu and that "it would be better to go to bed."[83] Mortification of the flesh then did not really stir her decidedly complex but inherently pragmatic soul.

There existed more appealing ways to approach the divine. One was communion, the high point of the Catholic mass and the fundamental ritual upon which rested the worshipper's union with the suffering body of Christ. The cult of the Eucharist had gained preeminence in the Tridentine church as an "anti-Protestant affirmation" and a focus of the baroque "Forty Hours" ritual.[84] But, characteristically, Francisca's desires for communion had sprung, not from the teachings of the institutional church, but because her childhood companion, the Child Christ, had taken her to a church and given her communion before she had reached the required age for the ritual. After this first communion, which, she reminded Margil, was without doubt sacramental, she was constantly "dying to take communion."[85] The pleasures of communion were threefold. First, Francisca's letters often describe the moments of anticipation before the priest or friar officiating lifted the host high above his head and the heavens opened and the miracle of transubstantiation occurred. She waited impatiently for it as the priest muttered the requisite prayer and was so in tune with the ritual that it was not necessary to be present with the congregation on the benches. It was enough to be in the confessional, even while deep in conversation, to hear the priest lift the host, and immediately her mind would be transported and filled with the sacramented Christ.[86] Second, once she had approached the altar and ingested the oblate and the wine, transformations always occurred. They could be violent feelings of being consumed by divine fire, or they could be the gentle presence of the sacramented Christ who stayed with her in peace until her next communion.[87] Such pleasures were not hers alone. Margil, making a last confession before his death, noted that during the consecration of the host Christ himself had often responded to him from the host with the formulaic words of the congregation but referring to the body of the friar: "*Hoc est Corpus Meum.*"[88] Francisca carefully preserved every crumb of the host until it melted in her mouth and was offended when one of her confessors, Fray Ángel, reminded her not to dislodge any particles from between her teeth.[89] And she certainly belongs to the large group of religious women who throughout the ages have felt physically revitalized by the host: in October 1698, she told Margil of feeling so "strengthened that I was left more satisfied than if I had eaten the most substantial and delicate delicacies."[90] In her youth she did claim to have been able to fast for extended periods and live only on the host, as scores of holy women had done before her. But neither she nor her *beatas* ever claimed to live off the host alone as did some controversial holy women such as María Janis in Italy.[91]

Third, Francisca's most avid descriptions of communion are of adoring the reserved Eucharist, undertaking long vigils, and bursting into ecstasy when the host was finally revealed. For these ends, she attended masses at her favorite churches, such as the Carmelite church, San Antonio, the Jesuit college, the Congregation of Guadalupe. Once the host had been unveiled she was transfixed and transported to the presence of God.[92] On the day of Saint John the Baptist, 1699, for example, she went to the Carmelite church for a vigil of the Señor Sacramentado. Once the veil had been taken off the Eucharist, Francisca nevertheless felt that it was still there, separating her from its sight. She took it as a sign of the impenetrable barrier between her and God and retreated behind a door to cry. The thought that the host was visible to all the churchgoers but herself was unbearable. The Carmelites who were "normally very unhurried in their masses, seemed on this day to go to extraordinary lengths to delay the mass." Those delays seemed like a whole year, and when the moment finally came it was as if the angels "pulled the curtains" and her soul "saw and adored the host and in it the loving master hidden in it." It was all over too quickly, for they covered it and Francisca "barely managed to enjoy his presence."[93]

### The Hermitage and the Desert

Margil's long sojourns in the deserts, mountains, and jungles of the New World must have inspired his new protégée because when she met him she not only declared herself a "wretched" woman, but began to turn her ambitions toward spiritual feats that could only be achieved through long periods of withdrawal from the community of men and women. In her father's hermitage, at the deep end of the orchard, Francisca entered the desert populated by Christianity's first desert monks. Her withdrawals varied in duration from a nine-day novena for a saint's feast to a forty-day retirement in imitation of Christ's days in the wilderness before Easter. Once separated from her family, Francisca felt as if she had entered an intermediate world between the worldly and the divine: "I will stay here as someone who does not live in the world, but has passed to the region of Purgatory where souls are purified."[94] Such experiences were a necessary preparation for the ecstasy that would inevitably possess her during the splendid church rituals that accompanied festive occasions. These otherworldly episodes so occupied her soul that she would ask permission to only attend mass on Sundays and feast days, during which she "would confess and take communion as if I was about to die."[95] In the hermitage, Francisca read religious instruction books and performed exercises in the Ignatian spirit in which she tried to imagine a certain mystery or biblical episodes. She also performed prostrations, disciplines, and said prayers, all the while applying these new practices to the cherished project of saving souls from purgatory. In October 1698, for example, she gave Margil a brief description of a typical, and perhaps utopian, day in the hermitage:

> After some exercises I read the text "The Travails of Jesus," then I began to perform the exercises on the Incarnation, that is, to accompany the Lord in the womb of our Lady, contemplating that most pure and enclosed womb, and with that consideration, in gratitude for the *fineza* of his divine love, I do one discipline in the morning and another in the evening. With each discipline I do ninety prostrations; in each one I perform the Act of Faith, while saying I believe in the mystery of the Incarnation in the Divine Word. . . . I try to follow the stations two or three times between day and night due to the graces and indulgences which are granted for it—as I do not say the altars to help the *animas benditas*—since it would not be just that they suffer and I who have the time and means to help them attend only to one thing. Therefore, beside the fasts, cilices, disciplines, prostrations, and prayer which I perform in reverence of the holy mystery of the Incarnation, I follow the stations and pray as much as I can for the necessities of the blessed souls.[96]

This Ignatian focus on rigorous mental exercises was a new phenomenon for the Francisca who had been too busy in her teens and early twenties simply receiving the visions and revelations sent by her benevolent Lord. She had not had to seek experiences previously through church-sanctioned means. On the contrary, members of the divine court had sought her out; she had simply transmitted the message. In 1701 she confessed to Fray José Díez her lack of interest in the Ignatian method until Margil's arrival, but while she was enthusiastic about her new practice, it simply did not require much effort to imagine the dramatic episodes of Christ's life. Nevertheless, she worked with gusto in the hermitage undertaking prostrations that she discovered were highly effective tools of religious practice: "In the prostrations I was shown some of the great sweetness and gentleness which the Queen of the Angels felt in her holy soul in these acts of profound humility and I understood that undertaken with the required reverence and a contrite and humiliated heart they are of great pleasure to God, meritorious for the soul and a great torment for the Devil."[97] Physically, she found the prostrations difficult, and her success depended ultimately on God's grace. In February 1699, for example, she wrote that "I began my exercises with the strength with which the beautiful Lord endowed me, for two days I did the prostrations without the help that I felt later, and after these two days were over I felt such a great lightness and such strength that it seemed to me that I could scale the tower of San Francisco [the parish church].[98] The prostrations, however, could at times be so physically demanding that the stigmata wounds she carried on her chest would open, and the blood would ooze "in great quantities and very alive."[99]

This new inward turn in Querétaro's otherwise sociable holy woman must have aroused interest in her circle, for visitors were now turned away at her door. On the first day of the new year 1699, for example, she wrote to Margil that several friars as well as a "lady" had come to her door, but all had been turned away and told that she was doing "exercises."[100] But if her labors in the hermitage were intense then so were the rewards. Knowing how much she cherished the daily rituals of mass, confession, and communion the Lord gave her the grace of attending them by means of bilocation from the isolation of her cell. After sunrise, she would make the sign of the cross and drink blessed water. This would induce in her a sensation of entering a church and finding herself physically in front of the sacrament. Suddenly, without realizing it she would be listening to mass.[101] Holy days might also catapult her into a state of sudden glory. On the eve of All Saints, 1698, Francisca found herself in a glory that "if it is not of heaven then I do not know where it comes from" and one that induced in her a feeling of finally being "*bienaventurada*" or blessed soul.[102] Even Francisca's newfound sense of the *nada* and sudden longings for the desert could not erase her thirst for the visual splendors of heaven. Thus, the feast of the Assumption, perhaps because it had to do with the merciful Virgin, never failed to elevate the "wretched" woman to visions of divine processions and feasts.[103]

If saints' days were important opportunities for intense religious experiences then the liturgical year presented one supreme moment in which to meditate on the salvation of mankind through the crucifixion and resurrection of Jesus Christ. And if Lent was an opportunity for ordinary Catholics to repent and take stock of their fallible nature, then for Francisca it was no less than a divine opportunity to put her formidable efforts to work for the salvation of her fellow humans. "Once a year," she remarked to Margil in April 1699, "the Holy Church remembers our misery." Lent was thus a dangerous time, for it reminded God of the inherently vicious and sinful nature of human beings who had crucified his son. At the same time it was an opportunity for the worldly to make peace with God. In Puebla, for example, the nun María de San José noted that after a particularly terrifying period of earthquakes, which had rattled the city, Lent had brought quietude at last. [104] In Margil's work cycle, Lent was his busiest time. He traveled between haciendas, villages, mines—every nook and corner of Catholic society that might not have received the appropriate attention during the year. The stakes indeed were high, and the missionaries of Santa Cruz had no time for sleep as they engaged penitents in round-the-clock confessions.

Into this torrential situation Francisca inserted her prayers and begged for God's mercy. She cried over "how little Christians make use of these rituals of the Church." The Lord appearing to her in person reinforced that conviction and ordered her to "cry and understand this truth that I give you my daughter, for if Christians gave any consideration of their nothingness, that they are dust and ash, then I would lift them up to a clear knowledge of me who am their God and Father and Redeemer." He also instructed her to cry "for the pomp and vanity with which the dust and nothingness of miserable flesh has lifted itself with such pride to insult, drag to the ground, and spoil the beauty of the soul which I raised with such power and authority over all things created."[105]

Easter thus presented Francisca's ultimate challenge of the religious calendar. Her most ambitious *retiros* would take place around that period. As Easter approached she would inevitably begin to feel intense desires to go out into the desert like Christ. During those periods she experienced, like her Lord, the temptations of the devil and suffered excruciating pain and tortures. In February 1699, Francisca detailed for Margil the severity of the tortures she suffered at the hands of the devil and their likeness to those faced by Jesus in the desert. Entering her cell one night she had walked into fire, and as she watched the flames circling her she experienced such excruciating pain that she felt as if she had been dismembered. The fire had taken her to terrible places populated by small animals that attacked her and began to eat her insides. It was a place so terrible that she could not even be certain that it was purgatory or hell. Her overwhelming sensation while there was simply that God had absented himself from her. It was a fear more powerful than any she had ever felt, for she did not know "of what or why." Telling herself that this place was hell and the animals demons she hoped to overcome this sensation, but it always got the better of her. The torment lasted twenty days.[106]

As Easter neared, her efforts became ever more intense. In March 1699, Francisca wrote to Margil that "Since Lent began, the Lord determined to send me various sufferings which I experience from ten o'clock in the evening until three o'clock in the morning; they are tremendous and only he who makes me feel them can fortify me so that I do not die." In spite of such torments, however, Francisca stepped up her prostrations, and claimed to do three hundred of them from six to nine in the evenings as well as ninety postures in a cross, intermingled with disciplines and the stations.[107] At times, her efforts at imagining the scenes of Christ's last days paid off. On April 2, 1699, she wrote to Margil of the extraordinary insight she had gained into the sufferings of Mary at seeing Christ on the Cross: "I have no words to say how my soul understood this . . . it seems to me that in spite of all I've heard of the pains and afflictions of Our Lady, until now I had not understood any of it."[108]

Later, the Lord sent her an army of demons who beat her and insulted in the same manner in which Christ had suffered in his *via crucis*. Remembering how Margil used to tell her that "the Lord suffers in each one of us" she asked Him for help and was granted union. He "moved His face to mine and with that grace He allowed me to enter into Him and He gave me an understanding of many mysteries of His holy passion."[109] The physical signs of the beating were so evident that she was very glad to have retired from company in order to be able to hide them. Finally, once Easter arrived she truly stopped taking notice of this world and began to only experience the supernatural. The climax of her suffering was reached on Holy Friday when she left the hermitage to reenact the *via crucis* in the churches of Querétaro. After her apocalyptic state of mind surrounding the crucifixion, resurrection would bring with it ample rewards, and Francisca would inevitably reach an ecstasy that was a divine gift. On Holy Friday in 1699, she noted that she had stayed in the church of Guadalupe "in a corner, retired as if I were alive, but my soul enjoyed a superior knowledge." The statue of Saint Francis had begun to bleed in the chest and hands in order that she "learn that lesson of profound humility." The saint had then spoken to her of the passion of Christ and had granted her the great favor of bringing her to the places in the Holy Land where Christ had really suffered. It had not occurred to her to ask for the indulgences usually granted for visits to the Holy Land since her visit had been a supernatural voyage. But upon returning the angel had told her that she could obtain the same indulgences as if her trip had been undertaken in the flesh. Having asked Margil's permission on the matter she then decided to apply all her indulgences for the souls in purgatory. She had also gone to the church of Santa Clara, where she had remained in vigil over the Holy Sepulcher the entire night.[110] On Holy Sunday, at dawn, while in prayer, her soul was filled with light and she saw

> our Redeemer and Lord, glorious Jesus, beautiful and shining with the holy cross in his hands and approaching me he said words that due to my indignity I cannot repeat; with his words he obliged me to take the cross in my hands, and he made himself an admirable throne of angels and with great velocity . . . he took with him this machine and beauty of angels and me at the feet of the cross as the tiniest ant amongst them; I found myself where the Lord had gone and it seemed to me to be heaven.

On that same day she was granted the privilege of "circulating the entire heaven and enter the choirs of Angels, Saints and the holy virgins; all of this happened rather violently so that I hardly remember any particulars, only that I kissed the hand of a holy pontifex who was in the choir of the holy apostles and that would be Saint Peter, elsewhere our Father Saint Francis blessed me and embraced."[111]

The Francisca who emerged from Margil's tutelage in 1701, in spite of a newfound interest in self-obliteration, solitude, and disciplined religious practice, was not an altogether transformed person from her more boisterous and youthful days. The visions still came with rapidity and luxuriousness; mystic darkness was still beyond her grasp. Instead, her true passion and energy in these years was spent on a triangular relationship between her, Margil, and the lay brother Fray Antonio de los Ángeles. Under the leadership of Margil, the trio scaled the mystical Mount Carmel together, a journey Francisca pursued with all the vigor of her sociable nature.

### Francisca, Fray Antonio, and Margil: Scaling the Mystical Mount Carmel
Fray Antonio de los Ángeles was a peninsular of hidalgo descent from Santander. After sojourns in Madrid and Seville, de los Ángeles had tried his

luck in the New World and in Querétaro became a well-off merchant and landowner. A spiritual crisis led him first to become a lay brother at Santa Cruz and later to profess there. He professed a few years after the convent's foundation and served as its *portero* for over twenty years until his death in 1711. He was renowned in the city for his charitable activities. Three times a day he distributed the remains of the friars' meals to the poor on the convent steps.[112] Francisca knew Fray Antonio from the time he was a wealthy merchant, and it seems he sought her out in his spiritual crisis and that she in turn encouraged him on the path to his final profession.[113] They became *hermanos* sometime in the early 1690s. From that time onward they enjoyed a friendship characterized, in the words of Fray Juan de Ortega, by "such intimacy that there were no secrets between the two of them."[114]

When Margil became guardian of Santa Cruz the two men formed an immediate and enduring bond. Together, they nursed poor vagabonds in the infirmary constructed at Margil's orders.[115] Margil mentored him in devotional practices. The holy man reputedly only slept from eight to eleven o'clock at night. Antonio de los Ángeles then woke him and together they read a chapter in the *Mística Ciudad de Dios* by his favorite Spanish visionary, Sor María de Agreda. After the reading they confessed their sins and took turns prostrating themselves in the form of a cross for penance. The holy man pronounced his penitence according to "what the Lord dictated." Most often the disciple lay on his back on the floor while the master trod on his mouth for the space of time it took to say three creeds. Afterward, they would exchange roles and continue to pray until the bell rang for matins.[116] Margil found his disciple possessed with the divine spirit. His opinion was later quoted in de los Ángeles's biography: "His glory was his communication with Christ in his fellow men, discerning Christ in each and every one of them. For this reason he had compassion for the sick who came to ask for confession, and to this he owed the care and love with which he treated the poor who came to his door."[117]

In Francisca's view the three of them formed an unbreakable bond, especially in light of the fact that Fray Antonio had been included in the *hermandad* that the *beata* had professed with Margil at the turn of the century. With the mentor's departure, his two disciples grew closer in their grief and began a long spiritual collaboration. The credit obtained in heaven for their pious behavior—or lack thereof—would be thrown into one pot, from which would be extracted an equal amount of indulgence for brother and sister. Francisca saw it as a culinary task performed by the mistress of heaven: "It is like the union of the groom with the holy bride; both achieve the same degree of perfection, so that if one is penitent and the other humble, the Virgin is to whisk these two virtues together in order that both achieve the same degree of humility and penitence." The ever cautious Fray José Díez, Francisca's interim confessor after 1701, quickly added a note to this rather blunt image: "She [Francisca] does not mean to say that if one surpasses the other in virtue, his achievement will be taken away to share with the *hermano* the corresponding indulgence, but that in this union they both participate and communicate, and the virtues of one mix with the virtues of the other so that the fruits of their efforts be communal and deposited in a box for the necessities of all."[118] Inspired, Díez went on to explain that this was how the primitive church operated: "There was but one soul and one heart between them, they were of course not equal in merit or grace, but they helped each other like brothers and there were no poor relatives." In the *hermandad* with de los Ángeles and Margil, Francisca then was not a poor relative.

The *beata* understood what great benefits could be reaped from their collaboration. In 1704 she related to Díez a vision she had seen of all her confessors and Santa Cruz friends in heaven, brilliant rays of sun emanating from them in varying degrees according to their holiness. With the exception of Margil, de los Ángeles of course outdid the rest. She saw him as a beautiful boy dressed only in tunic and stole, and he seemed a *bienaventurado*. "Oh, how tranquil you are," she exclaimed to him and was silenced and told that he was praying. Seizing the opportunity she asked the Lord to allow her to use some of the treasure He was gathering with His prayers for the souls of purgatory. Her wish was granted, and as she threw her earnings and His into one pot they resulted in the release of twenty souls from purgatory.[119]

Margil regarded Fray Antonio as his "heart"; he confessed to Francisca that the greatest rewards of his religious life had been his relationship with the friar. In Margil's absences, therefore, Francisca threw herself into an intensively mystical union between the two.[120] Fray Antonio regularly wrote to her of his own spiritual progress. In turn, Francisca produced a steady stream of notes to her friend containing exclamations of love and gratitude, spiritual advice, and lamentations for her own ruinous state. "You are the only one I really confide in, more than any other person, you are the one who consoles me, you who are the handkerchief for my tears," she wailed. Without restraint she poured out her various complaints over inattentive confessors and severe priests.[121] To Francisca's mind, she and Fray Antonio had been led to the true path toward spiritual perfection by Margil. Had Margil not taken up the guardianship of Santa Cruz, both of them would have been left to a lifetime of wrong turns and emptiness: "I give thanks to the Lord that you have now found your rightful place which is peace and tranquil enjoyment amidst all that is adverse. . . . This is the bed which our beloved father Margil has made us so that we can rest, and outside of this resting place everything is fatigue and sadness."

The path opened to them by Margil scaled the mystical Mount Carmel. Saint John of the Cross described the process as a journey through the night taking place in three stages: "The first one, the night of the senses, is the early part of the night when the soul is deprived of the attraction of things; the second part, faith, is like midnight, totally in the dark; and the third, towards the early morning hours, is God, when the light is about to arrive."[122] Francisca, probably echoing Margil's rhetoric, took pleasure in the metaphor of the mountain. The climb was a laborious one, not only due to its steepness, but to the many hindrances it presented, such as the flies swarming around the pilgrims. "Like you say, I will not let those *moscas* get in my way on my climb up Mount Carmel," she assured Fray Antonio. The rewards promised, however, by Margil were delicious, for at the summit of the "Olympic Mountain," where "there is no air, nor does a bird move," they would encounter "superior spirit and the peace of Christ."[123] While they were partners, at times she took care to underline his appropriate superiority over her wretchedness. Thus, in the climb up the Mount, he was always steps ahead of her: "I will go with you wherever you take me, which is to anoint the feet of our master with the balsam of our hearts and tears of love and pain for our ingratitude at not having been loyal and fine lovers of his Majesty." It was thus Fray Antonio, following in Margil's footsteps, who extended a hand to Francisca and pulled her up the steep incline. Thus, while in theory equal in their common enterprise, she at times became the poor relative: "I am like these beggars who walk from door to door, without shame due to my necessity, and you are like these rich men who have more than they need, and who pass through life endowed and rested. I will come to your door to ask charity; when you receive all these favors please invite me into your presence."[124]

Margil, as the forerunner, set the tone for this triangular Christocentric odyssey. In his letters he exhorted her to live in the passion of Christ with such language as "Oh, our poor Jesus, oh our poor one, there is no one who loves him."[125] Such messages were eagerly read and followed by both of them. They avariciously shared his letters and showed each other the letters they had written to him. Francisca watched Fray Antonio's progress with admiration:

"Every day I give thanks to the Lord for the state in which he has put your soul, for me that is like a sweet and soft *refresco*." Judging by the few letters that survive from Margil to his *hija espiritual*, his writing must indeed have been like a gust of fresh desert air into the often laborious and anxious daily striving of his devotees. In February 1707, for example, he sent a stirring missive from Zacatecas. "There are only three heretics in the world," he lectured Francisca. "I, the *portero* [Fray Antonio] and you are the worst; come now, you crazy woman, our heresy is that even if we believe in God, we have no faith in him [aunque creemos en dios . . . no creemos a dios]." The crux of his argument was that the threesome had become so wrapped up in their own experience of God—in discerning whether their mystical revelations came from God or the devil—that they had betrayed their original vow to live in a state of nothingness. Instead of letting God fill themselves with his presence, they had let their egos gain preeminence in their being. From all this had surged a false humility, when the only true humility was found in the example of the Virgin, who without questioning His motives had obeyed and placed her trust in God as He became flesh and blood in her own son, to the point of watching with resignation His crucifixion. In that great torment her spirit was "the most elevated and pacific *olimpo*."

Since his argument was primarily aimed at his *hija espiritual* who was the *worst* heretic of them all, Margil probably intended to curb her extravagant frenzies and anxieties over the authenticity of her visions, her own imperfections, and the long withdrawals of the divine presence from her soul. In short, she was too full of herself, of emotion and disorderly humanity. True "poverty of spirit" was only achieved by a soul empty of itself. Thus, he counseled his disciples, they should take the Virgin as the ultimate model of behavior. His own devotion to the Virgin was famous throughout New Spain and Central America, where he had made popular the Iberian custom of saluting with an *ave maría puríssima* when entering a house.[126]

Under Margil's influence, Fray Antonio had indeed early on become a particular devotee of the Virgin. Francisca encouraged him in his devotion, and began signing her letters with "*esclava de Jesús y María.*"[127] Fray Antonio's Marian devotion was stimulated by his constant reading of Madre Agreda who in her *Mystical City of God* (Mística Ciudad de Dios), written in direct inspiration from the Virgin, theorized a much greater role for the Virgin—"co-redemptress" and "co-judge" with Christ—in developing and disseminating early Christianity than any theologian before her.[128] On the day of the feast of Santa Isabel she told him she had seen him in a vision "accompanying our

Lady like a prince and a beloved son. . . . It is clear that our Lady has stolen your heart." As her friendship with Fray Antonio intensified after Margil's departure she began to incorporate his presence into her visionary realm, placing him in biblical scenes with the Virgin and notifying him of this sudden elevation of status in her letters. When Fray Antonio, like Francisca, periodically retired, she saluted his returns with greetings such as this: "I hope that you have been well in the house of our Lady, that you enjoyed the company of Jesus, Mary, and Joseph." His weight in the divine world was confirmed from celestial heights. One day, when arranging flowers, Francisca found that she had clumsily stacked a glass vase on top of another smaller one and had attached it so securely that she could not separate them. After many desperate attempts, she muttered, "vaya, en nombre de Antonio de los Ángeles!" As the vases came apart smoothly and easily, she stood aghast while the girls helping her cried, "miracle, miracle." To Fray Antonio's undoubted satisfaction—for he was a humble man—she admonished them not to act like *milagreras,* an admirable reticence that would also have pleased the Inquisition.[129]

But while Francisca encouraged Fray Antonio in his devotion to the Virgin, it is not at all certain that she was able to duplicate his single-mindedness. Indeed, her letters portray a far more restless soul, full of ambitions for her newly founded *beaterio* and her own spiritual accomplishment.[130] The Virgin's selfless devotional example, her peaceable passivity in the face of trials, however holy her attributes, would have been a difficult model to follow for the Francisca of this period. However much she tried to get rid of her nuisance of an ego, it survived and exhorted her to new victories. Instead, Francisca instinctively tried to follow in the footsteps of charismatic and active evangelical figures such as Saint Francis and Madre Agreda.

Fortunately, since Fray Antonio was not her confessor, she was not obliged, indeed not allowed, to unburden her soul to him. Unlike her confessors, he did not regularly send her *cuadernitos* of eight pages to fill laboriously with visions that might interest him. Fray Antonio provided her with paper and writing feathers, but the prohibition against confessing to him in effect set her free to choose her subjects. By virtue of this freedom, and because Fray Antonio was her partner on a mystical journey and not director, her letters to him from this period portray a more accessible image of her spiritual life and its pitfalls than do the long and clearly forced accounts she was obliged to render to Díez, her interim confessor in this period. As fellow travelers they adorned their notes with constant warnings of the hurdles they faced: "of all our passions, none frightens me as much as that of self-love since it knows so well how to hide," she began enthusiastically in one of her short notes to the friars. But she was unable to elaborate since the message boy stood at the door waiting impatiently for her note.[131]

Since they shared a *hermandad*, they prayed for each other every day and reminded each other in their letters of particular concerns, especially souls in torment in purgatory, that required a more concentrated effort.[132] When de los Ángeles's father died in Spain, she mobilized her fellow beatas for round-the-clock prayers, communions, *vias sacras*, and novenas for his soul. She then followed her friend's progress through grief carefully: "I am so glad to hear that you went out for a little diversion, Don Agustín told me this, and I think that the fresh air must have given you strength." This mother-hen attitude was common in her when it came to Fray Antonio. One day, during a visit from the *padre predicador* of the Franciscan convent Francisca smugly asked him what he liked the most about the convent of Santa Cruz. Overjoyed, she heard from his lips that it was the "silence and the *portero*." "Had he known how much mine the *portero* is, I would have thought he said it to please me," she wrote to Fray Antonio.[133] Since he was *hers* she worried over his health endlessly, sending him various powders for his delicate health and scolding him in winter if she had heard that he had been out in the porteria with all its *aires y frios*.[134]

On a happier occasion she reminded him that he helped her more with his "prayers, than others with all their reales." When problems arose, particularly in her dealings with the ecclesiastical class, she turned, not to her confessor, but to Fray Antonio. "There are things which one has to talk about, and not to have anyone is a terrible pain," Francisca complained. Her letters often warn him of her visit but do not specify her troubles. It was better, in her view, to talk face to face than to write since she believed that conversation teased out truths that could not be put on paper.[135] And he seemed to read her mind and articulate her spiritual life with a brevity she claimed to admire: "I received your *papelito* at noon, in which you tell me in brief what I am feeling with such pain." And when she confronted dilemmas concerning her soul, she skillfully circumvented the prohibition against confessing with him by putting the matter theoretically. "If a soul who practices ordinary prayer feels such novelty during it that it shrinks from continuing, and can feel no comfort since it has neglected its duties . . . ," she began cautiously but resolved to go no further since she realized that she could not even express what she felt. Should he think it wise, however, she resolved to write to Margil about it. Thus, while the *portero* was not given the responsibility of serving as her informal spiritual director, he was nevertheless an intermediary tribunal who decided whether she should appeal to the supreme authority itself.[136] But the holy man did not return to Querétaro again except for visits of a few weeks, perhaps months. Although he continued to write to her and advised her interim confessors on how to govern her soul, he was physically absent.

As the eighteenth century began its march, Francisca then found herself in need of impressing new friars with different appetites. This enterprise was a complex and laborious one for it no longer centered on her persona or success alone but on that of a fast-growing community of poor and orphaned Creole girls congregated in her family home.

## 6 The *Beaterio* of Santa Rosa, 1699–1712

### *"Virtuous Doncellas" in Need of Shelter*

In October 1700, Fray Antonio Margil de Jesús extended his spiritual partnership with Francisca de los Ángeles into the reformist realm in the tradition of "paired sanctity," the longstanding cooperation between holy men and women in conventual foundation.[1] He brought two orphaned girls, Antonia, seventeen years old, and María, fifteen, to live with Francisca, her mother, and two sisters. The girls were members of old Querétaro families but belonged to their impoverished branches. Margil, an active matchmaker, decided to enter the girls into a community where they could live above reproach until he returned from his mission to Guatemala, at which point he would either find them husbands or help them take the veil. The beginnings were not promising. The girls came every morning to breakfast in silence, "bathed in tears." Francisca was unable to get them to speak of their troubles, and their consternation only increased in the midst of the flood of questions posed by her mother and sisters. It was not until Margil visited and confessed the girls that they began to accept their new surroundings.[2] He solicited the help of Querétaro's ever generous civic booster, the cleric don Juan Cavallero y Ocio, who promised to include them in a group of orphaned Creole girls to receive a dowry of three hundred pesos (to help them find Creole husbands). They received the dowry in 1702, but by that time they seem to have adapted to their new situation and decided to remain with the community. In that year three more orphans from similarly poor but established Querétaro families joined the community. At that, the group of women grew to nine in number. They were sent hot meals once a day from the grumbling cook of the Santa Cruz kitchen, but as far as other earthly needs were concerned they were on their own.[3] Margil's absences were felt severely by the first members of the community. "They are not yet that spiritualized [*espiritualizadas*]," Francisca explained to Fray Antonio.[4]

By introducing the girls into the Alonso Herrera household, Francisca and Margil took a decisive step in the direction of founding some sort of a religious institution, whether it be a *recogimiento* or *beaterio*. Such places had proliferated in Spanish America from the Conquest onward and served various purposes vis-à-vis the region's emerging urban societies. They functioned as houses of correction, shelters for women rich in vocation and poor in resources as well as protective havens for young Spaniards—like Margil's protégées—caught up in the vicissitudes of the ever more complex New World society. In Peru, for example, *limeños* anxious to uphold social order could rest assured that such institutions would serve as sentinels against indigenous incursions into its flock of underprivileged Spanish *doncellas*.[5] Such sentiments probably motivated Margil, but Francisca's ambitions were likely more complex. From the community's inception her efforts focused on establishing an exemplary lifestyle, emulating that of the First Order of Saint Clare. At the same time the name she chose for her new community, that of the famous Italian fourteenth-century mendicant Santa Rosa de Viterbo, exemplifies her confidence in its utility for the propagation of the faith. Absolute poverty, a rigorous ritual schedule, constant self-examination, including public confessions of sins to the community, were to produce, in contrast to the pleasurable Santa Clara, a vigorous and ascetic apostolic mission comparable to Santa Teresa's Carmelite reforms. But the early years were chaotic, and the entrants of varied spiritual talent. Nevertheless, as for class and caste, *queretanos* could rest contented that the community served the decidedly holy purpose of preventing local girls without resources from mixing their Spanish blood with that of Indians, mestizos, and mulattos.

Over the years, the Santa Cruz friars continued to bring young girls in need to the house, and Francisca of her own initiative admitted girls she liked and whose circumstances supported their petition. The ambiguity that surrounded the foundational status of the *beaterio* in its early years led to frequent troubles over admissions between Francisca and the group of male benefactors who thought it their right to enter their protégés there. More girls were brought to the community that she found did not adapt to the sort of austerity and communal living she hoped to induce in her *beatas*. In one such matter she argued in a note to Fray Antonio that "Don Juan [Caballero y Ocio] does not know what I know and thus they might let her in . . . but I have my motives which I will not list here for you in order not to tire you"—perhaps hoping that he might have a say in the matter.[6] Another such case that dragged on for years was that of Juana Ysguerra, a Querétaro *criolla* of unstable mental disposition but desirous of the mystical life. It appears that she had been admitted to the *beaterio* on several occasions for spiritual exercises in one of its hermitages, but by the time that she applied for permanent entry Francisca could stand it no more. Only Fray Antonio's gentle persuasion seemed to calm the girl's fits of temper.[7] Arguing that Juana needed constant supervision and frequent confessing and that her mood swings severely affected the morale of the community, Francisca flatly refused to take her in. The guardian of Santa Cruz seems to have been easy prey to the many young women who sought him out with their families and persuaded him to allow them entry into the *beaterio*. "This behavior of his has me in a state. After two or three 'pleases' from them, and without further consideration, he is full of sympathy and wants us to suffer what only God understands," she exclaimed again to her patient friend, ordering him to try and talk the weak-minded friar out of his stupor.[8] Sometime around 1707, the guardian entered a young girl into the *beaterio* with the stipulation that she be given a separate cell. When Francisca told her that it was not good for healthy, young girls to sleep on mattresses, she began to brood "and go about very disconsoled." Taking her usual recourse, Francisca wrote to Fray Antonio that the guardian simply did not know the girl and thought too highly of her, "for it is one thing to know someone in the confessional, and another entirely to live together."[9]

Around this date it is clear that there were already around twenty women in the *beaterio*, and in Francisca's view it was not advisable to take in any more. "Better to be few and united" she extolled to Fray Antonio and did not discuss the case further. As for the few who should be admitted it was not enough to possess virtue. To find grace in Francisca's eyes a certain mystical spirit was needed: "she is simply not for here," she retorted in one of her explanations for refusal of entry to Fray José Díez.[10] Women who could not get used to sleeping on planks in their petticoats would certainly not be able to adapt to the rigorous life in the *beaterio*.[11] Usually, Francisca gleefully concluded that her premonitions about a girl's character were right. On one occasion while the holy woman was entertaining six priests and friars in the house, one of the girls came in and caused a scandal of some sort. "It seems that the devil possessed her," she retorted to the patient Fray Antonio. Indeed, the girl had not yet taken the habit and had only been admitted because the guardian in the presence of Fray Antonio (she was careful to drive home that point) had begged Francisca to take her in. At times she had to take extreme measures to stop the persistent and bossy Santa Cruz friars. Furious over a girl left in the community by Ortega the vicar, she wrote to Fray Antonio: "If he persists in this with the *niña*, I refuse to go to his feet until this matter has been resolved. She cannot stay here for she is a heavy burden for this community. If he tells me she has to stay I will retire to my hermitage and beg you to run this community for me." The poor *portero* thus frequently found himself in the middle of a brawl between his charismatic brethren and their bellicose *hija espiritual* and probably found himself forced to resolve the dispute.[12]

The *priora* had more subtle ways as well to deal with an unwanted entrant. When Díez brought a protégée of his to the house, she told him the woman was free to stay. But instead of incorporating her into the life of the colegio, she left her idle, free to roam around as she wanted, hoping that she might repent of her choice, especially since she had a more suitable candidate in mind. Acquaintances of hers had asked her to take in their daughter, who was inclined to the religious life, but they did not have any space in their small house to follow a serious prayer and exercise schedule. Francisca was of a mind to let the girl in, see how it worked out and only then talk to the *beaterio's* principal material benefactor, Caballero y Ocio, about her entrance. Although the girl was younger than Díez's candidate and would therefore have to learn everything from scratch the prospect sounded more appetizing to Francisca who preferred to mold her girls according to her own ideas.[13]

While Francisca tried to filter in the sort of entrants she believed had a special disposition for the religious life, the community of course contained all sorts, and like many *beaterios* in the New World it was a curious mixture of laywomen and religious. Some of the young girls, to her delight, showed great promise for the future, such as the one who entered over Lent in 1702. She seemed truly inclined to matins, springing out of bed at the sound of the bell before anyone else had even thought of stirring. In her, Francisca believed that she discerned God's grace. Others seemed to create discord wherever they went. The letter following her enthusiastic praise for the new entrant contained a complaint about one of the new members who turned out to be the most rebellious so far. "When I least expect it, there is war," she railed and could not sleep for worry. Indeed, the girl was so rambunctious that Francisca feared her "nature" and dragged her heels in punishing her. Besides, she claimed to know nothing about punishing or imposing discipline.

The friars sent her advice as to how to "govern" their protégées, and she was expected to undertake the spiritual guidance of searching souls.[14] Some souls may have suffered more mental instability than others. Francisca's sister Gertrudis, for example, was given to bouts of difficult behavior, such as isolating herself from the community during fits of rage.[15] María Phelipa, an Alonso-Herrera family friend, seems to have demonstrated similar symptoms, and Francisca warned a confessor on one occasion not to pay any attention to her *cositas* since the girl was "poor miserable soul."[16] But given the large numbers of young and poor Creole women who found themselves in marginal situations, as the town population grew and its class structure grew more complex, the *beaterio* logically became a desirable haven for such candidates. And in view of its poverty and Francisca's insistence on keeping the community small, the result was that many women seem to have filtered through, their stay arranged by benevolent confessors while a more permanent situation could be found.[17]

As for securing cooks and servants Francisca did not have much luck either. Neither could she offer the advantages of Santa Clara, a rich and bustling institution that contained hundreds of women and the required comforts; nor could she entice them with good wages. Francisca hired two Indian women for domestic service and an old man, who sat by the *beatas'* front door and served as doorman.[18] The eldest servant, Juana, slipped through the corral one night, taking her bedding, clothes, and other belongings with her and was never seen again. Similarly, errand boys stayed for only limited periods before disappearing into thin air. One such boy began to serve the women at an early age, but when he began to enter rebellious adolescence he turned up only when it pleased him.[19] As the community grew, the Santa Cruz friars seem to have come up with the option of placing *depositadas* in the community to serve in the kitchen. The advantages, of course, were that *depositadas* were women serving time for small crimes or other sins and thus had no recourse for flight other than exile from Querétaro. But Francisca found them far too rebellious and worldly in spirit and was not at all at ease with them. Thus, while she demanded strength of character and austere spirit from the *beatas* themselves, the matter of the servant population was much more ambiguous and fluid. Homeless, wandering types who strayed in and did small jobs around the house were provided with a floor to sleep on. Josepha de Jesús María, one of the first entrants, reported that an "*indiesuelito*" slept in the corridor in front of Francisca's cell for an unspecified amount of time.[20]

Thus, daily life at the *beaterio* certainly included men who were not ecclesiastics. It seems, for example, that Francisca raised a small boy in the *beaterio* by the name of Ignacio. He lived there until his death in his twenties and served the *beatas* faithfully. She grew very attached to the boy and claimed on his death that his soul was untainted by sin.[21]

The rapid pace with which the community grew may also have affected Francisca's mother and sisters. After the death of her husband, Antonia de Herrera had settled with her daughters into the life of a virtual recluse, her quiet days only interrupted by confession and mass at Santa Cruz. The presence of so many girls of a tender age must have been unsettling. However virtuous and docile, the sheer task of ordering their days into a peaceful and quiet routine was daunting. As the community grew, Caballero y Ocio built the *beatas* a new dormitory. In a letter to Fray Antonio from this period, Francisca mentions that she had gathered the girls together and asked them if they missed being in "the other house" (her family's). She determined to ask her mother if they might be permitted, in turns, to use the other house for some of their daily occupations. After deliberations she decided against it, and for some time, Antonia and her two daughters, Clara and Gertrudis, seem to have lived apart from Francisca and her protégées. Francisca found this to be a painful situation and confided in Fray Antonio that she had had to hide her displeasure from the girls and pretend that she was in agreement with all this. The new house did not have a kitchen installed. Don Juan had planned to put a kitchen and a stock room in there, but Francisca had refused, preferring that the community eat together in the old house, and citing how easily the devil overcame a divided community. With the separation, however, she found herself forced to fashion a kitchen and refectory in one of the cells. To Fray Antonio, Francisca made little of the community's discomforts and with bravado exclaimed that women who lived in "exile" should not expect luxury. Whether she meant "exile" from her mother's house or the "exile" on earth of God's creatures she did not say, but a double entendre would not have been out of character.[22] Francisca, herself, however, always guarded her privacy. She seems to have resided throughout her career as foundress in a separate cell on two floors, working upstairs and sleeping downstairs.[23]

Since its beginnings in the early 1690s, the construction of the *beaterio* had occurred in haphazard phases, beginning with Caballero y Ocio's construction of hermitages for Francisca and her female relatives and continuing in spurts as the community grew. But in the early years there was little to separate the *beatas* from the hustle and bustle of surrounding streets except a row of trees and a chicken corral.[24] In the patios of the new house Francisca kept parrots in cages, some of them given to her by the Santa Cruz friars. Their singing announced the grace of God, and she was very fond of them. The patios served various purposes, for in addition to maintaining a schedule of prayer and worship, the *beatas* were hard at work on their own material survival. They made flower arrangements commissioned by townspeople, wax figures of the saints decorated in glass boxes, pastries, and crucifixes.

As a result of their disordered living arrangements the *beatas* suffered various inconveniences. Since hospitality was a fundamental principle of the community, Francisca could not turn away the many priests who came to her door, often from other cities and towns, desirous of spending a few days in a place so graced by God and so different from the bustling convents many of them administered. Sometime around 1705, for example, Francisca reported to Fray Antonio that she had indeed taken in the priest he had sent her for a few days. However, he had had to stay in a room in the interior ("to my great mortification") since the room usually reserved for visiting ecclesiastics was in such a bad state that it had to be whitewashed again.[25]

## La Vida Común

After Margil's departure, Francisca and her community acquired another Santa Cruz protector, Fray José Díez, an avid missionary and ascetic. He was a rather problematic character, however, and at the heart of his contradictions and complexities lay the frustrated desire to convert pagans. He had arrived with the first group of Propaganda Fide friars in New Spain in 1683 and was among the founders of the college in Querétaro. Immediately upon taking residence in Querétaro, Díez had been dispatched on missions to the Spanish population. Having reached Yucatán it seemed that his dream would be realized, for there he met with the already legendary Margil and his companion Fray Melchor López. Díez, accompanied by another friar, embarked with the duo on a ship to head south to Central America, a land of ample opportunity for avid missionaries, but they were driven back by pirate ships. Once in Mérida, he had to suffer the humiliation of watching the veteran missionaries leave for their adventure while he, along with his companion, was assigned the task of founding a recollect monastery in Mérida. He served there over two years as master of novices until he was called back to Querétaro in 1686. There he continued his missions to Spaniards but kept his eyes open for another chance to go south. When he heard that Fray Escaray (another close friend of Francisca's) was heading to Mexico City to ask for authorization to go south, Díez renounced his post as vicar and met with the friar in secret to beg him to take him along.

The friars headed south but had to suffer the embarrassment of falling seriously ill in Chiapas and being recalled to Querétaro. In the following year, however, Díez's time seemed to have finally arrived; in 1691, the Indians of New Mexico rebelled and killed twenty-one missionaries. A general call was issued in New Spain for volunteers to the hostile territories, a call to which the ardent friar was quick to respond. In six months he was in Santa Fe, confessing and burying the sixty Indians executed there for their part in the rebellion. Afterward an epidemic killed off most of the remaining population of the town, and Díez suddenly found himself in a situation that far exceeded his wildest dreams in terms of drama and intensity. Appointed chaplain to the Spanish forces in Santa Fe, Díez immediately resigned from the task and asked to be sent to the gentiles instead. He then spent the next three years as a missionary to the Tequa Indians until 1696, when he was called back to Querétaro. He arrived in August only to discover that he had escaped—or been deprived of—martyrdom by a hair's breath. In June five Franciscans, among them a friar from Santa Cruz, had been killed by Indian rebels there.[26]

When Margil became guardian of Santa Cruz, he named Díez as his vicar. In the following year, the unfortunate friar tried to renounce his duties in order to head south to convert the Indians of Talamanca, but Margil would not let him go. In the following year, Margil himself headed south again for more glory and adventure while a disgruntled Díez had to resign himself to daily administrative tasks at the college, whose chronicler he had become. The remainder of his life would be spent at the college and in missions to *fieles*. Not that he did not achieve success in institutional terms; Díez served repeatedly as guardian of Santa Cruz and became in 1709 the commissary of missions. But his ardent thirst for the hands-on mission of converting remote and hostile tribes was never fulfilled, and it undoubtedly left him embittered.[27] In addition to these afflictions, his health kept failing. In his 1701 chronicle of Propaganda Fide's missionary efforts in the New World Díez described the hardships of the job. He said of himself that having arrived in New Spain in "robust" health at the age of twenty-six, twenty years of toil had left him frail, struck down by illnesses of various kinds, and a "nuisance" to everyone. To top Díez's afflictions, when Margil took his restless self away from the college he left Díez another source of mortification: the spiritual and material care of his *hija espiritual*, Francisca de los Ángeles, and her hoard of willful *beatas*. Thus, in 1701, Fray José Díez became Francisca's confessor. The two would form a relationship that became problematic to say the least.

Díez took seriously his new duties of governing women who, as of yet, did not even live in an officially sanctioned religious community. He decided to give no leeway for rebellion. The women were ordered to confess their sins in his and the community's presence. When he found their *pecados* excessive the friar ordered the person's belongings packed and thrown out of the house. The sinful soul, having thus been "reinvested with grace," was then obliged to beg him and the other women for mercy. Punishments were meted out in the creative spirit of the Counter-Reformation; they included carrying a stone around the neck and a stick in the mouth.[28] One girl who had not carried out an order promptly was ordered to stand out in the garden bareheaded under the noon sun from twelve until three o'clock in the afternoon.[29]

Díez also set about bringing some order to the womens' diverse vocations. In May 1702 he gave them a written manual, to be read out loud every week, setting out the general principles of their communal life. Francisca was named mother superior, an office she would hold until her death in 1744. The simplicity of the new community's life was expressed in their first oratory: its altar was merely a bench, bare of adornments except an image of the Child Jesus borrowed from a benefactor.[30] The friar ordered the women's liturgical life around the canonical hours, which were separated into hours of mental prayer, menial work, and attending mass, communion, and confession at Santa Cruz after prime. The religious practices and routines of the *beaterio* were as austere in character as Díez himself. The women awoke daily at four and recited communal prayers, matins, and lauds, after which they walked to Santa Cruz to be confessed and take communion. Upon returning they would eat breakfast, followed by manual labor until it was time for vespers, terce, sext, and none.[31] Imitating the Santa Cruz friars' nighttime wanderings, they would occasionally leave their house at three in the morning and begin to recite meditations while walking from the Franciscan cemetery to the Santa Cruz church where they would sing psalms and wait for the church to open.[32]

And while the *beatas* were to search for God in the secrecy of their prayers and privacy of their cells and hermitage, Francisca was clearly enamored of her mentors' ideal of communal exercises and openness of spirit between members. Thus, she frequently organized communal exercises during which, each morning, the *beatas* would be woken one at a time by a fellow *beata* singing a verse on the doorstep of their cell. A much favored practice was for each *beata* to write down in secret her favorite penitences. The slips of paper were then placed in a bowl and a secretary elected to draw. The lucky one would then have the pleasure of seeing the entire community perform her preferred penitence together.[33] During Advent, the communal exercise became more and more theatrical. A series of *hospedajes* in the spirit of the tradition of the *posadas* were held that centered on staging various biblical events. In one instance, the *beatas* enacted Jesus's visit to the sisters Martha and Mary. Francisca played the role of Martha, while María Isabel, one of the community's eldest members, was Mary. One of the younger members was dressed up as Jesus of Nazareth, and the entire community congregated to receive him singing verses. They then led him to a table prepared by Francisca and adorned with flowers and sat him at the head. Francisca and María

Isabel served the visitor, and the entire community was entertained with music and song. According to Francisca, it was a day of "much devotion" to the community.[34] Francisca's charges followed her example. Like her, they fasted and mortified themselves in preparation for the great events of the Christian calendar and felt haunted in their efforts by the devil. They took turns borrowing the keys to her hermitage at the far end of their orchard; there they stayed during nights in solitude communicating with God.[35]

In spite of these common principles of devotion her disciples shared with Francisca, their spirituality was a humble reflection of hers. Indeed, the few letters we possess from the early *beatas* indicate that their spiritual ambition was to experience the presence of God in their souls. But with that purpose achieved, they did not imagine themselves to be especially chosen as recipients of special powers, nor did they dare to persuade others that they were so blessed.

Such humility reflected perhaps their naturally melancholic disposition and a consciousness of their low station in life, but more importantly it was the result of the forceful hand of the Franciscans. Letters from two sisters, Isabel Rosa and Marcela, show that both were punished and had to face the scorn of others at some point in their lives for behavior considered to deviate from the principles of the community. Such difficulties are a prominent theme in the account of her life in the community that Marcela jotted down in December 1725. For unknown reasons, she spent the first five years in the *beaterio* as a novice, a period that usually lasted only a year. Perhaps the *beatas'* reluctance to give her the habit was caused by what they considered to be her unruly character. A few years later, once she had become a full-fledged member of the community, she was punished for her lack of obedience by being deprived of her habit and relegated to the kitchen. Her cell was taken over by a new member of the community, and she was given one that did not even have a bed in it. In her opinion, the punishment had a beneficial effect, for she began to recognize her faults, the gravest of which was "a lack of resignation to the will of God." Her distress had an impact on her health, and she was confined to her bed for the next three years with a pain in her heart. Perhaps she was accused by the other *beatas* of wanting to leave Santa Rosa, for in her account she was preoccupied with defending herself: "God knows that I did not feel this temptation to leave. . . . In this period I realized that I was already dead for I was already enshrouded and that therefore I had to be silent and suffer." Finally, she began to partake in the community's life, but she nevertheless continued to keep to herself: "I always retired whenever I could among the trees to enjoy solitude."[36]

The Franciscans instructed the *beatas* not to take God's love for granted. Such teachings were reflected in the women's writing. Intensely mystical, Marcela's sister, Isabel Rosa, used religious imagery that nevertheless recalled how unimportant and miniscule her existence was in the divine scheme of things: "sometimes I see my soul as a small fish in the great ocean of the Trinity and in others as a tiny butterfly embracing the immense fire of the presence of God."[37] Well informed by the Franciscans of the dangers and temptations her spirituality could inspire, Isabel remained wary whether she was following the right course to virtue: "I did not receive any formal support nor did I have anyone who could resolutely tell me if the path I was taking was secure and that I should not resist My Lord, that his holiness would take charge of my soul."[38] She was acutely aware of the likeliness that her petitions would fail to arouse God's approval: "one day, wishing for the salvation of souls, I presented to the Lord the hearts of all mortals and his Majesty told me that he did not receive enforced wishes . . . and he taught me the right way to ask."[39]

Guidance for these women was of varied quality. For example, the letters of spiritual counsel sent to Isabel by the Jesuit Juan Antonio de Mora, Francisca's vicar, are formulaic and sermonizing notes, exhorting her to live "transformed in Him through love and imitation." "It is also important," Mora reminded her, "that you apply yourself to the exercise of pure and fine love and disinterested humility." He warned Isabel of false humility and the dangers of disobedience, and his encouragements were predictable, such as carrying Christ crucified in her heart and to persevere in her path. Most of the letters then ended with a playful message to another of his spiritual charges, María Gertrudis, who was reminded that "if she was not *muy santa*, our Lord would get very angry."[40] His letters are light notes, probably written quickly without too much thought. They contain the sort of advice any guidebook could give and contain none of the intensity and character of Margil's letters to Francisca.

Such notes along with whatever texts the *beatas* read clearly delineated the maxims of their journey. The women had an innate sense of hagiography and dramatic appeal as they wrote about their own spiritual lives. An anonymous *beata*'s account of her life, for example, starts with a hagiographic childhood characterized by loss of family, threats to her chastity, and early revelations and pious devotion. Her adult life was characterized by a love for Christ so intense that it rendered her virtually incapable of partaking in community life. The love affair had begun sometime after her entry into the *beaterio*—she was eleven years old when she entered—while praying in the orchard. The thirty-three-year-old Nazarene, sad and tired, had fallen into her arms and stolen her soul. Oral prayer was impossible since the soul recoiled at uttering secret words and instead withdrew to its center where like a dove it entered Christ's entrails and was bathed in his blood. During certain periods of her life—in one instance for eight years—Christ stayed sacramented inside her, but during others he withdrew, and it was only the exercise of Saint Ignatius that brought him back.[41]

The frequent visits of priests and friars to confess the women, give communion, and say mass were integral to the survival of the community. The sacraments presented the bread and butter of the women's religious life, and should their hunger for these rites remain unsatisfied the inevitable results were the infiltration of the devil into the community and subsequent discord. As the community grew it was left to the foundress's powers of persuasion to maintain a steady stream of male ecclesiastical visitors to the beaterio to perform these services. Furthermore, the beatas all had their preferred confessor, a man with whom they felt the right chemistry to open their souls to. Francisca's letters are therefore frequently annotated with lines such as "Beatriz needs desperately to see Padre Campaner." Hurdles in the relationship could lead to classic cases of heartbreak, such as that of the beata whose confessor refused to continue their relationship, which led her to fall physically ill with despair.[42] Similarly, as a figure of supreme authority, the confessor was fundamental to maintaining discipline among women whose lives were confined within the relatively narrow boundaries that the era's piety prescribed for women who did not distinguish themselves and led ordinary lives of worship. Thus, in cases of naturally willful souls, a spirited confessor was needed. On April 8, 1714, for example, Francisca wrote to Santa Cruz that Chupita, one of the orphans brought by Margil at the turn of the century, was so rebellious that she thought the gentle Padre Dávila simply would not be able to handle her.

The friar was well intentioned and always ready to help. On many occasions he confessed the entire community after saying mass when the Santa Cruz friars failed. But Chupita had a habit of playing cat and mouse with her confessor. At times she refused to confess with him, and instead spent far too much time with don Nicolás Armenta the chaplain. Although Francisca would dish out punishments such as physical confinement, she did not possess the authority needed to subdue the determined girl. She thus wrote to her mentors that it was urgent that a new and strong-willed confessor be found.[43]

While Francisca demonstrated a strong hand in maintaining discipline, hierarchically conscious *beatas* probably held out until a confessor's authority had been wielded. Such was the case of her sister Gertrudis and the unruly Juana Ysguerra, who both required Margil to use a chastening note to quell their independent strivings.[44] Similarly, rebellious servants were sent up the hill to Santa Cruz to be given a good talking to.[45] Since the community could not thrive without confessions, Francisca's letters well into the 1720s never omit gentle admonishments, prodding, or outright angry demands for confessors. Santa Cruz had no formal obligation to the *beaterio*. Since the individual friars with whom Francisca had formed relationships were frequently away on mission or otherwise engaged, it was only the constant pressure she placed on her mentors' community that kept this lifeline open to her protégées.

The sacrament of confession was also necessary to clear the air before the community withdrew for periods of prayer and meditation. In an undated letter, Francisca bitterly complained that the entire community was about to enter exercises of the Virgin when not one single priest or friar had stopped by to aid them for days. Morale was terribly low, she wailed, and the *beatas* unprepared to begin their period of meditation.[46] Without confession there could be no communion, which had to be undertaken without a blemish on the soul. Indeed, Francisca at times aggressively threatened to deprive herself of communion if the guardian of Santa Cruz did not send over the required confessor to help her prepare.[47] At the same time, to women like Francisca's *beatas*, communion was a much more complex and vital matter than merely reaffirming ties to the church and body of Christ. It was the constant confirmation needed in a continuous love affair that was based on union in purity of spirit with the divine. In that sense, communion could also present the single most daunting obstacle to a religious woman bent upon her *camino de la perfección*. Torn by conflicting emotion, self-doubt, and the challenges of bending the ego to a process so clearly delineated by confessors, guide-books, and sermons, an aspiring soul might find communion an almost insurmountable obstacle.

It required the most single-minded commitment and purity of heart. For example, the *beata* Marcela felt herself during a time of crisis to be incapable of confessing or taking communion. Her predicament was solved when an understanding priest explained to her that in certain periods of their lives the saints had suffered similar crises. Francisca frequently denied herself communion during turbulent times, citing the existence of something "so doubtful and secret" in her soul that only an experienced confessor would know how to extract it. Several of her letters suggest that *beatas* going through crisis also refused communion.[48]

### "The Wisdom and Diligence of Her Pen"

Francisca's facility with the pen was used to the utmost advantage for her growing but as of yet unsanctioned community. This was acknowledged by the chronicler María de Jesús when she noted that "all the improvements and advances which at present [1730] this college enjoys are owed to the wisdom and diligence of her [Francisca's] pen."[49] Francisca's frequent correspondence with don Juan Caballero y Ocio convinced him that the women's saintly way of life must be supported. In addition to the material improvements he undertook to her family home, he secured permission to say mass at the community's new oratory. His benevolence with the poor women did not stop there, for he frequently said mass there himself and became a regular visitor.

Caballero y Ocio was an important ally. Fifty-five years old at the turn of the century and with a distinguished career behind him, he was connected to the important Querétaro family clans of Ocio, Ocampo, Corona, Medina, and Monroy, which originated in Extremadura, Castille, and Zamora. The patriarchs of three generations of his paternal lineage sported the title *capitán*. Don Juan himself had served as Inquisitor, alcalde, and *alguacil mayor* in Querétaro, was the founder of the rich order of Guadalupe, and had been the chief financial backer of church building in the city. His father, Capt. Juan Caballero de Medina y Corona, had been a *regidor* in Mexico City, and his sister Leonor was married to a chevalier of the Order of Calatrava. Another was married to a judge of the Real Audiencia in Mexico City.[50] Don Juan thus possessed excellent connections and used them in Francisca's cause. Desiring to bring more pious women who found themselves in dire straits into the community he sent a friend with a petition for a conventual foundation to Madrid but was unsuccessful. Francisca spurred him on nevertheless, sending him gentle but exhorting letters during his stays at his various country estates. In an undated letter, after gently fussing over his health and earthly worries she advised him to strike while the iron was hot:

> I bid you very good days, during which I am heartened to know that you have recovered from all your infirmities as the Lord wants you to and that the diversion of the country and fresh air will alleviate Your Grace's pains, and although I know that the administration of all your servants and workmen is a heavy burden, the Lord will give Your Grace strength and spirit so that

when you are angry you will not be impatient and I beg of Your
Grace not to forget your poor sinner; as I was writing this note
I received this letter which I send to Your Grace from Antonio
de los Ángeles Bustamante. Please read it Your Grace; I think
that the approval should be on its way soon since all the necessary
circumstances are in place to prevent any difficulties that we might
experience as it [the convent] would be founded in the most abject
communal and particular poverty and since his Sanctity or the
King will know that it is the city which asks for it and which will
maintain it. . . . Fray Antonio tells me in this letter that it is not
important whether your message is ready or not, it is enough for
this *puntito* to be included in a letter from Your Grace for the
same representative and please forgive me for any inconveniences
I might cause you; the Lord will pay you very well. I received
the dozen chickens you sent and esteem the love and charity of
Your Grace. Until tomorrow when I will go to *Nuestra Señora*
[Guadalupe] to ask for your holy blessing . . . your most grateful
servant Francisca de los Ángeles.[51]

Don Juan was not the only target of Francisca's publicity campaign. The
community quickly acquired a following of benefactors and well-wishers. Fray
Antonio de los Ángeles, after Margil's departure, became Francisca's staunchest supporter in all things. He went door to door among rich Querétaro
households begging for charity, arranged weekly deliveries of mutton from a
local hacendado, benefactor of the Santa Cruz friars; sent wine and bread for
the service of the Eucharist; served as intermediary between Francisca and the
guardians of Santa Cruz; and organized the lobbying drive for the foundation
of a convent.

To maintain the favorable attention that the community received, Francisca
had to articulate in attractive terms the logic of the women's contemplative
life. After all, they were not members of an elite convent like Santa Clara whose
wealth and glorious adornments served to enhance the city's prestige. They
were simply a group of poor, uneducated women, "each and every one only
thinking of how to become holy."[52] As a result, the story of their adventure
had to be well told in colorful terms that accentuated the importance of their
mission for the town at large, and the divine will that steered it.

Taking the lead from her mentors, Francisca sometime in the 1690s explained to Sitjar the miraculous attributes of a heavy wooden cross that was

The reformer: Don Juan Caballero y Ocio. *Crónica del Real Colegio.*

stuck in the ground in the middle of her orchard. The Indians of the neighborhood had once tried to remove it, but finding it immobile had begun to venerate it as a symbol of divine powers.[53] The Alonso-Herrera family house and orchard had thus been consecrated as sacred territory, battleground between God and the devil. The group of impoverished women, with no other resources, was thus God's army fighting evil. They were the least likely divine warriors conceivable, but then it was well known that God favors the weak. The activities that went on within their cells were thus of great importance to the town at large, no less so than the splendid liturgical rites observed at Santa Clara. In August 1696, Francisca told Sitjar of a terrifying battle between devils and angels that took place in Querétaro before the arrival of the archbishop. The devils' strategy had been to divide and infiltrate into the city's most holy territories, such as the great convent of the parish church in Santa Cruz, as well as into the houses of *beatas*. Before the creation of her own community, then, Francisca was already emphasizing the importance of this underprivileged class within ecclesiastical hierarchy in safeguarding divine benevolence toward human sinners.

As soon as Francisca's community got its conventual schedule of round-the-clock prayers and penitence underway the devil's attacks naturally intensified. Impressed by the ferocity of the attacks—the loud noises sometimes coming from the *beaterio* attested to the saintliness achieved within the community—one of the *beaterio*'s benefactors offered to stand watch in the night to catch the devil at his own tricks. One such charitable soul fashioned heavy bars to block the doors of the cells from the inside and then stayed up a few nights to stand guard in the orchard. Unfortunately, he did not witness any great battles, but his admiring eyes nevertheless perceived a strange light illuminating the cells of the pious women. His eager ears heard a vague ringing of bells that could not have emanated from any of the neighborhood's churches, but seemed situated somewhere in the sky above the orchard. His confessor clarified the matter for him; it was well known that God chose to signal his chosen places for worship in this manner.[54]

Francisca was eager to found a convent for her exemplary community. A conventual foundation was not at all far-fetched; the first female convent in New Spain was founded around a group of *beatas* in the capital who lived together for ten years before the foundation of a Concepcionista convent. The same can be said for many subsequent foundations, such as Santa Clara, Santa Catalina de Siena, and the *recogimiento*-convent of Balvanera—all founded in the late sixteenth century in the capital.[55] But while the fluidity of Conquest society had spurred royal approval for conventual foundations, the climate of the early eighteenth century was not nearly as propitious for such petitions. A steady torrent of complaint had been carried from ecclesiastical supervisors across the Atlantic throughout the second half of the seventeenth century against the idleness, extravagance, and worldliness of Mexican convents. More importantly, the new Bourbon king of a Spain weakened by the flow of money to the church was engaged in the Wars of Succession and not in the least favorable to the cause.[56] Blissfully unaware of these larger currents, Francisca through her patient entertaining and furious and constant letter writing maintained an arsenal of men, ecclesiastics, and seculars to keep alive the process. Her goal was to establish a convent of the First Order of Saint Clare, small, austere, and poor. The Marquis of Altamirano, a prominent, well-connected

Querétaro citizen, one of the Santa Cruz friars' principal benefactors, and the trustee of their convent, brought news and circulated letters between Querétaro and various corners of New Spain. The Franciscan commissary general, a frequent visitor at the house, petitioned the archbishop, and an unidentified "Señor Estrada" was a frequent presence at these meetings. With such powerful backers the prestige of the community grew. Fray Antonio also contributed as an intermediary to obtain Francisca's devotional objects blessed by God. "Here are the rosaries which you will give to Fray Alonso Monge," Francisca scribbled hastily in a note to her friend. "They will leave from here at two o'clock in the afternoon, with a secure messenger," she wrote, reminding him nevertheless that she wanted them back at some point.[57]

Spurred by their success the *beatas* decided to pepper their rituals with more extravagant rites. In honor of the purity of the Virgin, they established a ritual that mocked and humiliated the devil. Fashioning an image of him made of dirty rags, they tied it to a tree, beat it with sticks, and sang mocking verses that belittled his power and glorified the Virgin. With the help of two priests, they read him his sentence and threw him on a great bonfire. After Margil's return from Guatemala he added the touch of hanging the figure from a branch to strangle it, after which it was thrown on the fire. To finish the ritual he exorcised and blessed the house.[58]

With such promising beginnings, Francisca began to pursue even greater ambitions for the community's ritual life. Having celebrated the day of Santa Rosa de Viterbo at Santa Cruz every year, she informed the friars some years after the turn of the century that Santa Rosa had told her in a vision that she wanted the celebrities held at the *beaterio* from now on. The momentous event had occurred when Francisca was on the way to Santa Cruz to celebrate the saint's feast. She had been met by the image of Rosa herself, who informed her of her preference for the *beaterio*.[59] The friars obediently loaned Francisca the crosses, the image, robes, candles, and posies every year from then on.[60] Further, she decided that the *beatas* should celebrate a fifteen-day feast annually for the Assumption of the Virgin. And since this signified that mass had to be celebrated every day during the period, Francisca took advantage of the fact that there were now fifteen *beatas* in the community and ordered that each and every one of them should be responsible for the celebrations for one day. The townspeople enthusiastically supported the ambitious plan, even "the principal persons" of the community, who contributed with candles and money and participated in the mass.[61] In this manner, Francisca had now managed to secure the participation of seculars at masses at the *beatas'* small chapel. If such recognition was her objective, her success at this point was undisputed.

### The Devil at War

Fame and recognition carried with them pitfalls. With her unlimited ambition, Francisca in this case overstepped the role envisioned for her by her mentors. In celebrating mass every day and inviting seculars to assist and admire their efforts, the *beatas* were not exactly reinforcing the image of themselves as "wretched," which Santa Teresa had so often used to counter male anger and suspicion.[62] Furthermore, all this was happening with the active collaboration of Caballero y Ocio, who despite his friendship with the Santa Cruz friars, presented an active threat through his Congregation of Guadalupe to the power and privileges enjoyed by the Franciscan Order in Querétaro. As a result, the friars promptly acted when an unsuspecting and pious *queretano* informed the archbishop in Mexico City that Caballero y Ocio had for years maintained a *beaterio* in Querétaro that had a "great following" among the townspeople. Hearing that the archbishop had been much displeased to find that his permission for the foundation had never been solicited, Fray José Díez himself wrote a letter to his excellency advising against the *beaterio*.[63]

Other priests took fright. In a letter to Fray Antonio de los Ángeles, Francisca lamented that a certain cleric had been telling townspeople how worried he was about assisting the *beatas* given the news of the archbishop's reaction. From her various connections she also received news of malicious gossip circulating in the town regarding the community. She wrote to Fray Antonio in 1706: "Had I not been prepared by you this would have been yet another shock; it seems that you knew my ignorance as to how far the devil's arm stretches."[64] The havoc brought her down; she felt depressed and sick as if she were coming down with a cold.[65] At this point, however, aid came from an unforeseen direction. Don Matías de Hijar, a priest and a lawyer at the Real Audiencia in Mexico City who had long followed the *beaterio's* progress with interest, offered his help. Francisca seized the opportunity and cultivated the relationship assiduously, using the powers of her pen to secure his attention. In a letter to Fray José Díez, she admitted that she recounted visions to don Matías for "his recreation."[66] Spurred in his enthusiasm by Margil, Hijar quickly began to send the women money, and at the viceregal court, to lobby for a conventual foundation of some sort.[67]

Things did not proceed smoothly, however, for Francisca's camp seemed split in two as to how to react to the Santa Cruz friars' aggression. Don Matías argued for a report on the community's impeccable living standards, while Caballero y Ocio favored resting the case for the moment. Never one for inertia, Francisca favored the former's opinion and wrote to Fray Antonio to choose four seculars to sign the petition. Having asked, she then promptly supplied him with the answer she wanted: it would be best that the wealthy don José Merino "and such persons" sign, as well as Cabellero y Ocio (who she obviously thought she could turn to her way of thinking), the vicar of Santa Cruz, don Matías himself, and the prior of Santo Domingo.[68] By this time the group had decided to abandon plans for a conventual foundation and apply instead for the establishment of a *colegio*. The Marquis of Altamirano would be dispatched to the capital with the necessary documents, while the composition of the letter would be entrusted to Francisca's most faithful advisor, Fray Antonio de los Ángeles.[69] The marquis had by now agreed to take the responsibility for financing and acquiring the permission from Spain. Fray Antonio approved of the language of the petition and Francisca, encouraged, sent don Matías with the testimonies that had been gathered to Santa Cruz for the friar's scrutiny: "I do not feel secure about any of it until it has passed before your eyes." Since Fray Antonio had by now acquired quite a reputation for saintliness, she also believed it best that he write personally to Bishop Pedro de Urtiaga, an ally of theirs, to ask his help in the matter. Don Matías also thought it best, in view of Caballero y Ocio's prestige, that he send the king a personal letter to the same effect. However, Francisca worried about asking him, diplomatically understanding that he might feel hurt at being shoved aside by don Matías and the marquis. It was he, after all, who had initiated—if failed to secure—the foundation of a convent of the first rule of Saint Clare.[70]

Seething with excitement, Francisca and her allies considered plans for the layout of a new oratory.[71] The report was promptly dispatched to Madrid, but divine providence seemed to have other plans. The ship carrying it sank before reaching its destination.[72] And it was in the midst of this flurry of activity that Díez went further in his antagonism by taking it upon himself to remove all the objects needed to say mass at the chapel, thus pulling the ground from under Francisca's feet. He then ordered her to dissolve the community and send her *beatas* home or leave them on the street should they have no home to go to. At this, Francisca demonstrated that her obedience to her mentors had its limits. She simply refused to comply with the order and retorted that "it was her will to receive whoever came in need to her door, and that if his Majesty had united them, she would care for them, as with any others who might join them."[73] Díez was livid: "I have a confessor, but it is only in name for he does not say a word to me," Francisca reported to Fray Antonio.

In Díez's opinion, recent events were God's punishment of Francisca for spending so much time with secular priests.[74] But Francisca finally won the battle over the *beaterio*, and don Matías Hijar was successful in gaining renewed permission to say masses at her chapel. At the same time, though, she lost her staunchest supporter. In 1706, Caballero y Ocio died. His death reduced to ashes all her hopes of converting her community into a convent. The pious cleric had promised to leave the *beatas* twenty thousand pesos on one of his haciendas to secure the foundation. Instead, he left a legacy of three hundred thousand pesos to found a Capuchin convent, and twenty years later that money was used to found a convent whose first nuns were brought from Mexico City.[75] Furthermore, Caballero y Ocio's sudden death deprived them of their daily sustenance, which had flowed freely and informally from his pockets. With a community of twenty women on her hands and only six pesos a week left by Caballero y Ocio, Francisca also had to face increasing grumpiness from the Santa Cruz community, from which no material help was forthcoming.

Defiantly, she continued to take in applicants without economic resources. When a young girl in the *beaterio* died, mercifully transported swiftly into the other world by San Antonio, her relatives and grieving mother had barely turned the corner of the street with the coffin when a poor *gachupín*, widowed with a young daughter, appeared at Francisca's door, begging her to take in his daughter. The loss of whatever capital he possessed had forced him to take the traveling road, and he hoped to find work and better fortune on the Guadalajara frontier. He did not possess the three hundred pesos required by the nuns of Santa Clara to take the girl in. Francisca, perhaps motivated partly by a desire to underscore the contrast with that worldly institution, agreed to take his daughter in without pay. She did not regret her decision. Although the girl was lively in character, she seemed docile, with good inclinations, and was thereafter named *la mexicana* by the rest of the community.[76]

Don Matías's visits to the *beaterio* became more frequent and longer with the years. Francisca had a special cell constructed so her benefactor could spend his free days and weeks watching the fruits of his political endeavors through the struggles for *perfección* that defined the daily routines of his protégées. She anxiously watched over his health and tried to find him suitable companions in Querétaro. Aware that don Matías did not find the Querétaro clergy to his taste, she wrote to Fray Antonio de los Ángeles before one of his visits to exhort him to acquaint himself with a secular priest, a don Francisco Sánchez who was deliberating whether he should spend some time with the community. Francisca wanted Fray Antonio to persuade him to do so, since he was one of the few that don Matías could get along with, and she believed he would be the perfect companion for her benefactor's spiritual exercises.[77]

Don Matías contributed to the upkeep of the community, and don Francisco Sánchez eventually gained an interest in the *beatas*. He began to help out with their daily needs and say mass for them, as well as accompanying them in their spiritual exercises. His death a few years later again left them in dire straits. At this point Francisca seems to have shown considerable ingenuity and survival skills, for she organized the *beatas* into a full-time schedule manufacturing pastries and wax figures, flower arrangements, and the like. The energy before spent on mystical raptures now went into the more immediate enterprise of daily survival.

Judging by the admiring testimonies offered by her fellow *beatas* after her death—naturally peppered with the prospect of taking part in fashioning a myth—Francisca demonstrated considerable skill at "governing." Their statements all converge on two points: *su merced* had an uncanny ability to produce funds in times of dire needs, and she demonstrated considerable depth of understanding about human character. Narratives of periods of near hunger naturally involved miraculous interventions. Francisca begged the saints to intercede for mercy since she was unable to provide even a piece of bread or chocolate for breakfast. When she did so, she invariably found herself opening the door to a mysterious visitor offering a commission for flowers or sweets paid in advance. And funds kept in the drawer of her writing table seemed to last for an extraordinary length of time and replenish themselves. Whatever the motivation behind these statements by the *beatas*, they show that the *beaterio* did go through periods when sustenance and survival was a day-to-day challenge. Francisca's role as provider of food is a steady undercurrent throughout her letters, which not only contain petitions for mutton, chocolate, and the like but also for seeds for onions, beets, carrots, and lettuce. In her orchard Francisca tended to trees that produced avocados, pears, peaches, and apricots, among other exotic fruit.

When a disconsolate *beata* wandered about the grounds, deliberating whether to take measures to leave the community, the foundress seemed to have a knack for reading her moods. In such cases Francisca would summon them and tell them exactly what "was on their mind," persuading them to stay and seeking resolutions such as novenas and a new, understanding confessor. In some instances, her role as comforter even encroached on the sacred prerogative of the male cleric, the confessional. For four years Francisca acted as confessor every night to Josepha de Jesús María, who found herself in the impossible situation of being unable to communicate matters of her soul to the confessor. Francisca would listen to her confessions and tell her exactly what to tell the cleric in the morning. And Francisca proved a pragmatic rather than dogmatic caretaker of souls. When Josepha fell ill with a cold and felt herself consumed by the desire for *zapote prieto*, an exotic, sweet fruit normally forbidden to her, Francisca did not exhort her to resist her devilish temptations, but immediately provided some for her. To Josepha's astonishment she healed immediately. On another occasion, the *beata* struggled with her desire for hot chocolate while fasting in the hermitage and contemplated with dread the long hours before her afternoon drink would be handed to her. Then, she saw Francisca's hand come through the hole in the hermitage with a cup full of steaming hot chocolate. Rather than pushing her protégées to the extremes of ascetic self-denial, Francisca understood the value of small pleasures as incitement for greater spiritual achievements.[78] Similarly, she understood the dangers of constant soul-searching. In the case of Teresita, a young *beata* who mysteriously fell ill with headaches and fevers, Francisca advised bed rest and respite from the long general confessions that had consumed the woman of late. Indeed, Francisca was convinced that it was the *beata*'s passion for confession that had made her sick.[79]

## "Su más afecta hija"

Francisca's relationships with male clergy legitimized her efforts to found a religious community though she lacked an endowment of land or capital.[80] Unlike the convent of Santa Clara and other religious institutions for women that would be founded in Querétaro in the eighteenth century, Francisca could not claim a backer who was willing to cede haciendas or cattle herds in exchange for recognition as convent founder or for the satisfaction of seeing his family taking a central place in its church's elaborate ceremonies. Francisca's community served the unknown and unseen unfortunate, poor Spanish maidens or orphans of immigrant families lost in the region's increasingly more complex and fast-paced economy. For rich families, it was undoubtedly a pious gesture to support the community with donations, but such aid could not be counted on. It did not carry the public recognition associated with the convent of Santa Clara, and, in the first decade of the

The foundress: Francisca de los Ángeles. *Crónica del Real Colegio.*

eighteenth century, Francisca's *beaterio* stood on precarious ground. A group of poor women living together without royal or archbishopric sanction and ambitious for spiritual perfection that involved a dangerously intense mysticism invited suspicions of heresy. The affair smacked of the sort of mystical fervor that had led the city into the demoniac scandal, which, only a decade

Isabel María de Santa Rosa, founding member of the
*beaterio* of Santa Rosa de Viterbo. *Crónica del Real Colegio.*

old, probably served to check the enthusiasm of many *queretanos* for the idea
of pious women living alone.

Although Francisca herself enjoyed a reputation as a holy woman, had she
not after all been investigated by the Inquisition? The malicious gossip that
arose when the Santa Cruz friars, spurred by the archbishop's reaction to the
news of the *beaterio's* foundation, decided to withdraw their support of the
community only accentuated the difficult and ambiguous situation Francisca

found herself in during these first years. To maintain public goodwill and financial support, it was therefore imperative to uphold her ecclesiastical supporters' conviction of the significance of their cause. This was difficult since her supporters were divided in two camps. On the surface they were friendly and cooperative toward each other, but underneath there was wariness, anger, and suspicion on both sides. As evidenced in the struggle between the regulars and seculars for the archbishop's attention when it came to the *beaterio*, Francisca found herself embroiled in a larger political conflict that threatened to cut short her ambitions.

The Franciscan Order had dominated life in Querétaro since the city's early beginnings as a commercial outpost when its only raison d'être was its proximity to the silver mines of Guanajuato. The friars had arrived with the first wave of Spanish settlers and through the enduring travails of that first century had earned to right to control the parish that dominated the city's central plaza. By the eighteenth century the Order occupied not only the Great Convent attached to the parish church, but the convents of Santa Cruz, San Antonio, and Santa Clara. With the arrival of the friars of Propaganda Fide the Franciscans' missionary reputation was unsurpassed. The more comfortable and bureaucratic secular clergy did not seem to have a chance of competing. Caballero y Ocio's founding of the Congregation of Guadalupe and the erection of its church only a few street blocks above the Great Convent was a direct challenge to the dominance of the Franciscans, and they reacted testily. Francisca's growing community of *beatas* was but one of the battlegrounds on which the two camps confronted each other.

From the *beaterio*'s inception, Caballero y Ocio had been its chief benefactor in terms of its material necessities. The new building, the hermitages, and the chapel were constructed at his expense. As for most of their daily needs and spiritual direction, the *beatas* relied on the friars of Santa Cruz. Francisca's steady stream of notes to Fray Antonio de los Ángeles and the vicar and guardian of Santa Cruz during this period show the community to be in constant need of sustenance, material and spiritual. Flour for bread, maize for tortillas, chocolate for the morning and afternoon beverage, mutton, oblates, wine, spiritual talks, masses, and confessions mixed in her notes with the constant repetition of daily chores, be they for the benefit of the soul or body. This distribution of duties among Francisca's benefactors worked smoothly during Margil's tenure as chief engine behind the projected foundation. Between him and Caballero y Ocio there existed a friendship of sorts—Caballero, for example, had contributed toward the cost of Propaganda Fide's missions. Both men were committed to founding a conventional institution of some sort and shared the similar character traits of charisma and determination. Caballero y Ocio opened his church to the Santa Cruz friars during their missions to the townspeople of Querétaro.

Once Margil had departed, however, things were not that simple. The Santa Cruz friars found that the secular colleagues of Caballero y Ocio were increasingly making incursions into the spiritual administration of the *beaterio*, a territory they considered their own. Their grumblings in the beginning of the century got the headmistress into no end of trouble. Díez, in particular, showed unrestrained hostility toward the seculars. He began to miss visits to his charges and claim illness when Francisca climbed the hill to Santa Cruz to see him. And on the occasions in which she finally managed to see him, he told her curtly that his absences were God's punishment for dallying for so long with the seculars.[81]

Don Juan, for his part, seemed ready to step in whenever the Santa Cruz friars neglected their duties. He offered to pay for mass every day at the *beaterio* as well as over Semana Santa. But Francisca did not dare to tell the friars of his proposal. She rejected it and accepted only charity to buy candles and two pesos to have a priest come over and say mass. But when the Franciscans continued to neglect to say masses at the *beaterio*'s chapel, don Juan lost his patience. He told Francisca that he would send directly for license from Rome for any priest from any order to say mass there. He did not wait for her reply, but sent the letter off immediately. Francisca confided in Fray Antonio that she was overjoyed at the prospect of having masses said with so little trouble, but she worried that the guardian would be hurt and upset. A little later, however, things worsened as tensions ran higher than ever between the orders. The guardian of Santa Cruz asked Caballero y Ocio if the friars could use the church of Guadalupe for a mission. The request was logical since the two orders enjoyed a hermandad, which stipulated mutual help with confessions and masses on the orders' feast days and allowed the Franciscans the privilege of preaching missions at the church of Guadalupe. Don Juan personally was in favor of it, but the order rejected the petition. The Franciscans were so angered that they forbade Francisca from speaking to don Juan again. Caballero y Ocio himself was devastated at the friars' wrath and complained to Francisca that "if we cannot behave well with our brothers, then neither will we with our *projimos*." She reported to Fray Antonio that she had never seen him in such low spirits and did not dare tell him that she had been forbidden to speak to him.[82]

But in spite of mutual irritability, the relationship between the *beaterio* of Santa Rosa and the *colegio* of Santa Cruz was an inescapable fact. Francisca tried to reciprocate, to the best of her capacity, the favors that kept flowing down the hill to her humble abode. For some time, she and the *beatas* served as the friars' bakers. Flour and sugar arrived from Santa Cruz and were returned as buns and pastries. She also sent them apricots, melons, and other fruit from her orchard, turkeys from her corral, nourishing broths and meals when they were sick, as well as powders and pills that had proven effective with the women's various illnesses.

Francisca, who had been free from the age of nine to follow her own methods for achieving holiness, now found herself at the mature age of twenty-eight, tied up with the sort of tasks she had tried to escape while a child and young adult in her family's home. She baked, sewed, made pastries, and received secular and ecclesiastical visitors whom she cajoled and manipulated into rendering the service she required of them. She also marshaled a community of women with varied capacities and talents into following a ritual schedule mirroring that of a convent. After a few years of this, the famous Teresian maxim that "the Lord works among pots and pans" might no longer have seemed that spiritually attractive.[83] While she had dreamed of being a nun most of her life, she now found this new life far too constricting. Her own ambitions were not that easy to satisfy. She was after all still writing to Fray Antonio de Margil, the New World's most holy man, whose example she much preferred to follow to the less inspired Fray José Díez. And Margil had not let go of her. He fired off letters from far corners of the empire advising his peers on the best methods by which to confess her and demanded to remain informed of her progress.[84]

As her administrative duties multiplied Francisca began to retire more and more to her hermitage at the far end of the orchard, leaving a substitute to attend to her duties as mother superior. In the hermitage, she fasted, prayed, performed religious exercises, and attended to the urgent matter of the long abandoned missions in Texas, whence she still flew every Thursday with her guardian angel. Only to Fray Antonio did she confess her confusion at her dual existence. It seemed that whenever she tried to look at herself as a stranger, from the outside, she saw "a very bad woman, converted to the love of God, desiring to do penance with a hatred and fatigue for everything that is earthly, and yet I am not like that for I am of such a happy disposition that I would enjoy with perfection all this [earthly endeavors], and yet I feel so strange."[85]

In another letter she told him that "in my interior there seem to exist two persons, one of peace and tranquility, and another of anxiety and pain." Her confusion during these early years of the *beaterio* is comprehensible. Gaining public status at such an early age under the wing of the Franciscans had prepared her for a lifetime of service as an icon, a personage who was consulted and revered in her hermitage and was free of the worldly occupations that hindered the spiritual flight of common souls. Her daily duties, as well as her constant scheming to found an institution of some sort, kept her physically active and sociable instead of remaining locked away as a holy recluse. This life was a far cry from the one she had envisioned, and yet she found that she enjoyed it. Her pleasure brought guilt and misery at having forsaken the spiritual paradise that had been offered her. With Fray Antonio, at least, she did not have to pretend. While with Díez she needed to maintain her status, to demonstrate that she was still a preferred daughter of God, with her trusted friend she could admit to her internal confusion. Since self-deprecation was the basis of their spiritual quest Francisca could indulge her appetite for extravagance, making Fray Antonio her companion not only on the climb up the Mount Carmel but in her repeated descents into hell. She wrote to him anxiously: "I read your letters, and cried at the feet of my Lady, for it seems that you understand my pain and suffering so well. Sometimes I suffer more in a day than in many years altogether; hell has launched itself against me. I have no words to describe it. . . . Until the Lord deigns to take away the clouds that cover the beloved sun of my soul, I will suffer until the end of the world."[86]

The bedrock of Francisca's mission, Fray Antonio Margil de Jesús, was gone, and in his stead was the stern and depressive Fray Díez, his spirit blighted. She found him absolutely unsatisfactory from the very beginning. He was not a hands-on sort of a confessor, which caused her to complain to Fray Antonio that "he does not even write to me, he leaves me alone, and that does not suit me at all."[87] If he did not write then he did not visit either, telling her that he did not have the "will." The few surviving letters from Díez to Francisca demonstrate this lack of determination and enthusiasm. In an undated and hurried note he apologized for having forgotten that "today was my turn." In all probability this signified that he had forgotten that it was his day to say mass at the *beaterio*, and as for her coming to Santa Cruz he told her that he would leave that to her disposition.[88] Such indecisiveness was not part of Francisca's vocabulary, at least not when it came to relations with her fellow mortals.

Over the years the tension between them heightened. Díez did not seem to acknowledge—or perhaps chose not to—her special status as Santa Cruz's "*hija espiritual.*" In fact, he seems to have resented all the qualities that had made her interesting in Margil's eyes. He tried to get rid of her troublesome and fixed ideas regarding how she should proceed in her ritual life. Over Easter one year, he ordered her to participate in the procession that would descend the hill from Santa Cruz on Good Friday. Francisca was mortified since it had been her habit to undertake a vigil over the holy sacrament from the early morning on Holy Thursday until Friday night: "my dead confessors and my father Margil, have always given me freedom," she complained to Fray Antonio, "but now for my sins they order me to go home after the mass and to participate in the procession." It was "much more devout," she retorted angrily, to perform the Stations of the Cross without taking part in public demonstrations of faith.[89] Throughout the years, Francisca sought divine recourse and prayed that "God soften his heart and deliver it from the enemy." And while she vented her frustration in letters to Fray Antonio she was not afraid to remind Díez directly of his responsibilities: "Do not be afflicted Your Paternity, nor saddened, keep up your spirit; I tell of my travails for it is your office to know them in order to alleviate my pains and commend me to our Lord," she told him in the early stages of their relationship.[90] Over a month later, on February 2, 1704, she scolded him for his slovenly efforts at letter writing and informed him that if he cared so little about her while she was in the middle of a spiritual crisis she could just as well be "dead and in purgatory."[91]

Francisca believed that Díez's difficult disposition hindered his advances toward God. Repeatedly she saw him standing next to the joyous Fray Antonio and Margil, who turned their faces toward divine glory, while Díez's face expressed "pain and sadness." The result of all this was that Francisca's enthusiasm for letter writing diminished over the years to the point where even Díez complained that she could no longer fill even one *cuaderno* a week. In November 1706, in the midst of the crisis over the *beaterio*, headaches began to consume her. The well-meaning Sánchez staged healing sessions in which he took hold of Francisca's head, prayed magnificats, and said the Gospel. His techniques only seemed to aggravate the pain, but he would not give up and fetched some relics that he claimed were from the arm of San Nicolás. At that point, the patient felt as if a bone had broken in her head and fainted.[92]

The worst took place in the confessional. There, after Francisca poured out to Díez the great treasures that the Lord had bestowed on her soul since she had last seen him, the friar retorted impatiently that she really did not have to bother with all these descriptions—they would not make him love or esteem her more. This left her feeling strangely ashamed and unsure of herself, and she resolved not to confide the dearest secrets of her soul to her confessor anymore, for fear he might think she did so to gain his favor. Viewed in a larger perspective, these mortifications had to be another of God's gifts to achieve some balance in her otherwise favorable mystical life.[93] Despite such an optimistic mindset, however, Díez's attitude nagged at Francisca and caused her to doubt her own pleasure in the company of God. It reached the point where she dreaded going to his confessional and before doing so tried to eradicate anything that might be called self-love or arrogance in her. The tension made her feel physically ill, and during confession she only recounted the mundane *cosas de obediencia*. When Díez asked her questions afterward she answered them timorously, afraid that her answers would displease him. If he did not ask, she would spring relieved from the confessional.

As these events unfolded, the struggle between Díez and Francisca's secular priests intensified over the foundation of a convent or *colegio*. Díez clearly did not content himself with merely complaining to the archbishop and advising that the *beaterio* be dissolved. Instead, he vented his displeasure at his disciple's improper confidence and self-love through other channels or in the person of the Franciscan commissary general of the Indies, Fray Lucas Álvarez. On September 30, 1708, Álvarez wrote from Toledo to Díez that he had read his complaint of the "falsity of the *beaterio*," which was "what saddened me the most because I know of the damage that can originate from this kind of spirituality which, if it is not managed by experienced subjects of good and solid virtue, can serve to discredit the religious life." Díez and Álvarez had both been nurtured in a post-Tridentine Iberian climate in which *beatas* were problematic because they aspired to elite spirituality from a humble social position. Obviously, both shared the Mexican Inquisition's suspicions of such women in the colony.[94] Nevertheless, Álvarez asked the friar to show charity to the *beatas*, to assist rather than abandon them.[95]

Under such circumstances, the trust between *padre* and *hija* inevitably broke down. Sometime around 1710, Díez threatened to throw one of the oldest members of the community Magdalena "*la quintera*" from her room, presumably on the grounds that she could not pay for her upkeep. Francisca protested vehemently to Fray Antonio, citing her long years of service, poverty, and humility. "She does not know how to do anything else," she wrote to Fray

Antonio and with her usual resourcefulness resolved to alert Margil and don Matías to the problem.

Eventually, she became exhausted by her drawn-out battle with Díez over the dissolution or survival of the *beaterio*, and her waning enthusiasm gave way to a full-fledged spiritual crisis. In 1707, she sent several letters of complaint to Margil who at the time was engaged in reforming the errant population of distant and wild Zacatecas. As in Querétaro, he hauled out his community to perform public *via cruces* and had fourteen large crosses built on the outskirts of the city to remind its rowdy miners of who was responsible for their good luck.[96] In the midst of his busy schedule Margil still found time to compose diplomatic answers to Francisca's desperate missives. Do not stop trusting in God, he reminded her, even if the *padre espiritual* was unsatisfactory. As for Díez, Margil had but one piece of advice: "do not ever leave him, he will try you a lot but even if he curses you, never leave him." To conclude his exhortations he ordered her to prostrate herself "before the entire universe; the sky and the earth" and promise God to never to deny him in anything "which means forever; which means *in anything*, daughter forever, forever, forever, never deny him in anything, anything, anything."[97]

### "Midway"

In 1709, at the age of thirty-five, Francisca de los Ángeles penned a description of her mental life that some moderns might characterize as a mid-life crisis: "I feel like someone who has important business to perform and midway remembers that he has forgotten the crucial documents. That is how I feel, midway through my life."[98] Feeling old and harried, she made her way through the hundreds of small tasks that awaited her each day: assuring the continuing flow of charity to the *beaterio*, supervising the girls, resolving their squabbles, taking care of the sick, arranging for the visits of shoemakers and tailors, carpenters and artisans, priests and confessors. It all made her listless and melancholy, unable to turn to God except in communal prayer, during which she felt distracted and insecure. She knew the Lord was angry with her, for she had never experienced the holy fear known to the saints. Instead, all her life she had been nagged with doubts regarding God's presence and the devil's machinations. One day, as she made her way from her hermitage across the orchard to the house, she was suddenly struck immobile and had to sit down at the foot of a tree, where God showed himself to her ablaze with wrath.[99] Such visions made her timorous and unsure of herself. Whereas before she had felt included and favored by the celestial court she now sensed that the church, though heaven's representative on earth, might still call her her daughter but that such a status was no longer on offer up above.[100]

At times, visions appeared out of the darkness that comforted her and provided divine warmth, but they were few and far between. She was still given the privilege of feeling pain over Lent and Easter. Now, it was no longer a glorious suffering that gave way to the joy of the resurrection but a rather drab feeling that simply left her exhausted. Having in the past easily filled over thirty flowing pages with descriptions of her experiences over Easter, she now sent Díez a few insipid lines, ending with a despairing note: "of other things I will not give you an account since they are not important."[101] If there existed a celestial comforter in Francisca's affliction it was the ever steady and merciful Virgin. On September 20, 1710, Francisca wrote to Díez of a vision of the Lady. Her creative juices sapped, however, she had to borrow the words of a preacher she had once heard who described seeing the image of the Virgin of Guadalupe as seeming to contain and give birth to all the glory of heaven. Francisca's description of the image stopped short after a few lines, however, and she told Díez that she found herself "every day less able to explain these things."[102] She now only wrote, at her confessor's insistence, dutiful letters on her experiences on important feast days. However, her prose was more occupied with demonstrating the correctness and humility with which she performed the prescribed prostrations and other rituals, almost as if she needed to convince herself of their worth.

Aside from Fray Antonio's continuing friendship and Margil's occasional letters, spiritual nourishment was not forthcoming from Santa Cruz. As Francisca ceased to pen interesting mystical experiences, Díez stopped writing back, and if she turned to him, afflicted by the devil's persecutions, he told her she was suffering from headaches.[103] Taking his lead, she blamed herself and her difficult disposition for her affliction. On October 22, 1710, she wrote: "Many times now I have seen myself living several kinds of lives without ever being content in any of them, because in everything the Lord has found it to be his pleasure to send me bitterness, so that when looking at things from the outside it seems that what I want is sweet, but upon execution it is very bitter . . . only when I am alone in solitude are the enemies kept at bay."[104] This downtrodden woman was a far cry from the confident *mujer santa*, spiritual daughter of the founders of Santa Cruz and avid disciple of Margil's mysticism. She no longer had the will—or she felt, the physical strength—to climb the hill to Santa Cruz to seek solace in the desert.

Instead, consolation, surprisingly, came from a less interesting direction: don Matías de Hijar, the *beaterio's* great benefactor and admirer and friend of Margil, who had begun to spend ever longer periods of time in his little cell there. He prescribed frequent communion for Francisca, and she followed his advice, feeling better every time. By 1709, she was also writing short, friendly letters to Fray Juan de Ortega, Santa Cruz's new vicar. Díez seems to have caught wind of this new friendship and become jealous, for in a hurried note to Ortega that year she begged him not to show her letters to Díez since it seemed to affect him so.[105] Her crisis had not deflected Francisca's natural response to opportunity. She quickly began to fire off successive missives to the vicar inquiring after his delicate health, begging for only a few lines to assure her. When he was sick she promised not to write longer letters so as not to "calentarle la cabeza."

# 7   Mid-Life, 1711–1712

### Earthly Losses—Divine Gains

At the end of 1710, Francisca's sister Gertrudis fell ill and deteriorated rapidly. At one point, Francisca thought she had expired without receiving the sacraments, but thankfully divine intervention assured her a few more days to reconcile herself. Christmas celebrations at the *beaterio* were overshadowed by Gertrudis's illness. As her sister drew nearer death Francisca's heart "seemed to split open," but the Lord consoled her, informing her that her sister was one of the "predestined souls." Francisca told her not to forget her guardian angel, to call for him with fervor at the hour of death, and to be grateful to him for having liberated her from earthly misery. Her words seemed to have had some effect, for a few moments later Gertrudis pointed in the air, her face "filling with a strange light," and exclaimed that she had seen the angel wearing exquisite robes. Greatly relieved at the good death that Gertrudis seemed to be approaching, Francisca waited on her sister until she died a few days later, on January 2, 1711. At the moment of her death, Francisca asked God that if there was any waiting period required for her sister in purgatory to let her shoulder the pains so Gertrudis might proceed through and enjoy the peace of heaven. Her plea was heard, and Francisca was given such tremendous headaches and fevers for the next few days that she could not feel her interior pain.

Once the visits of townspeople to offer their condolences were over, however, Francisca, instead of rejoicing with her sister on her release, felt overtaken by a sudden grief that entailed greater darkness and travails than she had ever experienced before. If she had been allowed to hasten Gertrudis's stay in purgatory by taking on some of her pains, then she felt certain that her sister's suffering must be terrible indeed.[1] The experience lasted until the eve of the feast of the Virgin, or approximately one month, when Francisca was given divine hope that her sister had gone forth to eternal rest. The Santa Cruz friars honored their obligations to the *beatas* and buried Gertrudis with due ceremony in their cemetery. Later, her bones were disinterred and laid in her father's coffin, much to Francisca's pleasure.[2]

If spring brought release from grief and hope of peace, then summer renewed Francisca's pains. At ten o'clock in the evening on June 23, Fray

Antonio de los Ángeles died. Francisca had followed the rapid progress of his illness with dread, sent him garbanzo beans fried with greens, and inquired if he had been bled or not.[3] On the day of his death, she wrote to Ortega that she believed her friend was now enjoying a "beatific vision of our loving master." "I only cry and feel the absence of his lovely person, and cannot write at the moment due to the weight of my grief."[4] Two days after his death, she wrote Ortega another quick note, scribbled in large letters, in which she apologized for not having written and explained that she had been feeling so "absent from herself" that it had left her incapacitated. Ortega, who was as affected as she was, added to her letter a note describing the growing sentiment among *queretanos* of Fray Antonio's holiness. A pious servant present at the moment of the friar's last breath swore that he had seen him ascend to heaven in the company of five angels with such beauty and clarity that although he was in the darkness of his cell at the time, he saw the event in bright daylight. A laywoman in Santa Clara, Beatriz María de Jesús, unaware of Fray Antonio's death, testified how the friar had appeared to her on the morning of Saint John's mass and told her that he was about to go and enjoy the fruits of his suffering "in the paradise of religion." Then Ortega added that "another person of famed virtue and very experienced in divine favors, called Francisca de los Ángeles, spiritual sister of Fray Antonio for twenty years, so intimate with the friar that there existed no secrets between the two, said that he had appeared to her as his body was lowered into the grave, very beautiful and shining and had given her a tight embrace and told her he was about to enjoy the rewards of his travails."[5]

Francisca mobilized the entire community at Santa Rosa to facilitate his progress through purgatory in the unlikely event that any obstacles arose to hinder his speedy entry into paradise. The *beatas* performed novenas, the Stations of the Cross, attended as many masses as possible in the town's churches, and took communion frequently. When not thus engaged, they maintained silence and withdrew to their cells and hermitages for spiritual exercises.[6] Their labors, probably duplicated at Santa Cruz and other monasteries and homes, were rewarded when finally, at the end of the month, the town was given divine confirmation of Fray Antonio's new status in heaven. A person who had been given an object that had been in the dead friar's possession testified that upon receiving it he had prayed to God to "remedy the many necessities of the faithful, especially the drought which had become severe." As it was the end of June and the rainy season was late the city was in a state of panic. On that particular day, the sky had been an electric blue and the sun fierce. Suddenly, a cloud rose and poured such "copious rain that it seemed that the city of Querétaro would flood, and the water rose and spilled out of the drains and in a short time, the reservoir was filled."[7]

Fray Antonio's body was moved to the chapel of Nuestra Señora de Belén, approximately a year after his death. During the ceremony to celebrate the transferal further supernatural signs affirmed his presence in heaven. A storm tore boards off the roof of the church, which caused a stampede as the terrified congregation fought to get out. Francisca regularly visited the holy man's tomb and saw him frequently in dreams and visions. In July, she reported two sightings of the friar. One led to a serious headache, but the second announced that he would send her badly needed water, a promise he kept a few days later when a benefactor sent over several barrels.[8] She tried to still her grief by commissioning a painter to execute a portrait of her beloved, and when she did not find its resemblance close enough she commissioned another artist. Hearing that the Santa Cruz friars planned a biography of the holy man she was overjoyed and hoped that her heart would "serve as paper and that it say without saying a word all that it is feeling."[9] She tried to remember that Fray Antonio was now her advocate in heaven, and hoping that he would keep his friends "mui presentes" in his eternal happiness she set about arranging a schedule dedicated to his remembrance.[10]

On every Christmas Day thereafter, Francisca habitually kept vigil at the chapel of Belén in Santa Cruz where he was buried. And around the day of Saint Francis she dedicated three days to celebrate her friend's life: the first to his birth, the second to his entry into religion, and on the day of the saint his profession at Santa Cruz.[11] Such occasions would invariably lead to communication with her good friend and advocate up in heaven. In an undated letter Francisca mentioned having suffered terrible stomach pains to the degree that she thought she would die, when the friar appeared to her in a dream and administered medicinal water to her which healed her immediately. The next day she was able to celebrate his entry into religion.[12] There were further arrangements to be made, however, since Fray Antonio's death left hundreds of her letters unguarded, many of which contained harsh criticism of his brethren. She later begged her new confessor to find them and burn them, but he clearly did not comply with her wish.[13]

Sometime in the spring of 1711, however, Francisca's prospects began to brighten. By means unknown to us, she managed to finally extradite herself from Díez's melancholy grip and obtain a new confessor, Fray Ángel García, who was sympathetic and much more suited to her own spiritual flair. Francisca had been scheming toward this end for a while. Among her undated letters is a message to Fray Ángel in which she told him to by all means not remind Díez to come to the *beaterio*; however, if *he* would have any time to visit the community they would be delighted. Otherwise, the Lord would take care of them.[14] How Díez took this change we do not know, but for Francisca the tension between them had been unbearable for years. With a sigh of relief wafting through the pages, she explained to Fray Ángel how for four or five years now "I have found myself lacking in the liberty and sincerity, forthrightness and satisfaction which I should have felt in communicating the matters of my soul to the confessor."[15]

The end of the relationship with Díez came in a traumatic manner. He told Francisca finally that he had scruples about confessing her and that she should find another. Indeed, the benevolent but rather dull Padre Rodríguez should do for her. Gathering some of her scattered spirits about her, Francisca asked how she had failed in her obedience. When he refused to answer, she told him flat out that he was her confessor and that she would not go. Thankfully, a few days later, the Lord whispered in her ear that she should wait until after Easter, at which time a remedy would present itself. Díez then promptly fell ill, leaving Francisca in peace and quiet until after the resurrection. When Díez did come to the *beaterio* he explained to her that he really could not continue as her confessor when she would not give him a full account of her soul's life. Francisca answered that for the moment she had nothing to recount except despair, but that it was his sacred duty to "listen, teach and console." Díez stubbornly retorted that he would not confess her anymore, at which Francisca lost her patience and told him without further frills that "if she had to fall dead at his feet to be confessed she would," that he was "a minister of God and I a soul redeemed with the blood of Jesus Christ."

These last words seemed to have an effect on him, for when she gave him eight days to think about it he resolved that he would take her back and govern her soul until the end of his days. She should now forget her past travails. After this bitter victory, Francisca could not, however, and she resolved to leave him before he threw her out again.[16] Corresponding with other friars she had learned that she was not the only martyr chosen to suffer Díez. Ortega sent her letters he had received from the old man, bewildered as to how to tackle his fearsome person. An experienced Francisca advised holy patience in regard to Díez's "duro genio."[17]

And as soon as Francisca had made the decision to leave Díez she felt "an infinite relief and comfort" in her soul. It was not as if she did not have other friends and comforters. Every Monday, the rector of the Jesuits stopped by to help her reconcile and to give talks on divine love and peace through suffering. In the end it was the Jesuit who advised her to speak to Fray Ángel. The friar agreed to her proposal, which was to go on reconciling every Monday with the Jesuit and if a grave concern arose she would write promptly to the friar. Finally, once Margil was back in Querétaro, he would decide upon a future arrangement. Unaware of his disciple's stubborn actions, Margil had sent her a letter dated June 21 in which he exhorted Francisca to persevere, for in the person of Díez God incarnate was bent on testing her faith so she could be humiliated as Jesus had been humiliated. "I understand your worries," he wrote, "for they are mine as well," but in order to bend to the will of God it was imperative that she reconcile with Díez.[18] Francisca, however, had not attained the requisite degree of holiness to let the will of God ravage her further and ended her outpouring on a gloomy note: "I am nothing, and what might have made me saintly has ruined me."[19]

Nevertheless, a few days later she seems to have been feeling better, for she sent Fray Ángel a long list of mortifications she wanted to undertake. These included eight hours of prayer a day, three hundred prostrations in each of which she praised the names of Jesus and the Virgin, the Stations on her knees wearing all her cilices, discipline three times at the hour of the Lady, and all complemented by as much fasting as she could tolerate. But no sooner had Francisca sent off these ambitious plans than she had to confess to Fray Ángel that she simply was not cut out for these methodological and time-consuming approaches to God. First, her duties as headmistress of the *beaterio* took too many hours off her days, and, second, the Lord continued to whisk her away to divine regions without warning while she would be preoccupied in her daily tasks. Having made up her mind to follow her new regime, for example, something happened, and she could not remember what she did from Monday afternoon until Wednesday morning. Instead of following her scheduled rituals in her hermitage, she was taken away to purgatory where she met the souls of people she had known and was reminded of a duty she had neglected throughout her spiritual crisis: to pray for the exit of souls from purgatory. After this exciting journey Francisca grimly tried to focus on her lonely ritual but was only able to do one discipline and some prostrations, read a little, and write her letter to Fray Ángel. It occurred to her that now that she had obtained permission for her ambitious reforming plans, she simply did not feel like carrying them out and felt it ridiculous to separate herself from the others.[20]

Francisca then no longer felt that divine providence had wholly forsaken her. To undertake this next phase in her mystical life with flourish, she decided to ask Fray Ángel's permission for a general confession, an arduous task that might take days. Fray Ángel, perhaps aware of her reputation for long-windedness, gently advised her to stay with the established pattern of weekly confessions and letter writing. Her enthusiasm thus contained, Francisca nevertheless seems to have had a much brighter outlook on life during these summer months than in the preceding years. She wrote long, caring notes to her friend Fray Juan de Ortega in which she worried about his health, talked about her own and the various powders and medicinal waters she tried for her problems, and discussed her daily occupations, such as the size of the boxes used to carry the miniature saints' images made by the *beatas*.[21] In short, Francisca seemed back to her usual self, busy and inspired. This interval of peace, however, was broken at the end of 1712 when the Inquisition again entered her life.

### Relics and Memorias

The trouble arose, when on November 22 Fray José Guerra of the Propaganda Fide college in Zacatecas wrote to the Inquisitors in Mexico City reporting that the president of the College, Fray Antonio Margil de Jesús, was in the habit of circulating several crucifixes along with notes containing grants of indulgences among the population. Though they were objects of common value that could easily be bought in a store, Margil declared that they were "originals" and that carrying them would assure the indulgences promised in the grants that came with them. Apparently, they came from a *beata* in Querétaro, Francisca de los Ángeles, whose virtue was considered "tan relevante." The friar had his doubts, however. How could the virtue of a mere *beata* exceed that of Saint Francis and the Holy Pontifex? It seemed to Guerra that such persons did contain the keys to the treasures promised by indulgences, while these claims by a mere woman could lead to the slandering of Margil's good name, whose fame he well knew extended even to Spain, as well as the reputation of the apostolic colleges that were so *provechosos* to Christianity. Therefore, Guerra asked the Inquisition to clarify two matters for him. First, since the crucifixes obviously came from the Zacatecas region, why were they originals, and original to whom? Second, he wanted it clarified whether these indulgences had been certified by the church. If not, he pressed the Inquisition to do something about the matter, for it was intolerable that for such a person as a *beata* the colleges and Fray Antonio Margil de Jesús should suffer.

Fray José then revealed his own ambitions. He asked the Inquisition to grant him the power to act on behalf of the tribunal since there was no commissioner in Zacatecas. Whatever his motives—jealousy, scruples, or zealousness—he wanted to witness Margil's humiliation though, fearful of the famous friar, he like a good politician asked the Inquisitors not to reveal to Margil the identity of his accuser. Ironically, thirteen years later, upon Margil's death, Guerra would publish a laudatory sermon on the holy man.[22]

On December 6, the Inquisitor don Francisco de Garzaron wrote to Margil from Mexico City, demanding an explanation for the origins of the indulgences, their promises, and their value to the local population. Furthermore, he ordered a halt to their distribution until further notice from the tribunal. On December 19, Margil obediently sent the indulgences in his possession and declared himself ready to bow to the authority of the Holy Office since it took the "place of God on this earth."[23] Then he proceeded to relate the story of Francisca and thus revealed his pivotal role as chief propagandist of her fame.

Margil declared that it was common knowledge in Querétaro that God had chosen Francisca for Himself at an early age. Having made a youthful vow of chastity she now lived with other tertiaries in the *beaterio* of Santa Rosa with public virtue and example. While under the tutelage of Fray Sitjar, famed for his assured governance of souls, friars and seculars had begun to seek Francisca out, bringing her rosaries and other objects she took with her to be blessed during her reunions with God. Sitjar had made her write all her experiences down in little notebooks he gave her, which were now kept under lock and key at the college in Querétaro. Francisca's interim confessor, Escaray, had seen with his own eyes the grace of the stigmata in her bloody habit. He had told her he would have it washed and had given her a new one, but instead of washing it he had sent it to Mexico to show to other Franciscans who examined it in secrecy. The matter finally reached the Inquisition, which had made the usual inquiries. Margil then proceeded to lend his own weight to the matter and attested that in the twelve or thirteen years that he had governed Francisca's soul he had seen the stigmata marks a few times. Once, having fainted when the wounds in her chest opened and her habit became soaked, Francisca had had a vision that her guardian angel soaked up the blood with a handkerchief. She had given the handkerchief to Margil who had kept it and then given it to Díez, who possessed several more. Once he had asked to see her feet, and she had acquiesced with exemplary modesty. Examining them he had noted the lumps, thick and hard, without a sign of blood circulating through them.

He vouched for her integrity: "As for the aforementioned Francisca, I with my limited understanding have not found in her anything which might appear malevolent, but rather a profound humility with which she received all the favors God chose to communicate to his chosen; I have never heard anything contrary on her, not from the friars who have governed her, nor from the many *varones espirituales* who, with permission of their confessor, speak with her. Rather, all leave with great edification due to her modesty, humility and discretion."[24]

Margil then confirmed that Francisca had given the relics away at the order and behest of her confessor and "others." When Margil had left on mission, the relics had been included in his modest equipage. With "a purely natural faith" he had distributed them among his parishioners in Guatemala. He told them that they were from the famed María de Jesús de Agreda since one of their attributes was that they provided the same kind and amount of indulgences as objects from the Spanish holy woman. This small lie had been necessary to protect his *hija* but to no avail since many of the friars he met in Guatemala had already heard of Francisca. With discretion they had asked if these objects were really hers. Since they were men of confidence he told them the truth and gave them a copy of the indulgences they carried. In Mexico City and in Zacatecas Margil had continued to distribute these objects "with the same faith" but under the guise of Agreda's name. A lay friar in the great Franciscan convent in Mexico City, who already corresponded with Francisca, had guessed rightly as to their origin, and Margil allowed him to copy the grants. At this stage Margil decided to go out on a limb and stake his reputation on the power of her relics: "I have had experience of the impact they have had on many souls in terms of perseverance, renewed good intentions, and in the temporal, in difficult births and illnesses, and many people have told me the same, without neither them nor me, placing too much faith in these things than that which one can regarding a soul that lives in total obedience and like a conduct of all things that God permits."[25]

Since Margil and "others" had distributed the objects with such caution, they had not thought to ask permission of the Holy Tribunal. Had they done so, he added, they would not have been pressed to maintain the secrecy surrounding Francisca's name. Margil unabashedly attested to his belief in the power of objects from holy women, for he testified that he also kept locked in a box some objects from Madre Agreda as well as Saint Joan of the Cross so when he died they could be distributed to others who might need them. His treasure chest also contained a small Christ's image of known holiness since it had been given by Innocent XI to Fray Antonio Llinás, founder of the colleges of Propaganda Fide in the Indies.[26]

In Mexico City, the Inquisitors efficiently decided to process Francisca's case with that of a Madre Geronima, a *beata* of the same region whose grants, much longer and more detailed than Francisca's, had come to their attention. On January 14, 1713, the Inquisitors gave their opinion of the *memorias* of the two women. Such writing, they declared was "impious for it is indecorous to the sovereign majesty of the Queen of the Angels . . . in its general context it is erroneous doctrine formulated for vulgar, uneducated and novelty hungry people." They admitted that the Lord might "by virtue of his divinity" bestow such graces on devotional objects. Nevertheless, they should never be acknowledged in case they proved a challenge to orthodoxy. They concluded that such grants and relics demonstrated "false piety and superstition" and should be handed into the Holy Office by those who possessed them. Harsh criticism, indeed, but strangely enough the opinions named only Geronima by name, omitting Francisca's. Her *memorias* were definitely part and parcel of the vulgar piety the Inquisitors discerned in these documents, but in all probability it was Margil's fame and prestige as well as his defense of his spiritual daughter that prevented the Tribunal from mentioning Francisca's name. And when the edict was published, Geronima was mentioned first, her name in italics, while Francisca was mentioned at the end of the document and without italics.[27]

She did not escape punishment, however. The edict, which banned the grants and ordered all relics in relation with them brought to the tribunal within six days of its publication, was placed on church doors all over the colony. It was read in the cathedral of Mexico City on February 5, 1713, to an audience of the Real Audiencia and the *cabildo secular* as well as to a crowd of people.[28] A month later, the edict was read in the church of the Great Convent in Querétaro on a holiday after the sermon of the main mass and then hung on its doors. Five additional copies were hung on the doors of churches and convents throughout the city; their superiors were ordered to read it out loud during mass. Immediately, townspeople began to turn in rosaries, crosses, and medallions blessed by God in Francisca's presence, and although they were eventually returned to their owners—with a reminder that they were to be venerated only for what they were—some refused to take them back since that would be contrary to their "scruples." Francisca's relationship with townspeople was probably severely damaged. The chronicler of the *beaterio* of Santa Rosa, María de Jesús, hotly declared that the whole affair had been pure fiction emanating from malicious minds from beginning to end. Nevertheless, it is clear that many a pious *queretano*, fearful of deviating from established doctrine, broke off relations with their holy woman.[29]

Francisca sought solace from her new confessor, Fray Ángel, who conscientiously ordered her to write down her own account of the affair. In Fray Ángel, Francisca could expect a more sympathetic ear than in Díez since the friar had himself suffered a close brush with the Inquisition only a few months earlier. He had been denounced by a Querétaro cleric for publicly attacking the secular clergy for their insistence on marching before the Franciscans in the procession of Corpus Cristi. As his accuser grudgingly admitted, however, Fray Ángel was "much loved by everyone for his singular *cariño* and virtues" and *queretanos* listened to his advice and teachings as if he were an oracle. Probably because of Fray Ángel's good standing in town, the Inquisition did nothing about the matter, but it nevertheless affected the friar, as Francisca noted in a consoling note at the time.[30]

At Fray Ángel's orders, Francisca began to write down her recollections. She started her letter calmly, assuring the friar that in the beginning when her confessor, Sitjar, had come to her with relics he had wanted blessed, she had locked them up in a box, trying "a thousand times" to forget about them. It had seemed to her that anything she asked actively of the Lord, anything that showed her human desires, might "disturb the nudity and passivity with which I should approach prayer." She had been unable to foresee, however, that she might be deceived in the matter, though, she quickly reminded the friar, such fears had always been present in her soul. Just looking at the objects had given her pain, and she had said to the Lord, "look into the heart of your servant [her confessor], see his passion, and please do as he asks for your honor and glory." This she repeated day after day, until finally, while in prayer, her thoughts far away from the relics, she heard His voice whisper with love *His* agreement with her petition. This confirming experience occurred repeatedly, but nevertheless at times the Lord seemed neutral in the matter. The ultimate agreement with her petition came during her most mystical experiences. "Lost to myself, in that sea of grace without knowing anything, without remembering anything . . . so lost," she looked in God's presence at the rosaries and crosses and felt suddenly the power of His gift, which was "not only communicated through rosaries, crosses and medallions, but in our very essence."

The letter could not fail to arouse her confessor's sympathy, for it not only expressed Francisca's fears of such grave matters and emphasized Sitjar's role as manipulator, it demonstrated that she believed that though God might give gifts through tangible objects, he was more inclined to infuse mere mortals directly with his grace. In all things, then, Fray Ángel's new spiritual daughter, despite the doubts cast on her reputation by the scandal, appeared timorous, humble, and superbly spiritual in her understanding of her nothingness and the overwhelming, uncontrollable power of God. Affirming her orthodox timidity, Francisca finished her letter in an anxious tone. Fearing that this light she had seen had perhaps been an illusion of the devil's she condemned her own nature: "I do not possess true resignation when it comes to the grace of suffering, I am ungrateful, I confess my ingratitude, may the Lord watch out for me and bathe my soul in the blood he spilled for it."[31]

Having calmed her confessor's worries, Francisca nevertheless remained anxious at heart. In a subsequent letter to Ortega, she recounted an unsettling dream. Some important and respected people came to her. She was frightened but quiet and performed acts of resignation in preparation for her interrogation. They accused her of being ungrateful to God, and since she felt the same she listened with great care and attention. They claimed that hardly any of the things she had told her confessors about the demoniac scandal and her own Inquisition process in 1691 had been true. Then they proceeded to show her all the blessings and graces she had received from the Lord from the time she had use of her reason until the present day. She understood that they were right; she had wasted all her gifts without gratitude. It seemed to her that Judgment Day had come. Nevertheless, on her side she could discern a distant being, a superior judge who listened attentively to her accusers. The second time the tribunal convened, this judge seemed absent, and her prosecutors lashed into her, demanding whether "you remember this, and what did you think of this, and why did you not say this, how did you excuse yourself." As she reached the bottom of despair, however, she felt a "soft and sweet air" that consoled her suffering soul. This force took Francisca away from her tormentors to an unknown place and whispered to her that she had forgotten to tell them some things. As the voice spoke, a flood of memories gushed through her, and she recalled how the Lord had come to her in her youth as a lover: "for a time his visits were continuous, he was dressed in love, to recreate and lavish on my soul his gifts."[32]

### Love's Armor

Francisca was almost forty years old in 1712 and was herself convinced that she was nearing the end. In that year, she had lost two dear friends and assistants. Her sister Gertrudis had participated in the grand experiment that was the *beaterio* from the beginning and in spite of her mental problems had provided trust and comfort to its embattled headmistress. Fray Antonio de los Ángeles had been her dearest friend in the world, a man with whom she had enjoyed a loving, truthful, and trusting friendship. He had come to her aid whenever needed and had not judged or criticized her fervid experiences of the divine. Instead, he had thrown himself without prejudice head on into accompanying her on the mystical climb up Mount Carmel as well as her descent into hell. Aside from Margil, no other person had ever accepted her inspired and particular nature with such an open mind.

In the preceding years Francisca had suffered a spiritual dissication that accompanied her endless earthly duties and sufferings in the midst of internal divisions in the *beaterio*, her quarrels with her mentors over its fate, and the contretemps between her secular and regular benefactors. She had been saddled with a difficult and unpredictable confessor, and to clinch it all, the Inquisition had declared that the graces bestowed on fellow humans by God and through her were merely illusory, reeking of false piety and lack of scruples. She had been publicly humiliated in Querétaro, former friends and admirers had refused to have anything to do with objects they once had revered and praised for their miraculous powers, and her status as protégée of the Franciscans had not saved her this time. This wave of misfortune aroused in her anxiety and doubt regarding the authenticity of her spiritual life and of the graces she had felt so assured of. It all boiled down to the haunting feeling that she had reached a midway point on the road to something that mattered and had lost her bearings.

And yet she would not give in. Instead of packing up her booth and heading home to obscurity, Francisca found a new confessor and channeled whatever was left of her spirit into establishing a bond with him that might spur her toward perfection. And in the end, when all the accusing voices of confessors, townspeople, Inquisitors, and priests had died down, there remained only the loving whisper of the divine spirit, which reminded Francisca of the ecstasies she reached when ensconced in "His Love." Armed with that memory, she would embark on the last leg of her exile on this earth.

# 4  Old Age

# 8 Foundation

With the scandal behind her and the uninitiated Fray Ángel at her side, Francisca felt invigorated. She began to make ambitious plans for her spiritual endeavors, temporarily at least forgetting her complaints about old age and mental paralysis. Díez seemed depressed after their separation, but she brushed away feelings of guilt. She even resolved not to see him when he fell ill with fevers, for she surmised—perhaps accurately—that she was after all the cause of all his ailments.[1] Over Lent 1713, she bombarded Fray Ángel with letters asking for permission for various creative forms of penitence: twenty days without sleep and only slumber, only seven sips of water every twenty-four hours, and licking the floor in penitence for whatever pleasures and words might have tainted her tongue.

Francisca also felt herself to be greatly in debt to her community of protégées, whom she had abandoned during her "dark night." She resolved to throw herself at their feet and ask forgiveness for her errors. She would even go as far as performing the exercise of death, so favored by Madre Agreda, a task she had always disliked immensely. In it, she would lie on the floor in the middle of the chapel as if dead. The sacristan would place four candles at her head and feet, and the vicaress would read the exercise of death, which the *beatas* possessed in print. Afterward, all the *beatas* were to surround her and sing the litanies of the saints. For the exercise to truly have effect, Francisca asked Fray Ángel to come to the *beaterio* the following day to serve at morning mass and perform the funeral rites. To show him she was serious in her new endeavors, she sent him some new chains that a "person of respect" had loaned her, and asked him to bless them.[2] Over Easter, her Lent labors yielded ample rewards, though not as violent or euphoric as before. Christ demonstrated himself to her as a sweet and gentle presence during her prayers, and she smelled his blood in the chapel and was possessed by the desire to be bathed by it.

All was not peace and consolation, however. In May, Díez congregated the community in the chapel and declaring that "wounded love turns into fury" he publicly threatened to throw Francisca out of her own house. Afterward, she was forced to go to his confessional where she received further insults. As she left the confessional Francisca tried to gather some of her tattered dignity about her and walk "with resignation and peace" to her cell, but her mind was a "sea of fears, imagination, and anxiety," for Díez had used his trump card and refused her communion.[3]

The vengeful old man did not succeed in getting rid of her, and as the year progressed the new confessor and his *hija espiritual* seemed thrilled with each other. In July, Fray Ángel put Francisca to the test of praying for rain. To her relief, divine omnipotence chose to answer her prayers with a copious downpour. In the ensuing years it became a habit of his to request prayers from her during droughts, and they "never failed."[4]

With such encouragement Francisca began to hear clearly the divine voice again. For the first time in years she did not have any qualms about describing the experience to her confessor.[5] Naturally, as her spirits soared and achieved the long desired entry into heaven, the tests her mentor put her to became more severe. In November 1713, a scrupulous Fray Ángel added a note to one of her letters in which he explained that his protégée had seen a soul possessed by the devil and had begged the Lord to allow her to take on the suffering instead. The wish was granted, and Francisca was given the privilege of combating demons for eight days. Fray Ángel added that Francisca had also seen a vision of an eagle inhabiting a nest of crosses. He was convinced that the eagle was Francisca inhabiting the place God had prepared for her.[6] As the year progressed, then, Fray Ángel's downtrodden middle-aged protégée assumed the heroic proportions of her young and fiery days. She mused for her confessor on past milestones in her spiritual career, informing him, for example, that her vow of chastity—made at the age of ten in the orchard with her divine groom—had once been tested by a priest who made passionate advances on her.[7] Impressed, Fray Ángel heard her general confession in January 1714. Afterward, he testified that she had never had impure impulses against chastity, had never committed mortal sin, and retained the grace of baptism.

Fray Ángel rapidly found out, however, that his saintly protégée's boisterous spirit could easily spin out of his control. Over Christmas 1713, she found it impossible to go to mass because she felt so possessed by the Child Jesus who rested in her arms during the feasts. Fray Ángel told her to try and resist, to come to her senses and fulfill her Christian obligations, but she only retorted that she could not since that would wake the child. Francisca tried to go to mass but felt preoccupied and anxious that she might wake the child. In the end she resolved that she could not comply with the confessor's command since the mass simply did not sink in.[8] Once aroused, such inspirational bouts became more and more frequent. On one occasion Francisca remarked that she had not been able to walk home from Santa Cruz she had been so enraptured by a sermon; she thus had to take a carriage down the hill.[9] The loving divine presence stayed with her for long periods, which at times erupted into episodes with decidedly erotic undertones. In this period, for example, Francisca reported a constant sensation of burning in divine fire, which left her feeling an insatiable thirst for lemon water, *orchata* (rice milk), or other "fresh beverages." The sensation was so overwhelmingly scorching that Francisca could not eat hot meals at lunchtime, but had to content herself with salad, water, and bread.[10] In a letter from May 8, 1714, Francisca, apparently feeling consumed by fire for several days, asked Fray Ángel to give her blessed water as a remedy. As she bathed in the warm water—still wearing, with due modesty, her tunic—the Lord came to her as a lover and sweetly told her that "if my soul possessed his heart it would possess the heart's treasures." In the end she moaned, "I do not know why we do not all die for love of Him," and continued to go about as if in a "secret dream."[11]

Indeed, Francisca was so encouraged by her relationship with her new confessor that speaking with him of the matters of her soul took precedence over other pleasures. On April 8, 1714, for example, she only dropped in very briefly on mass at the Santa Clara convent, for she knew that the friar who said mass there in the mornings took so long, and she longed to have more time with Fray Ángel.[12]

If the friar found that his protégée's spiritual life could be an unruly affair, then the festive traditions of her *beaterio* were equally so. On a perfectly ordinary, calm day in April, he had made his way down the hill to visit the *beatas*, only to find that Querétaro's entire Carmelite community was there being royally entertained and fed by women Fray Ángel had thought had only been eager to follow him out of the confusion of society. Stern and disapproving, he immediately left the house, and the next day Francisca found herself forced to write him a long, soothing letter. But as always, she was quick on the attack and pointed out that the *beata*'s love of music had been sanctioned by higher powers than his. Indeed, Fray Antonio de los Ángeles, by now a figure of saintly status in Querétaro lore, had always asked for music when his superiors had allowed him to visit the *beatas*. Although she did not mention it in her letter, it must have been implicit that Fray Antonio, in his delight at small pleasures, was only following Saint Teresa's maxim that simple theatrical and musical festivities in the convents staved off their frequent "epidemics of melancholia."[13] Besides, such festivities were not entirely the *beata*'s fault since the archbishop had made such visits unavoidable by not granting enclosure to the community.

The Carmelite community had been visiting Francisca's house en masse once or twice a year since she was born. How could she deny them entry when the community was not even cloistered? Instead of complaining, Fray Ángel and other benefactors should pray to God that enclosure would be granted. The undercurrent to all this was, of course, that since the friars had not done their job properly by obtaining approval for locking Francisca's women up, they could not expect them to live as if they were. The poor friar was humbled and convinced by this missive and added a note to her letter referring to the well-known theological fact that music lifted the spirit higher to God and had the power of restoring the gift of prophecy to souls thus inspired.[14]

But if matters were going better than expected with her new confessor, Francisca and her community still had further trials awaiting them. While Díez had removed himself and his irritability to a remote mission, the person who replaced him would prove even more difficult to deal with: Dr. don Nicolás Armenta, a cleric of the Congregation of Guadalupe and eventually the chaplain of the *beaterio*. María de Jesús may have had hagiographic reasons for stating that Armenta's presence in the *beaterio* was "a bitter tempest which lasted for more than twenty years," but judging from Francisca's letters, the statement approached the truth.[15] Armenta was austere and vengeful and needed constant attention. Francisca came to the conclusion that he was "in the prison of his own passions" and prayed for him.[16] He would frequently punish the *beatas* by leaving them without confessor and at the mercy of the Santa Cruz friars, who by now had become far less enthusiastic on the subject of holy women.[17]

Indeed, by 1715, two years into Francisca's relationship with Fray Ángel, their courtship was over. The *beata* had become decidedly more guarded, and her confessor more short-tempered. Frustrated by her lack of humility Fray Ángel tried to persuade her that it was not the splendor of her talents that dazzled the divine into showering her with gifts but the good will behind her work. He told her an anecdote about an old Indian woman who brought a chicken to a king as a gift. Impressed by the thought behind the gift, the king had given her one hundred pesos. The moral of the tale was that the Lord's favors came in response to her understanding of her weaknesses, not the power of her talents.[18] Francisca's renewed self-confidence in God's love was not at all to Fray Ángel's austere tastes, which tended toward divine love in the dark. These were the sentiments that he expressed in a letter to another spiritual daughter of his at Santa Rosa, Isabel Rosa:

> love when the soul sees the light clearly and the open arms of the beloved is not good. It is not the love of the strong, but of children who love their mother because she nurses them. But to love when the soul feels as if it is in darkness and has fine desires to love, when it feels that it is useless and that it has offended God, this is pure love, these are desires that are highly acceptable to God because here it is not moved by the gifts but by the infinite qualities of the beloved. . . . These fears of the soul of whether it will lose it [God's grace] or not, if it has lost it or not, these fears are always agreeable to God . . . for they are not phenomena of the world, not for its delights or happy sweetness but only for God for whom the soul breathes, wounded like a slave.[19]

In retaliation, Francisca claimed that Fray Ángel made her afraid of writing—conscious as she was of "the dark battles of my intellect"—and of offending him with her disclosures. Indeed, shortly after having a vision of herself richly dressed in heaven, "all the doors closed on me" when Fray Ángel told her terrible things in the confessional, such as asking whether she thought these favors made her saintly and esteemed.[20] The friar impatiently brushed aside Francisca's claims of having seen souls in purgatory. On one occasion he told her that it was all in her imagination since she had never had anything to do with that particular *alma*. She would not give in, however. She sent for him more often than ever and provided evidence of divine dissatisfaction with him. Once when thinking of Fray Ángel's intemperate lack of understanding she had seen a vision of the naked Christ dripping blood, his eyes downcast. And if Fray Ángel doubted her, then the Lord had told her that *He* had not chosen to punish her, for she "had been of service to some souls." If Fray Ángel would not listen in the confessional Francisca had a vision in which the friar put between them a cloth with the imprint of Christ's face on it; she was immediately consoled, for it was as if the Lord himself was confessing her.[21] Indeed, having been accepted anew into divine graces, Francisca would not allow Fray Ángel to alter her conviction that she was beloved for her singular attributes and that her lover was a merciful God who did not punish those who loved him. Throughout this period Francisca continued to report visions of love, of feeling drunk, of being told by Christ that she was his bride, of being bathed in the "sweet liquor" of divine love, of seeing treasures of precious stones, and of being lifted to a "higher and nobler state," her soul among those graced by God.[22]

Four years later, in 1719, the rift between them was clear. Francisca still suffered ecstasies and agonies, felt beside herself over Lent, bathed in divine blood, and fought battles with the devil. But none of this was duly described in her letters; it was only mentioned in passing, for her confessor was simply no longer interested. On July 11, 1718, Francisca angrily reproached Fray Ángel for putting her in a situation where she was unable to speak freely with him. Aware of the great sins she committed by not baring her soul to him she retorted: "I can no longer speak to you as I did. One word from you, from the source that contained all my comfort in this miserable world has ruined all the honesty I had previously had with you." She then reminded him of his intermediary place in the structure of power, for it had indeed been the Commissary of the Franciscan Order himself who had ordered her to tell all during confession.[23] For some months between 1720 and 1722 Fray Ángel did not enter the *beaterio* even if he was in Querétaro. In a missive reminiscent of her earlier battles with Díez, Francisca reminded him that "this was his job."[24] And she took care to inform him of heartening conversations with the divine that confirmed her faith in His love. On January 22, 1720, she reported a conversation during which God told her: "do not take your two eyes off me, I will always be with you." She had responded: "Father of my soul, if love is paid with love than that is what I intend to do, disrobe me of all that is painful to you."[25]

In spite of their bickering though, the relationship—like that of a married couple that wants to separate but cannot out of habit—remained reluctantly steady. In 1719, for example, Fray Ángel went away, to Zacatecas to find some peace and quiet with his studies. There he wrote her a letter complaining of his terrible health. His knee hurt to such a degree that he could no longer bend it, and he had to say mass "con gravissimo trabajo." He could not remain seated even for the duration of one creed. No amount of cotton pads drenched in hot *agua ardiente* would relieve his suffering. He asked Francisca to take his letter to Ortega at Santa Cruz who was to consult with the infirmary as to the best course of action. Having satisfied his need to complain he added that he had secured her sheep and would send them with a Fray Joseph de San Antonio once he came down. He then finished the letter with a loving "tu hermano que en Christo te estima."[26]

In turn, Francisca missed Fray Ángel while he was away. She wrote to him that she felt like a "bird who flies constantly without having a branch to rest on," and that his absence had left her in a misery that would not be alleviated until she had put all her troubles in his hands.[27] In their squabbles they both turned to a higher tribunal in the person of Margil. Missives were fired to Zacatecas with such rapidity, at least from Francisca's side, that Margil found himself saddled with three before he had time to send one to Querétaro. On July 10, 1722, he wrote to her that Fray Ángel had complained about her "weakness." Meanwhile, Francisca had written to him in distress, for the friar had told her that she was "full of tears, demons; deceived and possessed by the devil." Margil responded by setting up a hypothetical conversation between confessor and spiritual daughter in which the latter behaved impeccably without allowing the confessor free rein:

> Father, my intention is not to offend the Lord. It is for that reason that you are my Father, to put me on the right path for I am here to obey you as I would obey God himself, provided the order does not go against the Lord.
>
> Well, give me an account of your life then.
>
> Well, Father, even if it means that all that is in me will come out; it is or has been this and that . . .
>
> You are a hypocrite, you tell me of these favors so that I will consider you good. To my mind this is arrogance.
>
> I know very well that if the Lord would leave me only a little bit, the entire army of devils would not be able to win me over; my intention is to only be faithful to God. . . . This is what I have to say to you; if it is bad then you can correct me. It is for that reason that you are my Father and custodian angel.[28]

Having provided her with this model of diplomacy, Margil nevertheless took the opportunity to humble Francisca and curtly told her that all her troubles with the confessor were caused by her own lack of resignation and faith in God. If she gave herself the time, she would understand that the Lord had placed the demon in her path in the form of these troublesome confessors. "The thing is that once upon a time before you got so sick with self-love you loved and trusted Fray Ángel; you got on well," he concluded in his letter, offering no other consolation. A year later he was feeling a bit more sympathetic: "I tell you daughter of my soul that my love, my will, my peace in the Lord will always remain with you and with everyone, but always with you in the customary special manner for our very special union in the Lord of which you are aware. . . . In Jesus you are mine, and in Jesus I am yours; and the two of us are only of one Jesus and to say it in one word; the two of us are to be only one Jesus, like two oblates."[29]

But Francisca had asked him to write to Fray Ángel and relieve him of his duties as her confessor and supervisor of her community. Margil declined to do so and admonished her that it was an unfair request after all Fray Ángel had done for him personally by taking charge of her.[30]

By 1722, at Fray Ángel's death, the affair was over. Francisca happily relied on the spiritual advice offered through the mail by Margil and her good friend the Jesuit Juan de Mora in Mexico City. Nevertheless, she cast about for a new confessor and came upon a most suitable choice: Fray Juan de Ortega, whom she had known for years and relied on for material provisions and other favors in his capacity as vicar of Santa Cruz. With him she felt confident. The friar seems to have been rather frail in physical and mental health, and her letters to him contain constant remarks fussing over his health and recommending cures. On one occasion, she mixed a special ointment of cochineal for him and waited expectantly for news of its effectiveness.[31] More importantly, she offered advice on Ortega's spiritual well-being that was remarkably daring. In 1712, for example, when Ortega had been made guardian of Santa Cruz he complained to Francisca that he absolutely did not want the office. Francisca commiserated with him at first and concurred with him that everyone had known that he did not want the responsibility—she herself had told everyone at the convent that he did not want it. But then she seemed to lose her patience and snapped at him with a remark that could have sprung straight from Margil's pen: "You really should try and resign yourself to the will of God, and to being absolutely nothing . . . then you would not be so full of fear and melancholy." Realizing she had gone too far, Francisca tempered her remark with a hurried excuse that she really had had no intention of saying it, the "pen had said what was said."[32]

The friar's passivity was encouraging, however, for in the next letter she thanked him for the humility with which he admitted her "rustic words."[33] This role play was a constant undercurrent in their relationship. Other letters include similar exhortations. In an undated note Francisca professed her sorrow at seeing Ortega carry his cross with "such sadness," but she could not refrain from driving home her point by exclaiming: "I do not know why it is so heavy for you since the cross the Lord gave us is sweet and gentle." And comparing his travails to hers, she found hers far more cumbersome and reminded him that he really should be the one to console her who was in charge "of so many *doncellas*."[34] And while she was in the process of securing him as a permanent confessor for her entire community Francisca reminded Ortega that it was the holy man himself, Fray Antonio Margil de Jesús, who placed his entire trust in Ortega's capacities to govern them. When he relented and finally asked for a *cuenta de alma* she replied triumphantly that this was his duty and that from there on, should there be anything she needed to get off her chest, she would write to him whether he had requested it or not. It was his duty to respond, for she wrote only at the order of Margil.[35] Indeed, Francisca felt so confident that when he confided in her his feeling of homesickness she admonished him angrily for failing in his duties: "Do not long for another life than the one you have got, God made you his minister and dispenser of his treasures; it would be as if a silversmith left his gold and silver which is his profession and began to make adobe; Your Paternity has never in your life told me anything that has left me feeling so disconsoled. . . . In your province you would also carry your cross and wherever you go you are to carry it until dying with Christ in the Calvary which is what I desire in this life."[36]

### Quotidian Life

As the Santa Rosa community grew in size and complexity the burden on its foundress to maintain provisions and the public's benevolent attitude naturally increased. As before, the *beatas* embroidered, sewed, arranged flower decorations, dressed and painted saints' images, and produced sweets of various kinds, especially *cajeta* (fudge). The Santa Cruz friars seem to have commissioned a steady stream of jars of *cajetas* and trays of biscuits, and they continued to send pounds of sugar, flour, and eggs for their production.[37] They also frequently requested flower decorations. Such artisanal production was a source of pride to the *beatas*. A great deal of work went into sewing the robes for the saints, and their handiwork made it into several convents and homes around the colony. Francisca's specialty were images of the baby Jesus in sugar. She boasted that her earnings for eight days of work on such *niños* far exceeded what the entire community made from sewing in a month. The manual labor required for the production was far from tedious; on the contrary, shaping and kneading the sugary mixture into the likeness of Christ often brought Francisca raptures and visions of cradling the newborn baby to her breast. At other times, of course, the devil managed to cut through her idyll, whispering in her ear that selling little baby Jesus images was comparable to Judas selling Christ into the hands of the Romans.[38]

By now, the community operated under a longstanding regime that in-cluded a vicaress, porter, and nurse among other administrative posts. It possessed a small library and held masses daily.[39] Daily life was no longer as dependent on the beneficence of pious citizens, but had acquired an au-tonomous rhythm that separated it from the *siglo* (secular society). At the same time, its governance grew more problematic. As in many convents the formation of factions among its members created turbulence. In an undated letter Francisca sought help from her mentors when a large group of Young Turks demanded her resignation as headmistress and expulsion from the community. "I am sorry about this," she wrote to Santa Cruz, "but the enemy is steady while they are not as they should be." To her correspondents, she only wished for more strong-willed souls to aid her in these constant battles with this group, which was terrorizing the others including her vicaress, the otherwise steady María Isabel.[40]

The increasing size and complexity of the *beaterio* also expressed itself in the difficulty of maintaining control over the women's connections with the outside world. In November 1729, Francisca struggled with brewing scandal when it emerged that a music teacher who was habitually present in the community giving lessons had seduced a *niña*, a lay member. Francisca tried to quell the scandal without the chaplain finding out, and eventually the teacher left the city, though the woman was not expelled.[41]

As the original community grew older, illnesses and infirmities naturally became a larger element in its daily life. Francisca seems to have been fre-quently engaged in caring for the sick. The Santa Cruz friars were also gaining in age, and recommendations for all sorts of powders and pills as well as descriptions of the ailments most common in the community began to pop up in her correspondence. From the apothecary at Santa Cruz she required a remedy named *el agua de la vida*, as well as *agua rosada* and aguardiente.[42] Water blessed by exceptionally holy friars was also a much sought after source of healing.[43] The sick were allowed to sleep on mattresses and eat meat, and Francisca concurred in the wisdom of the age that chocolate was essential to recovery.[44] Whether or not she possessed particular talents in this field is impossible to say, but on April 8, 1717, she reported to Fray Ángel that one of the community's eldest members, la Montaña, had had a dream while incapacitated in bed by pain in which a small girl had placed her hand on the wound, which immediately disappeared. When queried the girl replied that she was "la hija de los deseos de Francisca (daughter of Francisca's desires)." Although Francisca's days of recognition as a miracle worker were supposedly past after the 1712 Inquisition intervention, the anecdote indicates that such beliefs may not have been eradicated.[45]

## Sociability

By the mid-1710s, the forty-year-old Francisca, relatively old by the standards of the time, might have been expected to enter an age of quiet and rest after having overcome life's spiritual and material hurdles. By now, she might have realized Margil's maxim of the *nada* with greater maturity, her ego obliterated through years of rigorous training and abnegation. But Francisca was still being called to more active spiritual and material feats, and the wells of her ego remained plentiful. The souls from purgatory still called to her and feast days still revealed the mysteries of God who possessed her soul "alive and sacramented, dead and sacramented, resurrected and sacramented."[46] In spite of repeated efforts to perform acts of humility Francisca admitted that her self-love always triumphed. Such was the case in the instances in which she threw herself on the threshold of the oratory and begged every *beata* who entered to step on her mouth. At times, when no one arrived for long periods she became so impatient and full of longing for someone to see her that the whole purpose of the exercise was defeated.[47]

If her soul was still alive to the chaos induced by the divine presence, then it was equally alive to the things of this world. She simply felt too much emotion still at this age, she complained, was too happy when things went well for her, and liked to eat for the sake of eating. She also still became too downtrodden over insignificant things such as a perfectly good molar falling out or being unable to, due to her vow of poverty, entertain and feed important guests in the style that she liked.[48] Indeed, one of Francisca's greatest struggles, she confessed, were with her own urges for hospitality. She simply could not have an important person in the house without wanting to serve them a feast. Had she consulted textbooks on virtue to clarify the position of her soul on the path to God she would have been aghast. According to the standards of Saint John of the Cross, for example, her soul would not even have passed through the "first night" of purgation belonging to beginners. His stanza describes it thus:

> On a dark night
> Anxious, by love inflamed
> -O Joyous chance!-
> I left not seen or discovered
> My house at last completely quiet.[49]

Francisca's "house" was not quiet, the appetites did not lie dormant, her soul was not "freed from the sufferings and anguish" of sensuous experience.[50] Instead, "important persons" and "hospitality" were key features of the life of the *beaterio* during this period. More than a decade after its foundation, the *beaterio* of Santa Rosa de Viterbo had become an established feature of town life, supported by an intricate web of benefactors that reached to the capital. In Francisca's well-traveled confessors, of course, the headmistress possessed powerful advocates—should the mood take them. Margil, for example, introduced her to elite women in Querétaro and asked her in his letters to visit them.[51] He used his sojourns in a Mexico City filled with bustling, worldly, and aristocratic convents to spread the word of this exemplary community.[52] He also put Francisca in epistolary contact with several important figures in the city such as a Señor Castorena, a canon who wrote to Francisca frequently and often used her as messenger between himself and the holy man.[53] Francisca did as she was told, but she sent her letters to be edited at Santa Cruz before they were mailed, for she claimed that she did "not know how to write to distinguished persons."[54]

Francisca maintained intimate friendships with the Santa Clara nuns. In this, she crossed social boundaries since most of the nuns came from the town's most distinguished families. In 1715, she sent a hurried message to the Santa Cruz friars asking them to say mass for a departed Santa Clara nun, Luisa de Santa Clara, a dear friend of hers, whom she had seen in a vision of purgatory. In 1719 she mentions "watching over" the Altamirano nun.[55] And she engaged in correspondence with two nuns, especially with Madre Rosa María de Jesús, member of the established Urtiaga and Parra families, to whom she wrote regularly in the period between 1710 and 1720.[56] In spite of Madre Rosa's internment in a cloistered convent, Francisca visited her frequently and arranged for meetings between her and the Santa Cruz friars. She sent Madre Rosa lemons and flowers on occasion, and the nun in turn sent Francisca sweet jellied fruit. On her friend's behalf, Francisca visited a house of the nun's relative to console and calm a young girl who was probably suffering from bouts of hysteria or from some other nervous disorder.[57]

In her relative freedom as a *beata*, Francisca was of help to the nuns in various matters, for example, arranging for servant girls, both indigenous and mestizas, to enter the convent.[58] And it seems that she was present on occasions when novices were prepared for their profession. The *beatas* may even have sewn the elaborate costumes required for the occasion.[59] Francisca arranged for a special confessor for a young nun who probably needed a more experienced and sympathetic spiritual director than she had been given. In an almost triumphant tone she told Ortega: "Well, you know the complaints of nuns."[60] In a similar vein she sympathized with Ortega on troubles he had been experiencing with the elite nuns, referring again to their privileged but perhaps not deserved status: "what is permitted for some is not conceded to others and for my part I am glad that my rights in relation to Your Paternity spring from love and not obligation."[61] This latent jealousy sprang up on several occasions, for in many ways Francisca was competing directly with the nuns for the attentions of the ever busy Santa Cruz friars who habitually combined visits since the convent and *beaterio* were only separated by a few blocks. Thus, when Fray Ángel stopped by at Santa Rosa he was sometimes pressed to go to Santa Clara, and so did not have time to confess more than a few *beatas*.

Naturally, the Franciscans' prerogative was to maintain cordial relations with the elite, and Santa Clara presented a treasure chest of aristocratic connections. Thus, Francisca was forced to send missives up the hill asking the guardian to allot a separate day to the *beatas* since the nuns clearly were given precedence.[62] The friars sought her counsel regarding their relationship with the convent. This was a rather sensitive matter since its chaplains did not view favorably the Santa Cruz community's flair at winning over the souls of Querétaro's elite nuns. Francisca advised the guardian of Santa Cruz to think twice about continuing their visits. In her opinion they could harm the college since she had heard that malicious tongues were already spreading rumors.[63]

But naturally it was Querétaro society that provided the crucial support for the survival of the *beaterio*. Francisca's energies now focused on providing hospitality to the large group of *queretanos* for whom visits to the *beatas* and masses in their little chapel had become an integral element in a daily ritual schedule. The majority were women, members of Querétaro's upper Creole strata who sported the title doña. They would arrive in carriages accompanied by devoted priests seeking to improve their spiritual lives with such visits, or they would come alone to pray with the *beatas* or even to seclude themselves.[64] Many of them already enjoyed a sodality with the holy woman through the mediation of the Santa Cruz friars.[65] Francisca cultivated these relationships with fluent penmanship. She corresponded with Fray Ortega's sister, doña Juana Francisca de Ortega, as well as several other women in Querétaro.

Among them was her staunch benefactress, identified as la Señora Marquesa.[66] The marquise's haciendas provided the community with a steady stream of mutton, and Francisca seems to have felt confident enough of the marquise's support to borrow mutton from the Santa Cruz friars when her own supplies ran low, promising that her benefactress would pay them back. The lady also visited frequently and in the company of female friends. It was the marquise who introduced her to don Juan Fernandes Fontecha and his parents, all members of the Fernandes Fontecha family, among the most powerful landowners and merchants in Querétaro. The marquise suggested don Juan to Francisca as a benefactor to be cultivated and may have seen him as a possible successor to Caballero y Ocio. Francisca and the Santa Cruz friars followed that lead with gusto. In the following years the health and general situation of don Juan and his family emerge as prominent themes in Francisca's letters.[67] The *beata* did all sorts of sewing and handiwork for the marquise, as well as female members of the Fontecha family.[68]

In 1712, Francisca went with doña María Buenrostro to visit her two recently professed daughters, Antonia and Francisca, in the Santa Clara convent. María came from an old Creole family in Querétaro, and her husband, Capt. Juan Martínez y Lucío, a peninsular, was an eminent figure in the town.[69] In another letter she mentions visiting the Yanés, an old and prestigious local family, to offer her condolences. A doña Luisa Tagle was also a visitor at the *beaterio*. The Sanchez Tagle family were powerful landowners and merchants in Querétaro and included in their clan the marquis of Altamirano.[70] Evidence of the attentions of the elite is also found in a letter from Francisca advising the Santa Cruz friars to ask doña Luisa de Tagle and doña Josepha Susnavar to serve as godmothers for a *beata*'s profession. Francisca confidently claimed that they would do so with pleasure, indicating that she was familiar with them and that they had perhaps rendered that service to the *beaterio* in the past.[71] She acted as religious adviser and confidante for doña Rosa Urtiaga, a Querétaro woman with an inclination for the religious life and a probable relation to Captain Urtiaga, the Santa Cruz friar's benefactor.[72]

The clearest indication of Francisca's role as spiritual counselor is found in a letter in which she relates her visit that afternoon to a Querétaro family that had invited her in order to "Christianize" (*cristianizar*) a "criature."[73] The service referred to is obviously that of preaching the gospel or giving her blessing to a newborn. Whatever the precise connotation of the term, the reference illustrates that in their desire to consecrate their members to God, Querétaro families sought not merely the blessing of the church, but also that of individuals with known connections to the divine sphere.

It is likely that Francisca's social role within the feminine world was far more complex then her own letters reveal. This is suggested in part by an episode recounted by her biographer and based on her own account to her confessor. Although Francisca clothed the episode in her usual supernatural garb it reveals a matter of a far more earthly nature. While praying one evening, an unannounced female visitor entered Francisca's cell. The *beata* suspected that it was the devil clothed in a woman's apparel and promptly recited an Ave Maria. When the woman did not respond, Francisca's suspicions were confirmed. The unknown visitor then took a dead newborn infant from her coat, laid it on Francisca's floor, and left. Francisca prayed over the body all night, imploring God to take the devil out of it. She then wrapped it up and took it to the doorstep of the nearest church, the Santo Domingo, and left it there for a Christian burial. Here, Francisca acted as an intermediary between the church and a woman who for unknown reasons could not reveal the birth. While obliged to tell her confessor everything, Francisca hid the woman's identity in her magic-permeated recounting of the episode.[74]

In spite of the turmoil of the Inquisition scandal in 1712, Querétaro society continued to support the *beaterio* of Santa Rosa, acknowledging the benefits reaped after a decade of hard work by its foundress. Townspeople regarded Francisca's function not merely in the light of the service she rendered as an administrator, but continued to have faith in the power afforded to her by mystic authority. In 1714, for example, Francisca wrote to Fray Ángel that a sick woman had been brought to the *beaterio* hoping for an embrace from the foundress, which she believed would heal her. Francisca inserted the episode in her letter under the pretext of complaint, for she had indeed been very wrapped up with God on that day, but her tone was decidedly triumphant.[75] At other times, irresistible opportunities presented themselves to demonstrate her powers. In January of the same year Francisca sat under a tree in the orchard, conversing with Armenta the chaplain about the weather. The cleric was convinced that a crisis was imminent because of an extended drought. Francisca was not as worried, however, because she knew that immediate rain would ruin all her hard work in the garden. Nevertheless, as the couple continued talking, the foundress looked up and saw a small cloud trailing across the sky and was immediately transported to a region torn asunder by thunder, lightning, and terrible rain. Taking advantage of the moment, she asked the Lord to send a little of all that water to her part of the world. She saw the Lord hesitate as if he did not know whether he would say yes, and suddenly she knew that a hailstorm was imminent and urged Armenta to go inside with her. The cleric laughed at her when she told him he would be soaked if they did not leave immediately, but as they took the first steps the first hard grains hit, slowly building into a tempest the likes of which Querétaro had not seen in years.[76] Although Armenta was of a gloomy and taciturn disposition, it is likely that the episode reached the mill of town gossip. And should anyone care to point a finger, Francisca could refer to episodes like the one that occurred in 1725 when on his deathbed the Augustinian provincial was given a two-day respite from death to reconcile his soul thanks to a relic brought from the *beaterio*.[77]

There are indications in this period that *queretanos* did not merely turn to the person of the foundress as a fount of mystic power, but that the institution itself had begun to enter the "spiritual economy" of the region.[78] On December 5, 1716, for example, Francisca informed Fray Ángel that the daughter of a recently departed soul had brought her six pesos to have masses said for her mother in the *beaterio*. Francisca took care to cast herself as passive recipient in the matter, for it had been the Lord who informed her that he wanted the soul hurried out of purgatory as quickly as possible and toward that end six pesos would be brought to her. Fray Ángel sternly reprimanded Francisca for this transgression since the *beaterio* was to remain poor and do such favors out of charity. But the deed had been done, and all the disgruntled friar could do was to add a note to remind her "that it was her duty to obey me, and that in whatever else I might order her to do she should not try to fathom my reasons but leave matters to God."[79]

### Foundation and Its Troubles

In March 1715, the reluctant archbishop, don José Lanciego, finally came to Querétaro and visited the *beaterio* several times to see for himself this controversial community of truly poor women maintained by the goodwill of its neighbors. Having seen all her past initiatives to found a convent fail, Francisca seized the opportunity to ask him in person to grant the *beatas* at least enclosure. By strictly observing their enclosure, she vowed, the twenty-three *beatas* would demonstrate to the world at large the worthiness of their cause. The archbishop interrogated Francisca on "some of the mysteries of our holy Catholic faith." According to María de Jesús, she replied with such clarity that he remarked that she had responded like a great theologian. He granted the *beatas* enclosure and provided a small sum so they could divide their chapel with convent rails. The modest size of the chapel did not really allow for such division, and after the rails were installed only the *beatas'* small altar could fit in the upper choir, while the lower choir was extremely uncomfortable. A long battle had been won. Francisca seemed secure in her victory and finally separated from the society she so disdained and cherished. Matters improved dramatically when the jubilant Armenta, encouraged by the archbishop's goodwill, paid for the construction of a wall to close off the orchard and zeal the enclosure. He also funded the enlargement of the chapel, and one can only guess at the triumphant emotions of the foundress.

At this point, however, unforeseen and interesting developments began to take place in Querétaro. Disgruntled townspeople complained of being barred from the very place to which they had hitherto enjoyed free entry. Suddenly, aid that had been forthcoming dried up, and malicious rumors began to circulate.[80] Voices were heard exclaiming that the *beatas* showed great temerity to presume that they could enclose themselves with hardly any of the trappings of a conventual institution. The matter rapidly reached the archbishop's ear through the mediation of the Franciscan provincial and head of the Third Order in Querétaro. His predecessor, a longtime supporter of Francisca's, had tried to persuade the *beatas* to give up the idea of enclosure, or at least to leave the *beaterio* on Holy Thursday to participate in the procession of the stations. His request throws into relief what was possibly the chief concern of the townspeople regarding the enclosure. For years, the presence of the *beatas* along with other members of the Third Orders in public processions had probably been a matter of pride to the town. It demonstrated its intense and popular spirituality, for here was a community of religious women who truly lived in poverty and from charity and yet were accessible as devotional examples to the public. Their simple habits and modest behavior during such public festivities left no doubt as to the town's religious devotion and its ability to foster a faith that was pure and faithful to the doctrines of the church. Querétaro already had its aristocratic Clarisas to show the economic power of its orthodox faith. This group of poor Creole *doncellas* keeping its vocation with such rigorous example was much more valuable to town morale on display than buried behind walls.

But while Francisca's friend tried gentle persuasion, his successor was more ruthless. He dispatched a complaint to the archbishop in which he claimed that the *beatas* "had no further use than to raise problems and encourage vanities and since the *recogimiento* was so dependent on the aid of the parish it would be best that his Excellency have it demolished and destroyed."[81] The friar got so carried away that he concluded that the house should simply be set on fire. Taking him seriously, Francisca placed *beatas* on guard night and day. The archbishop, on reading the report took equally serious measures, ordering the ecclesiastical judge in Querétaro to notarize the provincial's testimony on oath and gather further commentary from the city's citizens. At that point, the provincial, uncertain whether he could actually convince the townspeople to burn down a community of pious virgins, decided to hold his peace and replied angelically that he "loved and esteemed the sisters very much." Similar testimonies soon poured forth from the citizenry. Its only complaint was that perhaps the women spent too much time on artisanal production such as embroidery, sweets, and religious objects that they sold for sustenance. When the archbishop received this new laudatory missive his bafflement was such that he did nothing about the matter. But he was clearly miffed and related his displeasure to Fray Ángel in a derisive commentary on Francisca and her divine connections.

Sometime during Lent of 1715 the humbled Franciscan examined Francisca rigorously on the effects that divine graces had had on her soul. Indeed, it seems that the archbishop had decided something had to be done to curb the *beata*'s willfulness, for he discussed with her confessor whether they should not deprive her of communion for a year. Francisca defiantly wrote to the friar that "the Lord will not desert me." Margil, at least, did not and wrote her an unusually gentle letter in July of that year from his solitary mission in Texas. He was very pleased with the archbishop's visit and his sanction of the enclosure. "Blessed be the Lord who so loves his roses," he exclaimed and reminded her that it was now all important that "the trees grow straight and be crucified more and more with their crucified Christ." Francisca had informed him of the troubles that ensued after the visit, but Margil brushed her worries aside with yet another gardening allegory: "although the roses are surrounded by thorns and torments these only make them exhale the sweetness of their aroma and fragrant virtues, so that all of us can enjoy the peace of that aroma." And as for Francisca's despair that the archbishop had named the troublesome Armenta as their chaplain when she had of course wanted her old friend and benefactor don Matías Hijar, the experienced Margil reminded her how well connected Armenta was in Querétaro society. He was convinced that Armenta, having been invested with such solemn duties, would now proceed with more *cuidado*.[82] Margil must have conveyed his pleasure to his brethren in Querétaro, for a year later it does not seem that Francisca's punishment had been meted out. Likewise, charity donations increased substantially after the first wave of discontent following the archbishop's 1715 visit. In 1717, Francisca reported that so many people now donated money to the *beaterio* that she no longer had to work as much as before. Indeed, she spent more time in bed sleeping, which aroused the wrath of the others who complained that Francisca was lazy, clearly not understanding that sleep underpinned a flourishing mystical life.[83]

Francisca had reached an impasse with the archbishop, who throughout his career had proved extremely reluctant to do anything to help her *beaterio*. Sometime in the 1720s she therefore turned to royal omnipotence in the person of its highest-placed servant in the colony, Viceroy don Baltazar de Zuñiga, Marquis of Valero. The marquis was well known for his devotion to female spirituality and would become in 1724 the founder of Corpus Christi, the first convent for indigenous women in the colony.[84] His interest had been aroused in the first place by the favorable relation by his secretary, don Bartolomé Crespo, of his 1722 visit to Santa Rosa de Viterbo. By then, Francisca's frustration must have reached boiling point. On July 21, 1721, a group of Capuchin nuns from the convent of San Felipe de Jesús in Mexico City had arrived to take possession of their new convent, funded by Caballero y Ocio's legacy. They were warmly greeted by *queretanos*. It must have seemed to Francisca a great injustice indeed to remain thus deprived, after two decades of serving the spiritual needs of her city. But a few days later, the divine wheels began rolling, and her benefactor was named president of the Council of Indies.

It was a most fortunate development, for Zuñiga took Francisca's cause with him to Madrid.[85] Having failed repeatedly in her quest to establish a convent Francisca now settled for rudimentaries such as the Eucharist, a cemetery, enclosure, and subjection to the Ordinary.[86] She left it to the marquis's discretion what form her institution should take. That proved a wise measure because the king endowed the community with the grand title of royal college and charged the archbishop with ensuring that its necessities were met. Thankfully, the archbishop by this time had died, and thus future prospects seemed bright. Francisca received the royal decree on July 2, 1728, on the Day of the Visitation.

The foundress had struggled for thirteen years—from the archbishop's visit in 1715—to maintain her community enclosed, a struggle that had failed in the face of town opposition. Her letters demonstrate that she frequently exited the *beaterio* in that period, visiting town households and walking to Santa Cruz. Her continuing visits were probably crucial to maintaining support and financial aid for her community among the Querétaro citizenry. But by this time Francisca had acquired an impressive auxiliary in her struggle. She could now count on an image of Santa Rosa de Viterbo, perhaps acquired by the *beatas* after 1715. When taken out on procession the image was in the habit of turning pale when no resolution was in sight for problems facing the community.[87]

In the midst of this difficult period, on August 6, 1726, Fray Antonio Margil de Jesús died in the infirmary of the Franciscan convent in Mexico City. The last decade of his life had been spent mostly outside of Querétaro. Between 1716 and 1722 he was in Texas attempting to resuscitate Propaganda Fide's missionary efforts there after its abandonment in 1693. He founded three missions between the Río Rojo and the Río Trinidad in the Bahía de Espiritu Santo and passed long periods of time in solitude, "aging sweetly" and living according to one of his biographers like the "anchorites, giving himself over to his labors and the sweetness of contemplation."[88] Margil cultivated a garden, cut timber, and lived on the edge of hunger, at one point reportedly eating raven meat. The Texas years were full of hardship caused, first, by the lack of support by the viceregal authorities and, second, by the incursions of the French. Margil, however, reportedly thought Texas was a paradise with—in the words of his biographer—its "sweet peace, abundant walnut trees, ravens and the long silences of winter." In 1722, he was forced to head south again after he was elected guardian at the college in Zacatecas. From there he continued to send Francisca fiery messages reminding her to rid herself "of whatever remained of the lady" in her and to look upon her community as "the ship where Jesus embarked with his [daughters]."[89]

In the period leading up to his death Margil visited Querétaro several times and traveled to Mexico City to try and save the flagging missions in Texas. In the capital he demonstrated that his oratorical skills had not suffered after years of solitude. Standing on a table near the main door of the cathedral he preached for three hours to the enraptured crowds that thronged the square.[90] In 1726, after a mission in Michoacán, he had returned to Querétaro in July. In the two weeks that he stayed in Querétaro Margil had made several visits to Santa Rosa and Santa Clara, but a few days into his stay he had fainted and lost consciousness for over an hour. The fainting spell was followed by high fevers. At the advice of doctors, Margil traveled to the capital to be treated at the Franciscan convent's infirmary; he was pushed by the ambition of his guardian who judged it opportune that Margil's death occur in a place where the glory owed to him could be expressed.[91] There, Margil made a general confession to an admiring friar, who found nothing in it that amounted to mortal sin. Nevertheless, Margil acknowledged having been tempted by the devil on numerous occasions and described himself as a "brute" who would have amounted to nothing had he not been led by the steady hand of God.

Hearing of his illness, the ecclesiastical community of the capital sent him various miraculous images, among them Nuestra Señora de los Dolores from the convent of Santa Clara. Reportedly, upon receiving the image Margil declared "until tomorrow," at which time, August 6, he indeed passed away.[92] His body immediately demonstrated signs of holiness since it stayed warm and flexible for at least ten hours after his death.[93]

Francisca anxiously awaited news of Margil's condition. According to the prior of the Carmelite convent in Querétaro, who inadvertently told her the news of his death, her reaction was a "sea of tears."[94] Margil's funeral was undertaken in Mexico City with great pomp and ceremony. His body was laid out in the sacristy of the church of San Francisco, where thousands came to have a last look at the legendary *bienaventurado*. The crowd that came to kiss Margil's naked feet was so numerous that according to witnesses it "made waves."[95] His funeral was attended by the viceroy and his court. The Jesuit friar Juan de Mora assured Francisca that the body's feet had been as pure and white as marble in spite of the thousands of leagues he had traversed in the New World and that the multitude had fought to kiss them. Indeed, the crowd's passion for touching the body was such that violence erupted as soldiers tried to fend it off. Mora was convinced that had the body not been so well guarded it would have been torn to pieces in a crazed hunt for miracle-working relics. The saintly friar's habit, however, was shredded for such purposes. After a "solemn mass" Margil was buried at the foot of the altar of the church of San Diego, in a vault belonging to the count of the Valle de Orizaba, between his two young children.[96] The Jesuit offered the consolation that Margil's time to enjoy glory in heaven had long been overdue and that his disciples should be happy to have such a powerful advocate in heaven. Francisca was not in the least consoled, however, and cried for him continuously. She dreamed of him giving her two slaps on the back, a customary greeting of his.[97]

Margil's death was preceded by the loss of María Isabel, one of the first members of the community and Francisca's close friend and assistant, and, in 1727, that of Antonia de Herrera, Francisca's mother. Like Margil, the two women continued to remain with Francisca in her dreams and visions. In 1727, for instance, she mentioned that the spirit of her late mother had given her counsel on the expulsion of a member of the community.[98]

In 1728, however, two years after Margil's death and after almost thirty years of running an institution that lacked solid official sanction and depended entirely upon the approval won by its good reputation, the foundress remained triumphant, the palm in her hand: a royal college whose maintenance was the obligation of the archbishop. The years of subsisting on a day-to-day basis, of politely reminding absent-minded benefactors of the most elementary needs, and of catering to two factions of squabbling ecclesiastics seemed at an end. But the stakes had been raised higher now, the *beaterio* was a royal college and thus an institution worthy of elite attention. And indeed, it seems that for some years before its royal sanction the upper echelons of Querétaro's Spanish society had regarded the community as a respectable depositing place for its perhaps more unfortunate members. Although we do not possess enrollment lists, Francisca in this period occasionally refers to new members of the community in her letters. Interestingly, she titles them doñas, whereas in the past she always referred to her companions by their first names, often adding the affectionate affix -*ita* to their names.[99]

When the process began is uncertain, but sometime after the death of Antonio de los Ángeles in 1711, Francisca wrote to Fray Juan de Ortega on the entry to the *beaterio* of the niece of a Santa Cruz friar. She claimed that the woman was of far too high a social station, and Francisca was not at all convinced she would work as an addition to the community.[100] And in the 1710s, some of the *beatas* lived with private servants.[101] Sometime in this period a woman from San Juan del Río petitioned to enter the community with her aunt. The woman had tried to get into Santa Clara but had not received enough votes to enter the novitiate. The fact that she expected to gain entry into the elite convent demonstrates that she possessed some social stature and that she considered Santa Rosa to be a respectable enough community to enter. Also, in this period it seems that a doña Rosa Vázques entered the *beaterio*. She may have been a member of the powerful Vázquez Terreros clan, which included several nuns in Santa Clara. It is clear at least that don Juan Terreros, one of the patriarchs of the group and the father of the future count of Regla was one of the community's benefactors.[102]

By 1728, then, the upper echelons of Querétaro society had begun to regard Santa Rosa as a viable and respectable depositing place for Spanish women (if not for their own daughters) who for whatever reasons did not gain entry into Santa Clara. How it was governed and by whom thus took on new significance. Almost immediately upon Santa Rosa's proclamation as a royal college conflict over its administration broke out with renewed vigor and eventually involved townspeople in yet another ecclesiastical scandal.

# 9  Eclipse

*An Ecclesiastical Standoff*
During the first months of 1729, the townspeople of Querétaro found themselves engulfed in a vicious quarrel between the secular and religious priesthood. The Franciscan Order and the city's ecclesiastical judge, Juan Fernández
de los Ríos, prefect of the Congregation of Guadalupe, were at loggerheads
over the question of who possessed jurisdiction over the *beaterio* of Santa
Rosa de Viterbo. The constant bickering between the Franciscan Order and
the town's increasingly more powerful secular clergy had become, by this
date, an integral element of its daily life. Santa Rosa had always been one
of the more important fields of conflict. As early as the turn of the century,
Margil had warned his brethren that the congregation of Guadalupe planned
a takeover of the *beaterio*. In spite of a brotherhood (*hermandad*) between
the two groups in which they pledged to aid each other with confessions and
missions, the seculars and the friars had been at loggerheads for years.[1]

The conflict had remained at low-level intensity for decades except for
a few blowups. One such event occurred in 1712, when the orders dragged
the townspeople with them into a tumultuous argument over precedence in
ceremonial processions. The affair severely affected Francisca's confessor, Fray
Ángel. The orders' placement in processions presented, of course, a delicate
problem since it demonstrated in no uncertain terms to the public the emi-
nence of the group involved. Thus, who went first and who second and third
was a matter worth many battles. The Dominicans had graciously accepted
third place in the important procession of Corpus Christi, but neither the
Congregation nor the Franciscans were prepared to emulate their pious example and take second place. The scandal had led to the feast day becoming a
spectacle; scribes could be seen on street corners taking down testimony from
onlookers. As the procession passed, the pious public, instead of staring in
rapt adoration at the statue of the Señor Sacramentado, would gossip openly
about who went and who did not while the women in the doors, balconies
and windows took notes and gossiped, "these ones won this time, and these
did not." The townspeople divided into opposing factions according to their
"own appetites" and relations with the ecclesiastics.[2]

The celebrations preceding the enclosure of Santa Rosa presented an occasion for public merriment free of such complications. On the eve of the event, the chaplain, don Nicolás de Armenta, celebrated a solemn mass and deposited the sacraments in their humble chapel. The night before had seen celebrations with music and pennants. Present at the mass was the entire Congregation of Guadalupe, which paid for this sumptuous ceremony; the ecclesiastical judge; representatives of the cabildo; and other elite members of the city. For three days the doors of Santa Rosa were thrown open, and the public was allowed to enter and explore every nook and corner, which would now forever be closed to it. According to María de Jesús, a multitude took the opportunity to wish the *beatas* well on their new journey.[3] Afterward the enclosure was announced publicly, doors were closed, and the community was left to its own devices. One fundamental question remained, however. Who should govern them? On January 1, a representative of the women wrote a letter to the archbishop inquiring as to whose authority the *beatas* should now be subject. On the one hand, they were members of the Franciscan Third Order, but they had belonged to secular ecclesiastical jurisdiction since 1715, when the archbishop took the *beaterio* under his protection. Two days earlier, having got wind of what was brewing in the *colegio*, the Third Order held a meeting. It convoked its members with a long, drawn-out ringing of the bells, which according to de Jesús caused upheaval among the townspeople, who sniffed scandal. The meeting resolved to send two Franciscans from Santa Cruz to Santa Rosa to demand unconditional obedience to the order or be disrobed.[4]

Once the *beatas* raised the question, however, the ecclesiastical judge, representative of the archbishop in Querétaro, acted equally swiftly. He had received an order from Mexico City conferring on him all authority regarding the *colegio*, including the *beatas'* possible change of habit, a change that was designed to resolve the ambiguity of their position as Franciscan tertiaries. When the Franciscans arrived they found the judge there along with several clerics from the Congregation of Guadalupe. A verbal brawl ensued, in which—in the words of eager-to-please de Jesús—the clerics defended the *beatas* from the "harsh, spiteful and rapid" questioning of the Franciscans. It must have been a bitter moment for Francisca, for both factions put her on the spot and demanded she declare her allegiance. Sensibly, she declined to do so verbally but offered to compose a written statement. Her silence enraged the Franciscans who ranted on until they departed in a fuss, demanding that the bells be rung when they left to signal to the town their displeasure with their protégées' disobedience. The ringing bells started the rumor that the friars had forcefully disrobed the *beatas* and taken away the sacraments.[5]

On January 24, de los Ríos went to Santa Rosa with a notary to take signed statements from the women to the effect that they would be willing to change habits. There he remained cloistered for three days in discussions with the divided community. The Franciscans were infuriated, and at this stage the affair became a scandal. On January 25 and 26, two Franciscan friars, assisted by a crowd of curious onlookers, repeatedly attempted to gain entry into the house, citing their authority as delegates of the Pope. They were denied entry by guards placed there by the judge, and so was any Franciscan confessor who approached the sealed-off community. The townspeople seem to have sided with the Franciscans, who were after all much more involved in the lives of all classes and ethnic groups than the elite congregationists of Guadalupe. The Franciscans also used more subtle and probably more effective means than public spectacles. For example, they set a Santa Clara nun who was a friend of Francisca's to the task of bombarding her with letters trying to persuade her to be steadfast to her old mentors.[6] But the cabildo sided with the Congregation, and on January 31, de los Ríos achieved his victory with a statement from all but nine of the *beatas* confirming that they would take the habit of Nuestra Señora de los Dolores of their own free will.

It had taken some time and ingenuity on the judge's part. Several women had stated that they would change their habits and then instead changed their minds. Some brought the new habits into their cells, where they battled for days with their conscience and finally found that they simply could not stop being Franciscans.[7] Most of those who did consent to the change stated that their reason was to secure the peaceful existence and internal life of the college. The Congregation graciously welcomed the women into its ranks as congregationists; they would thereafter wear the black robe of Nuestra Señora de los Dolores. De los Ríos then sued the Franciscan friars who had tried to interrupt his activities in Santa Rosa for attempting to usurp his jurisdiction.[8]

Three days earlier, however, the Franciscans had retaliated and escalated the public nature of the case. They took an image of Christ owned by the Cofradía del Santo Cristo de San Benito from the church of Santa Clara on a public procession attended by the entire Franciscan community, carrying candles through the city's principal streets. The act was in direct defiance of de los Ríos's authority since his permission was required for such a procession. The friars then further escalated the crisis by escorting the nine *beatas* expelled by the hot-tempered judge to shelter in Santa Clara. Two friars then spent several days in private consultation with the group in the *locutorios* of the convent, drafting statements about de los Ríos's tyrannical methods.[9]

At the heart of the matter, of course, lay not merely the question of control over Santa Rosa, but also the secular clergy's resentment toward the wealthy and powerful Franciscans who still monopolized the city's only parish. As tensions heightened in February, de los Ríos directly attacked the Franciscans' right to the parish. He complained to the archbishop that the Franciscan parish priest neglected to explain doctrine on Sundays at mass, thereby provoking angry admonishment of the friar. To humiliate the Franciscans further, he had the archbishop's orders hung up on the church doors in full view of the public. When they were taken down he had them refastened to the font of blessed water in the vestibule from which they could not be removed. He then ordered the Franciscans to read out the orders during the next Sunday mass. When the friar officiating did not begin with a reading of the document, the judge stood up, and in full view of Querétaro's most prominent citizens, heatedly accused the Franciscans of incompetence and treachery.[10]

Nor did he neglect the Santa Rosa affair. Provoked by a visit on February 12 from two Franciscan friars who wanted to discuss the matter, he issued a declaration that threatened them with excommunication if they proceeded with the case and ordered that the threat be posted on all church doors in the town. At this final public humiliation, the Franciscans lost their temper; they excommunicated de los Ríos. The infuriated judge ignored their action, claiming that they had no jurisdiction over him. He then proceeded to demand that the nine *beatas* sheltered in Santa Clara appear before him to offer an explanation of their behavior. On March 24, since they did not reply, he excommunicated the *beatas* and affixed the declaration on all the city's church doors. The Franciscan provincial immediately responded by ordering that new proclamations be hung next to the judge's, declaring that he had no jurisdiction to excommunicate the women. The cathedral chapter in Mexico City was then notified of the judge's actions by the *beatas'* representative. Horrified at the public scandal created by the judge, the council, on April 2, ordered that the *beatas* be absolved by secular priests and that de los Ríos immediately remove his declarations. The recalcitrant judge did not obey his orders, however, and the women remained excommunicated in Santa Clara.[11]

The Franciscans then proceeded to defend their case in the archbishopric's court. There it stalled for at least a year and a half owing to the judge's reluctance to hand over the relevant papers to the Order's lawyer. Unfortunately, we do not possess information about how the quarrel was concluded, but we do know that on July 11 an apostolic decree allowed the tormented Santa Rosa *beatas* to revert to their Franciscan habits while remaining under the jurisdiction of the archbishop.[12] On October 9, 1733, the archbishop finally gave the order that the community should change habits again, and a new, clearly more peaceable ecclesiastical judge collected from the women their written—and probably relieved—consent.[13]

To Francisca de los Ángeles, the affair must have represented an inexplicable and insurmountable trial by the divine hand. Only two years after the death of Fray Antonio Margil de Jesús she was forced to renounce the community that embodied his evangelical and popular Christianity. The Santa Cruz community had fostered and promoted her from youth, and in spite of their occasional grumbling had unflinchingly supported her particular brand of spirituality, which to many a learned cleric might have seemed downright distasteful. While don Juan Caballero y Ocio, founder of the Congregation of Guadalupe, had undoubtedly been her most devoted benefactor, her soul had been in the fiery care of the Franciscans. In their emaciated, travel-weary persons she had found an example worthy of imitation. The secular clerics of the Congregation, well fed, well clothed, and well intentioned, simply could not have presented a match to Francisca's other-worldly Franciscan soul mates.

But the Santa Cruz community of 1729 was not the community that in 1700 had included such individuals as Margil, de los Ángeles, Díez, and Fray Ángel. The men who had provoked such intense feelings of love and grief in their disciple were gone, and Francisca in turn was no longer an anxiety-ridden, ecstatic soul who placed her spiritual well-being entirely in the hands of a confessor. Díez had died in 1722 at the age of sixty-five, after suffering an accident while fixing the aqueduct at the college.[14] And after Fray Ángel's death that year she wrote no further on the matters of her soul to Santa Cruz, merely a few polite letters to Ortega inquiring after the friars' health and well-being. By 1729, she may well have been able to justify her decision to give the interests of her newfound *colegio* precedence over old attachments. The bond had already been broken. She probably entertained no illusions as to the benefits of her new friendship with the ecclesiastical judge, for he was a harsh, spiteful character who, according to the testimony of Francisca's fellow *beatas*, took every opportunity to humiliate her. Sometime during the height of the scandal the *portera* Josepha de Jesús María overheard a conversation between the two. De los Ríos unabashedly told Francisca that he had already written to the archbishop informing him that this "holy place so venerated, so esteemed, so applauded" was now worthless. The esteem in which it had been held was ruined; it was just yet another house, its sanctity fallen to pieces. According to the witness, Francisca listened to him with attention and allowed him to rant as he pleased. But as soon as he paused for breath she responded—peacefully according to the admiring Josepha—"you can send the message to the archbishop that although this holy place might be in pieces, none of its relics have been lost."[15] With her new friends, then, Francisca was already slipping into her well-worn role of defending the existence of the community.

But if ties between mortals no longer existed, celestial relationships were not as easy to break. Francisca and her *beatas* were Franciscan tertiaries, daughters of a great mendicant movement, its founder one of the most compelling figures produced by the church. For almost thirty years they had lived in his example, in true poverty and simplicity; beggars and vagabonds had slept on their floors. Saint Francis was Francisca's intercessor in all things, present at her ordination as tertiary, crossing wild rivers with her on expeditions to the *infieles*, and soliciting help in her most dire moments of despair. Thus, arrayed in heaven watching her shame were not only holy men such as Antonio de los Ángeles and Antonio Margil de Jesús, but the saint himself, source of their spirituality and example in all things. As the stupefied community, locked up and subject to incessant bullying from the stormy ecclesiastical judge, tried to make up its mind, many a *beata* was therefore seen on her knees before the saint's image imploring forgiveness, tears streaming down from their eyes. And when the moment arrived when the robe would have to be removed (added to their travails was the humiliation of having to wear secular clothes for three days until the new robes were tailored) moans and cries were heard from locked cells.

As in previous times of crisis within the community, however, Francisca hardened herself as a headmistress with her "heart between two stones." She snapped at the undecided ones and commanded others to follow her example, which prompted one Santa Clara refugee to declare that the foundress was solely responsible for the women's change of habit. The twenty-four-year-old María Teresa de los Dolores testified that Francisca, in the presence of the chaplain Armenta, another *beata*, and the judge, had ordered her not to answer the judge with any *tonterias* and that it was imperative "for the permanence of the house to change the habit."[16] Others were unceremoniously thrown on the street by the judge in Francisca's presence. Such was the case of thirty-year-old María Guadalupe de Santa Rosa, who had spent two-thirds of her life within Santa Rosa's walls. Because she refused to take the new habit, the judge, speechless with rage, ordered her out. It was only through the charity of the notary present that she found shelter.[17] When the judge was absent, however, Francisca changed tack and told her community that even if they changed habits they would never in their hearts and souls cease to be tertiaries and as such would still partake in the indulgences and graces granted the order.[18] At the same time, the headmistress herself kept a sharp eye on any messages sent from the supernatural side of the border. When a heavy mirror that had divided the upper and lower choir fell with great clamor on the floor, Francisca immediately told herself that if the mirror had not broken it would mean the discord would not ruin the community. Thankfully, it did not break. And during the worst crisis, there were signs of mercy; Margil appeared to her in a consoling dream eight nights in a row.[19]

The scandal deeply affected Querétaro society. Lay citizens took active positions with the parties in the matter, and witnesses described secret, strategic sessions by the Franciscans that were attended by the elite of the town. Both parties complained to the archbishop that their adversary's actions were arousing public scandals and disturbance and endangering the social peace within the city. Indeed, the matter must have posed a serious threat because the *alcalde ordinario* of Querétaro took up the case with the cathedral chapter in Mexico City, warning that any further developments could unsettle the community's peace.[20] The peaceful and harmonious existence of the city's religious women was essential to its own tranquility. And largely due to Francisca's public reputation and wide network of benefactors and friends, Santa Rosa had emerged from its obscure origins to occupy a prominent position among the religious institutions of Querétaro.

The townspeoples' response to the scandal was thus an acknowledgment of Santa Rosa's involvement in Querétaro's Spanish society. The scandal arose in the midst of a turbulent period for the town. On the surface it was stable and peaceful. The early eighteenth century seems to have been one of expansion for the town in general, and the 1720s in particular were a busy period for its notaries.[21] The town's activities were dominated by a relatively small group of entrepreneurs, the majority of whom had sent or would send their daughters to the Santa Clara convent.[22] They were mostly hacendados but also merchants and workshop owners who married each others' female relatives, sported military or political titles, and mostly conducted their business with each other alone.[23] But while the elite core of Spanish Querétaro grew ever more active economically and socially cohesive throughout the period, prosperity also brought many downturns. The "doñas" who begin to appear as members of Santa Rosa in this period probably belonged to that more unfortunate current within society.

By the 1730s, Santa Rosa served various practical purposes for the rich. In 1734, for example, the town watched with fascination as an extraordinary scandal brewed in the Ocio y Ocampo family, among its most distinguished citizens. Doña Josepha, daughter of don Agustín Ocio y Ocampo, deceased member of the city's cabildo and an entrepreneur of dynamic resourcefulness, was accused by a middling peninsular merchant of having broken her promise of marriage to him. As the story unfolded it became clear that Josepha, sixteen years of age, had maintained sexual relations with don Juan Antonio Montaño, who owned a store on the ground floor of her family's house and had become an intimate friend of the family. The ecclesiastical judge in Querétaro became involved, and Josepha was repeatedly taken from her house publicly to be placed in the *colegio* of Santa Rosa.[24] Santa Rosa played a public role in the affair. Curious onlookers could follow the unfortunate girl's carriage as it pulled up and the sinner was whisked inside by the headmistress. That Santa Rosa was no longer a "*rosal*" for pious souls seeking only to live in austere peace was thus a fact by the 1730s. In 1739 it was acknowledged by the ecclesiastical judge. According to him, the *colegio* was now filled with laywomen since population growth had generated increasing poverty. While life in the community was virtuous, "care is taken to provide the moderation and gentleness that the delicate state and temper of the female condition requires, especially in early childhood." As a result, the judge commented, Santa Rosa was not for those souls who "are called to the penitential life."[25]

## Death

The headmistress, by the 1730s, had grown quiet—at least on paper—as a mystic. In 1729, Francisca was fifty-five years old. In 1739, five years before her death, her community, in the opinion of many *queretanos*, was far from exemplary with respect to its ascetic piety and the established Creole lineage of its members. It contained fifty-five *colegialas* and at least fifteen servants. In spite of its virtuous enclosure there were many faults to be found in its operation. The women drank too much chocolate and deprived themselves of food in order to throw sumptuous feasts for visitors. Those who entered without the habit did not have to present certificates of *limpieza de sangre* to the Third Order before their profession. And while the women themselves maintained enclosure, visitors and servants came and went with the same freedom as before the establishment of the *colegio*.[26]

As old age descended on Francisca, she carefully hung on to life. In July 1725 she penned a compelling description of the travails of growing old. She had fallen while climbing down the stairs leading from the upper floor of her cell to the ground floor to receive the new Augustinian provincial. In doing so she had hurt herself severely and was convinced the devil was at work. After that episode, the *beata* always said an Ave Maria while carefully descending the stairs.[27] Similarly, sometime in the late 1720s, Francisca had to dictate a letter to Ortega because she was too ill in bed to write. It is the only note not written by her hand to the friars, another marker on the road to old age.[28] She had always claimed to be interested only in the afterlife, and her curiosity now began to reveal itself. She made a pact with a friend that whichever of them died first would contact the other to inform her what heaven was like.[29]

Nevertheless, in spite of her losses and advanced age, Francisca does not seem to have been prepared to leave her earthly existence. In 1727, she mentioned having heard on three occasions the squeaking of carriage wheels in front of her cell, but when she looked there was nothing there. Shortly after, a *beata* died of sunstroke, and almost all the *beatas* became sick with measles. Francisca then interpreted her experience with the squeaking wheels as a prediction of three deaths in the *beaterio*. She confided to her confessor that she was terrified of being the second or third to die. But by the 1730s, Francisca was surrounded by the spirits of several departed loved ones: Fray Antonio, Margil, Fray Ángel, Díez, her mother, sister, and closest friends. All that was left were testimonies of their lives. In January 1736, for example, the entire community took turns during meal times to read Margil's biography.[30]

As a dutiful disciple, throughout her career Francisca had followed her Santa Cruz friars' admonishment to not lose sight of death. She claimed to long for death as an end to her earthly travails and the beginning of a new life. In 1715, for example, she wrote to Fray Ángel that her soul had flown like a dove with the angels in the sky, but when she came to herself she cried over not being able to die and fly away. And in an undated note Francisca reported her desire to arrive at the day of her death dead to everything except her "dead and resurrected Jesus."[31] At the same time, she was terrified of death's prospect, at least in her youth and young adulthood, when she confessed to always having been afraid of performing the exercise of death so favored by the much admired Madre Agreda. It was not until around 1715, in a gush of enthusiasm following her drawn-out spiritual crisis, that Francisca decided to face the event and began to perform the exercise in the presence of her community. By that time her sister Gertrudis and Fray Antonio de los Ángeles had died and joined the celestial ranks, thus increasing the attractiveness of the other world.[32]

Francisca de los Ángeles died on June 7, 1744, aged seventy, seven months, and fourteen days. She died of dropsy after a long illness. In her last days she demanded to be carried to her cell so she could perform the three-day exercise of Santa Clara. The only people allowed in the cell were a *niña* she had raised and a *muchacho* who brought her food. A few days afterward, she awoke at eight o'clock, sent flowers to the altar, and the final agonies began at eleven. Significantly, there were no friars from Santa Cruz to assist her in these last moments, only two Jesuits. She died finally between four and five in the afternoon, thankfully for her hagiographer muttering "Jesus, Jesus." The stillness with which she died confounded the friars, who dared not approach the bed until after a proper interval.

Her body lay in the Santa Rosa chapel for nine days, after which the funeral ceremony was undertaken. Naturally, miracles occurred such as the gigantic candles rented by the *beatas* for the occasion failing to burn down at all during the event. Thus, the thrifty foundress persisted in saving money for her beloved community even after her death.[33]

# 10  Bourbon Querétaro

*Secularization and the New Elite*

The beginning of the Wars of Independence in 1810 marked perhaps less of a watershed in Querétaro than in many other regions. In spite of initial turmoil the city remained stable, its peninsular elite well entrenched among Creole families. Nevertheless, the event presents a turning point in the history of its religious institutions for women. After that date, the entry rates of new nuns into Santa Clara, which already had begun to decline in the last years of the colonial period, plummeted.[1] Although we do not possess the figures for Santa Rosa, one suspects much the same trend, especially since its religious membership had already declined by the end of the period. This development can be explained partly by the Bourbon administration's enlightened disdain for the church's pervasive influence in the life of New Spain as well as by the increasingly secular ethos that its policies implanted in colonial society. To the new absolutist monarchs of Spain, the revival of their flagging possessions depended not so much on the success of its citizens in prayer and penitence, as on social reform based on scientific and intellectual knowledge. Productivity had to be raised, not the wails of repentance. As Jo Ann Kay McNamara notes: "The concept of human nature, grounded in original sin, redeemed only through tears and penitence, gave way to the tabula rasa of John Locke, a human nature that was fundamentally good and perfectible through social reform."[2]

Cloistering women for the purpose of protecting their status and honor constituted an increasingly outmoded ideal to Enlightenment thinkers like Voltaire, Diderot, and Rousseau who blamed convent education for the moral flaws in women's characters.[3] In Mexico City, a more pragmatic approach to such institutions was reflected in a royal decree of 1780 that ordered all convents to open public schools. By 1800, most *recogimientos*, hitherto religious shelters for all types of women, had lost their protective role and had been closed or turned into prisons or schools.[4] In 1799, a royal decree permitted women of all ethnic groups to engage in "all labors and manufactures compatible with their strength and the decorum of their sex."[5] The convents did not escape unscathed. In 1774, the king ordered all Mexican convents to adopt the *vida común*, to eat and sleep in a common refectory, and to expel the large populations of laywomen who lived there. In the great convent of Santa Clara in Querétaro, the reforms halted professions during the next four years, expelled all laywomen except for a small group of very old residents, and cut the servant population of the convent by at least two-thirds, leaving merely one servant per nun.[6] Writing a few years after the tumult had passed, the abbess evoked the image of "desert" in describing the melancholy atmosphere pervading the convent. According to her, the community's life was now characterized by grayness and silence, and most of the nuns spent all their money paying the upkeep of their protégées and servants outside the convent.[7]

Between 1740 and 1770 the core of Creole elite families that had formed the web of power in Querétaro dispersed. This is clear from the Santa Clara convent's entry records. Family names, while pertaining to old circles, are missing from notarized business transactions, indicating that they were no longer involved in the booming entrepreneurship that had transformed the city once again in this period. The families of the Santa Clara nuns in this period had connections with families who preceded them, but they no longer had significant links with each other. By cloistering their daughters they dutifully carried on a tradition passed on from earlier generations, but they were no longer a socially or economically cohesive, interrelated group.

Undoubtedly this trend was related to a series of harvest failures and epidemics that occurred at the beginning of the decade. In 1749 the maize harvest failed. This caused famine among Indians and the castes, who attacked the city's corn exchange. The following year saw a second harvest failure, this time accompanied by an epidemic that spread across the country.[8] The harvest failures and epidemic must have had an impact on the fortunes of Querétaro's traditionally landed elite, which probably turned to conserving its estates rather than focusing on expansion or consolidation. Instead, economic activities in the 1750s in Querétaro were largely dominated by new family networks, with connections extending all over the region, as well as a handful of men, mostly peninsulars.[9] Furthermore, in contrast to the landed wealth of earlier families, many of these men were listed as merchants and miners, representing new and highly profitable enterprises. Indeed, although many of these newcomers married into old Creole families, their honorary posts and titles indicate that the Creole offspring of elite families had been excluded from the town's most powerful circles.

While the Creole elite disintegrated, Querétaro prospered. In the decades between 1740 and 1770 the wealth of the city was reflected in its architecture, which underwent a transformation. In the works of Ignacio Mariano de las Casas and Francisco Martínez Gudino, the flamboyant, ornate structures possess such originality that they are considered a particular provincial school of the *churriguresque* movement.[10] In spite of the city's increasing worldliness and efforts by reform-minded bishops within the Mexican church, the baroque piety of provincial cities such as Querétaro was untouched during the two decades between 1750 and 1770. The generous religious expression of its citizens did not diminish.[11] At the same time, however, there occurred subtle but significant changes within Querétaro's religious institutions. Following the Bourbon church reforms, which were aimed at curbing the riches and power of the colony's ecclesiastical institutions, the dominant Franciscans of Querétaro were stripped of their large central parish in 1757.[12] And owing to population growth, greater miscegenation, and social decline on the part of the city's Creole population, the process described previously at Santa Rosa was replicated in the Santa Clara convent. It began to function to an ever greater degree as a pious shelter for laywomen. During the three decades from 1745 to 1774, the number of girls admitted as paying boarders almost quadrupled when compared to earlier rates of admission.[13]

By the end of the eighteenth century, driven by a faster-paced and more complex economy, most of Querétaro's traditional elite families had been pushed aside by newcomers. The 1791 census reveals that the Plaza Mayor, Querétaro's traditional center of power, was now inhabited by twice as many peninsulars as Creoles, almost all of whom were merchants. The streets leading from the Plaza Mayor, a traditional residential area for the elite, had become segregated between peninsulars and Creoles.[14]

Querétaro's new, mostly peninsular elite did not establish the intimate ties to Santa Clara that earlier families had enjoyed. Comparisons between the early and late eighteenth century (1710–1740 and 1780–1810) show that the representation of nuns who had Creole fathers was far greater by the end of the century than in its early decades.[15] Querétaro's Iberian merchants probably followed the example of their predecessors and married Creole women of good families but increasingly broke with established tradition by not cloistering their offspring in Santa Clara. The majority of the city's Bourbon elite was clearly influenced by the practical spirit of the Enlightenment and by royal policy that regarded the fortunes spent on cloistering aristocratic women wasted when such money could be spent on public works of charity. It was influenced too by the declining importance of convents in the mother

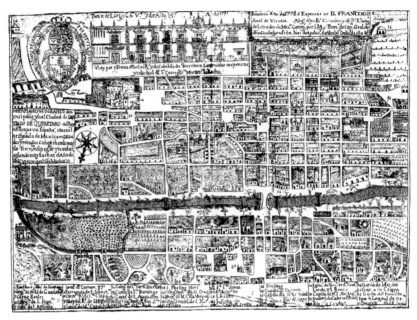

Querétaro, 1778. *Cartografía de Querétaro, colección de 35 planos de la ciudad capital y del estado.* Facsimile, 2nd ed., Querétaro, El Gobierno del Estado de Querétaro, 1978.

country. As a result, this elite did not associate status and fortune with having a daughter in Santa Clara as had the town's earlier elite.[16]

During the last four decades of the colonial period, the baroque religious life of the colony came under ever greater attack from the enlightened Bourbon administration. The signaling event was the expulsion of the Jesuits, the pillars of Creole religious culture, in 1767. The following decades saw heightened criticism of the populace's "superstitious" beliefs and increasing restrictions placed on baroque religious festivals and their characteristic public drama. Around the turn of the century, for example, Bishop San Miguel of Michoacán banned certain processions in León, Silao, and other areas of the Bajío.[17] The passionate Christocentrism preached by Margil suddenly seemed dubious. In 1784, for instance, the parish priest of Azatlán published a pamphlet in which he argued that Miguel de Guevara's famous sonnet, sung by every Jesuit schoolboy at bedtime, was heretical since it professed a direct, passionate love of God. The publication aroused such public dispute that both sides eventually appealed to the Inquisition to rule on the matter.[18]

On the surface, reformist policies do not seem to have caused marked changes in the religious expression of Querétaro's citizens. In 1802, José María

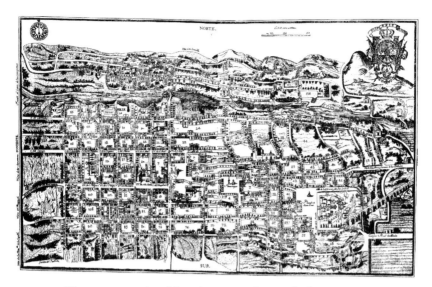

The prosperous city of Querétaro, 1796. *Cartografía de Querétaro*.

Zeláa y Hidalgo commented on the city's religious cult: "its annual feasts are notorious, its penitent processions, its devout confraternities, its perpetual chantries and its pious obligations."[19] The cult of sacred images was still integral to the city's religious culture, as is evident in the lay association formed by the city's wealthiest citizens around the image of Our Lady of Pueblito in the middle of the century. In 1803, the merchants of Querétaro paid for a new image of the Puríssima Concepción in the church of San Antonio, decorated it with elaborate jewelry, and undertook the obligation of paying for an annual feast surrounding it.[20] Religious associations were still active as was demonstrated both by the founding of the new and powerful confraternity of the Cordón in the same period and by the growing charitable activities of the Third Order.[21] The ayuntamiento continued to support public religious festivals. From 1776 to 1779 it spent 1777 pesos on novenas, masses, and celebrations of saints' days.[22]

Female religious still enjoyed a reputation outside their institutions. Zeláa y Hidalgo and the anonymous author of a Querétaro chronicle, *Varios acuerdos*, found it noteworthy to mention five nuns and *beatas* among important personages of the second half of the century.[23] Similarly, sermons preached during profession ceremonies or funerals of the city's nuns retained their ecstatic, baroque rhetoric, imbued with awe and adoration of their virtues.

One friar, for example, preaching on the profession of a Capuchin nun, argued that Christ had died not merely to save the soul of man but most importantly for the church, his wife, since the church, according to Christian doctrine, was born out of the Lord's side. And who, asked the preacher, building his argument to its pitch, was the "wife par excellence" if not the nun, according to San Cipriano "the most illustrious part of the Church"?[24]

One detects in these late-century sermons, however, a new element lacking in those of the early period. Early preachers extolled the virtuous and elevated status of the nun but were not particularly concerned with demonstrating to their congregation that such a life was better or holier than they could ever imagine. This indicates that there existed clear agreement between the speaker and listeners as to the advantages of conventual life. By contrast, later preachers used eloquent rhetoric to contrast the life of the nun with that of sinners in the world. They humbled their wealthy congregation in dramatic sermons that contrasted their own "unhappy land, fatherland of disorder, dominion of vice, reign of sin and the Devil" with the world of the cloister, "land of serenity and peace, a land of benediction and sweetness; a land of milk and honey."[25] The ills, vanities, and perishable nature of this world were meticulously detailed, while the audience was awed with vivid descriptions of the life of the nun, which was filled with austerity, poverty, humility, self-mortification, silence, and prayer. They were reminded of the constant heroic battle that the nun had to fight against the very nature that characterized all human life: "[she] will consequently have to moderate the passions of the spirit, to negate love of the heart, or the desires of her own will . . . austerities which seem unbearable to human forces."[26]

In return for her labors, however, the nun received a spiritual wealth and happiness of which "the human heart cannot form an adequate idea."[27] If such words indicate a dissatisfaction by their speakers with the populace's lack of respect for conventual life, other friars went even further in their rhetoric. In 1790, when the Santa Cruz friar Pedro Bringas de Manzaneda preached a sermon on his sister's profession, he openly attacked what he considered the irreverence of the laity for the religious life: "men of the world consider the cloister as a sepulcher of living beings, or as a prison which many young inexperienced men and many unsuspecting girls suffer when they lose their liberty."[28]

Such rhetoric may echo a greater esteem of material status and wealth among Querétaro's new elite at the expense of respect for ecclesiastical institutions. According to Zeláa y Hidalgo, the new families lived in aristocratic style: "The principal citizens use their carriages, which enlighten the populace with their beauty and magnificence, there are more than sixty-six of them [carriages] at this time."[29] The increased social and economic authority of the individual was expressed in the later decades of the century through new constructions that symbolized Querétaro's civic accomplishments, including buildings such as the Alhondiga, the Royal Tobacco Factory, the Casas y Cárceles Reales, and plans for an alameda to show off the luxurious and leisurely aspect of life that wealth afforded its citizens. Similarly, the architectural styles of the city's new edifices, such as the Carmelite convent built in 1803, followed the neo-classical movement, an enlightened reaction against the lively and ornate churriguresque that had characterized Creole architecture since the 1720s. The new style had been installed in the colony by the Bourbon administration with the founding of the Academy of San Carlos in the early 1780s.[30]

There clearly existed in Querétaro at the time a tendency toward a more "enlightened" manner of piety. The Franciscan Third Order was split over the question of whether to continue its support for extravagant baroque religious festivals such as Holy Thursday, and divided over its foundation and support of a primary school for boys, established in 1788. Other confraternities were turning to organized charitable activities in response to the social problems created by the city's expansion, while many traditional confraternities affiliated with the regular orders were falling into decline.[31]

### Santa Rosa de Viterbo: Institutional Splendor

By Francisca's death in 1744, Santa Rosa was a worldly institution in comparison with its biblical beginnings, a bustling community that contained all sorts with varied purposes. As the eighteenth century steered into its final decades the Bourbon climate took hold in Querétaro with all its uncertainties. With the turmoil, the *beaterio* of Santa Rosa gained a well-fixed purpose: to siphon off the unlucky *criollas* tossed to the side by the storm and left there to mingle their blood with undesirable castes. While some well-established families had begun to send their offspring to Francisca in the 1720s and the elite had supported the community, it was not until the 1750s that the city's elite truly caught on. In 1739, the majority of the community's fifty-five members came from the provinces and lived in relative poverty. In 1751, however, don José Velázques de Lorea, one of Querétaro's richest citizens and lieutenant colonel of the Royal Militia, built the community a sumptuous new church and cloister that would have gone beyond even Francisca's hopes. It was designed by the famed architect Ignacio Mariano de las Casas and is considered among the foremost architectural expressions of the baroque in the colony.[32] Large parts of the ancient edifice with its adobe structures were demolished to make space for boisterous new buildings. New Spain's most famous painter of the century, the Oaxacan Miguel Cabrera, was commissioned to paint elaborate retables of such noted figures as Saint Joseph and the Virgin of Guadalupe. Ignacio Mariano de las Casas also designed its baroque organ, now considered among the foremost examples of its kind in the world. The interior of the church rivals and almost exceeds that of Santa Clara with its orgy of gold, flamboyance, and ecstatic storytelling art. The confessionals, for example, were covered with golden and colored swirling patterns, which might have seemed jarring to the Margil who preached his doctrine of the empty vessel to Francisca.

Notarial records from the middle of the century and the following decades show that Santa Rosa's financial means steadily increased through donations from Querétaro citizens and its rapidly developing banking activities. Virtually nonexistent before the 1740s and relatively dispersed around the middle of the century, such transactions had become frequent by the end of the century and the beginning of the nineteenth. Between 1770 and 1810, the community notarized almost twice as many financial transactions—and double the sums of money—as in the period between 1730 and 1770.[33]

At the same time, the *beaterio*'s members began to identify more openly with their background. Until the 1740s at least, Santa Rosa's members always signed documents with their religious names, for example, Francisca de los Ángeles, Isabel de Santa Rosa, and so on. During the second half of the century, however, the women, most of whom belonged to old elite families, began to sign notarial documents with their family names. By the end of the colonial period all members of the community used their family names.[34] Moreover, some women owned extensive estates and left small fortunes when they died. Thus, Rosa de Zárate y Aranda, a member of an old Querétaro family, left donations of thirteen thousand pesos in her will in 1781, an amount that may have constituted only part of her estate. Others owned "urban and rural" real estate and purchased and sold houses in the city.[35] Many of these relatively affluent residents were members of families who earlier in the century occupied the upper stratum of Hispanic society.

It is likely then that Santa Rosa had begun to serve the same purpose for the town's downwardly mobile upper class families that it had for its more marginal members at the beginning of the century: as a buffer against greater social misfortune.[36] Lacking sufficient dowries to marry within their rank, Santa Rosa's residents could conserve their status and honor without having to take religious vows or pay the substantial dowries required at Santa Clara.

In several instances, Santa Rosa served as a type of reformatory shelter for women who in some way did not fit into, or who rebelled against, the norms and roles assigned to them in lay society. From the 1750s to the 1770s, several women entered the community for shorter or longer periods for such reasons. The Marchioness of la Villa del Villar del Águila entered the institution for a month to cure her "melancholy temperament" through the quietude and long confessions it provided her. Juana de la Campa, whose undefined "illness" effected a temporary separation from her husband, lived for a long period with the *colegialas*, and Gertrudis López was admitted into Santa Rosa when her husband accused her of adultery.[37] In 1770, when María Josefa Rosa Casimira Ramírez y Cervantes, the seventeen-year-old daughter of an affluent Creole family, denounced her own heresy to the Santa Rosa chaplain she was cloistered in Santa Rosa during and after the proceedings, which involved her confession and absolution.[38]

Santa Rosa now found itself in troubles typical of colonial religious institutions that were too big and too open. In a 1758 letter to the archbishop in Mexico City, the ecclesiastical judge of Querétaro admitted that a certain Franciscan friar had been engaged in illicit correspondence and perhaps relations with a member of the Santa Rosa community for several years. Discussing the problem, the judge also mentioned a separate case of a *beata* who, having borne a son in the *beaterio*, raised him there and only left a few years later. This, the judge claimed, took place at a time when the community had virtually ceased to live cloistered from the world.[39] The judge hastened to assure the archbishop that such problems had been overcome a year before when entrances to the college were fitted with such heavy and solid wooden doors that "better ones cannot be found at any other monastery."[40] Alarmed by such news, however, the archbishop sent the Santa Rosa community a dispatch containing orders for a more effective separation from the world.[41]

Two decades later the college had not succeeded in isolating itself from the world. In 1776, Inquisition procedures against a confessor who had been found to solicit illicit favors from his Santa Rosa protégées revealed that eighteen years before the same priest had solicited, in the confessional, the headmistress of the college and that these problems "were almost publicly recounted in Querétaro." The priest's present misdemeanors involved two laywomen who lived in Santa Rosa; a year later a third woman denounced him. All three testified that the priest arranged meetings in the street, outside the college's door, and one admitted that she had left the cloister once to meet him in his home. Although the women were lay residents of the college and not bound by a vow of enclosure, they clearly enjoyed extensive freedom of movement considering that they lived in a religious institution.[42]

## Enlightenment

By the end of the colonial period, *queretanos* were no longer the baroque population that had welcomed the ecstatic friars of Propaganda Fide and participated in their dramatic reform project. Secularization had begun to sprout roots, and religious faith, according to its new dominant class of wealthy Creoles and peninsulars, was to find its expression in the depths of the heart and soul, but not in extravagant public manifestation. While the change does not constitute what John Somerville has termed a transition from "religious culture to religious faith," its repercussions were nevertheless profound.[43] For the early Creole elite, lacking a substantial connection to the mother country, convents and religious culture established its place within Iberian civilization. By contrast, for its peninsular successors the ties with the mother country probably undermined their involvement in local culture.

Half a century after Francisca de los Ángeles's death the medieval culture of sociable mysticism and rapture she propagated was no longer endorsed by the city's new elite. Man was no longer a "wretched" creature capable at most of getting rid of his messy nature in order to become an empty vessel for God. The rich peninsulars and Creoles of Querétaro had the satisfaction of watching the fruits reaped by orderly entrepreneurship and were not tortured by questions relating to the inherent misery of human existence. Hard work paid off in this world as well as the other and promised to take them on a course toward a perfection that Fray Antonio Margil de Jesús would have maintained was only possible through God. What Francisca would have thought of this new world is another matter. Might not the ambitious and sociable headmistress in her have been tempted by the opportunities provided by a dynamic economy for expanding and enhancing her much-loved *beaterio*'s role in society? Or would the scornful ascetic in her have been appalled at its audacious faith in the inherently weak human being and the lack of respect shown to her Lord and Master in Heaven? We cannot know. Most likely, as always in her, there would have been an extended battle of conscience and a most baroque compromise.

# Epilogue

Posthumously, the reputations of Francisca de los Ángeles and her mentor, Fray Antonio Margil de Jesús, were granted different fates. After their deaths, evidence was gathered regarding the miracles attributed to them, and biographies were written. But while Margil's biography, written by Fray Isidro Félix de Espinosa, became a classic and was followed by at least ten other works, Francisca's, written by Fray Hermenegildo de Vilaplana, was either lost or languishes unpublished and unfound in a Roman archive.[1] Similarly, Margil was known as a saint in Mexico throughout the eighteenth and nineteenth centuries, while Francisca's reputation fell quickly into oblivion.[2] Soon after the friar's death, the colony began to take steps to preserve his myth and prepare the ground for a future canonization process. In 1728, the Congregation for the Propagation of Faith initiated the process, which was continued in 1729 when the municipal authorities of Mexico City petitioned the king to order an investigation of the holy man's heroic deeds.[3] His biographer, Espinosa, noted hopefully that just as San Antonio of Padua had not really been from Padua, so Margil could be named San Antonio de México.[4] By the late eighteenth century, miracles were still being attributed to Margil's various portraits, and funds were raised for the canonization process.[5] According to testimonies, Margil's cult had spread throughout the colony so that statues of him adorned the niches of houses in "the most humble villages."

In 1775, Francisca's biographer, Vilaplana, published a biography of Margil that gave added impetus to the process. By the end of the century things looked promising, and Rome seemed favorable to the Mexican cause. The situation changed dramatically, however, when Napoleon invaded the Holy City in 1798. Most of the papers pertaining to Margil's process were destroyed in the ensuing chaos.[6] Once that window of opportunity had been shut the subsequent century was one of disappointment for the Franciscan cause. As Antonio Rubial García notes, the Franciscans projected Margil as a symbol, not only of a "second Golden Age" of European evangelization in the New

World, but as connecting the missionary phenomenon of the seventeenth and eighteenth centuries with the original "Spiritual Conquest." Nevertheless, by the nineteenth century the failure of these missions had become evident. This is exemplified in the figure of Geronimo, the Indian leader raised in a mission, who became a serious challenge to white authority in the southwest of the United States. But already by the eighteenth century, Margil's saintly prospects were dubious at best. Rubial García notes that as "the West began to dismantle its forces against apocalyptic terror and the omnipotence of Satan" Enlightenment reformers were unlikely to embrace Margil's casting as a hero in such a plot, no matter how agreeable his activist and pragmatist stance.[7]

Francisca's fate is even more indicative of this trend. A poor *beata* who publicly proclaimed visions, preached, and through her divine connections gained influence with powerful men in her community ran contrary to the Enlightenment's practical and rational thrust. When the apostolic notary of Querétaro added his certification to the testimonies of Santa Rosa *colegialas* regarding Francisca's extraordinary powers, he noted that the manuscript "with the divine favor will soon see public light."[8] The friar was unaware of the great changes that the subsequent decades would usher in New Spain. Had Francisca died a century earlier her fate might have been different. At the height of the baroque period ecclesiastics pining for a Mexican saint enthusiastically promoted myths of holy women. Between 1640 and 1645, for example, Bishop Juan de Palafox y Mendoza sent manuscripts dictated by the famed nun María de Jesús to Spain in order to start her beatification process. After another noted Puebla nun, María de San José, died in 1717, her writings, never before published, were incorporated into a hagiographic biography published in 1723, and reissued in 1725.[9]

But even in that period, Francisca's reputation would not have been assured. It is sufficient to remember ecclesiastical authorities' repression of the popular cult of Catarina de San Juan in Puebla at the end of the seventeenth century to recall the precarious positions of such women. And in Spain, Teresa of Avila was the only female saint to be canonized during the Counter-Reformation. By the middle of the eighteenth century Enlightenment peninsulars considered what their baroque predecessors had found to be spiritual graces to be spiritual excesses. As Caffiero has noted regarding Italy of the eighteenth century, devotion, rational and "free of excess", became a spiritual model preferred over contemplation.[10]

Modernity did not simply arrive as an unexpected guest at the doorstep of the colony in the middle of the century. The signs had been there, obvious to modern scholars but naturally obscured to most contemporaries. In the Querétaro demoniac case of 1691, the Mexican Inquisition chose to swiftly punish the female perpetrators of the affair rather then delve into the nature of the possessions. It had needed to make clear to all that the orthodox could not accept the devil proposed by the women and their Franciscan protectors: a weak, ridiculous creature nevertheless given power by a cruel and arbitrary God. As Cervantes notes, this should not be taken as a sign of the influence of new cultural trends but simply as a measure to protect the devil's orthodox reputation.[11] Nevertheless, that gesture alone shows a growing discomfort with baroque extravagance and an inclination perhaps to view as excess what twenty years earlier would have been given due attention. A similar tendency is evident in the prohibition of the Jesuit Alonso Ramos's ecstatic biography of the *poblana* Catarina de San Juan in 1696.[12] In Rome, rationalist and scientific currents, permeated by the new thought rejected a century earlier in the trial of Galileo, generated new criteria for hagiography and beatification. Among the victims were the reputations of celebrated holy women such as Margil's beloved Sor María de Agreda, whose writings were banned a year after his death in 1727.[13] The new approach to female spirituality in the Holy See is best exemplified by the 1755 biography on the Blessed Clare of Rimini. With historical precision it picked apart an ecstatic, baroque version of her life published in 1718, deprived her of her glory as foundress and nun, and explicitly made no mention of her mystical exploits.[14]

Although mysticism and female visionaries enjoyed a popular revival in Italy in the late eighteenth century, the antibaroque sentiment that consumed the Vatican destroyed traditional hagiography. If the reputation of revered Italian medieval holy women was thus humiliated, what prospects were there for a provincial Mexican *beata*? Ironically, Francisca's story when seen through her letters contains many of the obligatory elements of the revisionist Jansenist approach to hagiography that became dominant in the late eighteenth century. Nuns were singled out who showed independence, organizational skill, and creativity when it came to the matter of foundations and who embraced an "active life, an external apostolate, and an involvement in society." Tertiaries, by virtue of their life in the secular world, "laid claim to new social and religious spaces for women."[15] But these elements would in all probability have been dwarfed in Vilaplana's biography by episodes demonstrating Francisca's miraculous powers and mystical triumphs. Unknowingly, then, Francisca de los Ángeles traversed a transitional period and died as it neared its completion. Devoted daughter of the post-Tridentine Church, her undisciplined mysticism and visionary boisterousness would not have found official sanction at the Vatican in any epoch of the early modern period. Instead, her "career" is a local variation of the Counter-Reformation theme, with its focus on sacramental devotion, evangelical action, and mystical experiences—a symptom of what Evennett terms the "quickening [of the] spiritual life-blood of Catholicism."[16]

Indeed, one of the most surprising aspects of Francisca's story is that in Querétaro, a pious but relatively unsophisticated city virtually on the periphery of the New World, her life was penetrated by surprisingly strong gusts of the cultural currents sweeping in from the larger world stage. The *beata* both suffered from and participated in the Counter-Reformation's project of imposing social order and discipline on Catholic societies under duress. In the New World, of course, only dim echoes could be heard of the cultural convulsions that had shaken Iberian society in the preceding century, but on the other side of the Atlantic other threats were at work in the strangeness of these regions, with their perceived inherent potential to morally corrupt a Spaniard living in the midst of Indians, Africans, and castes. With her ambiguous social position and spiritual aspirations Francisca presented one such undisciplined element to the Mexican Inquisition. While her career was not thwarted by the tribunal she nevertheless suffered at its hands. At the same time, her work as foundress and institutional reformer aided in the Counter-Reformation's disciplinary project by cloistering and providing religious indoctrination for women who presented similarly insecure factors in the colonial equation because of their vulnerability to assimilation into the castes.

But the authoritarian thrust of the Counter-Reformation was not what steered Francisca to her niche in life. In spite of its looming presence, the *beata*'s experience of exile on this earth became a far more flavorful affair. As a child and adolescent she was steeped in the sort of heterodox urban spirituality that her New World circumstances gave rise to. She expressed it in her charismatic visionary experiences and independent interpretation of the fundaments of the faith. Had Propaganda Fide never arrived in Querétaro, Francisca's internal life might have remained at that, extravagant and interesting but one dimensional. But in joining forces with the Spanish missionaries things took a different turn. In her mentors, particularly in Margil, the *beata* was exposed to the ecstatic mysticism and evangelism of the Franciscan tradition. She eagerly accepted the opportunity to become a spiritual *varón*, her visionary imagination kindled both by her mentors' almost biblical forays into the deserts of the New World and the mythical quality of the episodes of conversion that took place there. Her letters record not merely her participation in this millenarian project as reformer, mystic, and evangelist but project with honesty and humanist curiosity the turbulent life of her soul. They bring to light a personality with an immediate appeal to the modern reader for her sociability, complexity, and stubborn determination. Unlike the unfortunate souls persecuted for their religious expression in New Spain, a solid thread of acknowledgment of Francisca's gifts—in spite of her ups and downs with confessors—runs through her life. In this feminine and provincial Mexican variation of early modern Catholicism, charismatic piety and evangelical independence find acceptance and come to fruition.

# Notes

## Preface

1. A mystic worked her way through the soul's darkness toward union with God, while the visionary was the recipient of revelatory visions.

## Introduction

1. See Armstrong, *A History of God*, pp. 333–35.

2. Quoted in Kamen, *The Phoenix and the Flame*, p. 340. Kamen notes that between 1493 and 1820, fifteen thousand religious were sent to the New World by the king, "their peak emigration occurring precisely in the golden age of Trent, from about 1560 to around 1610." On religious education, see Hsia, *The World of Catholic Renewal*, p. 51. The term *Counter-Reformation* has become the object of much discussion. The clearest synthesis of this debate is presented in O'Malley's *Trent and All That*. O'Malley argues that the term must be used in context, that is, when discussing events and concepts that emerged as a direct reaction against the Reformation. Many developments in the Catholic world in the early modern period do not owe their character to this reaction but are a continuation of past traditions or popular innovations that eventually influenced church thinking and policy. Similarly, O'Malley argues, terms such as *Tridentine age, Catholic reforms, Confessional Catholicism*, and the like denote certain currents within Catholicism and should be used with precision. He adds his own suggestion, "Early Modern Catholicism," to these categories as an "umbrella" concept that provides them with "more precision on certain issues." In his argument, the term suggests both "change and continuity" within an open-ended chronology. In O'Malley's view, it is also a more popular term than the others mentioned, "all of which indicate more directly the concerns and actions of ecclesiastical, political, or politico-ecclesiastical officialdom." Rather, *Early Modern Catholicism* connotes local realities influenced by long-standing traditions rather than church policy, and it expresses that "popular attachment to Catholicism might sometimes be explained by the comfort people found in the everyday experience of it and not always by a grudging conformity to a grid imposed from above." I concur with this view and will use all such concepts intermittently only in the appropriate context.

3. On the Virgin of Guadalupe, see Brading, *Mexican Phoenix* and *The First America*, pp. 343–60.

4. See Jaffary, *Deviant Orthodoxy* for the case of New Spain.

5. Both terms used in Brading, *The First America*. The latter term is taken by Brading from the mendicant chroniclers Fr. Juan Meléndez and Fr. Diego de Córdova Salinas, see p. 335. The term the *new Jerusalem* is taken by Brading from Agustín de Betancur's *Teatro Mexicano*, see Brading, p. 373. On the extirpation of idolatry in the Andes, see, for example, McCormack, "The Heart Has Its Reasons," pp. 202–24.

6. Thus, the Mexican savant Carlos Sigüenza y Góngora eagerly used his kaleidoscope to study the 1691 solar eclipse, which sent the population of Mexico City scrambling in terror of the devil for shelter in the cathedral and churches. See Leonard, *La época barroca*, pp. 278–79.

7. Thompson, *Thomas Gage's Travels*, p. 70.

8. Paz, *Sor Juana*, p. 259.

9. Brading, *The First America*, p. 376.

10. Thompson, *Thomas Gage's Travels*, p. 72.

11. On Palafox, see Brading, *The First America*, pp. 237–38.

12. Brading, *The First America*, p. 239.

13. On that process in Spain, see, for example, Nalle, *God in la Mancha*, pp. 206–10.

14. Forster, *Catholic Revival*, p. 10.

15. Espinosa, *Crónica*, p. 59.

16. For biographies of Propaganda Fide missionaries see, for example, Espinosa, *El peregrino septentrional*, and the biographies written by the same friar referred to in later chapters.

17. Caffiero, "From the Late Baroque Mystical Explosion," p. 182.

18. McNamara, *Sisters in Arms*, pp. 521–22.

19. Quoted in Weber's *Saint Teresa of Ávila*. See p. 3 on such attitudes toward religious women and Saint Teresa in particular. See as well pp. 35–40, 52, 159, 165.

20. See, for example, Fray José Díez's admiring comment on the first Christians in his note to one of Francisca's letters in which he describes their communal life and prayers. Archivo Histórico de la Provincia Franciscana de Michoacán—Archivo del Colegio de Santa Cruz de Querétaro, AHPFM-ACSC, G-leg. 5.

21. This discussion and the quotation from Jerome is owed to Newman's *From Virile Woman to Female Christ*, pp. 3–5.

22. Quoted in Ahlgren, *Teresa of Avila*, p. 158.

23. See Weber, *Teresa of Ávila*, and Surtz, *Writing Women*, pp. 11–13, in which he discusses attitudes toward religious women in fifteenth-century Spain. He highlights, for example, Antonio de la Peña's prologue to a Castilian edition of the life of Saint Catherine of Siena in which de la Peña notes that "as compensation for their feminine weakness, God has given some women the flight of prophecy."

24. Hsia, *The World of Catholic Renewal*, p. 105.

25. See MacKendric and McKay, "Visionaries and Affective Spirituality," pp. 92–93.

26. Quoted in Surtz, *Writing Women*, p. 8 (his translation). The fascination with unlettered, affective spirituality, especially as expressed by females in Golden Age Spain, was accelerated by the cardinal's printing press in Toledo, from which issued works by Catherine of Siena and Angela of Foligno, both tertiaries and ecstatics. And it is useful to remember that Isabel de la Cruz, the heretical leader of the Iberian *alumbrados* who preached a total abandon to the love of God and mental prayer, was a Franciscan tertiary.

27. On the culture of the Jesuits, see O'Malley, "Was Ignatius Loyola a Church Reformer?" pp. 67–82.

28. See Muriel, *Conventos de monjas en la Nueva España, La sociedad novohispana y sus colegios de niñas*, and *Los recogimientos de mujeres*. Also see Asunción Lavrin, "The Religious Life of Women in Colonial Mexico," "The Role of the Nunneries," "La riqueza de los conventos," "Problems and Policies in the Administration of Nunneries," "The Execution of the Laws of Consolidation," "Values and Meaning of Monastic Life," "La vida femenina como experiencia religiosa," "La escritura desde un mundo oculto," "Indian Brides of Christ," *Monjas y beatas*, and "Sor María de Jesús Felipa."

29. See Soeiro, "The Social and Economic Role of the Convent" and "The Feminine Orders in Colonial Bahía, Brazil"; Gallagher, *The Family Background of the Nuns of Two Monasterios*"; Burns, "Convents, Culture and Society in Cuzco" and *Colonial Habits*; Ramos Medina, *Imagen de santidad en un mundo profano*; Amerlinck de Corsi and Ramos Medina, *Conventos y Monjas*; Aizpuru, *Las mujeres en la Nueva España*; Foz y Foz, *La revolución pedagógica en Nueva España*; Castañeda, *La educación en Guadalajara*; Ramos Medina, *El Monacato Femenino en el Imperio Español*; Van Deusen, *Between the Sacred and the Worldly*; and Loreto López, *Los conventos femeninos y el mundo urbano*.

30. See Jaffary, *Deviant Orthodoxy*; Rubial García, "Las Santitas del barrio," "Josefa de San Luis Beltrán"; and Alberro, *Inquisition y societé*.

31. See Ibsen, *Women's Spiritual Autobiography*; McKnight, *The Mystic of Tunja*; Myers, *A Wild Country Out in the Garden*; Lavrin, *Monjas y Beatas*; Sampson Vera Tudela, *Colonial Angels*; Myers, *Word from New Spain* and "Fundadora, crónista y mística"; Gunnarsdóttir, "Una visionaria barroca"; Loreto López, "Escrito por ella misma"; and Lavrin, "Sor María de Jesús Felipa."

32. Ibsen, *Women's Spiritual Autobiography*, p. 11.

33. On intense, near-heretical relationships between confessors and their *hijas* see, for example, Iwasaki Cauti, "Mujeres al borde de la perfección," p. 590.

34. Ibsen, *Women's Spiritual Autobiography*, p. 13.

35. Ibsen, *Women's Spiritual Autobiography*, p. 18.

36. Paz, *Sor Juana*, p. 17, 49.

37. In his study of Catholic life in southwestern Germany during the baroque period, Forster warns against viewing the region's Catholic revival as the product of a

policy of "confessionalization" by the secular and religious elite. The popular currents that he identifies in this revival are strikingly similar to those in the Querétaro of Francisca's epoch. As a feminine component of the Propagation of Faith's mission Francisca was an integral part of that flowering. See Forster, *Catholic Revival*.

38. See Evennett, "Counter-Reformation Spirituality," pp. 47–64.

39. See AHPFM-ACSC, G-leg. 5, no. 27, for a list of her guardian saints and angels. In October 1729, she promised an octave to San Antonio if he helped her find her keys (G-leg. 4).

40. AHPFM-ACSC, G-leg., no. 2, 1694.

41. AHPFM-ACSC, G-leg. 4, no. 7, undated.

### 1. The Emerging City

1. This date is calculated from a comment made by one of her confessors in 1714 where he noted that she was forty years old. See AHPFM-ACSC, G-leg. 5, no. 20.

2. Wright, *Querétaro en el siglo XVI*, pp. 39–44.

3. Brading, *Haciendas and Ranchos in the Mexican Bajío*, p. 18.

4. In comparing the agricultural production of the provinces of Michoacán, Puebla, and Oaxaca in the period 1700–1794, Richard L. Garner found that Michoacán (which included the Bajío region) grew at a rate of 1.6 percent per annum, twice the growth of Oaxaca (0.7) and Puebla (0.8). See Garner, *Economic Growth and Change in Bourbon Mexico*, p. 49.

5. Garner, *Economic Growth and Change in Bourbon Mexico*, p. 38.

6. On estate formation in the north, see Chevalier, *Land and Society in Colonial Mexico*. On the Bajío, see Brading, *Haciendas and Ranchos*, p. 17.

7. García Ugarte, *Breve Historia de Querétaro*, pp. 77–78.

8. Wright, *Querétaro en el siglo XVI*, p. 48.

9. Brading, *Haciendas and Ranchos*, p. 16. An intendancy report on the region from 1793 estimated that 48.7 percent of the working population was employed in agriculture; 34.1 percent as artisans, miners, industrial workers, and tradesmen; and 15.9 percent were day laborers. Brading, *Haciendas and Ranchos*, p. 20.

10. Super, *La vida en Querétaro*, p. 16. Super derives the 1642 population estimate of Spaniards from Fray Antonio Vázquez de Espinosa's description of New Spain in the seventeenth century.

11. Murphy, *Irrigation in the Bajío Region*, p. 92.

12. Murphy, *Irrigation in the Bajío Region*, p. 91.

13. Murphy, *Irrigation in the Bajío Region*, p. 94.

14. Super, *La vida en Querétaro*, p. 123.

15. On the importance of the textile mills by the end of the colonial period, see Brading, *El ocaso novohispano*, p. 197.

16. Celia Wu's analysis of the 1791 *padrón* shows that while peninsulars mostly congregated in the center and half of the Indian population lived in the neighborhood

of San Sebastian, the rest of the population did not live in segregated areas. Wu, "The Population of the City of Querétaro in 1791," p. 301.

17. Super, *La vida en Querétaro*, p. 274. The occupations listed for mestizos are those whose workforce was more than 50 percent mestizo.

18. AHPFM-ACSC, F-leg. 2, no. 12. "Papeles tocantes a varias oposiciones que se hicieron contra el Beaterio de Santa Rosa." Archivo General de la Nacion (AGN), Inquisición, vol. 693, p. 405.

19. Quoted in Murphy, *Irrigation in the Bajío*, p. 98.

20. Carlos Sigüenza y Góngora, excerpt *from Las Glorias de Querétaro* in Frías, *Las Calles de Querétaro*, pp. 26–27.

21. AHPFM-ACSC. G-leg. 2, no. 1, 2; leg. 7, no. 10.

22. AHPFM-ACSC, G-leg. 2, no. 1, 2; leg. 7, no. 10. To Margil, January, 1701, pp. 5–6.

23. de Jesús, *Crónica del Real Colegio de Santa Rosa de Viterbo*, pp. 117–24.

24. AHPFM-ACSC, leg-5, no. 8, to Margil, January 1, 1701, pp. 2–2v.

25. AHPFM-ACSC. G-leg. 2, no. 1. "Papeles pertenecientes al interior de la venerable Francisca de los Ángeles, escritos por sus confesores."

26. AHPFM-ACSC. G-leg. 2, no. 1. In the same document Francisca herself attested that her playmates were not only Christ but also other children that appeared from the rays of the sun whenever she called them.

27. AHPFM-ACSC, Francisca to Margil, April, G-leg. 2, no. 2, 1700, p. 6v.

28. On Sierra Gorda, see García Ugarte, *Breve Historia de Querétaro*, pp. 61–69.

29. Vilaplana, *Histórico y Sagrado Novenario de la Milagrosa Imagen de Nuestra Senora de Pueblito*, pp. 10–38.

30. See Landa Fonseca, *Querétaro; una historia compartida*, p. 7. For a discussion of popular devotion and miraculous images in seventeenth-century Puebla, see López, "Los conventos femeninos," pp. 231–53.

31. AGN, Inquisición, vol. 1036, exp. 6, pp. 151–60. The description is based on instructions from the Inquisition in Mexico City to their representative in Querétaro on the reading of an *edicto* on January 23, 1761.

32. Rincón Frías et al., *Breve historia de Querétaro*, p. 41.

33. Belanger, "Secularization and the Laity in Colonial Mexico," p. 13.

34. One of the complaints that led to the eventual secularization of the Franciscan parish around the middle of the century was that the Indians did not learn Spanish since the friars spoke their languages. One of the changes of the secularization was to mix the Indians with Spaniards and mestizos so they would learn Spanish, especially since the secular clergy did not speak their language. See Belanger, *Secularization and the Laity*, p. 95.

35. Septien y Septien, *Historia de Querétaro*, p. 112.

36. Super, *La vida en Querétaro*, pp. 15–16. On the foundations of the religious orders in Querétaro, see also Septien y Septien, *Historia de Querétaro*, pp. 111–93.

37. Navarrete, *Relacíon peregrina de Querétaro*, p. 51.

38. Belanger, "Secularization and the Laity," pp. 14–20, 32, 35, 38, 48, 50–60.

39. In 1793, for example, when the Archconfraternity of the Holy Sacrament attempted to have its constitution approved by the Crown, it claimed that it had contributed to the building of religious edifices, given charity for masses, paid the expenses of the parish of Querétaro, and attended the sick. See AGN, Clero Regular y Secular, vol. 195, exp. 9, pp. 130–89.

40. On the Marquis de la Villa del Villar del Águila and his intimacy with the Capuchin nuns, see Navarrete, *Relación Peregrina*. The chronicle is dated in 1739 and describes the city and the great aqueduct constructed for it largely at the expense of the marquis. Navarrete stated (p. 51) that the marquis built an expensive house (worth 30,000 pesos) next to the convent so he could "enjoy from greater proximity the spiritual delights which their [the nuns'] holy and ever beneficial conversation ignites in devout souls." On Urtiaga, see Anonymous, *Acuerdos curiosos* and AGN, Bienes Nacionales, vol. 242, exp. 8. Notarial documents from Querétaro show that townspeople would describe locations in the city by how many blocks south, west, east, or north they were from the nearest church or convent.

41. Biblioteca Nacional de Antropología y Historia, BNAH, rollo 39, Notarías, no. 5, Protocolos 1677–1678, p. 50. When he made his will in 1721, Capt. Francisco Alzaga, a peninsular, father of a Santa Clara nun, and Jesuit priest who had acquired a fortune in haciendas and factories in Querétaro, asked to be buried in the habit of Saint Francis. A tertiary during his lifetime, he also belonged to several confraternities, founded two chantry funds with the stipulation of thirty masses for each fund, donated four thousand pesos to the *beaterio* of Santa Rosa, paid for the feast of San Francisco in the Capuchin convent, and gave donations to all convents in the city. See Archivo Historico de Querétaro Notarias, (AHQ), Vitórica, 1721, p. 274, September 9.

42. Carlos Sigüenza y Góngora's description of the event is quoted in Leonard, *La época barroca*, pp. 184–90.

43. On illegitimacy in colonial Spanish America and attitudes toward it, see Twinam, *Public Lives, Private Secrets*.

44. AGN, Matrimonios, vol. 205, exp. 44, pp. 1–38.

45. AGN, Matrimonios, vol. 167, exp. 34, pp. 1–4v.

46. BNAH, rollo 39, Notarias no. 5, Protocolos 1677–1678, p. 77v.

47. On early Reformation Spain see Kamen, *The Phoenix and the Flame*, pp. 82–156.

48. See, for example, AGN, Inquisición, vol. 559, exp. 1, pp. 1–33, for the 1652 case of Juana de Chaide and vol. 631, exp. 4, pp. 1–96, for the case of doña Juana de Tovar.

49. AGN, Inquisición, vol. 741, exp. 23, pp. 217–22.

### 2. Women in Baroque Querétaro

1. For an analysis of the central role of Santa Clara in Querétaro society, see Gunnarsdóttir, "Religious Life and Urban Society." For an interesting discussion of the

importance the ecclesiastical hierarchy placed on maintaining order in the colony's convents, see Traslosheros's discussion of the case of Sor Feliciana de San Francisco of the convent of Santa Catalina in Valladolid, Michoacán, and her efforts to obtain a release from her vows. Traslosheros H., "Los motivos de una monja."

2. This was the role envisioned by Saint Dominic when he established the female branch of his order before the male branch so they could pray for the success of their mendicant brethren in their missions. See, for example, Wittberg, *The Rise and Decline of Catholic Religious Orders*, p. 35.

3. See Fitz-Maurice-Kelly, *The Nun Ensign*.

4. Calderón de la Barca, *Life in Mexico*, p. 153.

5. de la Rea, *Crónica de la Orden de Nuestro Seraphico Padre San Fransisco*, p. 99–103. Gallagher, *The Family Background of the Nuns of Two Monasterios in Colonial Mexico*, p. 77–79. On the foundation, see also Ramos Medina, Amerlinck de Corsi, *Conventos de monjas*, pp. 205–10.

6. Gallagher, *The Family Background*, p. 80.

7. In 1729, the convent bought the houses and gardens occupied by Juana María de Lara and her son in the Calle de San Antonio so as to expand its territory. In the same year, it also bought houses from María Gertrudis de Silva. The reasons for the purchase were the following: "the great necessity of this convent to acquire land for its offices and quarters for baking [menesteres de semillas] and other things which are pressing." See AHQ, Notarías, Vitórica, 1729, pp. 153, 182.

8. Septien y Septien, *Historia de Querétaro*, p. 169.

9. Septien y Septien, *Historia de Querétaro*, p. 101.

10. Gallagher, *The Family Background*, p. 79.

11. Loreto López argues for a similar function of convents in her study on convents in Puebla. In her opinion, holy nuns "maintained a direct relationship between the convent, the supernatural and society." See discussion in *Los conventos femeninos*, pp. 265–79.

12. Gómez, *Vida de la Venerable Madre Antonia de San Jacinto*, p. 11.

13. Gómez, *Vida de la Venerable Madre Antonia de San Jacinto*, p. 11. On attendance at masses, see p. 11; on her constant prayer, see pp. 11, 30.

14. Antonia took communion two to three times a week, during which her face "glowed and shone with such happiness and delight." A friar who often celebrated the Eucharist at Santa Clara stated that her face had always looked different from the others during the ritual ( p. 25).

15. On persecutions by the devil, see Gómez, *Vida de la venerable madre*, pp. 5–6, 24, 35.

16. For a discussion of the 1525 edict that defined *alumbradismo* in the peninsula, see Jaffary, *Deviant Orthodoxy*, p. 63 (page numbers refer to unpublished manuscript

of forthcoming book). Like the *alumbrados*, Antonia engaged in mental prayers and found excuses not to have to participate in communal rites.

17. Jaffary, *Deviant Orthodoxy*, p. 30. Antonia was not the only Santa Clara nun to experience the raptures of mental prayer. Gómez noted that Mother Petronila de la Purificación had been famous in the convent for her spirit and that during prayer she became so enraptured that she did not feel the whipping the novices were giving her. Another nun, Lucía de San José, was said to spend all her nights praying in the choir. See Gómez, *Vida de la venerable madre*, p. 27v.

18. Gómez, *Vida de la venerable madre*, p. 46.

19. Gómez, *Vida de la venerable madre*, pp. 37v, 38. The first time she saw the vision she consulted her confessor, but when it happened again on two separate occasions Gómez asked for the advice of two learned friars. They became convinced of the authenticity of the vision when the convent's infirmary caught on fire.

20. Gómez, *Vida de la venerable madre*, p. 46.

21. Gómez, *Vida de la venerable madre*, p. 45.

22. Gómez, *Vida de la venerable madre*, pp. 28, 47.

23. Gómez, *Vida de la venerable madre*, p. 45v.

24. Gómez, *Vida de la venerable madre*, pp. 49–58v.

25. AGN, Inquisición, vol. 693, 1694, pp. 408–24. The case of the abbess was brought to the attention of the Inquisition in connection with the accusations against Francisca de los Ángeles. The friar who gave the testimony mentioned that her powers were "common knowledge among many persons, secular as well as ecclesiastic."

26. Centro de Estudios de Historia de México (CONDUMEX), Buenrrostro, "Sermón por la profesión y velo de la Madre Teresa de San Joseph."

27. Bocanegra, *Sermón de los Dolores de María Santísima*, p. 3.

28. Such information usually appears in notarized testaments and other documents. Many list endowments for "her religious necessities and chocolate," as did María Rosalia Villareal when she left a clause in her testament recognizing the rights of her husband's daughter from a first marriage (and now a nun in Santa Clara) to six thousand pesos left by her father. See for example AHQ, Notarias, Parra, 1714, pp. 83–86, Parra, 1712, p. 112, Parra, 1719, pp. 114–121, Parra, 1724, pp. 57–63.

29. See, for example, AHQ, Notarías, Parra, 1729, p. 66, April 6. Isabel María de la Trinidad empowered Juan Manuel de Salinas of Mexico to represent her in court to obtain the inheritance left to her by José de Frías. See also Vitórica, 1721, p. 89, where Gertrudis de San Buenaventura empowered a lawyer to represent her in court in a case involving the ownership of a house in Querétaro given to her by her aunt.

30. An example that provides a comparison with the outside world is a sumptuous residence on the Plaza Mayor, which in 1717 was valued at 3,120 pesos. See Morales, *Arquitectura y sociedad*, p. 44. For examples on cells, see AHQ, Araujo, 1751, p. 99; AGN,

Bienes Nacionales, vol. 259, exp. 20, p. 10; and AHPFM, Santa Clara, Patentes de los Prelados Regulares, caja 2, 19 September 1715.

31. Daily activities within the convent have been deduced from the breakdown of expenditures in the "Libro de gastos" of 1748 to 1751, in AHPFM, Santa Clara. There, the abbess noted all those receiving a salary from the convent. Among others they included the chaplain, sacristan, doctor, barber, pharmacist, messenger boys, artisans who worked on repairs such as fixing the door to the church and a window in a cell, and two organists who had repaired the organ in the church. In the kitchen, communal servants, probably supervised by a nun, were often busy making sweets. Although the period in question is not the focus of this study, it is assumed that the traditions the book describes were longstanding.

32. The dispatches from the provincials to the nuns of Santa Clara on matters that needed correction are a valuable source on the daily life of the convent. It is prudent to take the friar's complaints with a grain of salt. In their indignation, they may have exaggerated the slack observance of the rules within the convent to induce the nuns to comply with their orders. Nevertheless, their complaints indicate the principal norms of deviant behavior within the convent throughout the eighteenth century, for the same complaints were repeated several times in this period. For a similar perspective on life in a convent, see Asunción Lavrin's description of the convent of Jesús María in Mexico City. Lavrin, "Cotidianidad y espiritualidad." pp. 213–19. On the resemblance between the convent and a farmhouse, see AHPFM, "Patentes," Fray Landeros, 1727.

33. See AHPFM, "Patentes", caja 1, 2. In 1727, the provincial prohibited the nuns from letting their servants come and go as they pleased and from keeping boys and girls in the convent without authorization. This order was reiterated in 1739 by Fray Cristóbal de Urrutia. In 1745, the provincial again declared that the servants who left the convent would be prohibited from coming back in.

34. AHPFM, "Patentes", caja 4. For a discussion of nuns' friendships with the outside world, see Lavrin, "La celda y el siglo."

35. AHPFM, "Patentes", caja 1–4: Juan Antonio Landeros, 1727; Cristóbal de Urrutia, 1739; Pedro Navarrete, 1739; Barreto, 1745; Felipe Velasco, 1748; Antonio de Ribera, 1752; José Santos, 1755; José Antonio de Riva, 1757; Domingo Villaseñor, 1774; Santiago Cisneros, 1778; Antonio Vicente Frías, 1781; Manuel Trujillo, 1796; Antonio Canaly, 1813. As several other dispatches from other provincials throughout the century contained the same admonishments, I have merely provided examples of the types of complaints the friars offered.

36. In 1735, the provincial tried to discipline the nuns by threatening excommunication, not only to those who wore *encarrujados* or pleats ironed into their sleeves, but also to those who even spoke of them. Traditionally, the abbess distributed 15 pesos to each servant every two years, but no attempt was made to hand out uniforms instead of money. See AHPFM, "Aranzel y distribución de los gastos del convento de Nuestra

Madre Santa Clara de esta ciudad de Querétaro," 1744. One suspects that the servants may have been the recipients of adornments, which the nuns were forbidden to use.

37. In 1709, the provincial, finding such attire indecent for young girls, ordered that all girls under the age of ten should wear the habit of Santa Clara, AHPFM, Patentes, caja 1, Fray Trejo, 1709. That exhortation went for the *cantoras* as well; they were not to wear open shoes or white stockings, decorations on their clothes, worldly aprons, or cambric.

38. AHPFM, Patentes, caja 1.

39. AHPFM, Navarrete, 1735, caja 2.

40. AGN, Inquisición, vol. 631, exp. 4, pp. 1–96.

41. AGN, Inquisición, vol. 571, exp. 9, pp. 234–45.

42. AGN, Inquisición, vol.597, exp. 3, pp. 597–605.

43. AGN, Inquisición, vol. 523, exp. 3, pp. 254–79.

44. AGN, Inquisición, vol. 523, exp. 3, pp. 280–99.

45. See Díez, *Apostólicos empleos*, pp. 32–36.

46. McCloskey, *The Formative Years*, p. 23.

47. Brading, *Church and State in Bourbon Mexico*, pp. 32–33.

48. McCloskey, *The Formative Years*, p. 27.

49. Brading. *The First America*, p. 377. Espinosa, *Crónica apostólica y seráfica*, p. 48. Espinosa recounts an episode that occurred during one of the friars' missions to Zacatecas. When the town heard of the imminent arrival of the Franciscan missionaries, the entire *cabildo*, ecclesiastical elite, and other dignitaries came out of the city to welcome them. The friars were then escorted to their quarters at the sanctuary of Guadalupe by over three thousand townspeople. See Espinosa, p. 67. Brading, in *Church and State*, also notes that the colleges quickly recruited Creole Franciscans to their missions in addition to peninsulars. The friars of the colleges formed a "spiritual elite," for they escaped most administrative tasks such as educating novices but could concentrate on their missionary activities. By the middle of the eighteenth century, Brading states, the colleges in Querétaro and Zacatecas had become segregated; Zacatecas housed Creole friars and Querétaro peninsulars. pp. 33, 36.

50. Díez, *Apostólicos empleos*, pp. 42–52.

51. Espinosa, *El peregrino septentrional atlante*, p. 41.

52. See Díez, *Apostólicos empleos*, pp. 90–91.

53. On this aspect of the Counter-Reformation in sixteenth-and seventeenth-century Spain, see Dedieu, "Christianization in New Castile," pp. 1–25; and Barnes-Karol, "Religious Oratory in a Culture of Control," pp. 51–78. On popular devotions in post-Tridentine Italy, see Carroll, *Veiled Threats*, pp. 79–91.

54. On their ages, see Díez, *Apostólicos empleos*, p. 76.

55. McCloskey, *The Formative Years*, p. 34.

56. Quoted in McCloskey, *The Formative Years*, p. 55.

57. See Gómez Canedo, *Sierra Gorda, un típico enclave misional*, p. 50.

58. Cervantes, *The Devil in the New World*, p. 114.

59. Espinosa, *Crónica*, p. 57. Espinosa also notes that the townspeople who used to bathe in a river near the town accompanied by music, singing, and other festivities ceased their activities under the friars' scandalized exhortations.

60. Espinosa, *Crónica*, p. 55.

61. Espinosa also reveals that in every town they came to the missionaries were usually welcomed by droves of women who were prepared to reform their way of life (*Crónica*, p. 66).

62. AHPFM-ACSC, G-leg. 5, no. 27, undated.

63. AHPFM-ACSC, G-leg. 4, no. 2, "Papeles pertenecientes a la dirección de almas; en particular a la de la venerable Francisca de los Ángeles."

64. AHPFM-ACSC, G-leg. 4, no. 2, "Apuntes para el gobierno interior de la hermana Francisca de los Ángeles."

65. On Beguines, *beatas*, and tertiaries in the Middle Ages, see, for example, Bynum, *Holy Feast, Holy Fast*, pp. 17–20.

66. AHPFM-ACSC, G-leg. 5, no. 20, 23, January 1714, to Fray Ángel reminiscing about her vow of poverty. On the plan to take her to Mexico City, see undated note to unspecified recipient, in G-leg. 5, no. 27.

67. AHPFM-ACSC, G-leg. 4, no. 2, "Papeles pertenecientes a la dirección de almas en particular a la de la venerable Francisca de los Ángeles."

68. For an analysis of the role of the written word in the relationship between confessor and protégée, see Donahue, "Writing Lives," pp. 230–39.

69. AGN, Inquisición, vol. 523, exp. 3, pp. 452–560.

70. AGN, Inquisición, vol. 685, exp. 3, p. 220.

71. AGN, Inquisición, vol. 547, exp. 30, pp. 457–65.

72. AGN, Inquisición, vol. 523, exp. 3, pp. 320–23.

73. On opposition to the College of Propaganda Fide in Querétaro, particularly within the Franciscan province of Michoacán, see McCloskey, *The Formative Years*, pp. 40–41.

74. McCloskey, *The Formative Years*, p. 222. According to the inquisitor in Querétaro, the Franciscans were known to shout to heaven, frightening those who did not believe the possession with such speeches as "Lord open the eyes of these blind and incredulous people, so that they can believe this truth." See Inquisición, vol. 547, exp. 30, p. 554.

75. From the letter of Manuel de Jeo to the Inquisition on November 13, 1691, quoted in Cervantes, *The Devil in the New World*, pp. 99–110. The Carmelite also commented that only single women became sick and that they were making a public exhibition of their possession by walking around the streets of the town "making a racket with

their cries at gatherings, terrorizing people, talking nonsense, and making many faces" (AGN, Inquisición, vol. 685, exp. 3, p. 223).

76. AGN, Inquisición, vol. 685, exp. 3, p. 231.

77. AGN, Inquisición, vol. 547, exp. 30.

78. AGN, Inquisición, vol. 685, exp. 3, pp. 480–87.

79. Cervantes, *The Devil in the New World*, pp. 119–24; Alberro, *Inquisition y Societé au Mexique*, pp. 258–62. Two other possessed women gave birth in the period after Juana.

80. For accounts of the case, see Cervantes, *The Devil in the New World*, pp. 113–24; Alberro, *Inquisition y Societé au Mexique*, pp. 253–64.

81. AGN, Inquisición, vol. 547, exp. 30, pp. 490–520 and vol. 523, exp. 3, p. 508.

### 3. Heresy

1. AGN, Inquisición, vol. 693, pp. 400–406, Testimony of Francisco Borda de Coronado, August 31, 1691.

2. AGN, Inquisición, vol. 693, p. 406.

3. AGN, Inquisición, vol. 693, p. 408.

4. AHPFM-ACSC, G-leg. 2, no. 2.

5. AGN, Inquisición, vol. 693, p. 418.

6. Holler, "More Sins Than the Queen of England," pp. 218–21.

7. Term borrowed from Holler, "More Sins Than the Queen of England," p. 220. On the development of the term *ilusa* to denote false mysticism, see Jaffary, *Deviant Orthodoxy*.

8. AGN, Inquisición, vol. 693, p. 428. Accounts of Francisca's stigmatas are also found among her confessors' papers and later inquisitional records. See AHPFM-ACSC, G-leg. 2, nos. 1, 2; and AGN, Inquisición, vol. 745, pp. 130–38.

9. AGN, Inquisición, vol. 693, pp. 429–34.

10. Statistics from Curcio-Nagy, in "Rosa de Escalante's Private Party," p. 268. The slowness of the Inquisition was not unrepresentative of its general working methods. As Alberro has shown, the Mexican branch of the Spanish Inquisition was forced to contend with local realities that often limited its effectiveness. As a result, the Mexican Inquisition was not nearly as successful as its peninsular counterpart. For a summary of Alberro's thesis, see the conclusion of her *Inquisition et Societé*, pp. 301–7.

11. AHPFM-ACSC, G-leg. 1, de Jesús, chap. 3.

12. AGN, Inquisición, vol. 693, pp. 432–34.

13. AGN, Inquisición, vol. 693, p. 424.

14. AGN, Inquisición, vol. 693, p. 410.

15. AGN, Inquisición, vol. 643, p. 410.

16. AHPFM-ACSC, G-leg. 5, no. 27, note from Margil to Fray Ángel, undated.

17. Bynum, *Holy Feast and Holy Fast*, pp. 23–25.

18. Elwood, "French Nuns and Fallen Women," p. 64. Elwood argues that for women of the seventeenth century in France, diabolical possession was a form of empowerment not available to women during and after the Enlightenment. In her study of the demoniacs of Querétaro, Alberro has constructed a similar thesis for the group of women based on an analysis of their socioeconomic circumstances. As impoverished women, reduced to the margins of Creole society and mingling with the castes, possession and the attention it gave them was their only medium for gaining the influence and stature that had automatically been awarded their Spanish forefathers. See Alberro, *Inquisition et Societé*, pp. 263–67.

19. Barker, *The Politics of Aristotle*; and Said, *Woman and Female*, pp. 3, 6.

20. Surtz, *Writing Women in Late and Early Modern Spain*, pp. 6–7.

21. Bynum, *Holy Feast and Holy Fast*, p. 22. She notes an increase in female saints in the period 1100 to 1400, especially of female lay saints who outnumbered lay male saints by the end of the Middle Ages.

22. See Caciola's argument in "Mystics, Demoniacs." Caciola argues that more attention should be paid to external perceptions of women mystics in order to understand whether they really attracted large cults. In her view, arguments that use statistics such as those of André Vauchez, showing that women represented 55.5 percent of the laity canonized in the Middle Ages, have their flaws. Looking at the hard figures behind the claims, Caciola shows that only four female saints among the laity were canonized between 1198 and 1500. In her view, "aspiring medieval women mystics were not universally regarded as channels of divine grace. Indeed, women claiming divine inspiration and supernatural powers elicited as much repugnance as they did reverence." She cites Inquisitorial documents, encyclopedias, and scholarly publications as alternative sources to hagiographies. See Caciola, "Mystics, Demoniacs," pp. 268–70.

23. de Certeau, *The Mystic Fable: The Sixteenth and Seventeenth Centuries*, pp. 85–86.

24. On the Beguines, see Bynum, *Holy Feast and Holy Fast*, p. 23. For a discussion of the phenomenon among women in Ital⟨ ⟩see Zarri, "From Prophecy to Discipline," pp. 87–90.

25. Bynum also notes that the growing intolerance of female mystics was influenced by the church's general suspicion both of mystics, whether female or male, and of popular religion (*Holy Feast and Holy Fast*, p. 23). See also Perry and Cruz, *Culture and Control*, pp. ix–xxiii.

26. McNamara, *Sisters in Arms*, p. 475.

27. McNamara, *Sisters in Arms*, p. 475.

28. Iwasaki Cauti, "Mujeres al borde de la perfección," p. 583.

29. Bell, *Holy Anorexia*, p. 151.

30. Bynum, *Holy Feast and Holy Fast*, p. 23.

31. The Council of Trent in 1563 had ordered the enclosure of all female religious communities, be they of the Third Order or those who enjoyed exemptions. For a

discussion of the reforms and their motives, see Hsia, *The World of Catholic Renewal*, pp. 33–41.

32. Modica Vasta, "Mystical Writing," p. 208.

33. Ortega Cosa, "Spanish Women in the Reformation," p. 99.

34. Ahlgren, *Teresa of Avila*, pp. 114–44.

35. Ahlgren, *Teresa of Avila*, pp. 163–64.

36. Weber, *Teresa of Ávila and the Rhetoric of Femininity*, pp. 3, 35–40, 52, 159, 165.

37. Weber, *Teresa of Ávila and the Rhetoric of Femininity*, p. 93.

38. Iwasaki Cauti, "Mujeres al borde de la perfección," pp. 581–613.

39. Iwasaki Cauti, "Mujeres al borde de la perfección," passim. On the 1625 proceedings, see Hsia, *The World of Catholic Renewal*, pp. 146–47.

40. Quoted in Franco, *Plotting women*, p. 7.

41. Myers, "Fundadora, cronista y mística," p. 76.

42. Godínez, *Práctica de la teología mística*, p. 117.

43. Myers, "Testimony for Canonization," pp. 272–73.

44. Myers, *Word from New Spain*, p. 3.

45. Alberro, "Herejes, Brujas y beatas," pp. 90–91. Mysticism was not the only female religious phenomenon to arouse the male clergy's suspicion. A woman's independent intellect created a similar opposition, as we see in Sor Juana Inéz de la Cruz's difficulties with her male confessors, and especially in her publicized quarrel with the bishop of Puebla, Manuel Fernández de Santa Cruz. See Penaloza, "La difícil relation de Sor Juana con el clero novohispano," pp. 326–30.

46. Rubial García, "Las santitas del barrio," p. 14.

47. Jaffary, *Deviant Orthodoxy*, pp. 73–76.

48. Jaffary notes that almost 90 percent of *ilusos* and *alumbrados* tried before the tribunal were unmarried, "a group amongst whom there was a high incidence of poverty in the colonial era" (p. 121).

49. Jaffary, *Deviant Orthodoxy*, p. 58.

50. For a summary of Jaffary's thesis, see *Deviant Orthodoxy*, pp. 9–38.

51. On the Romero case, see Rubial García's excellent discussion in "Josefa de San Luis Beltrán," pp. 161–77, and his article "Las santitas del barrio."

52. Zarri, "From Prophecy to Discipline," p. 87.

53. Myers notes that Puebla was the most productive of all the cities of New Spain in publishing the life stories of its holy people. See "Testimony for Canonization," p. 275.

54. On Madre Agreda's youth, see McNamara, *Sisters in Arms*, p. 509.

55. Wittberg, *The Rise and Decline*, p. 37.

56. de Jesús, *Crónica del Real Colegio*, p. 29.

57. AHPFM-ACSC, G-leg. 1, de Jesús, *Crónica*, chap. 2.

58. For studies of holy women in colonial Latin America, see McKnight, *The Mystic*

*of Tunja*; Myers, *Word from New Spain*; Ibsen, *Women's Spiritual Autobiography*; and Myers and Powell, *A Wild Country*. For a study of the tradition of reading and writing within colonial convents, see Loreto López, "Leer, contar, cantar, y escribir," pp. 67–95.

59. On this argument, see Vera Tudela, *Colonial Angels*, pp. 29–34. She notes that "hagiography seemed the perfect vehicle with which to trumpet the victories of the conquering and evangelizing Church in the New World" (p. 34).

60. As Vera Tudela argues in the case of the Mexican nun Sor Sebastiana, her "pain is the guarantee of her truth"; see *Colonial Angels*, p. 38.

61. On publication figures for Spain, see Hsia, *The World of Catholic Renewal*, p. 51.

62. Between 1540 and 1770, twenty-seven men and five women were canonized; all belonged to the clergy. See Hsia, *The World of Catholic Renewal*, p. 122.

63. For a discussion of Counter-Reformation saints, see Hsia, *The World of Catholic Renewal*, pp. 122–37.

64. Hsia, *The World of Catholic Renewal*, p. 141.

65. For a discussion of the genres used by religious female writers, see McKnight, *The Mystic of Tunja*, pp. 17–59.

66. See discussion by Myers, "Testimony for Canonization," p. 291.

67. Paz, *Sor Juana*, pp. 46–59.

68. Teresa of Ávila, *The Interior Castle*, p. 202.

69. See Lavrin, "Female Visionaries and Spirituality."

70. Godínez, *Práctica de la teología mística*, p. 99.

71. Clark, "The Cloud of Unknowing," pp. 273–93. On Saint John of the Cross, see de Certeau, *The Mystic Fable*, pp. 129–43.

72. de Certeau, *The Mystic Fable*, pp. 188–200.

73. Schroeder, *The Canons and Decrees*, pp. 215–16.

74. Schroeder, *The Canons and Decrees*, pp. 215–16. The first and last passages have also been quoted in Sánchez Lora, *Mujeres, conventos*, pp. 360, 366.

75. Schroeder, *The Canons and Decrees*, pp. 215–16.

76. Schroeder, *The Canons and Decrees*, p. 212, my translation.

77. Schroeder, *The Canons and Decrees*, p. 234.

78. Lavrin has noted the phenomenon described by Lora in her study of the religiosity of Mexican nuns. In a 1972 article, she argued that "During the seventeenth and a great part of the eighteenth century, as a result of the empty rhetoric of preachers and religious writers, pious ignorance, devoted mortifications and a world of religious revelation continued to be the main tone for the works aimed at the spiritual development of nuns." See Lavrin, "Values and Meaning of Monastic Life," p. 379. She reiterated this argument in a 1991 essay that argued that stifling women's intellectual development generated a self-expression steeped in mystic religiosity. See Lavrin, "Unlike Sor Juana?", pp. 61–86.

79. See Gómez, *Vida de la venerable madre*, pp. 18, 28.

80. AHPFM, Santa Clara, Fray Diego Mendívil, "Leyes de la esposa," not dated.

81. See, for example, AHPFM-ACSC, G-leg. 5, nos. 3,4, August 21, 1696, p. 14; April 19, 1697, p. 14v; October 18, 1697, p. 2v.

82. AHPFM-ACSC, G-leg. 5, no. 1, to Sitjar, November 29, 1693, pp. 7–8.

83. AHPFM-ACSC, G-leg. 5, no. 1, to Fray Antonio Margil de Jesús, undated.

84. AHPFM-ACSC, leg. G-2, no. 2, to Sitjar, June 1, 1696, p. 5.

85. Undated, but found in a pile of letters to Fray Ángel, her confessor from 1712, G-leg. 5, no. 20.

86. AHPFM-ACSC, leg. G-2, no. 3, to Sitjar, September 16, 1696, p. 23.

87. AHPFM-ACSC, leg. G-2, no. 4, to Sitjar, October 24, 1697, p. 15v.

88. See, for example, AHPFM-ACSC, G-leg. 5, no. 13, undated letter from 1706 to Díez.

89. AHPFM-ACSCG-leg. 5, no. 13, undated but in packet of 1706 letters.

90. AHPFM-ACSC, G-leg. 5, no. 20.

91. AHPFM-ACSC, G-leg. 5, no. 20, to Sitjar, October 2, 1714, p. 36v.

92. AHPFM-ACSC, G-leg. 5, no. 3, to Sitjar, September 21, 1706, p. 30, and October 2, 1696, p. 31.

93. AHPFM-ACSC, G-leg. 5, no. 4, to Sitjar, November 22, 1697, p. 18.

94. AHPFM-ACSC, G-leg. 5, no. 4, to Sitjar, May 5, 1697, p. 1.

95. As an example of the *fin amant* rhetoric, see AHPFM-ACSC, G-leg. 5, April 19, 1697, p. 16v. The Lord, having stayed with her throughout Easter, bid her farewell in the night. Embracing her softly, he said "stay in me without me." AHPFM-ACSC, G-leg. 5, no. 4, to Sitjar, August 20, 1697, p. 14; May 5, 1697, p. 3. On Beguine piety, see Newman, *From Virile Woman*, pp. 172–81. On the warrior-lord image, see letters to Sitjar, AHPFM-ACSC, G-leg. 5, no. 4, April 19, 1697, p. 8v., and October 19, 1697.

96. AHPFM-ACSC, G-leg. 5, no. 4, April 19, 1697, p. 7v, 15; May 5, 1697, p. 5; October 18, 1697, p. 1.

97. AHPFM-ACSC, G-leg. 5, April 19, 1697, p. 1; October, 18, 1697, p. 6.

98. AHPFM-ACSC, G-leg. 5, to Sitjar, October 24, 1697, p. 15.

99. AHPFM-ACSC, G-leg. 5, no. 3, October, 25, 1696, p. 41v.

100. AHPFM-ACSC, G-leg. 5, no. 1, to Sitjar, November, 29, 1693, pp. 1–9.

### 4. The Evangelist

1. Espinosa, *Crónica apostólica*, pp. 307–8.

2. AHPFM-ACSC, G-leg. 5, no. 1, to Sitjar, October, 29, 1693, p. 1v.

3. Díez, *Apostólicos empleos*, pp. 170–73.

4. AHPFM-ACSC, G-leg. 5, no. 4, to Sitjar, May, 5, 1697.

5. AHPFM-ACSC, G-leg. 5, no. 4, to Sitjar, April 19, 1697, p. 4.

6. AHPFM-ACSC, G-leg. 5, no. 4, to Sitjar, September, 9, 1697, p. 16.

7. AHPFM-ACSC, G-leg. 5, no. 1, Sitjar's narrative, "Noticia de algunas cosas que me dijo de palabra Francisca de los Ángeles . . .".

8. AHPFM-ACSC, G-leg. 5, no. 1, to Sitjar, June 1, 1696, 3v.

9. Sometime toward the end of the century, having decided to leave the city and spend her days as a hermit in a cave in the desert, Francisca disposed of her few belongings, thus revealing her circle of friends. She gave a crucifix to Santa Cruz; she donated some saints' images to the *enfermería* of Dr. Nicolás Armenta, a prominent cleric in Querétaro; and she gave other objects to unnamed benefactors. Francisca's hermitage was to go to a girl named Catalina whom Francisca commended to the care of the friars as if "she were the product of my entrails." She also possessed letters written to her by Fray Sitjar, as well as some books loaned to her by Juana de Isguerra and her sister Clara. Finally, Francisca instructed that a large crucifix be given to a Fray Pedro de San Buenaventura who was then in the service of Fray Llinás, founder of the apostolic colleges. AHPFM-ACSC, G-leg. 5, no. 20, undated letter to Margil.

10. AHPFM-ACSC, G-leg. 5, no. 6, July 1699, p. 45.

11. AHPFM-ACSC, G-leg. 2, no. 2, Sitjar's testimony, "Noticias de algunas cosas que me dijo Francisca de los Ángeles . . . .". See also, letters to Sitjar, G-Leg. 5, no. 4, May, 5, 1697, p. 1; May 29, 1697, p. 5; October, 18, 1697, p. 5v.

12. AHPFM-ACSC, G-leg. 5, no. 4, to Sitjar, October, 19, 1697, pp. 18–18v.

13. AHPFM-ACSC, G-leg. 2, no. 2, Sitjar's recounting of Francisca's stories from 1693, p. 1.

14. Armstrong, *A History of God*, pp. 312–35.

15. This habit of hers is mentioned in an April 19, 1697 letter to Sitjar, p. 5–7; see AHPFM-ACSC, G-leg. 5, no. 4.

16. AHPFM-ACSC, G-leg. 5, no. 4.

17. AHPFM-ACSC, G-leg. 5, no. 4, to Sitjar, October 2, 1697, p. 7.

18. Harbison, *Reflections on Baroque*, p. 54.

19. Díez, *Apostólicos empleos*, p. 44.

20. Soto Peréz, *Memorial de las Cosas Notables*, pp. 342–48.

21. On Le Goff's discussion of the "ideology of the desert," see Le Goff, *The Medieval Imagination*, pp. 47–66.

22. McCloskey, *The Formative Years*, pp. 29–30.

23. McCloskey, *The Formative Years*, pp. 30–31.

24. Espinosa, *Crónica apostólica*, pp. 46–48.

25. On the history of the *Santa Cruz*, see Espinosa, *Crónica apostólica*, pp. 10–29.

26. Espinosa, *Crónica apostólica*, pp. 50–54.

27. On more than one occasion, witnesses testified to having tried unsuccessfully to rouse the friar from his trance, only to see the lay brother to whom he had given his obedience do so with only a few words. See Espinosa, *Crónica apostólica*, pp. 154–56.

28. Espinosa, *Crónica apostólica*, p. 153.

29. Le Goff, *The Medieval Imagination*, pp. 66–77.

30. The term *apostolate to the dead* is coined by Barbara Newman in *From Virile*

*Woman.* This discussion is indebted to her chapter "On the Threshold of the Dead" on religious women and purgatory (pp. 109–36).

31. Newman, *From Virile Woman*, p. 111.

32. O'Malley, *Catholicism in Early Modern History*, pp. 138–39.

33. This brand of evangelism was also common to women condemned by the Inquisition for false mysticism. Josefa de San Luis Beltrán, for example, was reputed to have saved twenty-four thousand souls from purgatory during her "career." See Rubial García, "Las santitas del barrio," p. 29.

34. AHPFM-ACSC, G-leg. 5, no. 5, December 1698, p. 35.

35. AHPFM-ACSC, G-leg. 5, no. 6, August 1699, p. 57.

36. In 1717, for example, when Francisca was taking communion, the host got stuck in her throat. When the priest gave her another one, she happily applied the act for two souls instead of one. See AHPFM-ACSC, G-leg. 5, no. 23, January, 8, 1717, to Fray Ángel García Duque.

37. AHPFM-ACSC, G-leg. 5, no. 6, August 1699, p. 52v.

38. On the application of masses by the Santa Cruz friars for her soul, see for example, a letter from January 1714 to Fray Ángel, her confessor, in which she thanks him for his message that he had applied his mass for her. On the community's efforts, see, for example, February, 13, 1714, to Fray Ángel. On July, 19, 1704, for example, she thanked Fray Antonio de los Ángeles for applying the indulgences gained from the day of Saint Buenaventura for her.

39. AHPFM-ACSC, G-leg. 5, no. 17, to Díez, November, 10, 1710.

40. Newman, *From Virile Woman*, pp. 108–36.

41. Newman, *From Virile Woman*, pp. 119–22.

42. AHPFM-ACSC, G-leg. 5, no. 23, undated.

43. AHPFM-ACSC, G-leg. 5, no. 7, October 1700, p. 11.

44. AHPFM-ACSC, G-leg. 5, January 1700, pp. 2v–3.

45. AHPFM-ACSC, G-leg. 5, no. 12, July 4, 1704, to Díez.

46. AHPFM-ACSC, G-leg. 5, no. 8, August 1701, to Margil, p. 7.

47. AHPFM-ACSC, G-leg. 5, no. 4, to Sitjar, October, 22, 1697, pp. 12–13.

48. AHPFM-ACSC, G-leg. 5, no. 12, December, 20, 1704, to Díez.

49. AHPFM-ACSC, G-leg. 5, no. 12, December, 20, 1704, to Díez.

50. AHPFM-ACSC, G-leg. 5, no. 6, March 25, 1699, p. 14.

51. AHPFM-ACSC, G-leg. 5, no. 4, April, 19, 1697, pp. 10v–12.

52. AHPFM-ACSC, G-leg. 5, no. 11, July, 19, 1704, to Díez. On Madre Juana de la Cruz and the stones, see Newman, *From Virile Woman*, p. 121.

53. AHPFM-ACSC, G-leg. 5, no. 6, May, 3, 1699, p. 33.

54. AHPFM-ACSC, G-leg. 5, no. 3, to Sitjar, June, 1, 1696, pp. 4–5v.

55. The term is taken from Newman, *From Virile Woman*, p. 114.

56. AHPFM-ACSC, G-leg. 5, no. 6, to Margil, June, 3, 1699, p. 38.

57. Díez, *Apostólicos empleos*, p. 122, 148.

58. Díez, *Apostólicos empleos*, p. 154.

59. Díez, *Apostólicos empleos*, p. 179.

60. Díez, *Apostólicos empleos*, p. 229.

61. Espinosa, *Crónica apostólica*, pp. 290–97.

62. Espinosa, *Crónica apostólica*, pp. 290–97. He was also an intimate friend and confessor to some of the most beloved figures in Francisca's life, such as Fray Escaray, another legendary missionary; Fray Antonio de los Ángeles, her most trusted friend; and her greatest benefactor, don Juan Caballero y Ocio.

63. Vera Tudela, *Colonial Angels*, pp. 1–13.

64. On Francisca de la Natividad, see Loreto López, "Escrito por ella misma," p. 49; on María de San José, see Myers, "Fundadora, cronista y mística," p. 74.

65. Myers, "Testimony for Canonization," p. 280. Sampson Tudela in *Colonial Angels* argues that the hagiographic narrative underwent transformations in the New World as a result of the exotic ambience of these faraway lands. Thus, Catarina de San Juan's experience shows how "versions of the spiritual narrative of the cosmic tour often succumb to the allure of a kind of description most often associated with the account of "real" journeys." See p. 4.

66. On the repeated attempts to find the French expedition, see McCloskey, *The Formative Years*, pp. 62–63.

67. See McCloskey, *The Formative Years*, pp. 54–60.

68. Espinosa, *Crónica apostólica*, pp. 409–11.

69. It confirmed Sor María de Agreda's claim—she had traveled in spirit to New Mexico herself half a century earlier—that God had told her that "the creatures most disposed to convert, the ones toward whom his compassion was the most inclined, were the New Mexicans and the inhabitants of other remote kingdoms in that part of the world." Colahan, *The Visions of Sor María de Agreda*, p. 119.

70. Espinosa, *Crónica apostólica*, pp. 414–15.

71. AHPFM-ACSC, G-leg. 2, p. 4v.

72. AHPFM-ACSC, G-leg. 2, p. 4v.

73. Díez discusses the riots in *Apostólicos empleos* . . . . Two years later, such riots occurred in Mexico City. The Indian rebels burned down the vendor stalls in front of the viceregal palace and tried to crown one of theirs as king (see pp. 199–200). See also, Leonard, *La época barroca*, pp. 275–277.

74. Colahan, *The Visions of Sor María de Agreda*, p. 105.

75. Colahan, *The Visions of Sor María de Agreda*, p. 169.

76. Colahan, "María de Jesús de Agreda: The Sweetheart of the Holy Office," pp. 155–68.

77. Colahan, "María de Jesús de Agreda: The Sweetheart of the Holy Office," p. 121.

78. AHPFM-ACSC, G-leg. 7, no. 9, to Margil, April 1700, pp. 11–14.

79. AHPFM-ACSC, G-leg. 7, no. 9, to Margil, pp. 9–10.

80. AHPFM-ACSC, G-leg. 7, no. 9, May to July, 1700, p. 4v.

81. AHPFM-ACSC, G-leg.7, no. 9, to Margil, April 1700, pp. 9–10.

82. AHPFM-ACSC, G-leg.7, no. 9, to Margil, April 1700, p. 10v.

83. AHPFM-ACSC, G-leg.7, no. 9, to Margil, April 1700, p. 16.

84. AHPFM-ACSC, G-leg. 7, no. 9, to Margil, April 1700, pp. 11–15v.

85. AHPFM-ACSC, G-leg. 7, no. 9, to Margil, April 1700, p. 5.

86. AHPFM-ACSC, G-leg. 7, no. 9, to Margil, April 1700, p. 6.

87. AHPFM-ACSC, G-leg. 7, no. 9, to Margil, May to July 1700, pp. 18–18v.

88. AHPFM-ACSC, G-leg. 7, no. 9, to Margil, May to July 1700, pp. 18–18v.

89. AHPFM-ACSC, G-leg. 7, no. 9, to Margil, May to July 1700, pp. 18–18v. Francisca also noted that the Lord had asked her if she wanted the ardent friar to rest in eternal security. She replied yes, only to realize that it meant his certain death. The friar did indeed die in Texas of natural causes, but Francisca hinted that had she not interceded he might have been killed by the natives.

90. AHPFM-ACSC, G-leg. 7, no. 6, to Margil, 2 June, 1999.

91. AHPFM-ACSC, G-leg. 7, no. 9, to Margil, from April to July 1700, pp. 18v–19.

92. AHPFM-ACSC, G-leg. 7, no. 9, to Margil, June 2, 1699, pp. 35–36.

93. See Cervantes, *The Devil in the New World*, pp. 5–73.

94. AHPFM-ACSC, G-leg. 7, no. 6, to Margil, April 2, 1699, pp. 21–22.

95. AHPFM-ACSC, G-leg. 7, no. 6, to Margil, April 18, 1699, p. 24.

96. AHPFM-ACSC, G-leg. 7, no. 6, to Margil, August 1699, p. 51.

97. AHPFM-ACSC, G-leg. 7, no. 9, to Margil, May until July 1700, pp. 14v.-15v.

98. AHPFM-ACSC, G-leg. 7, no. 9, to Margil, April to July, 1700, pp. 18v–19.

99. AHPFM-ACSC, G-leg. 5, no. 3, to Sitjar, September 21, 1696.

### 5. Francisca and Margil

1. The development of the community is the subject of chap. 6 in part 3 of this book.

2. AHPFM-ACSC, I-leg. 9, "Papeles de Nuestro Padre Fray Antonio Margil de Jesús, Declaración de Francisca de los Ángeles."

3. Ríos, *Fray Margil de Jesús*, pp. 20–30.

4. Rubial García, *La santidad controvertida*, pp. 259–60.

5. AHPFM-ACSC, I-leg. 4, "Papeles de Nuestro Padre Fray Antonio Margil de Jesús," no. 12, "Declaración del Br. don Nicolás Armenta, clerigo presbitero, vecino de Querétaro."

6. Rubial García notes that testimonies of contemporaries focus much more on Margil's gestures during sermons than on his actual words. Margil then perfected the preaching style grounded in "Augustinian psychology," which played upon "the primary sensibilities of the public, manifested in tears and sighs." See Rubial García, *La santidad controvertida*, p. 273 (my translation).

7. See two of his biographies, Ríos, *Fray Margil de Jesús*, and Espinosa, *El Peregrino septentrional atlante.*

8. Ríos, *Fray Margil de Jesús*, p. 20.

9. Martínez, *Resumen de la vida*, pp. 93–95.

10. Quoted in Ríos, *Fray Margil de Jesús*, p. 92 (my translation). Margil used the skull to illustrate themes in his sermons.

11. Espinosa, *El peregrino septentrional*, p. 40–41, 66, 80–105, 114, 118, 127, 130–33.

12. Ríos, *Fray Margil de Jesús*, p. 95.

13. One of the laywomen tried by the Inquisition for "false mysticism" indeed reported having flown in spirit with Margil on his missions to the infidels. See Jaffary, *Deviant Orthodoxy*, p. 251.

14. On Margil's activities as guardian, see McCloskey, *The Formative Years*, pp. 94–95. In 1699, he sent friars to establish missions along the Río Grande, which proved more lasting than the Texas missions.

15. AHPFM-ACSC, G-leg. 2, no. 2, to Sitjar, May, 29, 1697, p. 9.

16. AHPFM-ACSC, G-leg. 2, no. 2, to Sitjar, May, 29, 1697, p. 7v.

17. AHPFM-ACSC, G-leg. 2, no. 2, to Sitjar, June 10, 1697.

18. AHPFM-ACSC, G-leg. 2, no. 2, to Sitjar, June 10, 1697.

19. AHPFM-ACSC, G-leg. 2, no. 2, to Sitjar, June 10, 1697, p. 11.

20. AHPFM-ACSC, G-leg. 2, no. 2, to Sitjar, August 20, 1697, p. 14.

21. AHPFM-ACSC, G-leg. 4, no. 2, "Apuntes para el gobierno interior de la hermana Francisca."

22. AHPFM-ACSC, G-leg. 5, no. 15, December 21, 1708.

23. AHPFM-ACSC, G-leg. 5, no. 15, December 21, 1708.

24. AHPFM-ACSC, G-leg. 5, no. 15, December 21, 1708.

25. AHPFM-ACSC, G-leg. 5, no. 15.

26. AHPFM-ACSC, G-leg. 8, June, 11, 1701, no. 1, "Novena de los quinze."

27. AHPFM-ACSC, G-leg. 5, no. 15, December 21, 1708, to Ortega.

28. AHPFM-ACSC, G-leg. 5, no. 5, to Margil, December 1698, pp. 33–34v.

29. AHPFM-ACSC, G-leg. 5, no. 6, to Margil, April 1699, pp. 23v–24.

30. AHPFM-ACSC, G-leg. 5, no. 6, to Margil, May 1699, p. 28.

31. AHPFM-ACSC, G-leg. 5, no. 5, August 1698, p. 16v.

32. AHPFM-ACSC, G-leg. 5, no. 15, December 21, 1708, to Ortega.

33. Espinosa, *Crónica apostólica*, pp. 154–55.

34. AHPFM-ACSC, G-leg. 4, no. 8, "Testimony of Josepha de Jesús María."

35. AHPFM-ACSC, G-leg. 9, *Vida de la Venerable Francisca de los Ángeles.*

36. AHPFM-ACSC, G-leg. 9, *Vida de la Venerable Francisca de los Ángeles.*

37. AHPFM-ACSC, G-leg. 4, no. 2, *Apuntes para el gobierno interior*, September 1729.

38. AHPFM-ACSC, G-leg. 5, no. 15, December 21, 1708, to Ortega.

39. AHPFM-ACSC, G-leg. 5, no. 15, December 21, 1708, to Ortega.

40. AHPFM-ACSC, G-leg. 5, no. 15, December 21, 1708, to Ortega.

41. Francisca's testimony, AHPFM-ACSC, G-leg. 4, no. 2, *Apuntes para el gobierno*, August 17, 1726.

42. On Francisca, see AGN, Inquisición, vol. 693, pp. 400–34. On Margil, see Ríos, *Fray Margil de Jesús*, p. 97.

43. Ríos, *Fray Margil de Jesús*, p. 97. A council of learned Querétaro ecclesiastics deemed that the charges against him did not amount to heresy, and thus the case never formally came to the Inquisition.

44. AHPFM-ACSC, G-leg. 2, to Margil, July 1, 1699, p. 45.

45. AHPFM-ACSC, I-leg. 4, no. 12.

46. AHPFM-ACSC, I-leg. 4, no. 12.

47. McNamara, *Sisters in Arms*, p. 516.

48. Van Deusen, *Between the Sacred and the Worldly*, p. 129.

49. Quoted in Ahlgren, *Teresa of Avila*, p. 98.

50. AHPFM-ACSC, G-leg. 5, no. 15, December 21, 1708, to Ortega.

51. AHPFM-ACSC, G-leg. 5, no. 15, December 21, 1708, to Ortega.

52. de Nicolás, *St. John of the Cross*, p. 159.

53. AHPFM-ACSC. G-leg. 2, no. 2, April 13, 1698, to Margil, pp. 7–9.

54. Myers, "Testimony for Canonization," p. 273.

55. AHPFM-ACSC, G-leg. 5, no. 8, to Margil, January 1, 1701, and September 14, 1701, 1–11v.

56. AHPFM-ACSC, G-leg. 5, no. 5, to Margil, July 1698, pp. 10–11v.

57. AHPFM-ACSC, G-leg. 5, no. 5, to Margil, July 1698, p. 11v.

58. AHPFM-ACSC, G-leg. 5, no. 5, to Margil, December 1698, pp. 32v–33.

59. AHPFM-ACSC, G-leg. 5, no. 6, to Margil, April, 18, 1699. p. 23. Francisca apologized for this trait in her writing and noted that Sitjar had always scolded her for it.

60. AHPFM-ACSC, G-leg. 5, no. 5, November 14, 1698, pp. 26–26v.

61. AHPFM-ACSC, G-leg. 5, no. 5, December 1698, pp. 31–32v.

62. See, for example, AHPFM-ACSC, G-leg. 5, no. 7, to Margil, April 1700, pp. 6–7.

63. AHPFM-ACSC, G-leg. 5, no. 5, August 1698, p. 17.

64. AHPFM-ACSC, G-leg. 5, no. 8, to Margil, January 1701, p. 9v.

65. This culture is described by Cervantes in *The Devil in the New World*, pp. 90–93.

66. Cervantes, *The Devil in the New World*, p. 93.

67. Cervantes, *The Devil in the New World*, p. 18.

68. Term coined by Cervantes, *The Devil in the New World*; see pp. 133–35.

69. AHPFM-ACSC, G-leg. 5, no. 7, 1699, to Margil.

70. Cervantes, *The Devil in the New World*, 133.

71. Cervantes, *The Devil in the New World*, p. 135.

72. In addition to cases mentioned by Cervantes, see, for example, AGN, Inquisición,

vol. 571, exp. 9, pp. 234–45; this is the 1675 case of Domingo de Silva, a dance and music teacher denounced for making a pact with the devil in the form of a human.

73. AHPFM-ACSC, G-leg. 5, no. 5, to Margil, November 14, 1698, p. 26.

74. AHPFM-ACSC, G-leg. 5, nos. 5, 6, to Margil, December 1698, p. 30; March 1699, p. 10v. In this sense, Francisca also demonstrated a confidence similar to many female mystics in New Spain, such as the unfortunate Josefa de San Luis Beltrán who inevitably emerged victorious from her battles with the devil. See Rubial García, "Las santitas del barrio," p. 31.

75. See discussion in Cervantes, *The Devil in the New World*, p. 81.

76. AHPFM-ACSC, G-leg. 5, no. 8, August 1701, p. 5v.

77. AHPFM-ACSC, G-leg. 5, no. 6, June 1, 1699, pp. 33–35.

78. AHPFM-ACSC, G-leg. 5, no. 7, January 1700, p. 2v.

79. AHPFM-ACSC, G-leg. 4, no. 2, *Apuntes para el gobierno*, September 22, 1729.

80. de Nicolás, *St. John of the Cross*, p. 163.

81. AHPFM-ACSC, G-leg. 5, no. 19, March 1713, to Fray Ángel.

82. AHPFM-ACSC, G-leg. 5, no. 5, October 1698, p. 24.

83. AHPFM-ACSC, G-leg. 5, no. 5, December 1698, p. 32v–33.

84. Rasmussen, "Liturgy and the Liturgical Arts," p. 282.

85. AHPFM-ACSC, G-leg. 5, no. 8, September 14, 1701, to Margil, pp. 8v.-9.

86. AHPFM-ACSC, G-leg. 5, no. 20, March 2, 1714, to Fray Ángel, describing one such scene.

87. On March 31, 1715, for example, she told Fray Ángel that she had received communion in a vision, but then later that same morning when she received communion from a priest flames had erupted inside her, the torture/ecstasy lasting for days. See AHPFM-ACSC, G-leg. 5, no. 21, March 31, 1715.

88. Ríos, *Fray Margil de Jesús*, p. 188.

89. AHPFM-ACSC, G-leg. 5, no. 23, April 8, 1717, to Fray Ángel,

90. AHPFM-ACSC, G-leg. 5, no. 23, April 8, 1717, to Fray Ángel, p. 24 See Bynum, *Holy Feast and Holy Fast*, on the satisfaction of eating the host. See, for example, p. 4: "The Eucharist and related devotions, such as those to the body, wounds, heart and blood of Christ, were at the very center of women's piety. Eating God in the host was both a sweet tasting that focused and transcended all hunger and an occasion for paramystical phenomena of the most bizarre and exuberant sort."

91. See Tomizza, *Heavenly Supper*.

92. On visits to these churches, see, for example, AHPFM-ACSC, G-leg. 5, no. 5, her letter of August 1699, to Margil, pp. 50–60.

93. AHPFM-ACSC, G-leg. 5, no. 5, August 1699, to Margil, p. 21v.

94. AHPFM-ACSC, G-leg. 5, no. 5, December 1698, to Margil, p. 35.

95. AHPFM-ACSC, G-leg. 5, no. 5, December 1698, to Margil, p. 35.

96. AHPFM-ACSC, G-leg. 5, no. 5, October 1698, to Margil, pp. 18–18v.

97. AHPFM-ACSC, G-leg. 5, no. 6, February 1699, pp. 7v–8.

98. AHPFM-ACSC, G-leg. 5, no. 6, February 1699, pp. 2v–3.

99. AHPFM-ACSC, G-leg. 5, no. 6, February 1699, pp. 2v–3.

100. AHPFM-ACSC, G-leg. 5, no. 6, January 1, 1699, pp. 1–1v.

101. AHPFM-ACSC, G-leg. 5, no. 6, February 1699, p. 5.

102. AHPFM-ACSC, G-leg. 5, no. 29, October 1698, p. 25v.

103. AHPFM-ACSC, G-leg. 5, no. 7, October 1700, pp. 7–7v.

104. Myers, "Fundadora, cronista y mística," p. 109.

105. AHPFM-ACSC, G-leg. 5, no. 6, April 18, 1699, pp. 26v–27.

106. AHPFM-ACSC, G-leg. 5, no. 6, February 1699, pp. 3–5.

107. AHPFM-ACSC, G-leg. 5, no. 6, March 1699, p. 10v.

108. AHPFM-ACSC, G-leg. 5, no. 6, April 2, 1699, p. 18.

109. AHPFM-ACSC, G-leg. 5, no. 6, April 2, 1699, pp. 18v–19v.

110. AHPFM-ACSC, G-leg. 5, no. 6, April 2, 1699, p. 21v.

111. AHPFM-ACSC, G-leg. 5, no. 6, July 1, 1699, p. 44v.

112. See AHPFM-ACSC, G-leg. 6. On his life, see Espinosa, *El cherubin custodio.*

113. Francisca's biographer claims that she turned Antonio de los Ángeles to the religious life. See AHPFM-ACSC, G-leg. 9, Hermenegildo Villaplana, "Vida de la Venerable Sierva de Dios," chap. 15.

114. AHPFM-ACSC, G-leg. 6. Fray Ortega's comments are attached to Francisca's letter of June 25, 1711.

115. Ríos, *Fray Margil de Jesús,* p. 95.

116. Espinosa, *El Peregrino septentrional atlante,* p. 128.

117. Espinosa, *Cherubin custodio,* p. 46.

118. AHPFM-ACSC, G-leg. 6, June 11, 1701.

119. AHPFM-ACSC, G-leg. 6, to Díez, October 11, 1704.

120. After de los Ángeles's death in 1712, Francisca commissioned portraits of him and later testified that Margil always regarded the portraits with a gaze so intense that it seemed "that they spoke to each other." See AHPFM-ACSC, G-leg. 4, no. 2, "Apuntes para el gobierno," August 17, 1726.

121. AHPFM-ACSC, G-leg. 4, no. 2, "Apuntes para el gobierno," undated.

122. de Nicolás, *St. John of the Cross,* p. 167.

123. The former quotation is found in AHPFM-ACSC, G-leg. 4, no. 2, "Apuntes para el gobierno." The latter is found in Pontificio Ateneo Antonianum, caja 203;56, Archivo de Propaganda Fide, letter from Margil to Francisca, Zacatecas, February 21, 1707.

124. PAA Archivo de Propaganda Fide caja 203; 56, letter from Margil to Francisca, Zacatecas, February 21, 1707. She emphasized her spiritual inferiority frequently, using sentences such as this: "I look up at you with loving anxiety from down here on the earth of my miseries."

125. PAA, Archivo de Propaganda Fide, caja 203; 67.

126. Martínez, *Resumen de la vida*, p. 92.

127. "I think our Lady is very happy with how you sign as her slave, and I will henceforth sign as *esclava de Jesús María*," she commented in an undated letter to the friar, AHPFM-ACSC, G-leg. 6.

128. This discussion is indebted to McNamara, *Sisters in Arms*, pp. 519–20.

129. AHPFM-ACSC, G-leg. 6.

130. On the *beaterio* of Santa Rosa de Viterbo, see the next chapter.

131. AHPFM-ACSC, G-leg. 5, no. 27, undated letter (probably from the first years of the century since it is found in a packet of letters containing at the end a notice of Don Juan's death in 1706).

132. "I am at work on what you asked of me, all three things, I'll do what I can," she wrote in an undated letter, referring to souls in particular need of help (AHPFM-ASCSC, G-leg. 5, no. 28).

133. AHPFM-ASCSC, G-leg. 6.

134. AHPFM-ASCSC, G-leg. 6.

135. "The last time I saw you at the porteria I felt so consoled and felt like we were so united, thanks to the Lord for that" (AHPFM-ASCSC, G-leg. 6, undated).

136. AHPFM-ASCSC, G-leg. 6. Written before Don Juan Caballero y Ocio's death in 1706.

### 6. The Beaterio of Santa Rosa, 1699–1712

1. Hsia, *The World of Catholic Renewal*, pp. 39–40.

2. Francisca recounted the first days of the *beaterio* to Fray Antonio de los Ángeles; see AHPFM-ACSC, G-leg. 6, "Cartas de la Venerable Francisca de los Ángeles."

3. María de Jesús, *Crónica del Real Colegio*, pp. 33–35.

4. AHPFM-ACSC, G-leg. 6, "Cartas de la Venerable."

5. For an analysis of the role of *recogimientos* in Lima, see Van Deusen, *Between the Sacred and the Worldly*. She notes that between 1669 and 1704 ten *beaterios* were founded in Lima. Their proliferation was due in large part to population growth, which motivated Lima's elite to fortify barriers between race, class and gender. See Van Deusen, *Between the Sacred and the Worldly*, pp. 140–54.

6. AHPFM-ACSC, G-leg. 6, "Cartas de la Venerable," undated.

7. AHPFM-ACSC, G-leg. 6, "Cartas de la Venerable," undated.

8. Since the letter is undated it is difficult to know which guardian she was speaking of. In all probability it was one of the following friars: "Fray Francisco Hidalgo, guardian from 1701–1703, Fray José Díez, guardian from 1703–1706, Fray Antonio Olivarez, guardian 1706–1709." For a list of Santa Cruz guardians, see Díez, *Apostólicos empleos*, p. 238.

9. AHPFM-ACSC, G-leg. 6, "Cartas de la Venerable," undated, but found in a packet of letters referring to the death of Caballero y Ocio, which occurred in 1706.

10. AHPFM-ACSC, G-leg. 5, no. 11, to Díez, January 8, 1704.

11. AHPFM-ACSC, G-leg. 5, no. 27, to Ortega, undated.

12. AHPFM-ACSC, G-leg. 6, undated.

13. AHPFM-ACSC, G-leg. 4, no. 9, "Principios del Beaterio de Santa Rosa," undated.

14. See, for example, an undated note in which she thanks an unnamed friar for his letter concerning the governance of Gertrudis, likely her sister, due to her delicacy. See AHPFM-ACSC, G-leg. 5, no. 28.

15. In an undated letter, Francisca notes that she had to bring Padre Dávila with her to persuade Gertrudis to join the community again. They managed to win her over by threatening to lock her up if she did not come out (*"la conquistamos"*). See AHPFM-ACSC, G-leg. 5, no. 28.

16. AHPFM-ACSC, G-leg. 5, no. 27: *"se deja llebar de qualquiera cosita,"* Francisca stated.

17. See, for example, the case of Francisca de San José; undated and recipient's name unknown but clearly sent to a Santa Cruz friar. See AHPFM-ACSC, G-leg. 5, no. 27.

18. AHPFM-ACSC, G-leg. 6, undated letters.

19. AHPFM-ACSC, G-leg. 6, undated letters.

20. AHPFM-ACSC, G-leg. 4, no. 8, testimony of Josepha de Jesús María, *portera*.

21. The boy Ignacio Cabrera died at the age of twenty-two, and Francisca claimed that he had hardly had to spend any time at all in purgatory. See AHPFM-ACSC, G-leg. 5, no. 27.

22. AHPFM-ACSC, G-leg. 5, no. 27, undated.

23. AHPFM-ACSC, G-leg. 4, no. 8, testimony of Josepha de Jesús María.

24. AHPFM-ACSC, G-leg. 4, no. 8, testimony of Josepha de Jesús María.

25. AHPFM-ACSC, G-leg., no. 5, undated.

26. On the rebellion, see McCloskey, *The Formative Years*, p. 73.

27. On Díez's career, see Díez, *Apostólicos empleos*, pp. 215–35.

28. de Jesús, *Crónica del Real Colegio*, p. 43.

29. de Jesús, *Crónica del Real Colegio*, p. 43.

30. de Jesús, *Crónica del Real Colegio*, p. 37.

31. de Jesús, *Crónica del Real Colegio*, pp. 38–39.

32. de Jesús, *Crónica del Real Colegio*, pp. 39–40. Their chronicler emphasized the risks and dangers they invoked on such a journey but reassured the reader that God had always held a protective hand over the little group.

33. AHPFM-ACSC, G-leg. 5, no. 27, undated letter, to Ortega.

34. AHPFM-ACSC, G-leg. 5, no. 27, undated letter.

35. On the devil and miracles, see Jesús, *Crónica del Real Colegio*, chap. 5. On the *beatas'* individual nightly meditations in the hermitage, see chap. 3. In a document dated September 27, 1720, the friars of Santa Cruz testified to their "rigorous regularity and withdrawal from the world, punctually observing to the utmost the rules of Christian perfection and the rule of the Third Order of our father San Francisco with

such example that it has come to the attention of the principal citizens of the city." See AHPFM-ACSC, F-leg. 2, no. 5: "Informe que hizo este Colegio Apostólico de la Santa Cruz de Querétaro al Señor Arzobispo de Mexico en abono del Beaterio de Santa Rosa de esta ciudad."

36. AHPFM-ACSC, G-leg. 3, no. 5: "Papel de Marcela en el beaterio de Santa Rosa el 6 diciembre por mandato de su confesor."

37. AHPFM-ACSC, G-leg. 3, nos. 1, 2. Testimonies of Isabel Rosa on November 27, 1713, and Fray Ángel on November 13, 1719.

38. AHPFM-ACSC, G-leg. 3, no. 3. Isabel Rosa, November 1725 to Fray Isidro Félix de Espinosa.

39. AHPFM-ACSC, G-leg. 3, no. 1, December 30, 1713.

40. AHPFM-ACSC, G-leg. 4, "*Apuntes* . . ."; letters from Juan Mora to Isabel, the vicaress, October 31, 1722; October 25, 1724; March 3, 1825; June 17, 1725.

41. AHPFM-ACSC, G-leg. 4, no. 2, "*Apuntes* . . .".

42. AHPFM-ACSC, G-leg. 5, no. 27, undated, and no recipient listed; name of *beata* and confessor are not mentioned; she is only named "*niña*."

43. AHPFM-ACSC, G-leg. 5, no. 20, April 8, 1714.

44. In an undated note to Margil she begs him to send these two a letter ordering them to confess with Padre Puga, something they had clearly refused to do. See AHPFM-ACSC, G-leg. 5, no. 28, undated.

45. AHPFM-ACSC, G-leg. 5, no. 28, undated. Undated note to Fray Juan Alonso de Ortega telling him she is sending two *muchachos* over and asking him to make sure they receive confession since the behavior of one of them was driving her mad.

46. AHPFM-ACSC, G-leg. 5, no. 28, undated.

47. "You know that communion is my only consolation," she wailed in an undated note to the guardian. Since she asks for Fray Ángel, it is safe to assume the note was written after 1712. See AHPFM-ACSC, G-leg.5, no. 27, undated.

48. AHPFM-ACSC, G-leg.5, no. 27, undated. See, for example, undated letter to Ortega in which Francisca relates an episode with one of the younger members of the community who had not yet professed as a *tercera*. The girl refused communion after morning mass and would not budge no matter how far the foundress and her confessor went in persuading her. In the end, Francisca was convinced that such a rebellious spirit did not belong in the community and suggested it would be best for the girl to leave them.

49. de Jesús, *Crónica del Real Colegio*, p. 55.

50. AGN, Inquisición, vol. 619, exp. 4, pp. 377–447, 1672, "Autos de la Pretención del Capitán don Juan Caballero y Ocio, para familiar del Santo Oficio."

51. AHPFM-ACSC, G-leg. 5, no. 27, undated.

52. de Jesús, *Crónica del Real Colegio*, p. 43.

53. AHPFM-ACSC, G-leg. 2, no. 2, undated to Sitjar.

54. de Jesús, *Crónica del Real Colegio*, p. 43.

55. Amerlinck de Corsi, Ramos Medina, *Conventos de monjas*, pp. 31–33, 44–51, 55–63, and Muriel, *Conventos de monjas*, pp. 167–75, 339–42. Of fifty-eight conventual foundations in the colonial period, fourteen had more informal antecedents, the majority of which had functioned as *beaterios*. See Muriel, *Los recogimientos de mujeres*.

56. From the late seventeenth century onward, reform-minded ecclesiastics had begun voicing their disapproval of the overly secular way of life led in most convents. In 1664, an outraged Franciscan friar, Antonio de la Annunciación, wrote to the king, begging him to eradicate *locutorio* traditions, an "intolerable abuse and offense to the eyes of God." The majority of Mexican convents, the scandalized friar maintained, had become the territory of the devil because the continual chatter between nuns and laity was filled with scandalous expressions that horrified spectators. In 1667, a Franciscan provincial had tried to limit the number of servants in the convents of his jurisdiction but to no avail. Between 1712 and 1718, Archbishop Aguiar y Seijas issued several orders to simplify and strip nuns' habits of their ornaments; see AGN, Inquisición, vol. 997, exp. 27. On attempts at reform in the seventeenth century, see Benassy-Berling, *Humanismo y religión*, and Lavrin, "Ecclesiastical Reform of Nunneries," pp. 182–203. These voices were echoed in seventeenth-century Spain. In 1619, for example, the Council of Castile petitioned the king to restrict entry into convents, for they contributed to "the impoverishment of the countryside." See McNamara, *Sisters in Arms*, p. 550.

57. AHPFM-ACSC, G-leg. 6, "*Cartas de la Venerable*," undated.

58. de Jesús, *Crónica del Real Colegio*, pp. 54–55.

59. Based on a reminiscence noted by an anonymous confessor, September 1729, in G-leg. 4, no. 2, "Apuntes para el gobierno."

60. Several references are made to the day of Santa Rosa and the celebrations at the *beaterio*. See, for example, G-leg. 5, no. 18, November 1711, to Ortega.

61. de Jesús, *Crónica del Real Colegio*, p. 55.

62. Weber, *Teresa of Ávila*, pp. 3, 35–40, 52, 159, 165.

63. de Jesús, *Crónica del Real Colegio*, pp. 55–57.

64. AHPFM-ACSC, G-leg. 6, undated, to Fray Antonio.

65. AHPFM-ACSC, G-leg. 6, not dated, but since it mentions the reaction of the archbishop I assume it was written in this period.

66. AHPFM-ACSC, G-leg. 2, no. 2, to Díez; undated but found in a stack of papers from 1706.

67. It is clear from Francisca's letters to Fray Antonio de los Ángeles that Margil corresponded with don Matías and asked her to keep him informed as to his actions concerning the foundation of a convent or a *beaterio*. See AHPFM-ACSC, G-leg. 6, "Cartas de la Venerable," undated.

68. AHPFM-ACSC, G-leg. 6, "Cartas de la Venerable . . . ." undated.

69. AHPFM-ACSC, G-leg. 6, "Cartas de la Venerable . . . ." undated.

70. AHPFM-ACSC, G-leg. 6, "Cartas de la Venerable . . . ." undated.

71. AHPFM-ACSC, G-leg. 6, "Cartas de la Venerable . . . ." undated.

72. Miramontes, *El Templo de Santa Rosa*, p. 30.

73. de Jesús, *Crónica del Real Colegio*, p. 56.

74. AHPFM-ACSC, G-leg. 6, not dated but found in a packet of letters containing references to the dispute with the archbishop.

75. Ramírez Álvarez, *Querétaro, vision de mi ciudad*, p. 165.

76. Ramírez Álvarez, *Querétaro, vision de mi ciudad*, p. 165.

77. Ramírez Álvarez, *Querétaro, vision de mi ciudad*, p. 165.

78. See the testimonies of Josepha de Jesús María, María Josepha de San Antonio y Luna, Josepha Bentura de los Dolores, María Manuela de Señora Santa Ana, and two anonymous testimonies. AHPFM-ACSC, G-leg. 4, no. 8.

79. AHPFM-ACSC, G-leg. 5, no. 27, undated.

80. "Su más afecta hija" means "Your most loving daughter." This was the term Francisca commonly used when signing her letters to Fray José Díez and other Santa Cruz friars.

81. AHPFM-ACSC, G-leg.5, no. 27.

82. AHPFM-ACSC, G-leg. 6.

83. Quoted in McNamara, *Sisters in Arms*, p. 496.

84. AHPFM-ACSC, G-leg. 9.

85. AHPFM-ACSC, G-leg. 6, undated to Antonio de los Ángeles.

86. AHPFM-ACSC, G-leg. 6, undated to Antonio de los Ángeles.

87. AHPFM-ACSC, G-leg. 6, undated to Antonio de los Ángeles.

88. AHPFM-ACSC, G-leg. 5, no. 27.

89. AHPFM-ACSC, G-leg. 5, no. 27.

90. AHPFM-ACSC, G-leg. 5, no. 11, to Díez, January 8, 1704.

91. AHPFM-ACSC, G-leg. 5, no. 11, to Díez, February 2, 1704.

92. AHPFM-ACSC, G-leg. 5, nos. 13, 15, November 1706, to Fray Ángel García Duque.

93. AHPFM-ACSC, G-leg. 5, nos. 13, 15, November 1706, to Fray Ángel García Duque.

94. For a discussion of the ambiguities surrounding *beatas* in Spain, see, for example, Van Deusen, *Between the Sacred and the Worldly*, pp. 24–26.

95. AHPFM-ACSC, F-leg. 2, no. 1, September 30, 1708.

96. Martínez, *Resumen de la vida*, p. 93.

97. PAA, Archivo de Propaganda Fide, caja. 203, no. 56.

98. AHPFM-ACSC, G-leg. 5, no. 16, August 10, 1709, to Díez.

99. AHPFM-ACSC, G-leg. 5, no. 16, August 10, 1709, to Díez.

100. AHPFM-ACSC, G-leg. 5, no. 17, April 29, 1710.

101. AHPFM-ACSC, G-leg. 5, no. 17, April 29, 1710.

102. AHPFM-ACSC, G-leg. 5, no. 17, September 20, 1710.

103. AHPFM-ACSC, G-leg. 5, no. 17, August 21, 1710.

104. AHPFM-ACSC, G-leg. 5, no. 17, October 22, 1710.

105. AHPFM-ACSC, G-leg. 5, no. 16, 1709, to Ortega.

### 7. Mid-Life, 1711–1712

1. AHPFM-ACSC, G-leg. 5, no. 18, to Fray Ángel or Díez, February 5, 1711.

2. AHPFM-ACSC, G-leg. 5, no. 27, undated letter from Francisca to Santa Cruz thanking the friars and begging them not to forget her father or sister in their prayers and masses.

3. AHPFM-ACSC, G-leg. 5, no. 27. Undated note written in June to Ortega. She also asked the friar to let her know if there was anything she could do for the friar, for she would do it "with all my love." On her food deliveries to Fray Antonio, see undated letter. It clearly dates from his last illness, however, for it includes anxious inquiries into his state (in G-leg. 6).

4. AHPFM-ACSC, G-leg. 5, no. 28, undated to Ortega.

5. AHPFM-ACSC, G-leg. 5, no. 18, to Ortega, June 25, 1711.

6. AHPFM-ACSC, G-leg. 5, no. 19, undated (1712), to Fray Ángel.

7. AHPFM-ACSC, G-leg. 5, no. 27, note from Ortega; undated but states that this occurred at the end of June.

8. AHPFM-ACSC, G-leg 8, to Fray Ángel, July 13, 1712.

9. AHPFM-ACSC, G-leg 8, to Ortega, May 5, 1712.

10. AHPFM-ACSC, G-leg. 5, no. 27, undated.

11. AHPFM-ACSC, G-leg. 8, undated, to Fray Ángel.

12. AHPFM-ACSC, G-leg. 5, no. 27, undated.

13. AHPFM-ACSC, G-leg. 5, no. 27; undated and untitled, but in all probability to Fray Ángel.

14. AHPFM-ACSC, G-leg. 5, no. 27, undated.

15. AHPFM-ACSC, G-leg. 8, to Fray Ángel, Day of Saint Joseph, 1712.

16. AHPFM-ACSC, G-leg. 8, to Fray Ángel, Day of Saint Joseph, 1712.

17. AHPFM-ACSC, G-leg. 5, no. 27, undated, to Ortega.

18. PAA, Archivo de Propaganda Fide, caja 203, no. 56.

19. AHPFM-ACSC, G-leg. 5, no. 18, Day of Saint Joseph, 1711.

20. AHPFM-ACSC, G-leg. 8, to Fray Ángel, April 21, 1712.

21. AHPFM-ACSC, G-leg. 8, to Ortega, July 7, 13, 22, 1712.

22. AGN, Inquisición, 1712, vol. 745, exp. 7, pp. 130–132v. PAA, Misc. 327.10. Fray José Guerra, *Fecunda nube del cielo Guadalupano y mística Paloma*, México, 1726.

23. AGN, Inquisición, vol. 745, exp. 7, p. 133v.

24. AGN, Inquisición, vol. 745, exp. 7, pp. 136–136v.

25. AGN, Inquisición, vol. 745, exp. 7, pp. 136–37.

26. AGN, Inquisición, vol. 745, exp. 7, p. 138.

27. AGN, Inquisición, vol. 745, exp. 7, pp. 150–56.

28. AGN, Inquisición, vol. 745, exp. 7, p. 157.

29. AGN, Inquisición, vol. 746, pp. 385–86; for de Jesús's comments on the affair, see *Crónica del Real Colegio*, p. 91. De Jesús maintained that Francisca's name had gotten mixed up with that of another *beata* denounced by the Inquisition, but the Inquisition documents and Margil's letter show this not to be the case.

30. AGN, Inquisición, vol. 750, exp. 37, pp. 591–604.

31. AHPFM-ACSC, G-leg. 6, to Fray Ángel, undated.

32. AHPFM-ACSC, G-leg. 6, to Ortega, October 31, probably 1713.

## 8. Foundation

1. AHPFM-ACSC, G-leg. 5, no. 27, undated, to Ortega.

2. AHPFM-ACSC, G-leg. 5, no. 19, March 1713, to Fray Ángel.

3. AHPFM-ACSC, G-leg. 5, no. 19, May 1713, to Fray Ángel.

4. See, for example, AHPFM-ACSC, May 22, 1714, note from Fray Ángel in G-leg. 5, no. 20.

5. AHPFM-ACSC, G-leg. 5, no. 19, July 1713, to Fray Ángel.

6. AHPFM-ACSC, G-leg. 5, Fray Ángel's note, November 27, 1713.

7. AHPFM-ACSC, G-leg. 5, no. 20, January 1714, to Fray Ángel.

8. AHPFM-ACSC, G-leg. 5, no. 19, December 30, 1713.

9. AHPFM-ACSC, G-leg. 5, no. 19, undated. The occasion for the rapture was communion on Corpus Christi. Once she came home she fell straight into bed. On another occasion, as she was speaking to Fray Ángel in the confessional during mass, she heard the friar lift the host and was immediately transported even though she continued to talk to him. Her mind was filled with the *Señor Sacramentado*, and the "lord caressed my soul and gave me all his love." See AHPFM-ACSC, G-leg. 5, no. 20, March 2, 1714.

10. See, for example, AHPFM-ACSC, G-leg. 5, no. 20, letter from April 27, 1714.

11. AHPFM-ACSC, G-leg. 5, no. 20, May 8, 1714, to Fray Ángel. On January 28, 1715, she exclaimed that "I want to be able to sleep soundly and be well awake and alert, but I go about like between sleep and waking in a secret dream" (no. 21, January 28, 1715, to Fray Ángel).

12. AHPFM-ACSC, G-leg. 5, no. 20, April 8, 1714.

13. McNamara, *Sisters in Arms*, p. 540.

14. AHPFM-ACSC, G-leg. 5, no. 20, to Fray Ángel, April 30, 1714. "How am I to stop the girls from playing and singing. I would be happy to see them behind convent grills and under the rule of the Capuchins so that even if they knew how to play music and sing they would not do so."

15. de Jesús, *Crónica del Real Colegio*, p. 87.

16. AHPFM-ACSC, G-leg. 5, no. 21, to Fray Ángel, February 3, 1715. On that occasion she noted that Armenta had had chocolate with her and blessed some candles, a sign of recovery since he had refused to speak to her for eight months.

17. AHPFM-ACSC, G-leg. 5, no. 27, undated.

18. AHPFM-ACSC, G-leg. 5, no. 27. Note from Fray Ángel on April 27, no. 20.

19. AHPFM-ACSC, G-leg. 4, no. 4. Fray Ángel to the *beata* Isabel Rosa, December 2, 1715.

20. AHPFM-ACSC, G-leg. 5, no. 23, January 31, 1717, to Fray Ángel.

21. AHPFM-ACSC, G-leg. 5, no. 22, to Fray Ángel, 1716 (no further date).

22. See, for example, AHPFM-ACSC, G-leg. 5, nos. 23, 24, January 16, 1717; April, 11, 1717; June 29, 1718.

23. AHPFM-ACSC, G-leg. 5, no. 24, July 11, 1718.

24. AHPFM-ACSC, G-leg. 5, no. 25, undated but found in a stack of letters dated between 1720 and 1722.

25. AHPFM-ACSC, G-leg. 5, no. 25, January 22, 1720.

26. "Your brother who loves you in Christ." AHPFM-ACSC, G-leg. 5, no. 27, from Fray Ángel to Francisca, 1718.

27. AHPFM-ACSC, G-leg. 5, no. 25, January 22, 1720.

28. PAA, Archivo de Propaganda Fide, caja 203, no. 59.

29. PAA, Archivo de Propaganda Fide, caja 203, no. 60, Zacatecas, July 1, 1723.

30. PAA, Archivo de Propaganda Fide, caja 203, no. 60, Zacatecas, July 1, 1723.

31. On the cochineal ointment, see undated note in AHPFM-ACSC, G-leg. 5. no. 28.

32. AHPFM-ACSC, G-leg. 5, dated 1712 but in no. 27.

33. AHPFM-ACSC, G-leg. 5, undated but follows letter with exhortations.

34. AHPFM-ACSC, G-leg. 5, to Ortega.

35. AHPFM-ACSC, G-leg. 4, no. 7, undated to Ortega.

36. AHPFM-ACSC, G-leg. 5, no. 27.

37. References to such exchanges are mostly found in undated notes to Ortega asking for ingredients or lamenting delays in the production, even apologizing for the product. See AHPFM-ACSC, G-leg. 5, nos. 27, 28.

38. AHPFM-ACSC, G-leg. 7, November 18, 1717, to Fray Ángel.

39. The library is mentioned as *libreria* in a January 19 letter to Fray Ángel; see AHPFM-ACSC, G-leg. 5, no. 27.

40. AHPFM-ACSC, G-leg. 4, no. 7, undated, to Ortega: "I wish God would give me one *hermana* who would fight for me without the fears and tremors of my vicaress Isabel."

41. AHPFM-ACSC, G-leg. 4, no. 7, November 1729. She was convinced that Armenta would find her "too lax" and would punish the woman severely.

42. AHPFM-ACSC, G-leg. 4, no. 7, undated letter to Ortega.

43. AHPFM-ACSC, G-leg. 5, no. 19, undated, but found in packet of 1713 letters to Fray Ángel. In the letter, she asked especially for water blessed by a friar by the name of Juan de la Cruz.

44. See, for example, AHPFM-ACSC, G-leg. 5, no. 25, January 22, 1720, on finding a

whole box of chocolate when she thought she did not have any and was desperately in search of it for a sick woman.

45. AHPFM-ACSC, G-leg. 5, no. 25, no. 23, April 8, 1717, to Fray Ángel.

46. AHPFM-ACSC, G-leg. 5, no. 25, April 26, 1721.

47. AHPFM-ACSC, G-leg. 5, no. 20, April 21, 1714.

48. In 1717, the devil whispered to her that she ate not merely out of necessity but because she liked to do so. See AHPFM-ACSC, G-leg. 5, no. 23, October 27, 1717. On the molar falling out, see November 18, 1717 to Fray Ángel.

49. de Nicolás, *St. John of the Cross*, p. 165.

50. de Nicolás, *St. John of the Cross*, p. 165.

51. AHPFM-ACSC, G-leg. 5, no. 27, undated letter mentioning that she went that morning to see a doña Petra, who Margil had asked her to "look after."

52. Sometime, in the 1710s, he managed to secure for a *beata* from Francisca's community a place as a chorist in one of the great convents in the capital. Francisca naturally agonized over who should go. There were already four enthusiastic applicants lined up, and problems arose as to whether seniority or liveliness of spirit should be the determining factor. From an undated letter but found in a stack of letters that primarily date from between 1710 and 1720. See AHPFM-ACSC, G-leg. 5, undated.

53. AHPFM-ACSC, G-leg. 5, no. 27, undated.

54. AHPFM-ACSC, G-leg. 5, no. 28, undated.

55. AHPFM-ACSC, G-leg. 5, undated, no. 21, letter to Fray Ángel, 1715; no. 27, not dated, to Ortega: "I am worried about the Altamirano nun."

56. Another nun, whom she calls Madre Buenaventura, is probably Teresa de San Buenaventura, from Querétaro. The daughter of unknown parents she professed in 1702 (AHPFM, Santa Clara, "Libro de profesiones," 1702, 1704). On Francisca's friendship with the nuns, see AHPFM-ACSC, G-leg. 5, no. 26, 27, 28. Letters from 1722 to Ortega; three letters not dated to Ortega but found among her correspondence from 1710–1720; and a note to Ortega, not dated: "I went to see the nuns and Mother Rosa is sick." In another note to Antonio de los Ángeles, she mentions the venerable Mother Rosa de Jesús. Since Antonio died in 1711, it is clear that she knew Rosa by then.

57. "Doña Petra has been acting like a little girl and not like a lady . . . it fell to me to stay with her in her house and I was mortified. I went more for Mother Rosa to whom I owe so much than for Petra." AHPFM-ACSC, G-leg. 5, no. 23: letter to Ortega, 1717.

58. AHPFM-ACSC, G-leg. 5, no. 23: letter to Ortega, 1717, no. 27; letter to Ortega, not dated.

59. In an undated note she mentioned how happy she had been to see the nun so beautiful and added that they were putting the finishing touches to her costumes. AHPFM-ACSC, G-leg. 5, no. 27, undated.

60. AHPFM-ACSC, G-leg. 5, no. 27, letter to Ortega, not dated.

61. AHPFM-ACSC, G-leg. 5, no. 27. Again, almost triumphantly, she told him that his troubles with the nuns were mortification sent by God. This perhaps echoed the friars' own counsel when she turned to them in her troubles.

62. AHPFM-ACSC, G-leg. 5, no. 27, several letters. In an undated letter, for example, she complains that the friar only had time to confess two *beatas* since he had to go to Santa Clara. The best remedy she thought would be to send him to Santa Rosa on Mondays and Santa Clara on Thursdays.

63. AHPFM-ACSC, G-leg. 5, no. 27, undated note. Francisca conceded that, of course, it was "very advantageous that you confess the nuns, but there are problems and continuing to confess the nuns might harm the college . . . . I can only tell you by mouth some of the things that have happened so if you are thinking only of the welfare of the nuns then go on confessing them, but if it is the peace and tranquility of the college you are thinking of then I would reconsider."

64. AHPFM-ACSC, G-leg. 5, no. 27. In an undated letter to Fray Ángel, she mentions, for example, that doña Nicolasa de Montaño wanted her to come and fetch her for a mass in the *beaterio*'s chapel. Francisca confessed to Fray Ángel that she really was not in the mood for it but would do so since the woman had "spirit and good will."

65. AHPFM-ACSC, G-leg. 5, no. 27, undated letter to Ortega, discussing the *hermandad* with a certain doña María Francisca.

66. AGN, Inquisición, vol. 634, p. 431.

67. AHPFM-ACSC, G-leg. 5, no. 27, undated letter to Fray Ángel inquiring after don Joseph and don Antonio Fernandes, who seem to be away. Francisca complains that she has not heard from them.

68. AHPFM-ACSC, G-leg. 5, no. 20, April 25, 1714, to Fray Ángel.

69. Francisca calls María Buenrostro "María Lucio," obviously confusing her with her husband's family name (AHPFM-ACSC, G-leg. 5, no. 18, letter to Ortega, 1712). María's daughters professed in 1711. In their *informaciones* their parents are stated to be "*gente conocida en esta República*" (AHPFM, Santa Clara, "Información de Doña Ana Francisca Martínez Lucio, 1711.") The girls' father, Juan Martínez y Lucio, had served in the honorary job of notary of the Inquisition in Querétaro and as *alcalde provincial de la Santa Hermandad.* AHQ, Notarías, Parra, 1724, pp. 57–63.

70. AHPFM-ACSC, G-leg. 5, no. 27, to Ortega.

71. Other well-rooted Querétaro clans may have been involved in her social world as well. In an undated letter to Fray Juan Alonso de Ortega, she asks him specifically as a favor to her to write to doña Josepha Soto, who may have belonged to the Soto family, which had several members in Santa Clara. Clearly, Francisca in this instance was involved in organizing spiritual counsel for the woman. Her letters frequently mention two women—doña Micaela Merino and doña Luisa—who frequented mass at the *beaterio*'s small chapel and whom Francisca recommended for confession by

the friars. Francisca also visited Luisa in her house. See AHPFM-ACSC, G-leg. 5, no. 19, 23–36.

72. AHPFM-ACSC, G-leg. 6. A note, not dated, to Antonio de los Ángeles from Francisca states: "[I hope] that our sovereign Lady give her the strength and spirit to embrace . . . the lofty religious state."

73. "They insisted that I come," she stated in her note. AHPFM-ACSC, G-leg. 5, no. 27.

74. AHPFM-ACSC, G-leg. 9, Hermenegildo Vilaplana, "Vida de la venerable madre Francisca de los Ángeles", chap. 16.

75. AHPFM-ACSC, G-leg. 5, no. 20, April 8, 1714.

76. AHPFM-ACSC, G-leg. 5, no. 20, January 19, 1714.

77. AHPFM-ACSC, G-leg. 4, "Apuntes para el gobierno," July 6, 1725. Francisca claimed that his eventual death did not detract from the power of the relic; indeed, God had simply decided to show that the provincial would die when He wanted him to die.

78. Term coined by Burns; see, for example, Colonial Habits.

79. AHPFM-ACSC, G-leg. 5, no. 22, December 5, 1716.

80. "Some persons who with piety and charity had visited the beatas and who were accustomed to being able to enter the innermost corners of the house . . . . felt it heavily that they not be let in, and for this reason began to withdraw and suspend the aid that some of these people had been providing and opposed the enclosure with various opinions and dictamens on the enclosure." de Jesús, Crónica del Real Colegio, p. 102.

81. de Jesús, Crónica del Real Colegio, pp. 103–4.

82. PAA, Archivo Propaganda Fide, caja 203, no. 58, Antonio Margil de Jesús, Misión de Nuestra Señora de los Dolores, July 19, 1715.

83. AHPFM-ACSC, G-leg. 5, no. 23, February 19, 1717.

84. On the foundation and the marquis's role in it, see Lavrin, "Indian Brides of Christ," pp. 241–51.

85. Miramontes, Templo de Santa Rosa, p. 30.

86. In this case, the "Ordinary" refers to the jurisdiction of the archbishopric of Mexico.

87. AHPFM-ACSC, G-leg. 4, "Apuntes para el gobierno," July 6, 1725.

88. Ríos, Apostól de América, p. 170.

89. AHPFM-ACSC, I-leg. 4, no. 48. Letter from Margil to Francisca, January 8, 1724.

90. Ríos, Fray Margil de Jesùs, p. 179.

91. Ríos, Fray Margil de Jesùs, pp. 183–84.

92. Ríos, Fray Margil de Jesùs, pp. 187–88.

93. Espinosa, El peregrino septentrional, p. 320.

94. AHPFM-ACSC, G-leg. 4, no. 2, "Apuntes para el gobierno."

95. Espinosa, El peregrino septentrional, p. 189.

96. Espinosa, *El peregrino septentrional*, p. 189.

97. AHPFM-ACSC, G-leg. 4, no. 3, letter from Juan de Mora in Mexico City to Francisca, undated but written immediately after Margil's death. On her grief and dreams, see confessor's notes on September 23, 1729. Ríos, *Fray Margil de Jesús*, pp. 188–90.

98. AHPFM-ACSC, AHPFM-ACSC, G-leg. 7, no. 7.

99. In an undated letter but probably from this period, she discussed the problems of a certain doña Juana who was suffering from hot flashes. Francisca had asked her to try and wear the habit of her sister doña Francisca, but that made her feel even hotter than before. In the same letter, Francisca mentioned that "they are coming from the parish for our doña Clara who is very tired but suffers with such love and patience that she is a great model for us all, may the Lord help her in her pain." Whether doña Clara was simply a temporary resident or a tertiary is difficult to know, but it demonstrates that women of a higher social station had begun to enter the *beaterio*.

100. AHPFM-ACSC, G-leg. 4, no. 7, undated to Ortega.

101. AHPFM-ACSC, G-leg. 4, no. 7, undated to Ortega.

102. A reference to this is found in an undated letter in AHPFM-ACSC, G-leg. 4, no. 7.

### 9. Eclipse

1. On the *hermandad* see Díez, *Apostólicos empleos*, pp. 112–18.

2. AGN, Inquisición, vol. 750, exp. 37, pp. 598–601: testimony of Br. don Juan Antonio Espinosa denouncing Fray Ángel García Duque, guardian of Santa Cruz, for his public "slandering" of the Congregation of Guadalupe. On February 15, 1712, the *calificadores* did not find anything to contradict Fray Ángel's good reputation and thus chose not to give the friar a reprimand. Nevertheless, the case was not closed, but unfortunately we do not now how it ended.

3. de Jesús, *Crónica del Real Colegio*, p. 111.

4. AGN, Bienes Nacionales, vol. 242, exp. 8: copy of the *Real Cédula* of July 9, 1728; December 11, 1728. Order from the dean of the *cabildo* declaring perpetual enclosure and a deposit of the sacraments to Santa Rosa. Letter of January 1, 1729, from Br. Sebastián de Olivares to the *cabildo*.

5. Such episodes were not altogether uncommon in the Spanish colonies. In 1656, for example, the nuns of Santa Clara in Santiago de Chile appealed to be released from the authority of the Franciscan order and transferred to episcopal jurisdiction. The friars promptly invaded the convent with the help of seculars and beat and abused the nuns, who remained their prisoners until 1662. See McNamara, *Sisters in Arms*, p. 505.

6. de Jesús, *Crónica del Real Colegio*, p. 114.

7. See the testimony on the situation in the college of the nine *beatas* who sought shelter in Santa Clara. AHPFM-ACSC, G-leg. 4, no. 9.

8. AGN, Bienes Nacionales, vol. 242, exp. 8, January 24: "Autos hechos en el Colegio

de Santa Rosa de Viterbo sobre la mutación de habito de las colegiales de dicho colegio." Testimony of the ecclesiastical notary on January 31 as to the Franciscans' attempted entry on January 25 and 26.

9. AGN, Bienes Nacionales, vol. 242, exp. 8, March 2: testimony of Juan Bautista majordomo of the Cofradía del Santo Cristo de San Benito. On the expelled *beatas'* consultation with the Franciscan friars, see letter from de los Ríos dated February 7, 1729, to the Dean of the Cabildo.

10. AGN, Bienes Nacionales, vol. 242, exp. 8. Letter of the parish priest of Querétaro to the archbishopric complaining over the judge's behavior, February 25, 1729.

11. AGN, Bienes Nacionales, vol. 242, exp. 8. Letter from de los Ríos to the *cabildo*, February 19, 1729. On the excommunication of the *beatas*, see letter from Franciscan representative, Lucas de Zareaga, to the fiscal of the archbishopric, March 26, 1729. On Franciscans excommunicating de los Ríos, see his letter to the *cabildo* on March 21, 1729. On *cabildo's* reaction, see its April 2, 1729 order. In his opinion, written on the margin of the letter sent by the beatas' representative, the fiscal recommended that the case be taken up and examined.

12. AGN, Bienes Nacionales, vol. 242, exp. 9.

13. AGN, Bienes Nacionales, vol. 242, exp. 9.

14. Díez, *Apostólicos empleos*, appendix I, pp. 232–35, Juan Domingo Arricivita, "Vida del V.P. Fr. Joseph Díez."

15. AHPFM-ACSC, G-leg. 4. Testimony of Josepha de Jesús María, undated but after Francisca's death.

16. AHPFM-ACSC, G-leg. 4, no. 9.

17. AHPFM-ACSC, G-leg. 4, no. 9.

18. AHPFM-ACSC, G-leg. 4, no. 9.

19. AHPFM-ACSC, G-leg. 4, *Apuntes*, 1729.

20. AGN, Bienes Nacionales, vol. 242, exp. 8. In June 1730, one of the friars involved in the affair complained that the *beatas* had now been in Santa Clara excommunicated for a year and half. On meetings with laymen, see testimony of Br. Francisco Pérez de Espinosa on such a meeting in the house of Colonel José de Urtiaga y Salazar (March 21, 1729).

21. The number of volumes left by Querétaro notaries drops steadily throughout the century. Between 1711 and 1743, forty-four thick volumes were filled. Between 1744 and 1770 this number fell to thirty-two volumes, and between 1780 and 1810 it had decreased to twenty-six volumes. We know that mid-century was a period of relative economic decline for the city, and the end of the century was a period of unstable economy, harvest failures, and social disturbance, all of which could explain the drop in volumes. Finally, volumes could have been lost, although officials of the Historical Archive in Querétaro are not aware of any such loss.

22. Its records therefore provide insights into the changes that took place within

Querétaro's elite during this period. Notarial records of the 1720s yield information on ten such economically active family fathers. They and members of their extended families were parents of twenty-one of the twenty-five *queretanas* who entered the convent in the ten-year period. On the relationship between Santa Clara and Querétaro's elite and the changes it underwent over time, see Gunnarsdóttir, "The Convent of Santa Clara."

23. AHQ, Notarías. The following documents are organized by name of notary, followed by year of transaction and page number of volume. On Agustín de Ocio y Ocampo, see Parra, 1721, p. 96; 1730, p. 83, May 23. On Pedro de Estrada Altamirano, see Parra, 1721, p. 160. On Juan Francisco de las Navedas, see Parra, 1721, p. 62; 1727, p. 136, July 24. On Francisco de Sarabia, see Parra, 1729, p. 102v; May 9. On José Fernández Fontecha, see Parra, 1722, p. 85, July 31, 1724, and January 14, 1724. On Pedro López Ballesteros, see Parra, 1723, p. 16. On Ignacio Lambarri, see Parra, June 14, 1725, p. 115. On Alonso Sánchez Grimaldos, see Vitórica, 1697, p. 95. On Juan Vázquez Terreros, see del Rincón, 1743, p. 68. (In those cases where the page numbers have been torn or blotted out I try to indicate with a date instead wherever possible.) On Diego de Andizábal y Zárate, see Morales, *Arquitectura y sociedad*, p. 43.

The connections between the hacendados were those of fathers and sons-in-law, brothers-in-law, and distant in-law relations. Finally, two of the men were connected through political office, both serving as *alcaldes* in the period. Thus, this small group of families formed an intricate web of relationships that involved the convent.

24. AGN, Matrimonios, vol. 43, exp. 20, 30, pp. 140–360v.

25. AGN, Bienes Nacionales, vol. 242, exp. 9. The judge's comments are found in his answer to an inquiry from the archbishop as to the utility of founding a Carmelite *beaterio* in the city.

26. AGN, Bienes Nacionales, vol. 242, exp. 9, April 21, 1739, report to the archbishopric on the state of the community.

27. AHPFM-ACSC, G-leg. 4, no. 2, "*Apuntes*," July 18, 1725.

28. AHPFM-ACSC, G-leg. 4, no. 2, "*Apuntes*," July 18, 1725.

29. AHPFM-ACSC, G-leg. 4, no. 2, "*Apuntes*," July 18, 1725.

30. AHPFM-ACSC, G-leg. 5, no. 26, January 1736, to Ortega.

31. AHPFM-ACSC, G-leg. 5, no. 27, undated.

32. AHPFM-ACSC, G-leg. 5, no. 21, July 3, 1715, to Fray Ángel.

33. AHPFM-ACSC, G-leg. 4, no. 9.

### 10. Bourbon Querétaro

1. From 1760 to 1809 112 women professed. During the fifty-year period from 1811 to 1857 only 47 women professed. See AHPFM, Santa Clara, "Libro de Profesiones, 1607–1857."

2. McNamara, *Sisters in Arms*, p. 526.

3. McNamara, *Sisters in Arms*, p. 548.

4. On the multifaceted function of *recogimientos* in colonial Latin America, see Van Deusen, *Between the Worldly and the Sacred*.

5. Arrom, *The Women of Mexico City*, pp. 27, 37, 47; Muriel, *Recogimientos*, pp. 223–24.

6. AHPFM, Santa Clara, *Libro de profesiones*, *"Patentes de los Prelados Regulares*," caja 4, November 18, 1774, December 3, 1774, December 6, 1774. See also, "Carta de la Abadesa y diffinidoras al Ministro Provincial," June 22, 1776, in "Patentes," caja 4.

7. AHPFM, Santa Clara, "Correspondencia de abadesas," May 8, 1774.

8. Anonymous, *Acuerdos Curiosos*. Pages are not numbered.

9. There is a preponderance of men in Querétaro's notarial records of the period, such as the infantry captain Manuel de Pasos; *regidor* and *alcalde provincial de la Santa Hermandad, alférez real* Pedro Bernardino Primo y Jordán; *regidor* Sebastian de Trejomil y Figueroa; *regidor* Francisco Antonio de Septien y Montero and his brother Capt. Juan Fernando de Septién y Montero; and Col. Lorenzo de Incháurregui. This suggests that economic and political power was no longer dominated by the traditional Querétaro families whose influence reached back into the seventeenth century. AHQ, p. 3, January 18, 1751; p. 68, May 22, 1755; p. 125, August 18, 1757.

10. George Kubler and Martín Soria, *Art and Architecture of Spain, Portugal and their American Dominions 1500–1800*, p. 82.

11. Santa Clara retained its importance to the city's ritual life. Besides daily masses, the convent celebrated approximately 117 feasts every year, together with devotional and requiem masses, in the period between 1748 and 1751.

12. On the Bourbon reforms, see Brading, *Church and State*.

13. See AHPFM, Santa Clara, "Licencias de entrada y salida de niñas, criadas y otras, 1708–1855" and "Patentes de los Prelados regulares," cajas 2, 3, 4.

14. Centro de Estudios de la Historia de Mexico (CONDUMEX), Fondo CCXXII, 1791, "Padrón general de la ciudad de Santiago de Querétaro, pueblos, haciendas y ranchos de su jurisdicción formado por Ignacio García Reballo de orden del Virrey Conde de Revillagigedo." Fifteen peninsular families lived in the Plaza Mayor at the time versus only eight Creole families. The Primera Calle de Guadalupe had one peninsular inhabitant and nine Creoles, and the second had five peninsulars versus fourteen Creoles. See also Wu, "The Population of Querétaro," p. 283. Wu also notes that the Plaza Mayor was not as important a residential area because the parish had been moved from the Franciscan convent.

15. In the later period, 80 percent of nuns' fathers whom we have background information on were Creoles and 20 percent peninsulars. Whereas in the early century, the proportion was more even: 64 percent Creoles and 36 percent peninsulars. From 1780 to 1810, twenty-nine queretanos sent their daughters to Santa Clara. Of these, twenty-three were Creoles, and six were peninsulars. In the earlier period, between 1710 and 1740, information on origins exists for twenty-eight nun fathers, ten of whom

were peninsulars and eighteen Creoles. Moreover, this increasing discrepancy took place in a period when the local elite clearly became more peninsular in character. Calculated from "Informaciones," AHPFM, Santa Clara.

16. This was a European phenomenon. Elwood sees the falling convent populations in eighteenth-century France as partly the result of Enlightenment thought. See Elwood, "Fallen Women," p. 324. On the enlightened Bourbon monarchs' religious policy toward New Spain, see the discussion in chap. 1 of this book and Brading, *The First America*, pp. 493–513. Asunción Lavrin notes a decline in female convent populations in certain cities of New Spain by the late colonial period, a phenomenon she believes could be explained by the increasing secular spirit of the age. See Lavrin, "Female Religious," p. 175. On royal policy toward the foundation of nunneries, see AGN, Historia, vol. 77, pp. 1–162. In response to the Marchioness of Selva Nevada's first petition to found a Carmelite convent in Querétaro, the king responded in a royal rescript of December 19, 1798, that the money should instead be spent on helping orphans, single women who lacked means, Indians, the poor, and the sick.

17. See Brading, *First America*, pp. 497–502; *Church and State*, pp. 163–69.

18. Casanova, "El pecado de amar a Dios," p. 536.

19. Zeláa y Hidalgo, *Glorias de Querétaro*, p. 27.

20. Anonymous, *Acuerdos curiosos*.

21. Belanger, "Secularization and the Laity," pp. 132, 160–65, 180–200.

22. AGN, Ayuntamientos, vol. 147, pp. 118–29, "Cuentas y Propios de la Ciudad de Santiago de Querétaro, años 1776, 1777, 1778, 1779, en que ha sido depositario de estos efectos don Juan Antonio Fernández del Rincón, regidor y depositario general de ella."

23. The author of *Varios acuerdos* mentioned the death, in 1809, of the daughter of an illustrious Querétaro citizen, Bernardo de Pereda, who had been a nun in Mexico City. Zeláa y Hidalgo noted a famous nun of Santa Clara, María Isabel Maldonado, who professed in 1750 as "examplar y virtuosa" (p. 43). He noted the death of the headmistress of Santa Rosa, Isabel María de Santa Rosa, Francisca de los Ángeles's right hand, in 1774 at the age of 100 (p. 51). He also noted (p. 59) the Capuchin abbess María Ignacia who died in 1792 (pp. 53–54) and the Carmelite *beatas* Rosalia del Sacramento (who died in 1762) and Mariana del Padre Eterno (who died in 1763).

24. Plancarte, *Sermón de Profesión*.

25. Plancarte, *Sermón de Profesión*; Fray José Francisco de la Rocha, *Ventajas del estado religioso*. Both sermons have been conserved in Biblioteca del Estado de Querétaro, Querétaro.

26. Plancarte, *Sermón de profesión*.

27. Rocha, *Ventajas del estado religioso*.

28. Pedro Bringas de Manzaneda, *Plática pronunciada en el Real Convento de Santa Clara*, p. 259.

29. Zeláa y Hidalgo, *Glorias de Querétaro*, p. 4.

30. Early, *The Colonial Architecture of Mexico*, pp. 191–93.

31. Belanger, "Secularization and the Laity," pp. 132–45.

32. AGN, Bienes Nacionales, vol. 242, exp. 9, April 21, 1739: letter from Alonso Francisco Moreno y Castro to the archbishop in Mexico City on the state of the college. Moreno y Castro explained that the women lived in abject poverty partly because their families did not live in the city and therefore did not support them financially.

33. Between 1730 and 1770, we have evidence of fourteen donations and loans to as well as those made by Santa Rosa. Between 1770 and 1810, this had grown to twenty-five such transactions. The total sum in the earlier period amounted to 18,100 pesos, while in the later period it amounted to 36,862 pesos. While the sums involve both notarized donations and loans, it is safe to assume that almost the entire amount was loaned out by Santa Rosa since the records show no other means of investment except for two purchases of houses. Of course, the sums shown here do not sufficiently portray the community's total financial base. Records of other donations may have been lost, and it is impossible to say whether the sums shown and loaned out on each occasion had not already been noted five, ten, or twenty years ago in another loan transaction. Thus, the same capital may easily have been counted twice. But whether the amount here is an under- or over estimate, the differences between the two periods nevertheless show the community's financial prosperity. See AHQ, Aguilar, 1758, p. 82; Patino, 1810, pp. 71–72; Del Rincón, 1743, p. 68–71; AGN, Tierras, vol. 3069, exp. 19, p. 20; AGN, Bienes Nacionales, vol. 137, exp. 186, p. 4; AHQ, Zárate, 1759, pp. 222–26; Zárate, 1762 (page number torn); Zárate, 1769; Zárate, 1777, pp. 151–151v; Zárate, 1784, pp. 65–66v; Patino, 1803, pp. 35–37; Zárate, 1795, pp. 40–51; 1767, p. 95; 1762, p. 47; 1766, p. 136; 1770, p. 2; 1778, p. 145; 1781, pp. 35, 99; Zárate, 1759, p. 12; 1762, p. 66; Vallejo, 1796, p. 175; 1798, p. 120; 1800, p. 196v; 1809, p. 344; 1809, p. 372; Ramírez de Prado, 1801, February 17, 1801.

34. AGN, Bienes Nacionales, vol. 1036.

35. On living allowances, see AHQ, Aguilar, 1758, p. 88; Zárate, 1769, 1770, pp. 87–90; 1777, pp. 129–130; Araujo, 1746, pp. 41–42; Cardoso, 1735, pp. 6–7; Zárate, 1782, p. 35; Vallejo, 1803, p. 278v; 1809, Vera, 1783; Ramírez, 1806, p. 26. On members of the community and residents buying and selling real estate, see Vera, 1785, p. 236; Armendariz, 1799; Vallejo, 1809, p. 357v. On Rosa de Zárate y Aranda, see Zárate, 1781, pp. 79–80; Vallejo, 1791, p. 114. In 1785, the former headmistress of the institution, Manuela de la Vía Santelices y Lizardi, empowered a representative to handle all her judicial affairs in Mexico City and administer her rural and urban estates. See, Vera, 1785, pp. 19–21.

36. One gains a glimpse of such circumstances, for example, in the 1756 testament of José Bernardo Rodríguez. He was the son or nephew of Regidor Bernardo Rodríguez, who had been an affluent and powerful man in local society in the 1720s. Clearly a victim of his family's socioeconomic decline, José now owned a *cacahuatería* and

a house valued at sixteen hundred pesos. He was unable to provide dowries for his daughters when they married, and indeed one worked in his shop. Another daughter managed to enter Santa Rosa through the generosity of an aunt, who paid the two hundred pesos required for her entry. AHQ, Araujo, 1756, p. 27v.

37. AGN, Bienes Nacionales, vol. 683, exp. 107, 1773. The file is a letter from José Mariano Ramírez de Prado to the archbishop in Mexico City on behalf of Gertrudis López's husband as well as the opinion of the ecclesiastical judge, José Antonio de la Vía, dated February 24, 1773. the file reveals that a number of married women besides the ones mentioned by name entered Santa Rosa for similar reasons in the period.

38. AGN, Inquisición, exp. 16, 1770, pp. 376–88.

39. AGN, Bienes Nacionales, vol. 474, exp. 22.

40. AGN, Bienes Nacionales, vol. 474, exp. 22.

41. AGN, Bienes Nacionales, vol. 474, exp. 22.

42. Laywomen living in Santa Clara were required to ask the provincial's permission to enter and exit the convent. It is likely that the Santa Rosa inhabitants were bound by similar rules. On the Inquisition case, see AGN, Inquisición, vol. 1178, exp. 3, pp. 42–215. According to one woman, the priest, having lured her to meet him outside the *colegio*, kissed and touched her. He explained that his actions were intended to cure the chest pains she had been suffering, for his hands had been blessed. On one occasion, the woman in question found it necessary to retire to a house in Querétaro to be cured of an illness. She was promptly visited by the priest who solicited similar favors from her. On amorous relations between a Franciscan friar and a Creole pretendant to Santa Rosa, see Lavrin, "Intimidades."

43. In his study on early modern England, Somerville describes a shift from a religious culture that "offers unmediated access to the realm of supernatural powers from almost any type of activity, or line of thought" to one in which religion lost its "social functions," while faith underwent "refinement or spiritualization." Thus, he emphasizes that such a secularization did not imply "an erosion of religious belief, resulting from some combination of intellectual and technological advance." Rather, it entailed the relegation of religiosity to the private sphere. See Somerville, *The Secularization of Early Modern England*, p. 9, 179.

## Epilogue

1. Records indicate that it was sent to Rome in the nineteenth century along with other documents pertaining to the activities of the Congregation for the Propagation of Faith in New Spain. An index of the documents includes the title "Biografía de la Venerable Sierva de Dios Francisca de los Ángeles." At the present time, however, it has not been found. See Vázquez Janeiro, "Documentación Americana en el Pontificio Ateneo Antoniano de Roma."

2. Vázquez Janeiro, "Documentación Americana en el Pontificio Ateneo Antoniano de Roma," pp. 18–19.

---

3. Martínez, *Resumen de la vida*, p. 95.

4. Martínez, *Resumen de la vida*, p. 95.

5. On Margil, see, for example, the testimony of Isidoro de Araujo Guerrero of Querétaro in 1749. He describes how their son's life was saved when a portrait of Margil was held to his chest as he lay on the verge of death. See also the 1793 testimony of Santa Clara nuns on the miraculous 1762 recovery in 1762 of Sor Bonifacia Josepha de Guadalupe y Chaves from crippling arthritis. See AHPFM-ACSC, I-leg. 4, nos. 28, 36.

6. Rubial García, *La santidad controvertida*, pp. 281–86.

7. Rubial García, *La santidad controvertida*, p. 283. As a historian of mentalities, Burke argues that "saints have to be treated as witnesses to the age in which they were canonized." The failure of Margil's canonization is a clear signal of changing mentality within the papacy. See Burke, "How to Become a Counter-Reformation Saint," pp. 130–42.

8. AHPFM-ACSC, G-leg. 1, no. 4.

9. On the former case, see Loreto López, "Escrito por ella misma," p. 25, and on the latter, see Myers, "Fundadora, cronista y mística," pp. 78–80.

10. Caffiero, "From the Late Baroque Mystical Explosion to the Social Apostolate," p. 178.

11. Cervantes, *The Devil in the New World*, p. 136.

12. See Myers, "*Testimony for Canonization*," pp. 270–95.

13. Caffiero, "From the Late Baroque Mystical Explosion," p. 188. See also Colahan, *The Visions of Sor María de Agreda*.

14. Caffiero, "From the Late Baroque Mystical Explosion," pp. 189–91.

15. Caffiero, "From the Late Baroque Mystical Explosion," pp. 191–97.

16. Evennett, "Counter-Reformation Spirituality," p. 62.

# Glossary

*alcalde* : mayor

*alférez mayor* : lieutenant

*alguacil* : bailiff

*alumbradismo* : illuminism, a heresy involving the rejection of the church as mediator on the road toward God in favor of an interior spirituality focused on *dejamiento* or abandonment of the will to God

*animas benditas* : souls in purgatory

*arriero* : mule driver

*atole* : hot maize drink

*bienaventurado* : a blessed soul

*bromista* : joker

*cabildo* : secular or ecclesiastical council

*cacique* : Indian chieftain

*camino de la perfección* : the road toward spiritual perfection

*camino real* : royal highway

*capitán* : captain

*castes* : people of mixed origin, Spanish, African, Indian

*chuparatones* : bloodsucker

*cofradía* : confraternity

*colegiala* : member of a college or religious-educational institution for women

*cosas de obediencia* : standard elements of Catholic confession for a person who has taken vows of obedience to the church

*cuadernito* : small notebook, in this case bound together with thread

*cuenta de alma* : general confession, lengthier and wider in scope than the usual confessional procedure

*curandera* : healer, in this context a person who engages in indigenous healing practices

*delitos* : crimes

*depositadas* : women placed in religious institutions such as *beaterios* so as to reform them

*desnudez* : nakedness

*doncella* : maiden

*duro genio* : difficult temper

*edictos de fé* : public edicts issued by the Inquisition as guidelines for orthodox religious practices

*encomienda* : royal grant of the right to demand labor or tribute from indigenous communities

*en-diosada* : a soul possessed by God

*evangelio* : evangelical action

*falsa beata* : woman who fakes her spiritual perfection

*fandango* : a dance

*fanega* : unit of capacity

*"fiel es el Señor"* : "The Lord is great"

*fieles* : the faithful, in this sense Catholics

*gachupín* : person from Iberian peninsula

*hacendado* : estate owner

*hechizera* : witch

*hermanos/hermandad* : spiritual sister/brother or brotherhood

*hija espiritual* : female confessant and protégée of male religious

*hijos naturales* : illegitimate children

*imitatio cristi* : imitation of Christ, centered on experiencing his passion

*indiesuelito* : "little Indian"

*infieles* : infidels, pagans

*informe* : report

*limeño* : habitant of Lima, Peru

*limpieza de sangre* : purity of blood, in this case referring to Iberian ancestry

*locutorio* : convent parlor dedicated to visits by outsiders

*Magnificat* : the hymn of the Virgin

*mascaradas* : parades

*memorias* : written grant of indulgence accompanying relics

*merced* : (1) grant of land, (2) "Your Honor"

*milagrera* : a person who demonstrates inappropriate confidence in miracles not sanctioned by the church

*milpa* : field

*muchacho* : small boy, servant in the context of this study

*mujer santa* : holy woman

*mujer varonil* : a woman who has aquired manly attributes

*naturales* : natives

*necesidad* : necessity

*niña* : (1) lay member of a religious community, (2) servant

*padre predicador* : friar in charge of preaching

*pecados* : sins

*portero (a)* : door or gatekeeper

*projimos* : intimate friends or members of a family or group

*propio* : private possessions

*pueblo* : town, in particular when referring to indigenous communities

*rateria* : malintentioned nonsense

*recogimiento* : (1) spiritual withdrawal, (2) house of retreat

*refresco* : refreshing drink

*regidor* : alderman

*rejas* : convent grills

*retiro* : hermitage, sanctuary for spiritual reflection

*rosal* : garden of roses

*sacrilega* : a person who commits sacrilege

*siglo* : the secular world outside of the cloister

*sitio de estancia* : plot of land

*supersticiosa* : person who engages in superstitious practices and beliefs

*tabardillo* : typhus

*tamal* : corn mush

*Tejas, Texía* : the area spanning large parts of the modern state of Texas

*tomar estado* : to assume one's station in life

*tonterias* : silly things

*varón* : male

*vecino* : inhabitant or citizen of a town

*verdaderas apostólicas* : true apostles

*via crucis/via sacra* : reenactment of Christ's climb from the place of judgment to the Calvary, marked by the fourteen Stations of the Cross

*vida* : religious biography or autobiography

*vida común* : communal life in a religious institution where members eat and sleep in same quarters

# Bibliography

*Archives*

Archivo del Colegio de Santa Cruz, Fondo Santa Clara (ACSC)

Archivo General de la Nación (AGN)

Archivo Histórico de la Provincia Franciscana de Michoacán, Celaya (AHPFM)

Arzobispos y Obispos, vol. 2, 13

Ayuntamientos, vol. 137, 147, 202

Bienes Nacionales, vol. 137, 242, 259, 474, 683, 886, 1036, 1335, 1409, 1548, 1767, 5757

Clero Regular y Secular, vol. 195

Criminal, vol. 290

Historia, vol. 77

Inquisición, vol. 523, 547, 559, 571, 597, 619, 631, 634, 685, 693, 741, 745, 767, 770, 844, 997, 1036, 1178, 1246, 1326

Reales Cédulas Originales, vol. 95, 149

Templos y Conventos, vol. 9, 10, 17, 20, 44, 157, 158

Tierras, vol. 3069

Archivo Histórico, Querétaro (AHQ) Notarías;

Antonio Fernández del Rincón, 1730–1751 (Year ranges indicate notary's term in office)

Diego Antonio de la Parra, 1712–1736

Domingo de Perea, 1715–1719

Felipe de Susnavar, 1730–1753

Félix Antonio de Araujo, 1744–1759

Francisco Ramón de Ojeda, 1768–1792

Francisco de Vitórica, 1711–1743

José Cardoso, 1720–1742

José Ignacio de Vera, 1768–1788

José Manuel de Zárate, 1787–1798

José Ramírez de Prade, 1791–1802

Juan Carlos de Eraso, 1760–1783

Juan Crisostomo Zárate, 1758–1786

Juan Domingo Vallejo, 1791–1810

Mariano Rosas, 1744–1764

Miguel de Aguilar, 1757–1767

Ramón de Armendariz, 1799–1801

Salvador de Perea, 1677–1715

Biblioteca Nacional, Universidad Autónoma de México (BNUNAM)

Fondo Reservado

Biblioteca Nacional de Antropología y Historia, BNAH, Notarías, no. 5, Protocolos 1677–11678

Centro de Estudios de Historia de México (CONDUMEX)

Fondos Virreinales

Pontificio Ateneo Antonianum, Rome,

Archivo de Propaganda Fide, Caja 203, no. 56, 59, 67

## Published Works

Agreda, María de Jesús. *La mística ciudad de Dios, 1670.* Study and edition by Rev. Augustine M. Esposito, O.S.A. Madrid: Scripta Humanistica, 1990.

Ahlgren, Gillian T. W. *Teresa of Avila and the Politics of Sanctity.* Ithaca NY: Cornell University Press, 1996.

Aizpuru, Pilar Gonzalbo. *Las mujeres en la Nueva España, educación y vida cotidiana.* Mexico City: El Colegio de México, 1987.

Ajofrín, Francisco de. *Diario del viaje que hizo a la América en el siglo XVIII,* 2 vols. Mexico City: Instituto Cultura Hispano-Mexicana, 1964.

Alberro, Solange. "Herejes, brujas y beatas: Mujeres ante el tribunal del Santo Oficio de la Inquisición en la Nueva España," *Presencia y Transparencia: La mujer en la historia de México,* edited by Carmen Ramos Escondion, pp. 79–94. Mexico City: El Colegio de México, 1987.

———. *Inquisition y societé au Mexique, 1571–1700.* Mexico City: Centro de estudios mexicanos y centromexicanos, 1988.

Amerlinck de Corsi, María Concepción. *Conventos y monjas en la Puebla de los Ángeles.* Puebla: Gobierno del Estado de Puebla, Secretaría de la Cultura, 1988.

Amerlinck de Corsi, María Concepción, and Manuel Ramos Medina. *Conventos de monjas, fundaciones en el México virreinal.* Mexico City: CONDUMEX, 1995.

Anonymous. *Acuerdos curiosos, escrito por un fraile anónimo de Santa Cruz en Querétaro.* Querétaro: Gobierno del Estado de Querétaro, 1988.

Armstrong, Karen. *A History of God.* London: Vintage, 1999.

Arrom, Silvia. *The Women of Mexico City, 1790–1856.* Palo Alto CA: Stanford University Press, 1985.

Bakewell, P. J. *Silver Mining and Society in Colonial Mexico, Zacatecas, 1546–1700.* Cambridge: Cambridge University Press, 1971.

Barker, Ernst, ed. and trans. *The Politics of Aristotle.* Oxford: Oxford University Press, 1958.

Barnes-Karol, Gwendolyn. "Religious Oratory in a Culture of Control." In *Culture and Control in Counter-Reformation Spain*, edited by Anne J. Cruz and Elizabeth M. Perry, pp. 51–77. Minneapolis: University of Minnesota Press, 1991.

Bauer, Arnold J. "The Church in the Economy of Spanish America: *Censos* and *Depósitos* in the Eighteenth and Nineteenth Centuries." *HAHR* 63, no. 4 (1983): 707–33.

Belanger, Brian. "Secularization and the Laity in Colonial Mexico: Querétaro, 1598–1821." PhD diss., Tulane University, 1990.

Benassar, Bartolomé. *L'Inquisition Espagnole, XVe–XIXe siécle.* Paris: Hachette, 1979.

Benassy-Berling, Marie Cécile. *Humanismo y religión en Sor Juana Inéz de la Cruz.* Mexico City: UNAM, 1983.

Bilinkoff, Jodi. *The Avila of Saint Teresa: Religious Reform in a Sixteenth-Century City.* Ithaca NY: Cornell University Press, 1989.

———. "A Spanish Prophetess and Her Patrons: The Case of María de Santo Domingo." *Sixteenth Century Journal* 23, no. 1 (1992): 21–34.

Bocanegra, Fray Juan de. *Sermón de los Dolores de María Santísima profesando la Madre Ana María de los Dolores.* Mexico City, 1712.

Boils Morales, Guillermo. *Arquitectura y sociedad en Querétaro, siglo XVIII.* Querétaro: Instituto de Investigaciones Sociales, Archivo Histórico del Estado, 1994.

Boxer, Charles R. *Mary and Misogyny: Women in Iberian Expansion Overseas, 1415–1815.* London: Duckworth, 1975.

Brading, D. A. ———. *Miners and Merchants in Bourbon Mexico, 1763–1810.* Cambridge: Cambridge University Press, 1971.

———. *Haciendas and Ranchos in the Mexican Bajío: León 1700–1860.* Cambridge: Cambridge University Press, 1978.

———. "Tridentine Catholicism and Enlightened Despotism in Bourbon Mexico," *Jus* 15 (1983): 1–22.

———. *The First America: The Spanish Monarchy, Creole Patriots, and the Liberal State, 1492–1867.* Cambridge: Cambridge University Press, 1993.

———. *Church and State in Bourbon Mexico: The Diocese of Michoacán, 1749–1810.* Cambridge: Cambridge University Press, 1994.

———. *El ocaso novohispano: Testimonios documentales.* Mexico City: INAH, Dirección General de Publicaciones del Consejo Nacional para la Cultura y las Artes, 1996.

———. *Mexican Phoenix: Our Lady of Guadalupe: Image and Tradition across Five Centuries.* Cambridge: Cambridge University Press, 2001.

Brown, Judith. *Immodest Acts: The Life of a Lesbian Nun in Renaissance Italy.* Oxford: Oxford University Press, 1986.

Brown, Peter. *The Cult of the Saints.* London: SCM, 1981.

Burke, Peter. "How to Become a Counter-Reformation Saint." In *The Counter Reformation: The Essential Readings*, edited by David M. Luebke, pp. 129–42. London: Blackwell, 1999.

Burns, Kathryn. "Convents, Culture and Society in Cuzco, Peru, 1550–1865." PhD diss., Harvard University, 1993.

———. "Conventos, criollos y la economía espiritual del Cuzco, siglo XVII." In *Memoria del II Congreso Internacional: El monacato femenino en el Imperio Español*, edited by Manuel Ramos Medina, pp. 311–18. Mexico City: CONDUMEX, 1995.

———. *Colonial Habits: Convents and the Spiritual Economy of Cuzco, Peru.* Durham NC: Duke University Press, 1999.

Bynum, Caroline Walker. *Holy Feast and Holy Fast: The Religious Significance of Food to Medieval Women.* Berkeley: University of California Press, 1987.

Caciola, Nancy. "Mystics, Demoniacs, and the Physiology of Spirit Possession in Medieval Europe," *Comparative Studies in Society and History*, 42, no. 20 (April 2000): 286–306.

Caffiero, Marina. "From the Late Baroque Mystical Explosion to the Social Apostolate, 1650–1850." In *Women and Faith, Catholic Religious Life in Italy from Late Antiquity to the Present*, edited by Lucetta Scaraffia and Gabriella Zarri, pp. 176–204. Cambridge: Harvard University Press, 1999.

Calderón de la Barca, Frances. *Life in Mexico.* Berkeley: University of California Press, 1982.

Callahan, William J., and David Higgs, eds. *Church and Society in Catholic Europe of the Eighteenth Century.* Cambridge: Cambridge University Press, 1979.

———. *Church, Politics and Society in Spain, 1750–1874.* Cambridge: Harvard University Press, 1984.

Candau Chacón, María Luisa. "Mundo rural y monacato femenino en el siglo XVIII: Sevilla, 1685–1787." In *Memorias del II Congreso Internacional del Monacato femenino en el Imperio Español*, edited by Manuel Ramos Medina, pp. 155–92. Mexico City: CONDUMEX, 1996.

Carmen Reyna, María del. *El convento de San Jerónimo: Vida conventual y finanzas.* Mexico City: INAH, 1990.

Carroll, Berenice. *Liberating Women's History.* Champaign-Urbana: University of Illinois Press, 1976.

Carroll, Michael P. *Veiled Threats: The Logic of Popular Catholicism in Italy.* Baltimore: Johns Hopkins University Press, 1996.

Castañeda, Carmen. "Relaciones entre beaterios, colegios y conventos femeninos en Guadalajara, época colonial." In *Memoria del II Congreso Internacional del Monacato femenino en el Imperio Español*, edited by Manuel Ramos Medina, pp. 455–76. Mexico City: INAH, 1990.

———. *La educación en Guadalajara durante la Colonia, 1552–1821.* Guadalajara: El Colegio de Jalisco, 1984.

Certeau, Michel de. *The Mystic Fable: The Sixteenth and Seventeenth Centuries*, translated by Michael B. Smith. Chicago: University of Chicago Press, 1992.

Cervantes, Fernando. *The Devil in the New World: The Impact of Diabolism in New Spain*. New Haven CT: Yale University Press, 1994.

Christian, William, Jr. *Local Religion in Sixteenth Century Spain*. Princeton NJ: Princeton University Press, 1981.

Clark, John P. H. "The Cloud of Unknowing." In *An Introduction to the Medieval Mystics of Europe*, edited by Paul E. Szarmach, pp. 273–93. New York: State University of New York Press, 1984.

Colahan, Clark. *The Visions of Sor María de Agreda*. Tucson: University of Arizona Press, 1996.

———. "María de Jesús de Agreda: The Sweetheart of the Holy Office." In *Women in the Inquisition, Spain and the New World*, edited by Mary E. Giles, pp. 155–70. Baltimore: Johns Hopkins University Press, 1999.

Conde Martínez, Fray Rogerio, O.F.M. *Resumen de la vida del V.P. Antonio Margil de Jesús, Misionero Apostólico de Nueva España en los siglos XVII y XVIII*. Madrid: Imprenta de Hijos de T. Minuesa, 1929.

Cortés Pena, Antonio Luis. *La política religiosa de Carlos III y las ordenes mendicantes*. Granada: Universidad de Granada, 1989.

Cruz, Anne J., and Elizabeth M. Perry, eds. *Culture and Control in Counter-Reformation Spain*. Minneapolis: University of Minnesota Press, 1991.

Curcio-Nagy, Linda A. "Rosa de Escalante's Private Party." *Women in the Inquisition, Spain and the New World*, edited by Mary E. Giles, pp. 254–69. Baltimore: Johns Hopkins University Press, 1999.

Dedieu, Jean Pierre. "Christianization in New Castile: Catechism, Communion, Mass, and Confirmation in the Toledo Archbishopric, 1540–1650." In *Culture and Control in Counter-Reformation Spain*, edited by Anne J. Cruz and Elizabeth M. Perry, pp. 1–24. Minneapolis: University of Minnesota Press, 1991.

Deroy-Pineau, Francoise. *Marie de l'Incarnation: Marie Guyart, femme d'affaires, mystique, mére de la Nouvelle-France, 1599–1672*. Paris: Editions Robert Laffont, 1989.

Díez, Fray José. *Apostólicos empleos de los hijos del seraphín llagado obreros evangélicos del colegio de la Santíssima Cruz de la Ciudad de Santiago de Querétaro*, edited by Ferdy Langenbacher. Grottaferrata: Colegio San Bonaventura, 1999.

Dillard, Heath. *Daughters of the Reconquest: Women in Castilian Town Society, 1100–1300*. Cambridge: Cambridge University Press, 1989.

Donahue, Darcy. "Writing Lives: Nuns and Confessors As Auto/Biographers in Early Modern Spain." *Journal of Hispanic Philology* 13, no. 3 (spring 1989): 230–39.

Early, James. *The Colonial Architecture of Mexico*. Albuquerque: University of New Mexico Press, 1994.

Elwood, Ann Barclay. "French Nuns and Fallen Women: Social Control and Autonomy in Early Modern France." PhD diss., University of California, Berkeley, 1990.

Espinosa, Fray Isidro Félix de. *El cherubin custodio del Árbol de la vida del venerable siervo de Dios Fray Antonio de los Angeles Bustamante*. Mexico City, 1731.

———. *El Peregrino septentrional atlante: Delineado en la exemplar vida del venerable Padre Antonio Margil de Jesús*. Mexico, 1737.

———. *Crónica apostólica y seráphica de todos los colegios de Propaganda Fide de la Nueva España de los missioneros Franciscanos observantes*. Querétano: Gobierno del Estado de Querétano, 1997.

Evennett, H. Outram. "Counter-Reformation Spirituality." In *The Counter Reformation: The Essential Readings*, edited by David M. Luebke. London: Blackwell, 1999.

Fitz-Maurice, Kelly. *The Nun Ensign*. London: T. Fisher Unwin, 1908.

Florescano, Enrique. *Precios del maíz y crisis agrícolas en México, 1708–1810*. Mexico City: Ediciones Era, 1986.

Flynn, Maureen. *Sacred Charity: Confraternities and Social Welfare in Spain, 1400–1700*. London: Macmillan, 1989.

Forster, Marc R. *Catholic Revival in the Age of the Baroque: Religious Identity in Southwestern Germany, 1550–1750*. Cambridge: Cambridge University Press, 2001.

Foz y Foz, Pilar. *La revolución pedagógica en Nueva España, 1754–1820*. Madrid: Consejo Superior de Investigaciones Científicas, Instituto Gonzalo Fernández de Oviedo, 1981.

———. "Hipótesis de un proceso paralelo: La Enseñanza de Zaragoza y la Enseñanza Nueva de México." In *Memoria del II Congreso Internacional del Monacato femenino en el Imperio Español*, edited by Manuel Ramos Medina, pp. 63–82. Mexico City: INAH, 1990.

Franco, Jean. *Plotting Women, Gender and Representation in Mexico*. New York: Columbia University Press, 1989.

Frías, Valentín. *Las Calles de Querétaro*. Querétaro: Gobierno del Estado, 1984.

Gallagher, Ann Miriam, R.S.M. "The Family Background of the Nuns of Two Monasterios in Colonial Mexico: Santa Clara, Querétaro; and Corpus Christi, Mexico City (1724–1822)." PhD diss., The Catholic University of America, 1972.

García, Ayluardo, Clara, Manuel Ramos Medina, eds. *Manifestaciones religiosas en el mundo colonial americano*, vol. 1. "Espiritualidad barroca colonial; Santos y demonios en América (1993), vol. 2, "Mujeres, instituciones y culto a María" (1994), Mexico City: Centro de Estudios de Historia de México CONDUMEX, Consejo Nacional para la Cultura y las Artes, INAH, UIA.

García Ugarte, Marta Eugenia. *Breve Historia de Querétaro*. Mexico City: El Colegio de México, Fondo de Cultura Económica, 1999.

Garner, Richard L., with Spio E. Stafanoc. *Economic Growth and Change in Bourbon Mexico*. Gainesville: University Press of Florida, 1993.

Gemelli Careri, Giovanni Francesco. *Viaje a la Nueva España*, edited by Francisca Perajo. Mexico City: UNAM, 1976.

Gilchrist, Roberta. *Gender and Material Culture: The Archeology of Religious Women.* London: Routledge, 1994.

Giles, Mary E., ed. *Women in the Inquisition, Spain and the New World.* Baltimore: Johns Hopkins University Press, 1999.

Godínez, Miguel. *Práctica de la teología mística.* Madrid: Imprenta de José Doblado, 1780.

Gómez, Fray José. *Vida de la venerable Madre Antonia de San Jacinto, monja profesa de velo negro y hija del Religioso y Religiosíssimo convento de Santa Clara de Jesús de la Ciudad de Santiago de Querétaro.* Mexico City: viuda de Bernardo Calderón, 1689.

Gómez Canedo, Lino. *Sierra Gorda, un típico enclave misional en el centro de México, siglos XVII–XVIII.* Querétaro: Gobierno del Estado, 1988.

Gonzales Casanova, Pablo. "El pecado de amar a Dios en el siglo XVIII." *Historia Mexicana* 8 (July 1952): 529–48.

Guerra, Fray José. *Fecunda nube del cielo Guadalupano y mística Paloma.* Mexico City, 1726.

Gunnarsdóttir, Ellen. "Religious Life and Urban Society in Colonial Mexico: The Nuns and Beatas of Querétaro, 1674–1810." PhD diss., University of Cambridge, 1997.

———. "The Convent of Santa Clara, the Elite and Social Change in Eighteenth Century Querétaro." *JLAS* 33, no. 2 (May 2001): 257–90.

———. "Una visionaria barroca de la provincia mexicana: Francisca de los Ángeles, 1674–1744." In *Monjas y beatas: La escritura femenina en la espiritualidad barroca novohispana, siglos XVII y XVIII,* edited by Rosalva Loreto López and Asunción Lavrin. Puebla: Universidad de las Americas, Archivo General de la Nación, 2002.

———. "Los misioneros franciscanos y sus hijas espirituales en el nuevo mundo; el caso de Querétaro, 1674–1810," *Studi e materiali di Storia delle Religioni* 68, no. 26 (2002): 363–77.

Hamnett, Brian. *Social Structure and Regional Elites in Late Colonial Mexico, 1750–1824.* Glasgow: Institute of Latin American Studies, 1984.

Harbison, Robert. *Reflections on Baroque.* London: Reaktion Books, 2000.

Heller, Thomas C., Morton Sasna, Pam Swidler, and David E. Wellbery with Arnold I Davidson, Ann Swidler, and Ian Watt, eds. *Reconstructing Individualism: Autonomy, Individuality and the Self in Western Thought.* Palo Alto CA: Stanford University Press, 1986.

Holler, Jacqueline. "More Sins Than the Queen of England." In *Women in the Inquisition, Spain and the New World,* edited by Mary E. Giles, pp. 209–28. Baltimore: Johns Hopkins University Press, 1999.

———. "Escogidas Plantas," *Nuns and Beatas in Mexico City, 1531–1601.* New York: Columbia University Press, 2001.

Hsia, R. Po-chia. *The World of Catholic Renewal.* Cambridge: Cambridge University Press, 1998.

Humboldt, Alexander von. *Political Essay on the Kingdom of New Spain*, translated by John Black. London, 1811. Reprint, New York: AMS Press, 1966.

Ibsen, Kristin. *Women's Spiritual Autobiography in Colonial Latin America*. Gainesville: University Press of Florida, 1999.

Icazbalceta, Joaquín García, ed. *Cartas de religiosos de Nueva España*. 2nd ed. Mexico City, 1941.

Ignatius of Loyola, Saint. *The Spiritual Exercises*. Edited by W. H. Longridge. Oxford: Oxford University Press, 1975.

Iturburu, Fernando. *(Auto)biografía y misticismos femeninos en la colonia*. New Orleans: University Press of the South, 2000.

Iwasaki Cauti, Fernando. "Mujeres al borde de la perfección: Rosa de Santa María y las alumbradas de Lima." HAHR 73, no.4 (1993): 581–613.

Jaffary, Nora E. *Deviant Orthodoxy: A History of "False" Mysticism in Colonial Mexico*. Lincoln: University of Nebraska Press, forthcoming.

Jesús, María de. *Crónica del Real Colegio de Santa Rosa de Viterbo*. Edited with introduction by Josefina Muriel. Querétaro: Gobierno del Estado, 1996.

Johnson, Penelope D. *Equal in Monastic Profession: Religious Women in Medieval France*. Chicago: University of Chicago Press, 1991.

Kamen, Henry. *Inquisition and Society in Spain in the Sixteenth and Seventeenth Century*. London: Weidenfield and Nicholson, 1985.

———. *The Phoenix and the Flame: The Counter Reformation in Catalonia*. New Haven CT: Yale University Press, 1993.

Kubler, George, and Martín Soria. *Art and Architecture of Spain, Portugal and Their American Dominions, 1500–1800*. London: Penguin, 1959.

Ladd, Doris. *The Mexican Nobility at Independence, 1780–1826*. Austin: University of Texas, 1976.

Landa Fonseca, Cecilia. *Querétaro: Una historia compartida*. Querétaro: Gobierno del Estado, 1990.

Lavrin, Asunción. "The Religious Life of Women in Colonial Mexico." PhD diss., Harvard University, 1962.

———. "Ecclesiastical Reform of Nunneries in New Spain in the Eighteenth Century." *The Americas* 22, no. 2 (October 1965): 182–203.

———. "Problems and Policies in the Administration of Nunneries in Mexico, 1800–1835." *The Americas* 28 (July 1971): 57–77.

———. "Values and Meaning of Monastic Life for Nuns in Colonial Mexico." *Catholic Historical Review* (October 1972): 367–87.

———. "El Convento de Santa Clara de Querétaro, la administración de sus propiedades en el siglo XVII." *Historia Mexicana* 97 (1975): 76–117.

———. "Female Religious." In *Liberating Women's History*, edited by Berenice Carroll. Champaign-Urbana: University of Illinois Press, 1976.

———. "In Search of the Colonial Woman in Mexico: The Seventeenth and Eighteenth Centuries." In *Latin American Women: Historical Perspectives*, edited by Asunción Lavrin, pp. 23–59. Westport, CT: Greenwood Press, 1978.

———. *Sexuality and Marriage in Colonial Latin America*. Lincoln: University of Nebraska Press, 1989.

———. "Unlike Sor Juana? The Model Nun in the Religious Literature of Colonial Mexico." In *Feminist Perspectives on Sor Juana Inés de la Cruz*, edited by Stephanie Merrim, pp. 61–85. Detroit: Wayne State University Press, 1991.

———. "La vida femenina como experiencia religiosa: Biografía y hagiografía en Hispanoamérica colonial." *Colonial Latin American Review* 2, nos. 1–2 (1993): 27–52.

———. "Cotidianidad y espiritualidad en la vida conventual novohispana, siglo XVIII." *Memoria del coloquio internacional, Sor Juana Inés de la Cruz y el pensamiento novohispano*, pp. 203–19. Mexico City: Instituto Mexiquense de Cultura, 1995.

———. "La celda y el siglo: Epístolas conventuales." In *Mujer y cultura en la colonia hispanoamericana*, edited by Mabel Moraña, pp. 139–60. Pittsburgh: Instituto Internacional de Literatura Iberoamericana, 1996.

———. "Intimidades." In *Des Indes Occidentales a l'Amérique Latine*, edited by Alain Musset and Thomas Calvo, pp. 195–218. Paris: ENS Editions, 1997.

———. "Indian Brides of Christ: Creating New Spaces for Indigenous Women in New Spain." *Mexican Studies/Estudios Mexicanos* 15, no. 2 (summer 1999): 225–60.

———. "La escritura desde un mundo oculto: Espiritualidad y anonimidad en el convento de San Juan de la Penitencia." *Estudios de Historia Novohispana* 22 (2000): 49–75.

———. "Sor Maria de Jesus Felipa: un diario espiritual de mediades del siglor XVIII" (1758). In *Monjas y beatas*, pp. 111–60.

———. *Monjas y beatas: La escritura femenina en la espiritualidad barroca novohispana, siglos XVII y XVIII*, edited by Asunción Lavrin and Rosalva Loreto López. Puebla: Universidad de las Americas, Archivo General de la Nación, 2002.

———. "Female Visionaries and Spirituality in New Spain." Unpublished paper.

Le Goff, Jacques. *The Medieval Imagination*. Translated by Arthur Goldhammer. Chicago: University of Chicago Press: 1988.

Leonard, Irving A. *La época barroca en el México colonial*. Mexico: Fondo de Cultura Económica, 1993.

Loreto López, Rosalva. "Leer contar, cantar y escribir. Un acercamiento a las prácticas de la lectura conventual. Puebla de los Ángeles, México, siglos XVII y XVIII." *Estudios de Historia Novohispana*, no. 23, pp. 67–95. Mexico City: UNAM, 2000.

———. *Los conventos femeninos y el mundo urbano de la Puebla de los Ángeles del siglo XVIII*. Mexico City: El Colegio de México, 2000.

————. "Escrito por ella misma; vida de la madre Francisca de la Natividad." In *Monjas y beatas: La escritura femenina en la espiritualidad barroca novohispana, siglos XVII y XVIII*, edited by Rosalva Loreto López and Asunción Lavrin, pp. 24–66. Puebla: Universidad de las Americas, Archivo General de la Nación, 2002.

Luebke, David. M., ed. *The Counter-Reformation: The Essential Readings*. London: Blackwell, 1999.

Lynch, John. *Spain, 1516–1598: From Nation State to World Empire*. London: Blackwell, 1991.

Mannarelli, María Emma. *Hechiceras, beatas y expósitas: Mujeres y poder inquisitorial en Lima*. Lima: Ediciones del congreso del Perú, 1999.

Maravall, José Antonio. *Culture of the Baroque: Analysis of a Historical Structure*, translated by Terry Cochran. Minneapolis: University of Minnesota Press, 1986.

Marshall, Sherrin, ed. *Women in Reformation and Counter-Reformation Europe*. Bloomington: Indiana University Press, 1989.

Martínez Lucio Buenrrostro, José. *Sermón por la profesión y velo de la Madre Teresa de San Joseph predicado en el convento de Santa Clara de Querétaro*. Mexico City, 1720.

Maza, Francisco de la. *Catarina de San Juan: Princesa de la India y Visionaria de Puebla*. Mexico City: Consejo Nacional para la Cultura y las Artes, 1990.

MacKendrick, Geraldine, and Angus McKay. "Visionaries and Affective Spirituality during the First Half of the Sixteenth Century." In *Cultural Encounters: The Impact of the Inquisition in Spain and the New World*, edited by Mary Elizabeth Perry and Ann J. Cruz, pp. 93–104. Berkeley: University of California Press, 1991.

McCloskey, Michael B., O.F.M. *The Formative Years of the Missionary College of Santa Cruz of Querétaro, 1683–1733*. Washington DC: Academy of American Franciscan History, 1955.

McCormack, Sabine. "The Heart Has Its Reasons: Predicaments of Missionary Christianity in Early Colonial Peru." In *The Counter-Reformation: The Essential Readings*, edited by David M. Luebke, pp. 199–225. London: Blackwell, 1999.

McKnight, Kathryn Joy. *The Mystic of Tunja: The Writings of Madre Castillo, 1671–1742*. Amherst: University of Massachusetts Press, 1997.

McNamara, Jo Ann Kay. *Sisters in Arms: Catholic Nuns through Two Millennia*. Cambridge: Harvard University Press, 1996.

————. "The Need to Give: Suffering and Female Sanctity in the Middle Ages." In *Images of Sainthood in Medieval Europe*, edited by Renate Blumenfield-Kosinski and Timea Szell, pp. 199–221. Ithaca NY: Cornell University Press, 1991.

Miramontes, Ana Cristina Díaz. *El Templo de Santa Rosa de Viterbo*. Querétaro: Gobierno del Estado, 1997.

Modica Vasta, Marilena. "Mystical Writing." In *Women and Faith: Catholic Religious Life in Italy from Late Antiquity to the Present*, edited by Lucetta Scaraffia and Gabriella Zarri, pp. 205–18. Cambridge: Harvard University Press, 1999.

Muriel, Josefina. *Las indias caciques de Corpus Christi*. Mexico City: UNAM, 1963.

———. *Los recogimientos de mujeres*. Mexico City: UNAM, 1974.

———. *Cultura femenina novohispana*. Mexico City: UNAM, 1994.

———. *Conventos de monjas en la Nueva España*. Mexico City: Jus, 1995.

———. *La sociedad novohispana y sus colegios de niñas: Fundaciones del siglo XVI*. Mexico City: UNAM, 1995.

Muriel, Josefina, and Alicia Grobet. *Fundaciones neoclásicas: La marquesa de Selva Nevada, sus conventos y sus arquitectos*. Mexico City: UNAM, 1969.

Murphy, Michael F. *Irrigation in the Bajío Region of Colonial Mexico*. Boulder CO: Westview Press, 1986.

Myers, Kathleen. *Word from New Spain: The Spiritual Autobiography of Madre María de San José, 1650–1719*. Liverpool: Liverpool University Press, 1991.

———. "Testimony for Canonization or Proof of Blasphemy? The New Spanish Inquisition and the Hagiographic Biography of Catarina de San Juan." In *Women in the Inquisition, Spain and the New World*, edited by Mary E. Giles, pp. 270–90. Baltimore: Johns Hopkins University Press, 1999.

———. "Fundadora, cronista, mística, Juana Palacios Berruecos, Madre María de San José, (1676–1719)." *Monjas y beatas: La escritura femenina en la espiritualidad barroca novohispana, siglos XVII y XVIII*, edited by Rosalva Loreto López, Asunción Lavrin, pp. 67–110. Puebla: Universidad de las Americas, Archivo General de la Nación, 2002.

———, and Amanda Powell. *A Wild Country out in the Garden: The Spiritual Journals of a Colonial Mexican Nun*. Bloomington: University of Indiana Press, 2001.

Nalle, Sara T. *God in la Mancha: Religious Reform and the People of Cuenca, 1500–1650*. Baltimore: Johns Hopkins University Press, 1992.

Navarrete, Francisco Antonio. *Relación Peregrina de Querétaro*. Querétaro: Gobierno del Estado, 1987.

Navarro y Noriega. *Memoria sobre la población del Reino de Nueva España*. 1820. Reprint, Mexico City: Instituto mexicano de investigaciones historico-jurídicas, 1943.

Newman, Barbara. *From Virile Woman to Woman Christ*. Philadelphia: University of Pennsylvania Press, 1995.

Nicolás, Antonio T. de, ed. and trans. *St. John of the Cross: Alchemist of the Soul*. New York: Paragon House, 1989.

Nuñez, Fray Antonio. *Distribución de las obras ordinarias y extraordinarias del día. Para hacerlas perfectamente conforme al estado de las señoras religiosas instruidas con doce maximas substanciales para la vida regular y espiritual que deben seguir*. Mexico, 1712.

O'Crouley, Pedro Alonso. *Description of the Kingdom of New Spain*. Edited and translated by Sean Galvin. Madrid, 1774. Reprint, San Francisco: John Howell Books, 1972.

O'Malley, John, ed. *Catholicism in Early Modern History: A Guide to Research*. St. Louis: Center for Reformation Research, 1988.

———. "Was Ignatius of Loyola a Church Reformer? How to Look at Early Modern Catholicism." *The Counter-Reformation: The Essential Readings*, edited by David M. Luebke, pp. 65–82. London: Blackwell, 1999.

———. *Trent and All That; Renaming Catholicism in the Early Modern Era*. Cambridge: Harvard University Press, 2000.

Ortega Cosa, Milagros. "Spanish Women in the Reformation." In *Women in Reformation and Counter-Reformation Europe*, edited by Sherrin Marshall, pp. 89–119. Bloomington: Indiana University Press, 1989.

Paz, Octavio. *Sor Juana, Her Life and Her World*. London: Faber and Faber, 1988.

Pérez Baltasar, María Dolores. "Beaterios y recogimientos para la mujer marginada en el Madrid del siglo XVIII. In *Memoria del II Congreso Internacional: El monacato femenino en el Imperio Español*, edited by Manuel Ramos Medina, pp. 381–94. Mexico City: CONDUMEX, 1995.

Perry, Mary Elizabeth. "Magdalens and Jezebels in Counter-Reformation Spain." In *Culture and Control in Counter-Reformation Spain*, edited by Anne J. Cruz and Elizabeth M. Perry, pp. 124–44. Minneapolis: University of Minnesota Press, 1991.

Perry, Mary Elizabeth and Ann J. Cruz, eds. *Cultural Encounters: The Impact of the Inquisition in Spain and the New World*. Berkeley: University of California Press, 1991.

Petroff, Elizabeth Avilda. *Medieval Women's Visionary Literature*. New York: Oxford University Press, 1986.

———. *Body and Soul: Essays on Medieval Women and Mysticism*. New York: Oxford University Press, 1994.

Plancarte, Fray José Antonio. *Sermón de Profesión que en la que hizó Sor María Antonia Ildefonsa en el convento de San Joseph de Gracia de Reverendas Madres Capuchinas*. Mexico City: don Mariano José de Zúniga y Ontivero, 1799.

Ramírez Álvarez, José Guadalupe. *Querétaro, vision de mi ciudad*. Querétaro: Editorial Provincia, 1966.

Ramírez Leyva, Edelmira, ed. *María Rita Vargas, María Lucía Celis, beatas embaucadoras de la colonia*. Mexico City: UNAM, 1988.

Ramos Medina, Manuel. *Imagen de santidad en un mundo profano*. Mexico City: Universidad Iberoamericana, 1990.

———, ed. *Memoria del II Congreso Internacional: El monacato femenino en el Imperio Español*. Mexico City: CONDUMEX, 1995.

———. *Místicas y descalzas*. Mexico City: CONDUMEX, 1997.

Rasmussen, Niels Krogh, O.P. "Liturgy and the Liturgical Arts." In *Catholicism in Early*

*Modern History: A Guide to Research*, edited by John O'Malley. St. Louis: Center for Reformation Research, 1988.

Rea, Fray Alonso de la. *Crónica de la Orden de Nuestro Seráphico Padre San Francisco, Provincia de San Pedro y San Pablo de Michoacán, 1639*. Mexico City, 1991.

Rincón Frías, Gabriel, José Rodolfo Anaya Larios, María Isabel Gòmez Labardini. *Breve Historia de Querétaro*. Querétaro: Gobierno del Estado de Querétaro, 1986.

Ríos, Eduardo Enrique. *Fray Margil de Jesús, Apostól de América*. Mexico City: Editorial Jus, 1959.

Rocha, Fray José Francisco de la. *Ventajas del estado religioso sobre la vida del siglo; oración panegírico-moral, eucarística y gratulatorio que en la entrada que hizó Doña María Ignacia de la Rocha al exemplar convento de* RR MM *Capuchinas de la muy noble Ciudad de Querétaro*. Mexico City: don Mariano José de Zúniga y Ontiveros, 1799.

Romero Swain, Susan. "One Thousand Sisters: Religious Sensibility and Motivation in a Spanish American Convent; Santa María de Gracia, 1588–1863." PhD diss., University of California, San Diego, 1993.

Rubial García, Antonio. "Josefa de San Luis Beltrán, la cordera de Dios: Escritura, oralidad y gestualidad de una visionaria del siglo XVII Novohispano" (1654). *Monjas y Beatas: La escritura femenina en la espiritualidad barroca novohispana, siglos XVII y XVIII*, edited by Rosalva Loreto López and Asunción Lavrin. Mexico City: Universidad de las Americas, Puebla, Archivo General de la Nación, 2002.

———. "La santa es una bellaca y nos hace muchas burlas," El caso de los panecitos de Santa Teresa en la sociedad novohispana del siglo XVII. *Estudios de histoira novohispana*, vol. 24 (January–June), Mexico City, 2001, pp. 53–75.

———. *La santidad controvertida: Hagiografía y conciencia criolla alrededor de los venerables no canonizados de Nueva España*. Mexico City: Fondo de Cultura Económica, 1999.

———. Las santitas del barrio. "Beatas" laicas y religiosidad cotidiana en la ciudad de México en el siglo XVII, in *Anuario de estudios americanos*, vol. LIX-1 (January–June), Seville, 2002, pp. 13–37.

Ruether, Rosemary Radford, ed. *Religion and Sexism: Images of Woman in the Jewish and Christian Traditions*. New York: Simon and Schuster, 1974.

Said, Suzanne. *Woman and Female in the Biological Treatises of Aristotle*. Odense, Denmark: Odense University Press, 1982.

Saint-Saënz, Alain. "Al margen del convento: Santeras en la España del Siglo de Oro." In *Memoria del II Congreso Internacional: El monacato femenino en el Imperio Español. Monasterios, beaterios, recogimientos y colegios*, edited by Manuel Ramos Medina, pp. 511–22. Mexico City: CONDUMEX, 1995.

Saint Teresa of Ávila. *The Interior Castle: Saint Teresa of Ávila*. Edited and translated by Allison Peers. New York: Doubleday, 1989.

Salazar de Garza, Nuria. *La vida común en los conventos de la ciudad de Puebla*. Puebla: Secretaría de la Cultura, 1990.

Salvucci, Richard. *Textiles and Capitalism in Mexico: An Economic History of the Obrajes, 1539–1840*. Princeton NJ: Princeton University Press, 1987.

Sampson Vera Tudela, Elisa. *Colonial Angels: Narratives of Gender and Spirituality in Mexico, 1580–1750*. Austin: University of Texas Press, 2000.

Sánchez-Barba, Mario Hernández. *Monjas ilustres en la Historia de España*. Madrid: España Sorprendente, 1993.

Sánchez Lora, José L. *Mujeres, conventos y formas de la Religiosidad Barroca*. Madrid: Fundación Universitaria Española, 1988.

Scaraffia, Lucetta, and Gabriella Zarri, eds. *Women and Faith: Catholic Religious Life in Italy from Late Antiquity to the Present*. Cambridge: Harvard University Press, 1999.

Schroeder, H. J. *The Canons and Decrees of the Council of Trent*. Rev. ed. Rockford IL: O.P. Tan Books, 1978.

Seed, Patricia. *To Love Honor and Obey in Colonial Mexico: Conflicts over Marriage Choice, 1574–1821*. Palo Alto CA: Stanford University Press, 1988.

Septien y Septien, Manuel. *Historia de Querétaro desde los tiempos prehistóricos hasta el año de 1808*. Querétaro: Gobierno del Estado, 1967.

Serrera Contreras, Ramón M. *La Ciudad de Santiago de Querétaro a fines del siglo XVIII*. Querétaro: Gobierno del Estado, 1973.

Sigüenza y Góngora, Carlos de. *Glorias de Querétaro*. Querétaro: Gobierno del Estado, facsimile, 1945.

Soeiro, Susan. "The Social and Economic Role of the Convent: Women and Nuns in Colonial Bahía." *HAHR* 54, no. 2 (1974): 209–222.

———. "The Feminine Orders in Colonial Bahía, Brazil: Economic, Social and Demographic Implications, 1677–1800." In *Latin American Women: Historical Perspectives*, edited by Asunción Lavrin, pp. 173–97. Westport CT: Greenwood Press, 1978.

Somerville, John. *The Secularization of Early Modern England: From Religious Culture to Religious Faith*. Oxford: Oxford University Press, 1992.

Soto Peréz, José Luis, O.F.M., ed. *Memorial de las Cosas Notables de este Colegio de Herbon, III*. Santiago de Compostela, 1948.

Super, John C. *La vida en Querétaro durante la Colonia, 1531–1810*. Mexico City: Fondo de Cultura Económica, 1980.

Surtz, Ronald E. *The Guitar of God: Gender, Power and Authority in the Visionary World of Mother Juana de la Cruz, 1481–1534*. Philadelphia: University of Pennsylvania Press, 1990.

———. *Writing Women in Late and Early Modern Spain: The Mothers of Saint Teresa of Ávila*. Philadelphia: University of Pennsylvania Press, 1995.

Thompson, Eric J., ed. *Thomas Gage's Travels in the New World*. Norman: University of Oklahoma Press, 1985.

Tomizza, Fulvio. *Heavenly Supper: The Story of Maria Janis,* Translated by Anne Jacobson Schutte. Chicago: University of Chicago Press, 1991.

Torres Sánchez, Concha. *La clausura femenina en la Salamanca del siglo XVII, Dominicas y Carmelitas descalzas.* Salamanca: Universidad de Salamanca, 1991.

Tostado Gutiérrez, Marcela. *El álbum de la mujer: Antología ilustrada de las mexicanas.* Vol. 2, *Época colonial.* Mexico City: INAH, 1991.

Traslosheros H., Jorge E. "Los motivos de una monja: Sor Feliciana de San Francisco. Valladolid de Michoacán, 1632–1655. *Historia Mexicana* 47, no. 4 (1998): 735–63.

Tutino, John. *Creole Mexico*. PhD diss., University of Texas, Austin, 1976.

Twinam, Ann. *Public Lives, Private Secrets: Gender, Honor, Sexuality and Illegitimacy in Colonial Spanish America.* Palo Alto CA: Stanford University Press, 1999.

Underhill, Evelyn. *Mysticism*. New York: Doubleday, 1990.

Vallarte, Martín de. *Luz que guía al camino de la verdad y dirección de religiosas por un sacerdote deseoso del approvechamiento de las almas que se consagran al cordero immaculado que es luz de la gloria eterna.* Mexico City, 1746.

Van Deusen, Nancy. *Between the Sacred and the Worldly: The Institutional and Cultural Practice of Recogimiento in Colonial Lima.* Palo Alto CA: Stanford University Press, 2001.

Van Young, Eric. *Hacienda and Market in Eighteenth Century Mexico: The Rural Economy of the Guadalajara Region, 1675–1820.* Berkeley: University of California Press, 1981.

Vásquez Janeiro, Isaac. "Documentación Americana en el Pontificio Ateneo Antoniano de Roma" *Archivo Ibero-Americano*, no. 52 (1992): 767–809.

Vilaplana, Fray Hermenegildo. *Histórico y Sagrado Novenario de la Milagrosa Imagen de Nuestra Señora del Pueblito de la Santa Provincia de Religiosos Observantes de San Pedro y San Pablo de Michoacán.* Mexico City, 1765.

Villaseñor y Sánchez, José Antonio. *Teatro Americano, descripción general de los reinos y provincias de la Nueva España y sus jurisdicciones.* Mexico City, 1746.

Weber, Alison. *Teresa of Avila and the Rhetoric of Femininity*. Princeton NJ: Princeton University Press, 1990.

Weinstein, Donald, and Rudolf M. Bell. *Saints and Society: The Two Worlds of Western Christendom, 1000–1700.* Chicago: University of Chicago Press, 1982.

Wittberg, Patricia. *The Rise and Decline of the Catholic Religious Orders: A Social Movement Perspective.* New York: State University of New York Press, 1994.

Wright, A. D. *Catholicism and Spanish Society under the Reign of Philip II, 1555–1598 and Philip III, 1598–1621.* New York: Edwin Mellen Press, 1991.

Wright, David. *Querétaro en el siglo XVI: Fuentes documentales primarias.* Querétaro: Dirección de Patrimonio Cultural, 1989.

Wu, Celia. "The Population of the City of Querétaro in 1791." *JLAS*, 16 (1984).

Zahiño Penafort, Luisa. "La fundación del convento para indias cacicas de Nuestra Señora de los Angeles en Oaxaca." In *Memoria del II Congreso Internacional: El monacato femenino en el Imperio Español. Monasterios, beaterios, recogimientos y colegios*, edited by Manuel Ramos Medina, pp. 331–40. Mexico City: CONDUMEX, 1995.

Zarri, Gabriella. "From Prophecy to Discipline, 1450–1650." In *Women and Faith: Catholic Religious Life in Italy from Late Antiquity to the Present*, edited by Lucetta Scaraffia and Gabriella Zarri. Cambridge: Harvard University Press, 1999

Zeláa y Hidalgo, José María. *Glorias de Querétaro, 1680–1802*. Querétaro: Gobierno del Estado, 1985.

Zemon Davis, Natalie. "Boundaries and the Sense of Self in Sixteenth Century France." In *Reconstructing Individualism: Autonomy, Individuality and the Self in Western Thought*, edited by Thomas C. Heller, pp. 53–63. Palo Alto CA: Stanford University Press, 1986.

———. *Women on the Margins: Three Seventeenth-Century Lives*. Cambridge: Harvard University Press, 1995.

# Index

Ángeles, Francisca de los (*continued*)
social world of, 197–202, 268n71; spiritual virility of, 8–9, 55–56, 74, 151–52,
183–84; success of, 100, 156–57; supporters
of, 164–65; suspicion surrounding, 161–
64, 169; tension between José Díez and,
157–61, 167–70, 175–76, 187–88; themes
in the writings of, 11–12; trust in God
of, 14; view of Indians of, 98–99, 118–19;
visions of, 110, 171, 191–92; visit to New
Mexico of, 95–96; wrestling with God, 72;
wretchedness of, 115–17; writing skill of,
70–74, 152–57, 190, 191
Annunciación, Antonio de la, 262n56
Antigua, Madre, 70
Antonio de Mora, Juan, 149
Aquinas, Thomas, 56
Araujo Guerrero, Isidoro de, 277n5
architecture: of Querétaro, 69–70, 240n40
Aristotle, 56
Armenta, Nicolás, 150, 190, 201–2, 210, 251n9
Armstrong, Karen, 78
Arroyo Sandoval, Phelipe de, 28–29
art: of Querétaro, 66–69, 72
asceticism, 4
Augustinian missionaries, 25–26, 121

Bajío region of Mexico, 17–19, 238n4
Baltazar de Zuñiga, Marquis of Valero,
Viceroy don, 205–6
Barca, Calderón de la, 28
Barco, Pedro de, 80
*Battle of the Spirit*, 70
*beaterio* of Santa Rosa: background of
members of, 226–27, 275n36, 276n42;
communal exercises at, 147–48; confessions at, 150; conflict over jurisdiction
of, 209–16; daily life at, 195–97, 216, 227–
28; Dr. don Nicolás Armenta at, 190;
establishment and growth of, 139–45,
275n33; festivities at, 189–90, 198, 209–10;
Francisca de los Ángeles's governance
of, 142–43, 160–61, 177; José Díez as vicar
of, 145–52; opposition to, 157–61, 167–
70, 203–4; punishment of, 146–47, 148,
150–51; Querétaro community support
for, 199–200, 208; recognition of, as a
royal college, 207–8; success of, after the

death of Francisca de los Ángeles, 225–
28; support from Juan Caballero y Ocio
for, 164–65; support from the Santa Cruz
mission for, 140, 164–66, 171, 195–97; visit
by the archbishop to, 202–5
Bell, Rudolph, 57
Bellarmine, Cardinal Robert, 1
bienaventurados, 13; Antonio de los Ángeles
as, 133; Antonio Margil de Jesús as, 207;
Francisca de los Ángeles as, 128; Miguel
Font-Cuberta as, 96–97
bilocations, 93–95, 96–97, 130–31, 253n69
Bocanegra, Hernán Pérez de, 18
Bonilla, Fray, 46–47
Borromeo, Carlo, 1
Bourbon, Jeanne-Baptiste de, 6–7
Brading, David, 3, 4
Bridget of Sweden, 57
Bringas de Manzaneda, Pedro, 224
Buenrostro, María, 200
Bynum, Caroline Walker, 55–56, 57

Caballero de Medina y Corona, Juan, 152
Caballero y Ocio, Juan, 27, 34, 46–47, 54, 62,
77–78, 139, 140, 144, 154, 157–58, 158, 213,
253n62; correspondence of, with Francisca
de los Ángeles, 152–53; and support for
the *beaterio* of Santa Rosa, 164–65, 200
Cabrero, Ignacio, 226
Caffiero, Marina, 6, 230
Calderón de la Barca, Francis, 30–31
*el camino de la perfección*, 5, 64, 67, 72, 119,
124, 151
Campa, Juana de la, 227
Campaner, Padre, 150
Capistrano, Juan, 98
Carroll, Michael P., 41
Casañas de Jesús Maria, Francisco, 93
Casaos, José de, 28
Casas, Pablo de, 38
Castillo, Madre, 10, 64
Castro, Joseph, 88
Catherine of Siena, Saint, 57, 73, 237n26
Catholicism: decline of, in Spain, 11; during
the Enlightenment, 222–25, 228, 229–30;
heresy and, 37–48, 55–62; indulgences
in, 73, 130–31, 178–83; introduction of,
in Querétaro, 24–28, 232; missionaries

In the Engendering Latin America series